Towards an International Law of Co-progressiveness, Part II

Developments in International Law

VOLUME 71

The titles published in this series are listed at *brill.com/diil*

Towards an International Law of Co-progressiveness, Part II

Membership, Leadership and Responsibility

By

Sienho Yee

BRILL
NIJHOFF

LEIDEN | BOSTON

Library of Congress Control Number: 2014954650

ISSN 0924-5332
ISBN 978 90 04 25060 4 (hardback)
ISBN 978 90 04 28922 2 (e-book)

This book is printed on acid-free paper.

MIX
Paper from responsible sources
FSC® C109576
FSC www.fsc.org

Printed by Printforce, the Netherlands

Table of Contents

Preface

Shortly after the collection of my essays *Towards an International Law of Co-progressiveness* appeared in early 2004, the documents made publicly available revealed that one of the papers was discussed by governments and quoted by one Judge in the *Legality of Use of Forces* cases before the International Court of Justice. The book itself or some of the essays subsequently also have featured in interesting company in the syllabi of some august universities. The attention received emboldened me to propose the publication of a second volume of my essays with the same orientation, which is now presented before the readers.

This collection of eighteen old and new papers opens with a revisit to the concept of the "international law of co-progressiveness", which I proposed and coined the phrase to describe in 2001, elaborating it first as a descriptive observation and then as a normative position and identifying some core tenets of this law, a law that is characterized by a spirit of being all-encompassing (hence "co"), preoccupied with advancements at an appropriate speed in moral and ethical terms more than in other respects and having human flourishing as its ultimate goal (hence "progressiveness"). The volume is then divided into three parts organized roughly around membership, leadership and responsibility, exploring how these matters may reflect and inform that law. Part I, on membership, includes papers discussing various issues relating to the place of a State, civilization and region within the international system and their relationship with that law, and how various factors may affect that place or the perception thereof, such as the alleged "civilizedness" of a State, declarations of independence, and the roles of civilizations, regional perspectives, law, intrinsic and instrumental values, as well as public opinion. Part II, on leadership, includes papers dealing with the legitimacy of strong States, great States and leader States, vis-à-vis the "equal State"; their roles in the international system and the harmonious or co-progressive world; and their relationship with military activities in the exclusive economic zone, sustainable development and world politics, particularly Security Council decision making and implementing. This part also contains papers addressing leadership in treaty-making and international adjudication—reform proposals regarding the International Court of Justice and the presidency of the International Tribunal for the Law of the

Sea. Part III, on responsibility, includes two papers on member responsibility for acts of an international organization and one on the concept, logic and reality of universal jurisdiction, a tool to enforce responsibility across the world.

These issues are hefty. Hopefully, if one is interested in such matters, one can find in each paper my personal reflections, the results of my exploration for a considerable period of time.

The essays have been written for a variety of occasions and fora. I have however attempted to do some coordinating so that these papers are organized around the above-mentioned three topics into a more or less coherent book. However, my desire to retain all the essential arguments prevails over all other considerations, as they have been discussed by others.

The original publication dates of the papers included here span over a period of 10 years. I am pleased that the passage of time does not seem to have diminished the currency of the central themes and the main arguments in them. Some of these papers have received scrutiny, in some cases only recently. As most of the criticisms do not seem to have affected my main points, I do not attempt to respond to them here meaningfully, except noting some interesting subsequent developments and criticisms in postscripts here and there. Sometimes I feel that some criticisms do not seem to engage my arguments on the merits but use them simply as a sort of attack target in order to elevate the attackers' own agenda. For example, one may see attacks on my idea of "leader State" without a proper understanding of, or even attempt to understand, my arguments. As to these attacks, no response would seem to be called for or be of help to the attackers.

Although events such as 9.11 and its aftermath that took place shortly after the concept of the international law of co-progressiveness debuted gave one some hesitation as to the co-progressive nature of the world, I pointed out in the *Preface* to the 2004 volume that these were just aberrations and that the advancement of international law continues unabated. Since that time, the world has undergone further soul-searching and is now reexamining perhaps the very basics for its proper functioning, and I remain optimistic about the co-progressive nature, or future, of the world and international law.

1 October 2014

Note on Style and Abbreviations

The essays collected in this volume have been written for a variety of forums and thus have followed a variety of styles. In order to keep changes to a minimum, a decision has been made not to uniformize the styles, citations or abbreviations. One can see a hundred flowers of style bloom here.

In some cases if a paper originally published contains a long and interesting abstract, that abstract may be reproduced at the end of the paper as a postscript or in the bio footnote.

A large number of the essays first appeared in the *Chinese Journal of International Law* and thus followed its style guide (www.chinesejil.org/style.htm). The style of the *Chinese Journal of International Law* has three notable features regarding footnoting. Firstly, only regular fonts are used, without any need for small cap, italics (except for emphasis) and other interesting attractions prevalent in other journals. Secondly, citation formats follow those used by the official sources, with a view to helping to keep citations to official documents uniform across the world.

Thirdly, abbreviations are used with a view to ensuring that official abbreviations are followed and that the readers need not carry a book of abbreviations in order to understand one. When abbreviating journal titles, efforts are made to keep the *unique components* of a title but abbreviate the other words in it. For example, "Chinese JIL" is used for "Chinese Journal of International Law".

The common non-unique components of journal titles are as follows:

(1) "LR" for "Law Review";
(2) "JIL" for "Journal of International Law";
(3) "JTL" for "Journal of Transactional Law";
(4) "JILP" for "Journal of International Law and Policy";
(5) "CL" for "Comparative Law";
(6) "YIL" for "Yearbook of International Law" or "Year Book of International Law";
(7) "JLS" for "Journal of Legal Studies".

Notwithstanding the above, the following commonly used abbreviations may be used in this collection:

(1) "AFDI" for "Annuaire français de Droit international";
(2) "AJIL" for "American Journal of International Law";
(3) "BYIL" or "BYBIL" for "British Year Book of International Law";
(4) "EJIL" for "European Journal of International Law";
(5) "EPIL" for "Encyclopedia of Public International Law";
(6) "Hague Lectures" or "Recueil des Cours" or "RCADI" for "Recueil des Cours de l'Académie de la Haye (RCADI)" or "Collected Courses of the Hague Academy of International Law";
(7) "ICJYB" for "International Court of Justice Yearbook";
(8) "ICLQ" for "International and Comparative Law Quarterly";
(9) "ICTYJR" for "ICTY Judicial Reports";
(10) "IDI" for "Institut de droit international";
(11) "ILA" for "International Law Association";
(12) "ILC" for "International Law Commission";
(13) "ILCYB" for "Yearbook of the International Law Commission";
(14) "ILM" for "International Legal Materials";
(15) "ILR" for "International Law Reports";";
(16) "NJW" for "Neue Juristische Wochenschrift";
(17) "RGDIP" for "Revue generale de droit international public";
(18) "UNJY" or "UNJYB" for "United Nations Juridical Yearbook";
(19) "UNYB" for "United Nations Yearbook
(20) "YIHL" for "Yearbook of International Humanitarian Law".

Finally, the index is prepared with a view to providing entries only for those ideas that are discussed in the book. As a result, it is to a great extent an index to selected matters only, rather than a comprehensive one.

Acknowledgements

Most of the essays included in this volume are reprints or revisions of essays that have been published elsewhere, mostly in the *Chinese Journal of International Law*, published by Oxford University Press, and in the books published by Martinus Nijhoff. In some instances substantial revisions have been made to the form and format and even content, though not the core substantive arguments, giving rise to the question as to whether permission or acknowledgement is necessary. Furthermore, the right of an author to include his or her earlier publications in a subsequent personal collection seems to be universally recognized. In any event, the publishers either have a standing policy permitting such use or have given me specific permission for such use in the original license or subsequently. The earlier publication of a paper included herein is noted and acknowledged in the bio/first footnote in each instance where appropriate. I am grateful to all the journals and fora as well as the publishers for their kindness.

The preparation of this collection in current form as well as many of the original papers benefited from the comments of various scholars as well as my assistants at various places. This is noted in the footnotes where appropriate.

I am grateful for the kind assistance from the Peace Palace Library, especially Ms. Ingrid Kost who has been giving me most effective assistance since I stepped into that Library for the first time in the autumn of 1995; Wuhan University Library and the Law Library; the National Library of China; the University of Colorado Law Library, especially Ms. Jane Thompson; and the Northwestern University Law Library, especially Ms. Irene Berkey.

The preparation of this collection in final form as well as many of the original papers benefited financially from Research Project No. 08&ZD055 of the China Social Sciences Foundation and the Fundamental Research Funds for the Central Universities in China. The preparation of some papers also benefited from my visiting positions as Fowler Hamilton Visiting Research Fellow, Christ Church, Oxford and Resident Fellow at the Rockefeller Bellagio Center, Italy. The funders for the grants and the fellowships, however, had never seen any of the papers before they were first published.

A lot of thanks go to Martinus Nijhoff and its commissioning editors for their confidence in my projects and their flexibility in the production process.

Finally, I am most grateful for the support from Wuhan University, where I am Changjiang Xuezhe Professor of International Law and Chief Expert at the China Institute of Boundary and Ocean Studies as well as the Institute of International Law. The leaders of the Institutes and the President of the University have given me very favorable working conditions which, in part, made this book possible.

Chapter 1

The International Law of Co-progressiveness: The Descriptive Observation, the Normative Position and Some Core Principles*

I. Introduction

1. I am delighted to be here to participate in the commemoration of the 60th anniversary of the debut of the Five Principles of Peaceful Co-existence (the "Five Principles") and to ponder the development of international law under the current circumstances or perhaps for the future. I have been on an adventure to promote the international law of co-progressiveness since early 2001 when I published my paper *Towards an International Law of Co-progressiveness*.[1] In my presentation today, I will first highlight, as a descriptive observation, what I consider to be the international law of co-progressiveness, a phrase I coined to describe the international law that is characterized by a spirit of being all-encompassing (hence "co"), preoccupied with advancements at an appropriate speed in moral and ethical terms more than in other respects and

* This is a revised version of my remarks made at the Colloquium on "The Five Principles of Peaceful Coexistence and the Development of International Law" organized by the Ministry of Foreign Affairs of China and the Chinese Society of International Law on 27 May 2014 in Beijing. First published in 13 Chinese JIL (September 2014), 485, this paper was completed on 9 July 2014 and the websites cited were current as of this date unless otherwise noted.

1 Sienho Yee, Towards an International Law of Co-progressiveness, in Sienho Yee and Wang Tieya (eds), International Law in the Post-Cold War World: Essays in Memory of Li Haopei (2001), 18-39. My efforts first resulted in a series of essays, some of which were collected and published as Towards an International Law of Co-progressiveness (2004) (hereinafter, "Yee, Towards (2004)"). This volume represents part of this effort. This paper draws substantially from my earlier works in terms of both substance and language.

having human flourishing as its ultimate goal (hence “progressiveness”). I will then attempt to move from that descriptive observation to a normative position about the international law of co-progressiveness and argue that the international law of co-progressiveness not only *is* the law that governs international relations in the post-Cold War world but also *should be* the law that governs international relations *generally*. Finally I will tentatively attempt to identify some core tenets of this law.

II. The descriptive observation

2. After the end of the Cold War, efforts were made to characterize the nature of international society and international law. Just as there are many ways of seeing the world, there are many ways of seeing international law. In the above-mentioned paper published in 2001, I chose to focus on and highlight the spirit of international law at a particular moment or period in time, as that spirit is exhibited in the component parts of the system: its subjects, its formation, its content and its enforcement and other aspects. That is to say, the spirit of international law was my vantage point for observation and analysis. The leitmotif of international law was co-existence at the height of the Cold War, co-operation during the period of détente and is now co-progressiveness in the post-Cold War era. As there was no pre-existing word that follows perfectly from co-existence and co-operation, I had to coin the phrase “co-progressiveness” to describe what I had observed. By the “world of co-progressiveness” is meant a society that is all-encompassing (hence “co”), preoccupied with advancements at an appropriate speed in moral and ethical terms more than in other respects and having human flourishing as its ultimate goal (hence “progressiveness”). Of course, the leitmotif in each period is not the only theme audible to us: in co-existence there was co-operation; co-existence was the background note to co-operation; and co-existence and co-operation are the background notes to co-progressiveness.

3. The international law of co-existence regards primarily States as its subjects. Its formation primarily depends on the customary international law formation process. Its content concerns itself mostly with the separate existence—and the resulting co-existence—of States. Its enforcement primarily depends on the separate, unco-ordinated action by States such as counter-measures or, at best, resort to reciprocity. Peace was assured, but it was a standoffish peace, perhaps assured by or under the threat of mutual assured destruction.

4. The international law of co-operation begins to include more subjects and/or participants such as individuals, at least for some purposes. Its formation is also helped by a great variety of non-traditional forms of law such as gentlemen's agreements and declarations, or soft law, etc. Its content primarily concerns itself with promoting détente and co-operation between States and with mutual benefit. The idea of community interest strengthens with the appearance of the notion of *erga omnes* obligations in international law.[2] The co-operative spirit made it possible for several grand concepts to be formulated during the period of détente. As pointed out by Wolfgang Friedmann,[3] its enforcement is often characterized by a sort of "membership" sanction so that the co-operative community simply excludes a non-performing State from the community and therefore the benefits deriving from membership.

5. The international law of co-progressiveness is all-encompassing as far as its subjects and/or participants are concerned, so that individuals and even non-governmental organizations have become such subjects and/or participants, if not yet to the full extent. This makes it possible that in terms of input and influence, no participant is left outside the system. The formation of the law is improved by the participation of these new players and the innovative resort to the resolutions of the UN Security Council to establish international criminal tribunals, etc., or, in the view of some, even to implement humanitarian intervention or, now, the responsibility to protect. Its content is preoccupied with advancements at an appropriate speed in moral and ethical terms more than in other respects and has, as its ultimate goal, human flourishing to the fullest extent, so that each individual is able and willing to realize his or her own worthwhile pursuit, or perception of the good life. This is reflected in the various further concretization of the grand norms and the conclusion of the large numbers of agreements. The enforcement of the law takes centre-stage and is characterized more and more by a sort of "membership identification" by which a State wants to be identified as a good member in the community and

---

2 Barcelona Traction, Second Phase, Judgment, ICJ Reports 1970, 3, 32, para.33 ("an essential distinction should be drawn between the obligations of a State towards the international community as a whole, and those arising vis-à-vis another State in the field of diplomatic protection. By their very nature the former are the concern of all States. In view of the importance of the rights involved, all States can be held to have a legal interest in their protection; they are obligations *erga omnes*.").

3 Wolfgang Friedmann, The Changing Structure of International Law (1964), 88-95.

by a sort of "image sanction" by which States and the international community resort to the public shaming of a violator of the law, in order to induce it to come back to the road of law compliance. There is some acceleration in the strengthening of the idea of "community interest" and in the institutionalization or common enterprising in the management of world affairs or global governance, or more simply, in the enforcement of international law. The rule of law occupies a special place in international relations and law, with great efforts being made to ensure that rights and obligations are respected.

6. The ultimate goal of this law, just like that of any society, is human flourishing. By human flourishing is meant the situation where an individual lives his or her life driven by a worthy project, goal or value. This orientation moved me to be dissatisfied with the normal ideas of negative liberty and positive liberty. I proposed that we consider the role of "induced liberty", in the sense that efforts to seek meaning do not result from any innate quality of the atomic individual, but are induced, though not to be coerced, by the community, its culture and history, and its web of relationships. Thus, without the State the individual would not have thought about many choices. Sovereignty thus informs and influences the perception of personhood. From this perspective, strong States are essential to human flourishing. I also believe that the idea of inducement has a broader application than I have just described.

7. Of course, this picture of the international law of co-progressiveness is not completely blemish-free. There are still a lot of problems in various parts of the system, but the overall tenor of this law is co-progressiveness. These problems include occasional occurrence of militant humanitarianism or "humanitarian intervention". As a result of these blemishes or problems, when I was working on the coining of the phrase "international law of co-progressiveness", I was content with the calmer word "progressiveness", as compared to others such as "liberalness" or "democracy". The choice of the term "progressiveness" also reflected my dissatisfaction with certain radical tendencies or overmoralization and, thus, perhaps a certain super-speed—if this is the only problem—in moving forward, in international relations. In my view that would not be sustainable or desirable in the long run.

8. Since the publication of my original paper in the spring of 2001, the world has witnessed some dramatic events such as September 11 and the ensuing war against terror, "shock and awe" warfare, the Arab Spring, extreme weather conditions such as Hurricane Katrina, internet attacks and chaos including Prismgate, the increased tension in the East and South China Seas, and the incorporation of Crimea into the Russian Federation. Conventional and

non-conventional challenges thus conspire to remind us that the world is not yet ideal and to give us a rude awakening that we are indeed on the same boat of common destiny, facing common pains, common challenges and common aspirations. Despite the aberrations and zigzagging, the overall tenor of the international community is still co-progressiveness, and the advancements in international law continue unabated, if more soul-searching is going on now than before.

III. The normative position

9. I hope I have painted a good picture of the international law of co-progressiveness, albeit with a broad brush. If the picture is more or less accurate although a bit impressionistic, what can flow from this? If we can say that, as a descriptive observation, the international law prevailing since the end of the Cold War is characterized by a spirit of co-progressiveness, what normative proposition can we draw from this?

10. Usually one is tempted to move from the descriptive observation to the normative position without any bridging step, that is, asserting that *what is* is also *what ought to be*. But we were taught long ago by philosophers that we should not go so fast; we have to provide good reason for that jump. Here I argue that indeed, regarding the international law of co-progressiveness, we can make this jump and conclude that the international law of co-progressiveness *should be* the law that governs international relations *generally*, not just *is* the law that governs international relations in the post-Cold War world. And I will give you some good reasons for this jump.

11. First of all, it is essential for law to reflect the general spirit—as opposed to the material phenomena—of society as much as possible and as accurately as possible. Otherwise there will not be a situation of general obedience to law and therefore no law will exist. On this score, the international law of co-progressiveness does better than the other candidates. The descriptive observation I have made about this law is a more or less accurate one. The law of co-existence, for which the Five Principles have been a strong promoter especially in terms of *opinio juris*, has been criticized for being focused on the separate existence of States and saying little on the states coming together, or the institutionalization of international relations which now plays a most important role in global governance. The law of globalization and the law of cooperation are mostly focused on the material aspects of international relations, which are of course only part of the story in our society.

12. Secondly, law must reflect not only the general spirit of society, but more importantly, the good part of that spirit. Otherwise this law will have no future; another kind of law will take its place. This point finds support in an analogy to one of the principles enshrined in the Constitution of the Chinese Communist Party, which says that the party has to represent the advanced productive forces as well as the orientation of the advanced culture in society.[4] On this criterion, the international law of co-progressiveness also does better than the other candidates. As discussed, the good part of the spirit of the current international environment is co-progressiveness. It is not clear that the law of co-existence, with its focus on peace or independence, equality and reciprocity, can take proper account of the progressive spirit. The other "laws", with a focus on material development, do not do a good job, either. Furthermore, material development is said to be driven by wealth accumulation and efficiency, but the most capable advocate of the economic view of the law, Richard Posner, has admitted that wealth accumulation—at least, in my view, the single-minded pursuit of it—as a value has encountered powerful challenge.[5] Indeed, that point finds no better proof anywhere than in Asia: the infamous and disastrous campaign of Japan to build a Greater East-Asia Co-prosperity Sphere before and *during* the Second World War is still vivid in our memory. The pursuit of prosperity without progressiveness is scary, to put it lightly. Therefore, "common development" or "common prosperity" as such should not be the *ultimate* goal of law or society; co-progressiveness should be. The law of development or prosperity should not be the law that governs international relations generally; the international law of co-progressiveness should be.

13. Thirdly, law must be able to help to solve the pressing issues of

---

4 See http://english.cpc.people.com.cn/65732/6758063.html ("The Communist Party of China is the vanguard both of the Chinese working class and of the Chinese people and the Chinese nation. It is the core of leadership for the cause of socialism with Chinese characteristics and represents the development trend of China's advanced productive forces, the orientation of China's advanced culture and the fundamental interests of the overwhelming majority of the Chinese people.").

5 Richard Posner, 1997 Oliver Wendell Holmes Lectures: The Problematics of Moral and Legal Theory, 111 Harvard LR (1998), 1637, 1670 & n.62 ("I speak from experience. See Richard A. Posner, Utilitarianism, Economics, and Legal Theory, 8 J. Legal Stud. 103 (1979), powerfully criticized in Ronald Dworkin, Is Wealth a Value?, in A Matter of Principle 237 (1985).").

society by providing for frameworks and good rationales for the problem-solving operations. On this criterion, the law of co-progressiveness also does better. For example, it would be difficult for the law of co-existence with an emphasis on separate existence and separate action, not on States coming together, to do a good job in meeting common challenges and common aspirations, which requires high intensity in cooperation and institutionalization on a world scale. More difficult would be for the law of co-existence, which stresses equality and reciprocity, to deal with, on a normal understanding of legal principles, the new pattern or model of big power relations or international relations generally as proposed by Xi Jinping, the "common but differentiated responsibility" principle or the big power's responsibilities in addressing the common problem of climate change, the proper framework of rights and responsibilities under which some are to give up some rights or to assume greater responsibilities, or a leader State's powers and obligations or responsibilities. The latter type of problems also exists with the law of cooperation unless one says that cooperation means agreeing to everything without principled criteria. The international law of co-progressiveness with a bent for progressiveness and an emphasis on the application of fitting criteria and enlightened equality and on our sharing a common destiny and tackling common problems, provides a better analysis of these problems, a better framework for solving them, and a better narrative or rationale for the practical operations to solve them.

14. Finally, international law should not only reflect the general spirit or even the good part of that spirit of the international community, or help to solve the pressing issues of society by providing for frameworks and good rationales for the problem-solving operations, but also help to change that community for the better. Some who have concerned themselves with the functioning of the legal system, social system or "scheme of things" in general have expressed this idea in various ways. For example, an immortal poet said:

> [...] could you and I with fate conspire
> To grasp this sorry Scheme of Things entire,
> Would not we shatter it to bits—and then
> Re-mould it nearer to the Heart's desire![6]

---

6 The Ruba'iyat of Omar Khayyam, trans. by Edward Fitzgerald, as quoted in Georges Abi-Saab, Cours général de droit international public, in: 207 RCADI (1987-VII), 463.

US President John F. Kennedy reportedly chastised Paul Freund, a prominent professor of constitutional law who declined his invitation to become the Solicitor General, the chief United States advocate before the US Supreme Court, on the ground that he had planned for too long a time to write a history of that court, by saying that he was sorry and had hoped that the professor "would prefer making history to writing it".[7] One of course remembers Karl Marx's teaching that philosophers have interpreted the world in various ways, but the point is to change it.[8] One can easily imagine that international law should not be content with the "reflection" role, but should be the handmaiden of general social progress across the world in material as well as moral and ethical terms.

15. On this criterion, the international law of co-progressiveness will also do much better than the other candidates. As can be seen from the core principles set out below, the international law of co-progressiveness puts emphasis on a bent or tendency for progressiveness regarding every issue and requires each State or appropriate participant to measure progressiveness externally against a common standard or at least internally against its own standard or its own past achievements. This would serve as a self-propelled engine for progressiveness. In this way, this law emphasizes voluntary action and the internal forces that move States and persons to action. True, advancements coming from such an emphasis may not be at a super speed, but each incremental step forward in every State and participant will lead to an appreciable sum total in the world. Furthermore, some outside inducement, not coercion, is permitted to boost the primarily internal engine for advancement and progressiveness. Current events in the aftermath of the Arab Spring prove that one cannot go too fast and jump into a perfect world when the people are not yet ready. This also applies to places where "constitutional backsliding" is said to be taking place, or perhaps to the faltering of the grand vision of a European Constitution.

16. As a mild form of value-oriented law, the international law of co-progressiveness hopefully will be sufficient, as a result of its preference for

---

7 Time Magazine (Feb. 17, 1992, US ed.), 73; Baltimore Sun (June 6, 1993), 6C (1993 WL 7368883). It is often said that the professor's rejection of the Solicitor General position was the cause for Kennedy's subsequent refusal to nominate him to fill a vacancy on the Supreme Court.

8 Karl Marx: Selected Writings (David McLellan ed., 1977), 156, 158: Theses on Fuerbach, pt. XI.

internal soul-searching in decision-making and external coaxing but not coercing, to thwart in the future any soulless militant adventures or something similar and to nudge the world into an ascending, progressive direction, but will not lead to "steroidized universal values" except the most fundamental ones, or the enforcement of such steroidized values across the world. That is to say, such an approach will not lead to artificial and boring sameness across the whole international community. The increasing recognition of a community of common destiny and the concept of *jus cogens* in the world since its codification in article 53 of the Vienna Convention on the Law of Treaties of 1969, to which China is a party, gives one the confidence to say that such a mild form of value-oriented law is not too much to ask for; the few most fundamental universal values that it recognizes are the ones that no State or participant can escape from. There cannot be common destiny without some universal values being shared by all. Nor can a State or participant be an effective promoter of the common destiny without sharing some fundamental universal values. In reality, the most fundamental values are usually already being shared, promoted and implemented in the domestic legal orders. For a participant that promotes and implements shared values domestically, a question may be asked: why not also do the same internationally? The more difficult question is to agree on which fundamental values should be so promoted and implemented across the world. Making that decision can only be a dynamic exercise, in which all players in the international system or the international community as a whole should participate.

IV. Some core principles

17. Now I come to what constitutes the international law of co-progressiveness in terms of concrete rules and principles. As we know, it would be a "mission impossible" for me to enumerate all the principles that can be put in this basket. I will leave a fuller exposition for the future. After all, the title of my original paper starts with the word "Towards". Thus, this law is not yet fully formed. Nor is it static. Ours is only a march towards this law. Since quite some time ago—before my 2001 paper was written—I have been trying to understand, elaborate and propose the nuts and bolts that would form part of this law and will continue to do so in the future. For now, I will only try to highlight several principles that have some sort of macro or framework effect and offer some observations (without detailed elaboration), as informed by my previous works and my on-going efforts. These rules and principles can be put in two

categories: primary rules of conduct and secondary rules, as they have been called, that deal with the consequences of primary rules or the making and changing of the primary rules. I would prefer to call these secondary rules "systemic rules". This categorization may be difficult and controversial but will be made here anyway. I will start with the second category: the systemic rules or the secondary rules.

18. First, where possible international law should decide a question with a bent for or a bias in favor of co-progressiveness, that is, the spirit of being all-encompassing, preoccupied with advancements at an appropriate speed in moral and ethical terms more than in other respects and having human flourishing as its ultimate goal. This functions as the overall orientational directive for the system as well as its components—system participation, law formation, law content as well as law enforcement.

19. Second, progressiveness is to be measured both internally against one's historical achievements and externally across the world against those of other participants in the system, but the content and pace of such advancement should be informed by the special circumstances of each State or an appropriate participant and be ultimately set by that State or participant involved, on the conditions that the most fundamental obligations under international law be complied with. In this way the world will remain richly diverse, which in itself is a most important value. Progressiveness should be usually internally-initiated or self-propelled within each State or participant, and can also be externally induced, but not coerced. Hopefully the bent for or bias in favor of co-progressiveness is sufficient to act as some kind of self-propelled engine within each State or participant. If not, efforts can be made to induce it to move towards progressiveness. If a common standard can be agreed upon and can be complied with, it will be ideal; if not, at least internally within a State or participant there should be some advancement. If each State or participant can achieve some advancement even if measured internally vis-à-vis the past, with all the advancements in the different States and participants combined, the whole world would be in a better shape.

20. Third, clashes between intrinsic and instrumental values should be decided by decision-makers in a conscious and explicit way and by giving preference to a more important value but, at the same time, to the applicable intrinsic value where possible.[9]

---

9 See Sienho Yee, The Intrinsic and Instrumental Values of Diversity: Some Philosophical and Legal Considerations, in: Sienho Yee & J.Y. Morin (eds),

21. Fourth, every State or appropriate participant (including international organizations, regional organizations, civilizations and perhaps individuals) in the international system is a holder of rights and bearer of obligations vis-à-vis each other as well as the international system or the international community of common destiny and common interests.[10] Whether a participant is an appropriate one in this connection will depend on the particular circumstances. States are still the primary manageable end units in the world and the primary subjects of international law. There can be a difference between the international system and the international community as well as between the interests of the international community and the sum total of the interests of all the States and other participants in the community. These issues will be left for the future. In any event, an enlightened assessment and calculation of national interests or self-interests is incumbent upon every State or participant. The international system is a public good. It is imperative for this system to be maintained and to function reasonably properly and stably, even if there are trouble-spots scattering around in the international community. The international legal system is the spine of that system. In turn the UN Charter is the spine of the international legal system, and the UN Security Council is the ultimate protector—with article 103 of the UN Charter as the ultimate legal protector—of this spine and therefore the system. The UN system no doubt has been established for the protection of the "common interest" and for the attainment of certain "common ends", as can be seen from the preamble to and article 1(4) of the Charter. Article 103 of the Charter is the ultimate embodiment of the importance of the international system as a whole or the common interest or common ends, because the article gives priority to obligations arising under the Charter over obligations from all other agreements. The idea of "common interest" received further recognition quite

---

Multiculturalism and International Law: Essays in Honour of Edward McWhinney (Martinus Nijhoff 2009), 207-226 [Chapter 6 below].

10 See Sienho Yee, Sovereign Equality of States and the Legitimacy of "Leader States", in: Ronald St.J. Macdonald and Douglas M. Johnston (eds.), Towards World Constitutionalism (2005), 737-772 [Chapter 8 below]. On a pluralistic vision of the system, see Edward McWhinney, A New, Multicultural World Community and an Emerging New, Pluralistic World Order System, 11 Chinese JIL (2012), 469-486; On the role of civilizations in this scheme of things, see Sienho Yee, The International Law of Co-progressiveness and the Co-progressiveness of Civilizations, 12 Chinese JIL (2013), 9-17 [Chapter 4 below].

early on, such as in the Genocide Convention, under which, according to the International Court of Justice, the parties "merely have, one and all, a common interest",[11] as well as in the concept of *erga omnes* obligations, as mentioned above. Since the end of the Cold War, the "common interest" idea has been gaining strength in a big way. States have put into operation the concept of "common heritage of mankind" under the UN Convention on the Law of the Sea. They have also established and energized the World Trade Organization. Now they are together tackling the problem of climate change. Acting separately States are also starting to protect the common interest. Glimpses of this can be seen in the recent protests filed by Korea and China against Japan's submission[12] to the Commission on the Limits of the Continental Shelf for an outer continental shelf regarding Okinotorishima, which is far from any zone claimed by Korea or China, and in the recent *Whaling in the Antarctic* case which Australia brought and won at the International Court of Justice against Japan regarding the latter's whaling program in waters which Australia did not claim sovereignty over or sovereign rights in.[13] Whether or not Australia's status as a party to the convention on whaling, the interpretation of which was at issue in that case, was sufficient to give it standing was not pressed by Japan or the Court, for whatever reason. The standing of Korea, China and Australia to take these actions seems to be grounded in their interest in the international system or in the international community as a whole, or based on the systemic or community interest in the matters in dispute.

22. Fifth, equality to be pursued should be enlightened equality, not mechanical or superficial equality; it should be based on a fitting and progressive criterion in each instance appropriate to the particular subject matter at issue and the occasion so as to maximize or to make sophisticated the twin states of affairs called "like cases should be treated alike" and "different cases should be treated differently". As a result, allowances should be made for

---

11 Reservations to the Convention on the Prevention and Punishment of the Crime of Genocide, Advisory Opinion, ICJ Reports 1951, 23. On some ramifications, see Sienho Yee, Universal Jurisdiction: Concept, Logic, and Reality, 10 Chinese JIL (2011), 503–530.

12 See http://www.un.org/Depts/los/clcs_new/submissions_files/submission_jpn.htm.

13 Whaling in the Antarctic (Australia v. Japan: New Zealand Intervening), Judgment, ICJ Reports 2014, http://www.icj-cij.org/docket/index.php?p1=3&p2=3&code=aj&case=148&k=64&p3=0.

legitimate difference arguments based on a fitting criterion,[14] such as, for example, a proper respect for professionalism, value and wisdom. Of course, how to arrive at such a fitting criterion is no easy business. Every participant is to make peace with, and accept with a smile, such legitimate differences and not let jealousy overtake rationality or even trigger a rage. A corollary of enlightened equality is the principle of common but differentiated responsibility, which has been emphasized and put into operation in environmental law, especially in the measures regarding climate change.

23. Sixth, great States and leader States enjoy special powers and shoulder special responsibilities in the international system. They owe special, substantial contributions to the system as a whole and shall ensure its survival and proper functioning. Leader States are to comply with international law in an exemplary fashion and to help formulate or refine a proper vision of the world and build it up so that the flourishing of humanity can be achieved to the greatest extent.[15] Furthermore, when acting as a promoter of peace and security, especially peaceful settlement of disputes, a great State or leader State is to act evenhandedly, rather than to lean toward its allies, which is tantamount to a gangster boss settling scores between his ally and another group. The extraordinary powers granted to the permanent members of the UN Security Council under the UN Charter as well as the interesting arrangement under Article 16 of the Rome Statute of the International Criminal Court[16] are already reflections of the special positions of the great States and leader States in the international system.

24. Seventh, every State or appropriate participant in the international system is to observe the rule of law in every respect and to take the best account of rule of law concerns in making every important decision. An ideal state of affairs, the perfect rule of law means law is complied with simply because it is law, serving as the ultimate reason for voluntary action.[17] This requires that the existence of law or the concept of law coincides with law as the ultimate reason

---

14 Sienho Yee, Sovereign Equality, above n.10, 746-759.

15 Ibid., 759-772.

16 See Rome Statute of the International Criminal Court, http://legal.un.org/icc/index.html, art.16; Sienho Yee, A Proposal to Reformulate Article 23 of the ILC Draft Statute for an International Criminal Court, 19 Hastings Int'l & Comp. LR (Spring 1996), 529-537, reprinted in: Yee, Towards (2004), above n.1, 105.

17 Sienho Yee, The Perfect Rule of Law, in: Yee, Towards (2004), above n.1, 41, 52-58.

for action and with the state of affairs called the rule of law. This coincidence of various factors centers on law serving as the ultimate reason for voluntary action. "What is law" is an important issue, and this question is decided upon through the process by which the actors in society internalize law so as to treat a certain course of conduct as the standard of conduct and to use it as the basis for critiquing (including self-critiquing) the conduct of the actors as well as for demands for conformity, and only then does law come into existence. This idea was considered by H.L.A. Hart to be the internal aspect of "rules" in general and law as well.[18] The perfect rule of law thus embodies an internal point of view of the law. The internalization process might result from and be aided by many factors, *one of which* may be certain rules of recognition. When coercive measures are brought to bear upon any aspect of the legal process, the rule of law is already broken, at least in the first instance. Every State or appropriate participant is to do its best to promote the rule of law not only by making concrete rules and building concrete institutions and ensuring their proper functioning so as to police the compliance with the law in a *post-facto* accounting fashion but also, perhaps more importantly, by establishing mechanisms to promote voluntary compliance with the rule of law principles before an important decision is made so that such principles inform, or are internalized or factored into, important decision-making in an *ante-facto* seed-sowing fashion. In short, every effort should be made to promote the idea that law, imbued with a spirit of co-progressiveness, should be the ultimate reason for voluntary action.

25. Regarding primary rules of conduct, there are even more to enumerate. I promise I will do more in the future to identify a core set of

---

18 See H.L.A. Hart, The Concept of Law (1961), 54-57, 79-91, 102-103. As Hart observed, some people wrongly misrepresented the internal aspect of rules as a "mere matter of 'feelings' in contrast to externally observable physical behavior", ibid., 57. After saying that the phychological experiences analogous to those of restriction or compulsion may exist, he gave this response: "But such feelings are neither necessary nor sufficient for the existence of 'binding' rules. There is no contradiction in saying that people accept certain rules but experience no such feelings of compulsion. What is necessary is that there should be a critical reflective attitude to certain patterns of behavior as a common standard, and that this should display itself in criticism (including self-criticism), demands for conformity, and in acknowledgements that such criticism and demands are justified, all of which find their characteristic expression in the normative terminology of 'ought', 'must', and 'should', 'right' and 'wrong'." Ibid.

fundamental principles of the international law of co-progressiveness. But for now I would like to first temporarily incorporate all the Five Principles (to the extent identifiable as legal rules and principles), i.e., mutual respect for each other's territorial integrity and sovereignty, mutual non-aggression, mutual non-interference in each other's internal affairs, equality and mutual benefit, and peaceful co-existence.[19] I also would like to incorporate the principles of the UN and those stated or restated in the Friendly Relations Declaration,[20] i.e.:

(a) The principle that States shall refrain in their international relations from the threat or use of force against the territorial integrity or political independence of any State, or in any other manner inconsistent with the purposes of the United Nations;
(b) The principle that States shall settle their international disputes by peaceful means in such a manner that international peace and security and justice are not endangered;
(c) The duty not to intervene in matters within the domestic jurisdiction of any State, in accordance with the Charter;
(d) The duty of States to co-operate with one another in accordance with the Charter;
(e) The principle of equal rights and self-determination of peoples;
(f) The principle of sovereign equality of States;
(g) The principle that States shall fulfil in good faith the obligations assumed by them in accordance with the Charter.

26. Recognizing that the Five Principles did help to launch the project that resulted in these above-enumerated principles[21] but leaving aside whether the

---

19 See 1954 Agreement between the People's Republic of China and the Republic of India on Trade and Intercourse between the Tibet Region of China and India, preamble, as reproduced in China Institute of International Studies, On the Five Principles of Peaceful Coexistence—Essays in Commemoration of the Five Principles of Peaceful Coexistence (2004), 525.

20 The Declaration on Principles of International Law concerning Friendly Relations and Co-operation among States in accordance with the Charter of the United Nations, GA resolution 26/25 (XXV) (1970), http://www.un.org/en/ga/search/view_doc.asp?symbol=A/RES/2625(XXV)&Lang=E&Area=RESOLUTION.

21 Edward McWhinney, The Renewed Vitality of the International Law Principles of Peaceful Coexistence in the Post-Iraq Invasion Era: The 50th Anniversary

Five Principles are completely subsumed in them, I would like to offer two points of elaboration. First, it is not intervention in the domestic affairs of a State for another State or another proper participant in the international system to attempt to dialogue with or influence a government undergoing difficulties in order to induce it, without coercion or use of force, to conduct its affairs in a better way, or even with the dissenting voices so as to promote a peaceful resolution of any problems with which they are faced. I am not sure whether this may sound earth-shattering, but I do believe that this approach has important implications and jibes with the second principle enumerated above in paragraph 19. I am pleased to observe that China's efforts in the Syrian crisis, such as sending a special envoy to consult with the Syrian president, as well as talking with the rebels, and those of Russia, provide evidence in State practice supporting this elaboration. And we can see so far that the Chinese and Russian approach seems to be playing a very important role in dealing with the Syrian crisis. China's involvement in the efforts to resolve the civil war in South Sudan, as reported in the mass media,[22] is proof that this approach may be taking hold, perhaps even as a general one, or moving in that direction.

27. Second, the duty of cooperation is incumbent upon every State or appropriate participant in the international system in order not only to attain general good-neighborliness and conduct projects for the common benefit of mankind such as the International Seabed Area regime but also, more importantly and more urgently, to tackle pressing common problems and conventional as well as non-conventional challenges, such as counter-terrorism, cyber war and climate change. Such common problems may lead to disasters to be visited upon all participants. The duty moves from being "imperfect" to

---

of the China/India Pancha Shila Agreement of 1954, 3 Chinese JIL (2004), 379-384; Milan Sahović, Codification des principes du droit international des relations amicales et de la coopération entre les Etats, 137 RCADI (1972-III), 243-310.

22 See Drazen Jorgic, China takes more assertive line in South Sudan diplomacy, Reuters, 5 June 2014, http://www.reuters.com/article/2014/06/05/us-south sudan-china-insight-idUSKBN0EG00320140605. On China's role in general, see Dai Bingguo, Asia, China and International Law, 11 Chinese JIL (2012), 1-3. On the implications for third States, see Tom Ruys, Of Arms, Funding and "Non-lethal Assistance"—Issues Surrounding Third-State Intervention in the Syrian Civil War, 13 Chinese JIL (2014), 13-53; Stefan Talmon, Recognition of Opposition Groups as the Legitimate Representative of a People, 12 Chinese JIL (2013), 219-253.

binding, as the subject matter moves from the former to the latter category, regarding which rules and principles may impose other obligations. The duty should strengthen according to the nature of the subject matter, the severity and urgency of the problem to tackle and how "common" it is to the world. In the absence of a *lex specialis*, the duty to cooperate may be measured in general by analogy to the principle of common but differentiated responsibility in international environmental law, with the best efforts from each participant as the minimum.

V. Concluding remarks

28. In a general way, I have laid out the case, in terms of descriptive observation and normative position, for saying that the international law of co-progressiveness—a law that is suffused with the spirit of being all-encompassing, preoccupied with advancements at an appropriate speed in moral and ethical terms more than in other respects and having human flourishing as its ultimate goal—is the law that governs international relations in the post-Cold War world and should be the law that governs international relations *generally*. I have also identified some of the core principles that constitute this law. Without attempting a summary of the observations and arguments, I would like to highlight that, as is clear from the above discussion, the most important aspects of this law are the bent for co-progressiveness and the emphasis on self-propelled or internally-initiated action.

29. In a special way, the recurring change of scenes between war and peace in places such as Libya and Iraq seems to demonstrate the importance of the international law of co-progressiveness. It is no exaggeration for one to say that if indeed war is "the continuation of politics by different means", law can be the waging of war by different means and that, for a true strategist, lawfare is warfare, and the more important part at that.[23] The fiercest battle in a

---

[23] Cf. Carl von Clausewitz, On War (Alfred A. Knopf, 1993), 7-8 ("War is not an independent phenomenon, but the continuation of politics by different means", as quoted by Peter Paret). On similar themes, Niccolò Machiavelli said in The Prince (Bantam 2003), 51: "The two most essential foundations for any state, whether it be old or new, or both old and new, are sound laws and sound military forces. [… T]he absence of sound laws assures the absence of sound military forces, while the presence of sound military forces indicates the presence of sound laws as well. […]" And Napoleon organized the Napoleonic Code and spread it wherever his military forces reached. These strategists

contemporary war appears to be no longer that of aiming to defeat a country or to effect a regime change by kinetic force, which the shock and awe warfare—something that no one likes to endure for sure but has happened—can achieve relatively easily, but that of aiming to restore order and win over the hearts and minds of the people. In this battle, international law with a bent for co-progressiveness and an emphasis on self-propelled or internally-initiated action has a special role to play. Only such law can help to solidify stability and make it possible for people to thrive and flourish.

---

seemed to believe not only that power comes out of the gun barrel, but also that power can only be consolidated under the law. Apparently Napoleon took great pride in the vitality of his Code; legend has it that his last words included: "My Empire is gone but my Code lives. I can die now." At that moment, his legal feat was not just a worthy enough tradeoff for his military limits. The promising prospect that his law's empire would outlast and transcend his military empire permitted this proud man to make peace with himself and close his eyes. That was strong medicine. Lawfare thus can also be a "legacyfare".

Part I

Membership

Chapter 2

We Are All "Civilized Nations": Arguments for Cleaning up Article 38(1)(c) of the Statute of the International Court of Justice*

I. Introduction

The Statute of the International Court of Justice (ICJ or the Court)[1] states in Article 38[2]:

---

* Revised from: Sienho Yee, Arguments for Cleaning up Article 38(1)(b) and (1)(c) of the ICJ Statute, 4 Romanian JIL (January-June 2007), 33-43.

1 UNCIO (Selected Documents version, US Government Printing Office, 1946), 966. For useful commentaries on the Statute, see, e.g., Andreas Zimmermann, Karin Oellers-Frahm & Christian Tomuschat (eds.), The Statute of the International Court of Justice: A Commentary (2006) [subsequent to the first publication of this paper, a second edition of this book appeared in 2012, but the references to this work in this chapter are not updated, due to the desire to retain as much as possible the former paper]; Shabtai Rosenne, Law and Practice of the International Court: 1920-2005 (4th ed. 2006); Agora: The International Court of Justice at 60, 5 Chinese JIL (2006), 1-128 (Part I); 269-322 (Part II); Alain Pellet, Remarks on Proceedings before the International Court of Justice, 5 The Law and Practice of International Courts and Tribunals (2006), 163-182 (Alain Pellet, Remarks); Gennady M. Danilenko, Law-making in the International Community (1993); Max Sørensen, Les sources du droit international (1946).

2 UNCIO (Selected Documents version, US Government Printing Office, 1946), 973. For good or ill, this list of sources of international law has had enormous influence on the mindset of international lawyers. Of course, there have been disputes on whether or not the list is proper, or whether or not it is exhaustive. Writers often would add some other items to the list. A frequently added item is "unilateral acts", regarding which the International Law

1. The Court, whose function is to decide in accordance with international law such disputes as are submitted to it, shall apply:

    a. international conventions, whether general or particular, establishing rules expressly recognized by the contesting states;
    b. international custom, as evidence of a general practice accepted as law;
    c. the general principles of law recognized by civilized nations;
    d. subject to the provisions of Article 59, judicial decisions and the teachings of the most highly qualified publicists of the various nations, as subsidiary means for the determination of rules of law.

2. This provision shall not prejudice the power of the Court to decide a case *ex aequo et bono*, if the parties agree thereto.

This article has attained a special place in the system of international law and no substantive changes have been generally considered necessary as it has been working reasonably well since 1922. Proposals have been made however that Article 38(1)(b) should be amended by changing the phrase "evidence of" to "evidenced by" in order to correct an already recognized logical mistake[3] and Article 38(1)(c) be amended by deleting "civilized" in order to remove the questionable word for which no "hard" or real meaning was intended by the drafters, in each case without affecting the substantive meaning of the article.[4] This chapter will address only the proposal for cleaning up Article 38(1)(c). I do not claim originality on this proposal, but I hope to present some observations that are not often heard. First, I will relate the criticism made by others of the phrase "civilized" that it conveys discrimination between different kinds of nations. Then I will move on to present my own argument that the phrase should be deleted because it has not been given any concrete, real meaning, as

---

Commission adopted in 2006 a set of "Guiding Principles applicable to unilateral declarations of States capable of creating legal obligations". See ILC Report 2006, A/61/10, 362-381.

3 See Danilenko, n.1 above 76-77.

4 See Sienho Yee, n.* above. I will not deal with the amendment process itself, which is addressed in Wolfram Karl, Article 60, in Andreas Zimmermann, et al., n.1 above, 1469; id., Article 70, in ibid., 1487.

proved by the drafting history and subsequent practice in the Court and elsewhere. I will explain why, even though the phrase has no real substantive meaning, Article 38(1)(c) should still be amended by deleting it.

II. Criticism that the term "civilized" conveys discrimination

By directing the Judges to apply "the general principles of law recognized by civilized nations", Article 38(1)(c) retains the vestiges of a bygone era that divided the world into "civilized" and "uncivilized" provinces. It is a kind of imprint of the times. For some, this term conveys discrimination between different kinds of nations and thus is inappropriate. The most vocal condemnation of this term was already made in as early as 1960 by Judge Ammoun in his separate opinion in *North Sea Continental Shelf*. The Judge may be giving more weight to the term than was intended, as I argue below, but his eloquent words are worth quoting:

> It is important in the first place to observe that the form of words of Article 38, paragraph 1(c), of the Statute, referring to "the general principles of law recognized by civilized nations", is inapplicable in the form in which it is set down, since the term "civilized nations" is incompatible with the relevant provisions of the United Nations Charter, and the consequence thereof is an ill-advised limitation of the notion of the general principles of law.
>
> The discrimination between civilized nations and uncivilized nations, which was unknown to the founding fathers of international law, the protagonists of a universal law of nations, Vittoria, Suarez, Gentilis, Pufendorf, Vattel, is the legacy of the period, now passed away, of colonialism, and of the time long-past when a limited number of Powers established the rules, of custom or of treaty-law, of a European law applied in relation to the whole community of nations. Maintained and sometimes reinforced at the time of the great historical settlements—Vienna 1815, Berlin 1885, Versailles 1920, Lausanne 1923, Yalta 1945—European international law had been defended by jurists of indisputable authority in the majority of branches of international law, such as Kent, Wheaton, Phillimore, Anzilotti, Fauchille, F. de Markas, Westlake, Hall, Oppenheim, Politis: thus the last-mentioned writer's *La morale internationale* is striking by reason of the fact that it is centered on Europe alone and Europe's exclusive interests. However great and powerful the

> thinking of these renowned jurists may be, their concept of a family of European and North Atlantic nations is nonetheless beginning to be blurred by the reality of the universal community, in the thinking of the internationalists of a new age such as S. Krylov, M. Katz, W. Jenks and M. Lachs. What is more, the universalist jurists of Europe had been preceded by those of Asia and the Middle East: Sui Tchoan-Pao, Bandyopadhyoy, Rechid.[5]

Another view may be that the term does not convey such discrimination but implies it. As a result, it is inapplicable, or silently or tacitly ignored in practice. And indeed it has been.[6]

III. Drafting history showing the term "civilized" having no real meaning

Further study and reflection persuade me however that the sense and content that Judge Ammoun ascribed to the term "civilized" is much stronger than intended by the drafters or actually given to it in subsequent practice, whatever impression the phrase may give us. This is first and foremost demonstrated in the drafting history of Article 38(1)(c).

The Advisory Committee of Jurists at The Hague, tasked to draft a statute for the PCIJ, did not appear to give the phrase any "hard" meaning, but appeared to use it as a sort of symbolic projection of an image that the jurists thought States should aspire to. In fact, there was no explanation on the content of the term when it appeared, first apparently in the proposal on applicable law made by Descamps, as "les règles de droit international telles que les reconnaît la conscience juridique des peuples civilisés" (in translation, "the rules of international law as recognised by the legal conscience of civilised nations").[7]

The discussions of the Committee focused on other issues such as the nature of the principles. Concerned that States would not consent to the Court's jurisdiction unless the Court would decide cases within the confines of treaties

---

5 North Sea Continental Shelf, ICJ Reports 1969, 133-34 (Sep. op. Ammoun).

6 See Part IV below.

7 Permanent Court of International Justice Advisory Committee, Procès-verbaux of the Proceedings of the Committee, June 16th—July 24th, 1920 (1920) (PCIJAC PV), 306. All members of the Committee spoke in French except Mr. Root, and so the English version should be deemed as translation except the remarks by Mr. Root. Ibid., iv.

and recognized rules, Root reformulated this category of sources as "the general principles of law recognised by civilised nations".[8] This appeared also in Ricci-Busatti's proposal.[9] The Root formulation was subsequently incorporated into the Root-Phillimore Plan.[10] That formulation was ultimately adopted.

The meaning of the term "civilised" was not touched upon until de Lapradelle objected to the phrase "civilised nations". Phillimore's first response was that Ricci-Busatti's scheme also used the same phrase. De Lapradelle said that the phrase was "superfluous, because law implies civilisation",[11] and proceeded to make other points.

Then Phillimore explained that "the general principles [...] were these which were accepted by all nations in *foro domestico*".[12] The term "all nations" is worth noting; it makes no distinction between or among nations.

After that, de Lapradelle agreed that "the principles which formed the bases of national law, were also sources of international law. The only generally recognised principles which exist, however, are those which have obtained unanimous or quasi-unanimous support."[13] He then proposed that a simpler formulation "general principles of law" be used,[14] but did not fight hard to prevail. Perhaps a certain tendency of being "diplomatic" without pressing one's arguments to the sharpest set in. In any event, the Root-Phillimore formulation more or less has prevailed.

These statements by Phillimore and de Lapradelle do not indicate any value-added in the phrase "civilised". According to de Lapradelle's view, every State that has law is civilized. So viewed, all nations are equally civilized. These statements were influential in finalizing the provision discussed here. It would seem reasonable to conclude that expressly or even consciously the drafters intended to make no distinction between different nations or States. Unconsciously, however, the phrase "civilized nations" was probably a picture that froze the times, as explained below.

Because these comments show quite clearly that no real meaning was given to the phrase "civilized", we need not resort to any inference (normally resorted to when ambiguity exists) that one may draw from the use of "various

---

8 Ibid., 344.

9 Ibid., 351.

10 Ibid., 548.

11 See, ibid., 335.

12 Ibid.

13 Ibid., 335.

14 Ibid., 336.

nations" in article 38(1)(d). Furthermore, the second part of Article 38(1)(d) containing that phrase deals with individuals, and, thus, not the same kind of matter as dealt with in Article 38(1)(c). In addition, the idea that has become Article 38(1)(d) was proposed later than was Article 38(1)(c). There was no explanation for the use of the phrase "the various nations" in the drafting record, apparently believed to be a clear term. In any event, if inferences could be and were made from the phrase "various nations", a phrase obviously making no distinction between different nations used in the same article where "civilized nations" appears, these inferences would counsel reading the two phrases as having the same meaning and making no any distinction between different nations. It would be strange for the drafters to make a distinction between various nations in paragraph 1(c) but no distinction in paragraph 1(d) of Article 38.

An attempt to give some meaning to the phrase "civilized" by reading the term "nations" not as "States" but as "peoples" and then making a distinction between "civilized" and "uncivilized" peoples ultimately is unconvincing. This view fixates its attention on the original formulation of "la conscience juridique des peuples civilisés" by Descamps,[15] and then makes a distinction between various peoples. First of all, while his French original used this formulation, the English translation used "nations". During his speeches, Descamps used both "la conscience juridique des peuples civilisés"[16] and "la conscience juridique de nations civilisées".[17] We know that a common meaning of "nations" during that period of time was "States", as we can tell from the term "League of Nations", which is followed in the subsequently used term "United Nations". It is not so clear that Descamps was using the term as meaning "not State"; it is quite clear that there was a loose choice of words prevailing there, not a rare occurrence during international conferences. Descamps may just as well have had "States" in mind when he talked at the same time about "la conscience juridique des peuples civilisés" and "la conscience juridique de nations civilisées".

Second, Descamps used the term "la conscience juridique". Normally if a people is not organized into a State or some sort of political structure, there is probably no such a thing as "la conscience juridique", but only "la conscience

15 PCIJAC PV, n.7 above, 306.

16 Ibid., 318.

17 Ibid., 323.

morale". This is the insight from general jurisprudence.[18] So probably Descamps could not have meant plain old "peuples", pure and simple, but had in mind "peuples" organized into "States", and the term used was meant to express this idea.

Third, when Root's formulation debuted with the phrase "general principles of law as recognised by civilised nations" in the English original (Root spoke English during the discussions), although the French translation still retained the term "peuples civilisés", "nations" was used by Root in the sense of "States". This is not just because of the implications of the term "law". He used "nations" to mean "States" in his proposed description of custom as "international custom, being recognised practice between nations accepted by them as law",[19] since no one has argued that international custom can be general practice of peoples that are not States. It is reasonable to expect that he used "nations" in the same sense in the next paragraph on "general principles" in his proposal.[20] More importantly, Root would turn in his grave if he were taken as endorsing principles of various peoples not organized into States, as he was the most vocal advocate for placing particular emphasis on the need to take account of the attitudes of States.[21] He stated bluntly that "the States would not accept a Court which had the right to settle disputes in accordance with rules established by the Court itself, and by the interpretation of more or less vague principles".[22] Phillimore's remarks, as quoted above,[23] introducing the Root-Phillimore formulation incorporating Root's formulation also had "States" in mind.

As Root's formulation was what was subsequently adopted, his use of terms in the original English would be most important. This factor militates against, perhaps is fatal to, the argument for construing "nations" as "peoples".

Moreover, other members of the Committee understood the term as "State" because they used expressions such as "les principes qui sont à la base du droit national".[24] It would be difficult to argue that here "droit national" was referring to "people's law". Consistency would militate in favor of finding the concept of "State" in both "droit national" and "civilized nations".

---

18 Cf. H.L.A. Hart, The Concept of Law (2d ed. 1994), 79-99.

19 PCIJAC PV, n.7 above, 344.

20 Ibid.

21 See Danilenko, n.1 above, 254 n.6.

22 PCIJAC PV, n.7 above, 286.

23 See text to n.12 above.

24 PCIJAC PV, n.7 above, 335 (de Lapradelle).

Subsequently, Fernandes used "States", speaking of "le pouvoir de juger—à défaut de droit conventionnel ou coutumier—selon les principes de droit international non rejetés avant le differérend par la tradition juridique de l'un des Etats en conflit".[25]

In due course, the Drafting Committee's proposal had the French version as "les principes généraux de droit reconnus par les nations civilisées".[26] This phrase ultimately ended up in the Final Report of the Committee,[27] and then in the Statute of the PCIJ[28] and that of the ICJ.[29]

There does not appear to be any meaningful discussion of the phrase during the drafting conferences at the League of Nations, the meetings of the Washington Committee of Jurists or the San Francisco Conference adopting the United Nations Charter including the Statute of the ICJ. These subsequent exercises thus added nothing to the meaning of the term "civilized".[30]

This progression of the use of terms shows that if there were any confusion in the beginning of the debates, that was cleared up as the discussions moved forward. There is thus no support for reading "nations" as "peoples".

Those arguing for construing "nations" as "peoples" also sought support in an arbitration decision made in 1951 in which the Tribunal excluded the local legal system from the sources to resort to, because the local system did not contain the relevant rules or principles as a result of its primitive state.[31] This reliance is misplaced. Even assuming the Tribunal did sufficient work and was correct, the better view is that the local system could be excluded not because it was uncivilized or simply primitive, but because it so happened that the system did not contain the relevant rules. No legal system however sophisticated can be expected to contain all rules and principles adequate for all issues. The argument that there is no more non-liquet at present[32] in my view is only a

---

25 Ibid., 346.

26 Ibid., 567.

27 Ibid., 730.

28 League of Nations, n.13 above.

29 UNCIO (Selected Documents version, US Government Printing Office, 1946), 973.

30 See below, Part V.

31 See Bin Cheng, General Principles of Law as Applied by International Courts and Tribunals (1953, Grotius Classic Reprint Series 2006), 25, & n.7 citing to the Abu Dhabi Oil Arbitration (1951) (1 ICLQ (1952), 247; 18 ILR 144).

32 See, e.g., Legality of the Threat or Use of Nuclear Weapons, ICJ Reports 1996,

statement of aspiration, not reality, unless one would completely agree with the arguments of Ronald Dworkin that all the relevant legal data or background always point to a legal solution that fits the scheme of things, which solution a judge should adopt.[33] Local systems, interestingly, sometimes may contain some rules and principles that deal with the pains and aspirations of the local people in a sophisticated way. Thus, one should not consider a local system primitive or uncivilized simply because it does not have applicable laws on a particular topic. In any event, one should be slow in building any edifice on an arbitration decision made some 30 years after the original PCIJ Statute was drafted and adopted and several years after the new ICJ Statute entered into force.

Accordingly, not having any concrete, hard meaning, the appearance of the phrase "civilized" in the draft Statute, then the Statute, of the PCIJ may be simply an imprint of the zeitgeist of that era, in a subconscious way. It is simply an acoustic tool that makes certain people from certain background feel happy. The general preconceptions and/or prejudices simply found their way in the work product of the group of elite jurists, their elite upbringing notwithstanding. This shows that even this group of high-calibered jurists was not immune from the normal mortal's pitfalls. There is something unseemly or perhaps invidious in such a reality of life, probably showing a measure of subconsciousness which embodies the worst form of the invidiousness. It was so bad that it came naturally without any express elaboration.[34]

A more vivid illustration of this prevailing, indiscriminating and insensitive mood can be found in the very drafting records of the Committee of Jurists. Altamira, of Spain, made a drafting proposal. The content of that proposal is unimportant for our purposes. Apparently it was considered to be unrealistic. Another member of the Committee responded that he "had followed with great interest M. Altamira's proposals, that he respected M. Altamira's views, but that he could not forget that Spain was the land of Don Quixote".[35] Altamira felt compelled to make a written response, and did so several days later. That sentence must have left on him a deep impression; indeed, "scar" would be the better word. His response read: "despite my best endeavours I fail to understand the point of this witty allusion to my country

226, para.105(2)(E) (*dipositif*); but contra Higgins, Diss. Op. at ibid., 583.

33 See generally Ronald Dworkin, Law's Empire (1986).

34 PCIJAC PV, n.7 above, 335.

35 Ibid., 125.

and Don Quixote".[36]

IV. Subsequent practice on point in the Court and elsewhere disregarding the term "civilized"

That *was* reality and is, happily, history now. Subsequent practice in the Permanent Court of Intenrational Justice as well as the current Court—granted that either has seldom resorted to Article 38(1)(c) at all[37]—and elsewhere has studiously eschewed this usage. There is no evidence that this phrase was ever given concrete and substantive meaning in judicial practice or legal practice generally. That is to say, what one can glean from the drafting history of Article 38(1)(c) has no doubt been confirmed and solidified in practice.

As Rosenne noted as recent as in 1996 in his famous treatise on the International Court, "The reference in head (c) to 'civilized nations' is, whatever its historical origins, untoward to the extent that it implies a value-judgment on the degree of 'civilization' attained by different nations. It is tacitly dropped in today's literature on the Court and on international law."[38] In his new edition of that treatise, he omitted the latter sentence without any explanation.[39]

Whatever literature may say, official practice no doubt has consistently eschewed the term "civilized" where a situational context exists similar to that giving rise to Article 38(1)(c). For example, the International Covenant on Civil and Political Rights (1966),[40] in Article 15(2), uses the phrase of "the general principles of law recognized by the community of nations", making no distinction between any States. The Vienna Convention on the Law of Treaties (1969),[41] in Article 53, speaks of the "international community of States as a whole", making no distinction between any of them. The International Law

---

36 Ibid., 139, 145-146 (Annex 3).

37 Alain Pellet, Article 38, in: Andreas Zimmermann, Karin Oellers-Frahm & Christian Tomuschat (eds.), n.1 above, 771, Margin Note 260.

38 Shabtai Rosenne, 3 Law and Practice of the International Court: 1920-1996 (1997), 1601-02, n.81.

39 See id., n.1 above (4th ed. 2006), 1546, n.86. Perhaps he was moved to make this change because of the appearance of some articles on this issue between the two editions of his treatise. See, for example, David P. Fidler, The Return to the Standard of Civilization, 2 Chicago JIL (2001), 137.

40 999 UNTS 171.

41 1155 UNTS 331.

Commission's Articles on State Responsibility (2001),[42] in article 48(1)(b), speaks of "the international community as a whole", once again making no distinction between any players or components. The American Law Institute's Restatement Third of the Foreign Relations Law of the United States of 1986, in §102(1)(c), speaks of "general principles common to the major legal systems of the world", once again without making any distinction between any of them. The commentary to §102 speaks of "common to the systems of national law",[43] and the Reporters' Notes, "common to national legal systems".[44] Neither shows any signs of any distinctions being made between the various national legal systems.

That is to say, the obnoxious part of the phrasing "civilized nations" in Article 38(c) of the ICJ Statute has been disregarded, though not discarded yet. No doubt the views of the contemporary commentators that the phrase "civilized" is redundant[45] or that "one must not give too much importance to the 'archaistic' requirement of recognition 'by civilized nations'"[46] are correct.[47] This is not to say that now and then politicians may not utter this phrase, but their resort to it is for a purpose other than giving it any concrete and practical consequence in the legal field.

Such is the state of affairs that there is no need for one to go into the treacherous waters as to which State is more civilized than another. A person

---

42 A/RES/56/83 (2001), annex; A/56/10 (2001), 59.

43 ALI, n.17 above, §102, comment *l*.

44 Ibid., §102, Reporters' Notes, n.7.

45 Bin Cheng, General Principles of Law, n.31 above, 25.

46 Alain Pellet, Article 38, in: Andreas Zimmermann, Karin Oellers-Frahm & Christian Tomuschat (eds.), n.1 above, 769.

47 If the analysis and assessment made here are correct, the argument that the "category 'civilized nations' was not defined once and for all in 1920; it remains open, and subject (at least in theory) to fluctuation", Hugh Thirlway, Law and Procedure of the International Court of Justice, 61 BYIL (1990), 124, or that the term should be read to be consistent with the contemporary moral sentiments, could not be correct as a matter of law in this context (although in human rights law, such an argument may have currency), but can only be expressed as what someone believes to be a "smart" idea. Of course, not every State is truly equal in reality, but no difference was justified on grounds of degrees of civilized-ness. For a discussion of various "difference arguments", see Sienho Yee, Sovereign Equality of States and the Legitimacy of "Leader States", in: Ronald St. John Macdonald and Douglas M. Johnston (eds.), Towards World Constitutionalism (2005), 737-772 [Chapter 8 below].

with a critical mind and a sense of history will know how to answer this question.

V. Reasons for not disturbing Article 38(1)(c)

One then wonders why the Statute of the Court should not be brought into line with these developments in the use of terms by amending Article 38(1)(c) to read "the general principles of law recognized by nations of the world". This should have been done earlier, particularly when the new Statute was adopted in 1945. Before 1945, many people, including Chinese scholars,[48] had harbored outrage over their national States being excluded from the "family of civilized nations". The undesirability of the old usage was known to the world, at least to a large part of it. The general imperfection of the wording of Article 38 was also most likely understood. With nations smarting from an atrocious war, with severe time pressure for establishing a new United Nations, probably the attitude or feelings of inertia—"if something ain't seriously broken, don't fix it"—prevailed. However, the concerns underlying the argument made at the drafting of the new Statute that Article 38 had worked well in practice and should not be reopened were with reopening the debate on the substantive content of the provision. The jurists may be afraid that once reopened, Article 38 may not survive the debate intact, or that time was not in its favor.

One can see this sentiment in the drafting records. Basdevant was reported to have said at the UN Committee of Jurists at Washington, DC:

> [W]hile Article 38 was not well drafted, it would be difficult to make a better draft in the time at the disposal of the Committee. He also called attention to the fact that the Court had operated very well under Article

48 This issue was one of some significance during that period of time to many scholars. For a discussion of the influential views of that particular period of time, see Georges Abi-Saab, International Law and the International Community: The Long Road to Universality, in: Ronald St. John Macdonald (ed.), Essays in Honour of Wang Tieya (1994), 39, 41. Chinese scholars were familiar with how Western scholars viewed China. Professor Wang Tieya, who studied international law at the London School of Economics during 1936-39 or thereabouts, several times mentioned, during various discussions, to me this issue and his experiences at the London School of Economics and Political Science. Professor Wang's experiences were also described, in part, in: Ronald St. John Macdonald (ed.), ibid., 6-7 (Introduction by the Editor).

38. He felt, therefore, that time should not be spent in redrafting it.[49]

The Report of the Committee, with Basdevant as its Rapporteur, stated:

> Article 38, which determines, according to its terms, what the Court "shall apply" has given rise to more controversies in doctrine than difficulties in practice. The Committee thought that it was not the opportune time to undertake the revision of this article. It has trusted to the Court to put it into operation, and has left it without change other than that which appears in the numbering of the provisions of this article.[50]

Again, just as the fact that de Lapradelle did not press his argument hard enough during the drafting of the original Statute may bespeak a sort of "polite diplomatic tendency", perhaps the same sort of tendency set in during the drafting of the new Statute.

The concerns about disturbing the substantive content of Article 38 are not relevant to our discussion here because deleting "civilized" does not affect the substantive content of Article 38(1)(c). As related to earlier, despite the obnoxious phrasing, this provision does not really restrict any enlightened search for general principles to only those recognized in some so-called civilized nations.[51] One can surmise that if a redrafting of Article 38 was done, some cleaning up might have been done.

VI. Reasons for Cleaning Up Article 38(1)(c)

In this paper, I have argued in favor of the proposal that Article 38(1)(c) should be amended by deleting the word "civilized". This proposal does not affect the substantive meaning of Article 38, but aims to clean up the infelicities left behind by the imperfect drafting processes as described above.

One may ask if no substantive content is being affected, what is the fuss

---

49 14 UNCIO, 170-71 (statement by Basdevant).

50 Ibid., 843 (Report of the Committee of Jurists (Basdevant, Rapporteur)); UNCIO (Selected Documents version, US Government Printing Office, 1946), 868.

51 The subsequent practice shows that perhaps Judge Ammoun was over-estimating the force of the phrase "civilized nations" in his sep. op. in North

about the phrase? Or, as they ask, what is in a name? After all, Shakespeare tells us that rose will smell the same even if we give it a different name. *Pace* Shakespeare, a proper term is important. In the East, Confucius cautions us that,[52] when we do not get the name right, we cannot expressly ourselves properly; when we cannot express ourselves properly, we cannot accomplish our mission. An improper name confuses the ear and confounds the eye, particularly those who are at their first exposure to international law. I have encountered students and scholars who took the phrase "civilized nations" at its face value, apparently unaware of the issues pointed out here. While further study may cure the defect of taking the beguiling phrase at face value, the improper wording is no doubt one of the culprits. So generally there is value in ensuring accurate phrasing. Apparently "natural reason"[53] has been misled by the phrase.

Secondly, from time to time in public discussions, one does see invidious invocations of the phrase "civilized nations", apparently with the intent to inflame and injure. Although such invocations normally take place in informal discussions, the fact that they occur at all calls for action to remove the convenient tool for inflaming passions.

Finally, the appearance of the word "civilized" in Article 38(1)(c) is a wound to those States and their nationals that have suffered dearly and unjustly in the past. The world should do all it can to eliminate the emotional suffering triggered by a reminder in a frequently used instrument with enormous symbolic value such as the Statute. This is not too much to ask for, at a time when international law has raised high the banner of human dignity and entered

---

Sea Continental Shelf, as quoted in the text to n.5 above.

52 Confucius, Lunyu, Zilu.

53 In Catherine D. Bowen, The Lion and the Throne: The Life and Times of Sir Edward Coke (1957), 304-05, the author described Coke arguing with the King regarding whether the King protects the common law or vice versa. Coke wrote: "Then the King said that he thought the Law was founded upon Reason, and that he and others had Reason as well as the Judges. To which it was answered by me, that true it was that God had endowed his Majesty with excellent science and great endowments of Nature. But his Majesty was not learned in the Laws of his Realm of England; and Causes which concern the Life, or Inheritance, or Goods, or Fortunes of his Subjects are not to be decided by natural Reason but by the artificial Reason and Judgment of Law, which requires long Study and Experience before that a man can attain to the cognizance of it….".

a phase of co-progressiveness, as I have observed elsewhere.[54] At this moment, peoples all over the world are now supposed to go out of their way to make others happy, so that the whole world may enjoy a high index of happiness, why not let us make those who do not like the term happy by deleting it, especially when doing so does not do any violence to the Statute, or incur any meaningful cost at all? It would seem that it one were to pay real respect, not lip service, to human dignity, the first thing one would do would be to fix this sordid phrase, unless one wanted to keep it as a souvenir of human imperfection.

The singular importance of the ICJ Statute as a pillar in the international legal system, and Article 38 is a more important part of that pillar, especially in the system of international legal reasoning, something that every international lawyer or scholar puts on the pedestal and from which there is no escape, is such that each of the points discussed above is magnified greatly. Thus this special place where the term "civilized" appears adds special force to each of the arguments I have made here for its removal. Hopefully in the fullness of time this term will disappear from Article 38(1)(c).

---

54 See Sienho Yee, Towards an International Law of Co-progressiveness (2004), 1-26, reprinting an earlier article of the same title in: Sienho Yee & Wang Tieya (eds.), International Law in the Post-Cold War World: Essays in Memory of Li Haopei (2001), 18-39. A fuller elaboration is found in Chapter 1 of this volume.

Chapter 3

The *Kosovo* Advisory Opinion of the International Court of Justice*

I. Introduction

1. The Advisory Opinion proceeding concerning *Accordance with International Law of the Unilateral Declaration of Independence in Respect of Kosovo* (the *Kosovo* Advisory Opinion)[1] is the first in which all of the permanent members of the Security Council have participated in both the written and oral proceedings,[2] a situation

* First published as: Notes on the International Court of Justice (Part 4): The Kosovo Advisory Opinion, 9 Chinese Journal of International Law (2010), 763-782. The opinions are personal. I am grateful to the reviewers for their comments. This note was completed on 2 December 2010, as part of the work for Research Project No. 08&ZD055 of the China Social Sciences Foundation. All websites were last visited on this date unless otherwise noted. I find the use of the phrases "proceedings", "proceeding" and "case" quite difficult in the context of advisory opinion proceedings and will not try hard to distinguish them. Furthermore, "Federal Republic of Yugoslavia" and "Serbia" are used as interchangeable.

The original version contains this abstract: "This note first summarizes the Kosovo Advisory Opinion of the International Court of Justice of 22 July 2010 and then makes observations regarding several issues involved in the proceedings: the reformulation of the question presented by the United Nations General Assembly, the interpretation of Security Council resolution 1244 and the Constitutional Framework, self-determination and remedial secession and the unlawful use of force by the NATO in 1999."

1 Accordance with International Law of the Unilateral Declaration of Independence in respect of Kosovo, Advisory Opinion, 22 July 2010 (Kosovo AO), ICJ Reports 2010. All materials regarding this matter are found at the ICJ website (http://www.icj-cij.org).

2 Ibid., paras.6, 14, listing written statements received and oral statements heard.

not found even in the *Nuclear Weapons* Advisory Opinion proceedings.[3] During the period leading up to the proceedings, a great deal of literature appeared, including the *Agora: Kosovo*[4] published in the *Chinese Journal of International Law*. One could easily feel the high stakes in the proceedings.[5]

2. Against this background, the Advisory Opinion given by the Court on 22 July 2010 appears anti-climatic. To the question asked by the United Nations General Assembly (UNGA)—"Is the unilateral declaration of independence by the Provisional Institutions of Self-government of Kosovo in accordance with international law?"—the Court replied that it "*Is of the opinion* that the declaration of independence of Kosovo adopted on 17 February 2008 did not violate international law".[6] Earlier on in the opinion, the Court decided that it would not deal with the issue as to whether, outside the defined context relating to previous colonial experience or alien subjugation, international law provides for a right of self-determination or "remedial secession",[7] a question helping to engender much of the attention to the request for advisory opinion.

3. In this note, I will first summarize the background to the proceedings and the *Kosovo* Advisory Opinion itself. I will then make observations regarding several issues involved in the proceedings: the reformulation of the question presented by the UNGA, the interpretation of Security Council resolution 1244 and the Constitutional Framework, self-determination and remedial secession and the unlawful use of force by the NATO in 1999. In so doing, I do not aspire to present comprehensive arguments about, or solutions to, the potential problems identified.

II. The background

4. Often it is said that Kosovo has been the cradle of Serbian culture. According to one encyclopaedia, the name Kosovo is derived from a Serbian place-name

---

3 Legality of the Threat or Use of Nuclear Weapons, Advisory Opinion, ICJ Reports 1996, 226, paras.5, 9, listing written statements received and oral statements heard.

4 Agora: Kosovo, 8 Chinese JIL (2009), 1–61, 285–298, 573–592.

5 For an analysis of these high stakes, see Rein Müllerson, Precedents in the Mountains: On the Parallels and Uniqueness of the Cases of Kosovo, South Ossetia and Abkhazia, 8 Chinese JIL (2009), 2–25.

6 Kosovo AO, paras.1, 123(3).

7 Ibid., para.83.

meaning "field of blackbirds".[8] For some time, Kosovo was the centre of the Serbian kingdom. In 1389, it was the site of the Battle of Kosovo that formed part of the legacy of the Serb folklore. After the Serbs lost the battle, Kosovo was ruled by the Ottoman Empire from the mid-fifteenth to the early twentieth century, and the population of Albanian speakers in the region increased. In the early twentieth century, Kosovo was incorporated, as an autonomous province, into Serbia, later one of the constituent republics of Yugoslavia. By the second half of the century, the Muslim ethnic Albanians constituted a majority of the inhabitants in Kosovo, and interethnic tensions frequently became difficult to manage.

5. In 1989, Serbia revoked autonomy for Kosovo, and the Kosovo War ensued between the central government and the local Kosovo forces such as the Kosovo Liberation Army. The armed conflict was so fierce and the humanitarian crisis was so severe that the NATO intervened militarily in 1999, aiming ostensibly to stop the atrocities. The Western powers organized a Rambouillet Conference, attempting to induce Serbia to accept the Rambouillet Accords, to no avail. The NATO military campaign continued. Then an agreement to cease fire was reached, with many conditions incorporated into United Nations Security Council resolution 1244,[9] adopted under Chapter VII of the United Nations Charter. That resolution in its preamble "reaffirmed the commitment of all Member States to the sovereignty and territorial integrity of the Federal Republic of Yugoslavia and the other States of the region".[10]

6. The resolution instituted an international security presence to maintain peace as well as an international civil presence (the UNMIK) under the authority of the UN Secretary-General (UNSG)

> in Kosovo in order to provide an interim administration for Kosovo under which the people of Kosovo can enjoy *substantial autonomy within the Federal Republic of Yugoslavia*, and which will provide transitional administration while establishing and overseeing the development of provisional democratic selfgoverning institutions to ensure conditions for a peaceful and normal life for all inhabitants of Kosovo. [Emphasis added.][11]

---

8 www.britannica.com/EBchecked/topic/322726/Kosovo.

9 S/RES/1244 (1999).

10 Ibid., 10th preambular paragraph.

11 Ibid., para.10.

This interim regime was in due course established. Under this regime, all legislative and executive authority with respect to Kosovo is vested in the UNMIK and is exercised by the Special Representative of the Secretary-General. A Constitutional Framework was promulgated on 15 May 2001, defining the responsibilities relating to the administration of Kosovo between the Special Representative of the Secretary-General and the Provisional Institutions of Self-Government of Kosovo.[12] These institutions include the President of Kosovo, the Assembly of Kosovo, and a Government of Kosovo headed by the Prime Minister. The interim regime was intended to exist, "pending a final settlement".[13] One of the responsibilities of international civil presence was "Facilitating a political process designed to determine Kosovo's future status, taking into account the Rambouillet accords".[14]

7. Efforts were stepped up to seek a negotiated, political final settlement of the status of Kosovo, spearheaded by Mr. Martti Ahtisaari, UNSG's Special Envoy on Kosovo's future status. But the parties involved were slow to make any progress, leading to the Special Envoy's conclusion in his 2007 Report that the parties were not able to reach any agreement on Kosovo's future status.[15] He also concluded that "Reintegration into Serbia is not a viable option" and that "Independence with international supervision is the only viable option".[16] He thus made a "Comprehensive Proposal for the Kosovo Status Settlement",[17] which would ultimately give Kosovo independence.

8. On 17 February 2008, a declaration of independence in respect of Kosovo was made by a group of persons who were designated as "the Provisional Institutions of Self-government of Kosovo"[18] in the question presented by the UNGA but whose identity became a matter of controversy in the proceedings.

9. Serbia rejected that declaration and the proclaimed independence of

12 UNMIK regulation 2001/9, 15 May 2001; Kosovo AO, para.62.

13 S/RES/1244 (1999), para.11(a).

14 Ibid., para.11(e).

15 S/2007/168, Report of the Special Envoy, para.1.

16 Ibid.

17 Ibid., and S/2007/168/Add. 1, 26 March 2007. For an analysis of this proposal, see Rüdiger Wolfrum, Kosovo: Some Thoughts on Its Future Status, in: Sienho Yee and Jacques-Yvan Morin (eds.), Multiculturalism and International Law (2009), 561–574.

18 Kosovo AO, para.1.

Kosovo. But a sizeable number of States recognized the independence of Kosovo within a short period of time. Serbia then went to the UNGA to sponsor a resolution asking the Court for an advisory opinion on the question, as stated above, "Is the unilateral declaration of independence by the Provisional Institutions of Self-government of Kosovo in accordance with international law?"[19]

III. The *Kosovo* Advisory Opinion

10. The Court's reply to the question presented by the UNGA follows from a two-part framework of analysis. In the first part, the Court identified what it considered to be the essence of the question: "whether or not the applicable international law prohibited the declaration of independence".[20] The Court first contrasted the UNGA's question with that presented to the Supreme Court of Canada in the *Secession of Quebec* case[21] and proceeded to the point:

> 56. The question put to the Supreme Court of Canada inquired whether there was a right to "effect secession", and whether there was a rule of international law which conferred a positive entitlement on any of the organs named. By contrast, the General Assembly has asked whether the declaration of independence was "in accordance with" international law. The answer to that question turns on whether or not the applicable international law prohibited the declaration of independence. If the Court concludes that it did, then it must answer the question put by saying that the declaration of independence was not in accordance with international law. It follows that the task which the Court is called upon to perform is to determine whether or not the declaration of independence was adopted in violation of international law. The Court is not required by the question it has been asked to take a position on whether international law conferred a positive entitlement on Kosovo unilaterally to declare its independence or, *a fortiori*, on whether international law generally confers an entitlement on entities situated within a State unilaterally to break away from it. Indeed, it is entirely possible for a particular act such as a unilateral declaration of

19 Ibid.

20 Ibid., para.56.

21 [1998] 2 S.C.R. 217, 115 I.L.R. 536.

> independence not to be in violation of international law without necessarily constituting the exercise of a right conferred by it. The Court has been asked for an opinion on the first point, not the second.

11. The second part of the analysis consists in a search for any applicable prohibitions in international law. The Court found none.[22] The Court first looked for such prohibitions in general international law. In a rather summary fashion, the Court said:

> 79. During the eighteenth, nineteenth and early twentieth centuries, there were numerous instances of declarations of independence, often strenuously opposed by the State from which independence was being declared. Sometimes a declaration resulted in the creation of a new State, at others it did not. In no case, however, does the practice of States as a whole suggest that the act of promulgating the declaration was regarded as contrary to international law. On the contrary, State practice during this period points clearly to the conclusion that international law contained no prohibition of declarations of independence. During the second half of the twentieth century, the international law of self-determination developed in such a way as to create a right to independence for the peoples of non-self-governing territories and peoples subject to alien subjugation, domination and exploitation [citation to cases omitted]. A great many new States have come into existence as a result of the exercise of this right. There were, however, also instances of declarations of independence outside this context. The practice of States in these latter cases does not point to the emergence in international law of a new rule prohibiting the making of a declaration of independence in such cases.

12. It then proceeded to reject the argument that a prohibition of unilateral declaration of independence is implicit in the principle of territorial integrity.[23]

13. The Court then explained why it would not deal with the issue of self-determination or remedial secession:

> 82. A number of participants in the present proceedings have claimed,

22 Kosovo AO, part IV.

23 Ibid., paras.80–81.

> although in almost every instance only as a secondary argument, that the population of Kosovo has the right to create an independent State either as a manifestation of a right to self-determination or pursuant to what they described as a right of "remedial secession" in the face of the situation in Kosovo.
>
> The Court has already noted (see paragraph 79 above) that one of the major developments of international law during the second half of the twentieth century has been the evolution of the right of self-determination. Whether, outside the context of non-self-governing territories and peoples subject to alien subjugation, domination and exploitation, the international law of self-determination confers upon part of the population of an existing State a right to separate from that State is, however, a subject on which radically different views were expressed by those taking part in the proceedings and expressing a position on the question. Similar differences existed regarding whether international law provides for a right of "remedial secession" and, if so, in what circumstances. There was also a sharp difference of views as to whether the circumstances which some participants maintained would give rise to a right of "remedial secession" were actually present in Kosovo.
>
> 83. The Court considers that it is not necessary to resolve these questions in the present case. The General Assembly has requested the Court's opinion only on whether or not the declaration of independence is in accordance with international law. Debates regarding the extent of the right of self-determination and the existence of any right of "remedial secession", however, concern the right to separate from a State. As the Court has already noted (see paragraphs 49 to 56 above), and as almost all participants agreed, that issue is beyond the scope of the question posed by the General Assembly. To answer that question, the Court need only determine whether the declaration of independence violated either general international law or the *lex specialis* created by Security Council resolution 1244 (1999).

14. The Court then looked for any applicable prohibitions in Security Council resolution 1244 or the measures adopted thereunder, primarily the Constitutional Framework.

15. Before the Court conducted this search, it first concluded that the authors of the declaration of independence were not the "Provisional

Institutions of Self-Government within the Constitutional Framework, but rather as persons who acted together in their capacity as representatives of the people of Kosovo outside the framework of the interim administration".[24] The Court made this finding despite the express language of the UNGA's question characterizing the authors as the "Provisional Institutions of Self-Government". The momentousness of this finding was already noted earlier on in the Court's opinion.[25]

16. Searching for applicable prohibitions from this new vantage point, the Court found that Security Council resolution 1244 did not "bar the authors of the declaration of 17 February 2008 from issuing a declaration of independence from the Republic of Serbia".[26] The reasons are two-fold. Firstly, the resolution was intended to create an interim regime, while the declaration of independence was an attempt at final status. The two, therefore, operated at two different levels. Secondly, the authors of the independence, as re-characterized by the Court, were not the addressees of any obligations under that Security Council resolution 1244.[27]

17. Furthermore, the Court found that because the declaration of independence was not made by the Provisional Institutions of Self-Government, the declaration was not intended to take effect within the legal order in which those Provisional Institutions operated. Therefore, the declaration did not violate the Constitutional Framework.[28] A simpler way to put all this would be that neither Security Council resolution 1244 nor the Constitutional Framework applies to the authors of the declaration of independence, re-characterized by the Court as "persons who acted together in their capacity as representatives of the people of Kosovo outside the framework of the interim administration".[29]

18. The Court then proceeded to its general conclusion: "the adoption of the declaration of independence of 17 February 2008 did not violate general international law, Security Council resolution 1244 (1999) or the Constitutional

---

24 Ibid., para.109.

25 Ibid., para.52 ("a matter which is capable of affecting the answer to the question").

26 Ibid., para.119.

27 Ibid., paras.110–119.

28 Ibid., para.121. Probably, other measures could be relevant (see the Court's heading for this section: "the measures adopted thereunder"), but the Court focused on the Constitutional Framework.

29 Ibid., para.109.

Framework. Consequently the adoption of that declaration did not violate any applicable rule of international law."[30]

IV. Observations

19. The *Kosovo* Advisory Opinion, although anti-climatic, does give us a great deal of food for thought. This was attested to by the large number of declarations and individual opinions that the Judges appended to the Court's opinion.[31] The issues identified and positions expressed by the Court may have important impact. Here I will highlight some of the issues that I find to be of interest.

IV.A. Reformulation of the question of the UNGA

20. As has been noted, "At first sight, the text of the request [of the UNGA] might surprise us".[32] Obviously, such a question, which is surprising and perhaps somewhat awkward if indeed—in the words of the Court—"narrow and specific",[33] is ripe for reformulation by the Court before receiving an answer. The dispute is how to reformulate it. The Court's reformulation of this question goes to two aspects of the question: (1) the identity of the authors of the declaration of independence[34] and (2) the meaning of the question.[35] Regarding the first aspect, the Court itself admitted that it is "a matter which is capable of affecting the answer to the question".[36] Vice-President Tomka described this as "outcome-determinative".[37] In fact, the same can be said about the second aspect of the reformulation, as this determined the framework of analysis of the Court, which Judge Simma protested in his declaration.[38]

---

30 Ibid., para.122.

31 A total of nine Judges appended their declarations or individual opinions. See Kosovo AO, at the end, for the list of these and the ICJ website for the full text of them.

32 Peter Hilpold, The Kosovo Case and International Law: Looking for Applicable Theories, 8 Chinese JIL (2009), 47, 60, para.24.

33 Kosovo AO, para.52.

34 Ibid., paras.52–54, 102–109.

35 Ibid., paras.56, 83.

36 Ibid., para.52.

37 Vice-President Tomka, Declaration, para.1.

38 Judge Simma, Declaration.

Furthermore, in the light of the ultimate outcome in this matter, one wonders whether Vice-President Tomka's phrase has gone far enough in describing the relationship between the reformulation and the ultimate result.

21. Regarding the identity aspect of the reformulation, despite the express language of the UNGA's question characterizing the authors as the "Provisional Institutions of Self-Government", the Court found that the authors indeed were not these, but "persons who acted together in their capacity as representatives of the people of Kosovo outside the framework of the interim administration".[39] The Court reached this finding by delving into the facts surrounding the making of the declaration of independence. This finding has been subjected to weighty challenge by Vice-President Tomka:

> This conclusion has no sound basis in the facts relating to the adoption of the declaration, and is nothing more than a *post hoc* intellectual construct. The majority's conclusion implies that all relevant actors did not know correctly who adopted the declaration on 17 February 2008 in Pristina: Serbia, when it proposed the question; other States which were present in the General Assembly when it adopted resolution 63/3; the Secretary-General of the United Nations and his Special Representative; and, most importantly, the Prime Minister of Kosovo when he introduced the text of declaration at the special session of the Assembly of Kosovo![40]

22. More interestingly, one wonders whether it is appropriate for the Court to reform the question this way, given the fact that the UNGA was not entirely wrong, and there could be a properly delimited understanding of the question as going to the "competence of the Provisional Institutions" only, which a Note of Issues from the UK Permanent Representative has identified.[41] Even assuming the question as reformulated by the Court were a better one, one wonders whether the UNGA is necessarily not entitled to an answer to a not-so-good question. Perhaps even if the UNGA got the fact of the identity wrong, one wonders whether the UNGA is necessarily not entitled to an answer to a question based on an assumed fact, when the Court is not seised of a contentious case in which factual disputes may be of the essence but of a

39 Kosovo AO, para.109.

40 Vice-President, Tomka, Declaration, para.12.

41 Ibid., para.15, describing and quoting the Note from the UK.

request for advisory opinion on a legal question, which we know need not be one that is taken from a real situation. These can be questions that are worth exploring.

23. Regarding the meaning of the question, as described above in paragraph 10, the Court first highlighted the question put to the Supreme Court of Canada in the *Secession of Quebec* case, which asked about a right to effect secession, then reasoned this way: "By contrast, the General Assembly has asked whether the declaration of independence was 'in accordance with' international law. The answer to that question turns on whether or not the applicable international law prohibited the declaration of independence."[42] This reformulation of the question about whether the declaration was "in accordance with international law" to whether it "was adopted in violation of international law" has been criticized rightfully by Judge Simma as adopting the *Lotus* rule[43] as its underlying rationale in this case.[44] One may add that it is worse than usual that the Court did so without expressly citing the *Lotus* case. Probably, the world is now more nuanced than what one can get under the binary lens of the *Lotus* rule.

24. Given the second aspect of the reformulation of the question, the terms of Security Council resolution 1244 and the Constitutional Framework, and the outcome in the case, the identity aspect of the reformulation may have been considered the only way to assure a smooth travel to the result, because once one agrees that the authors of the declaration of independence are not the Provisional Institutions of Self-Government, it is not too difficult to accept the position that neither Security Council resolution 1244 nor the Constitutional Framework applies to them. From this perspective, it is not too difficult to understand the essence of the double reformulation of the question.

25. The most important part of the reasoning given by the Court in the "meaning" reformation of the question is: "the General Assembly has asked whether the declaration of independence was 'in accordance with' international law. The answer to that question turns on whether or not the applicable international law prohibited the declaration of independence."[45] With due respect, the second sentence quoted here does not logically follow from the first sentence. But the Court gave no further explanation for its conclusion in the

---

42 Kosovo AO, para.56.

43 PCIJ, "Lotus", Judgment, Series A, No. 10 (1927), 18.

44 Judge Simma, Declaration, esp. paras.2 and 3.

45 Kosovo AO, para.56.

second sentence. The sentences following that sentence, as quoted above in paragraph 10, describe the consequences from the conclusion stated therein. There, the Court was right in noting that the "no violation" sphere in law (which may be described as "this does not violate the law") is broader than the "in accordance with" sphere (which may be described as "this is in accordance with the law"). Still it would be difficult to agree with the Court's view that the UNGA asked it for an opinion on the first point, not the second, because the express language of the question did address the second point, whether the declaration is "in accordance with" international law. The Court here seemed to have turned the question on its head, and opted for the broadest scope of the issue.

26. When presenting to the UNGA the question that it did, Serbia, as the sponsoring State for the request for advisory opinion, may have collapsed several questions into one, for whatever reasons. This is no reason, however, for the Court to reformulate it into one that has the broadest scope which would yield an answer that happens to be most favourable to Kosovo: often a statement that the declaration of independence does not violate international law gives those untutored in law the misimpression that it is lawful. One may call this the "*Lotus*-maximum", drawing inspiration from the *Lotus* rule. This may be considered an important political message; it may provide fodder for political drumbeating and manoeuvring. In fact, a politician holding an office as high as Minister of Foreign Affairs of an important Western State is reported to have claimed in the mass media that the Advisory Opinion "confirms our legal view that the declaration of independence of the Republic of Kosovo was lawful".[46] The mass media brandished headlines in many forums proclaiming a similar message, such as "World court says Kosovo's independence is legal".[47] So it seems that the human mind is simply drawn to this *Lotus*-maximum. One wonders whether when reformulating the question this way the Court sufficiently considered this tendency.

27. In fact, the question can be more properly and more neutrally

---

46 Statement by the German Foreign Minister, as quoted in Wikipedia (en.wikipedia.org/wiki/Reactions_to_the_International_Court_of_Justice_advisory_opinion_on_Kosovo's_declaration_of_independence#cite_note-35). The original link given by Wikipedia no long works and the general caution against using Wikipedia materials should be borne in mind here.

47 See, e.g., AP News, "World court says Kosovo's independence is legal" (www.boston.com/news/world/europe/articles/2010/07/22/world_court_to_rule_on_kosovo_independence/).

dissected into three questions. Firstly, are there any international law rules and principles applicable to the declaration of independence in issue? Secondly, if yes, what are these rules and principles? Thirdly, is the declaration of independence in accordance with these rules and principles? So dissected, the question can be more easily and more neutrally answered. If the answer to the first question is no, then the Court can simply state that there is no international law applicable to the matter and need go no further. Probably with respect to general international law, this is the proper position. It is also a position that was made known to the Court, as it recapped it in paragraph 26 of its opinion.[48] Judge Simma also made this point in his declaration: "The Court could [...] have considered the possibility that international law can be neutral or deliberately silent on the international lawfulness of certain acts."[49] It would seem that taking this approach would give a more accurate and neutral message to the world. The Court, however, did not even explain why this approach was not an appropriate one. Of course, if, under this approach, there are more than one species of law applicable, the Court can give different answers under different categories of applicable law. There may be a conflict of norms or sources to be resolved at the end.

IV.B. Security Council resolution 1244 and the Constitutional Framework

28. The Court started the task of interpreting Security Council resolution 1244 by providing some general comments as follows in paragraph 94 of its opinion:

> While the rules on treaty interpretation embodied in Articles 31 and 32 of the Vienna Convention on the Law of Treaties may provide guidance, differences between Security Council resolutions and treaties mean that the interpretation of Security Council resolutions also require that other factors be taken into account. Security Council resolutions are issued by a single, collective body and are drafted through a very different process than that used for the conclusion of a treaty. Security Council resolutions are the product of a voting process as provided for in Article 27 of the Charter, and the final text of such resolutions represents the view of the Security Council as a body. Moreover, Security Council resolutions can

48 Kosovo AO, para.26 ("international law does not regulate the act of making a declaration of independence, which should be regarded as a political act").

49 Judge Simma, Declaration, para.3.

> be binding on all Member States (*Legal Consequences for States of the Continued Presence of South Africa in Namibia (South West Africa) notwithstanding Security Council Resolution 276 (1970), Advisory Opinion, I.C.J. Reports 1971*, p. 54, para. 116), irrespective of whether they played any part in their formulation. The interpretation of Security Council resolutions may require the Court to analyse statements by representatives of members of the Security Council made at the time of their adoption, other resolutions of the Security Council on the same issue, as well as the subsequent practice of relevant United Nations organs and of States affected by those given resolutions.[50]

29. The Court then proceeded to analyse the relevant factors and concluded that the Security Council resolution 1244 did not "bar the authors of the declaration of 17 February 2008 from issuing a declaration of independence from the Republic of Serbia".[51] Firstly, the resolution was intended to create an interim regime and did address the issue of a possible declaration of independence as an attempt at final status. Secondly, the authors of the declaration of independence, as re-characterized by the Court, were not the addressees of any obligations under that Security Council resolution 1244.[52] Furthermore, neither were they addressees of the Constitutional Framework and the declaration therefore did not violate it.[53] The Court's conclusion was reached despite the contrary views of two veto-wielding permanent members[54] of the Security Council.

30. This aspect of the Court's opinion and analysis has been subjected to strong criticism by some Judges,[55] especially Vice-President Tomka. These arguments need not be rehashed here. I will highlight three points that may be

---

50 Kosovo AO, para.94. For an academic discussion of this issue, See Michael Wood, The Interpretation of Security Councils Resolutions, 2 Max Planck YBUNL (1998), 73.

51 Kosovo AO, para.119.

52 Ibid., paras.110–119.

53 Ibid., para.121. Probably, other measures could be relevant (see the Court's heading for this section: "the measures adopted thereunder"), but the Court focused on the Constitutional Framework.

54 See Oral Statement of China, CR 2009/29 (7 December 2009); Oral Statement of Russian Federation, CR 2009/30 (8 December 2009).

55 See Vice-President Tomka, Declaration; Judge Bennouna, Dissenting Opinion; Judge Koroma, Dissenting Opinion; Judge Skotnikov, Dissenting Opinion.

relevant to future peace-keeping and territorial administration.

31. Firstly, the Court's approach to the interpretation of Security Council resolutions as explained in majestic generality in paragraph 94 of the Court's opinion no doubt appears proper and this paragraph is destined to be cited frequently in the future. However, it seems that the Court may have over-played the autonomous or self-contained nature of these resolutions and given insufficient weight to their context and the understandings of other parties which may have informed the intent of the Council. This is particularly important when a resolution may also function as a sort of agreement or incorporate one, settling a dispute or bringing peace with another party involved. In such a situation, the views of the party at the other end of the deal, so to speak, deserve appropriate weight, although how much may vary according to the circumstances. This is to ensure that the other party would not be given too much of a raw deal. In short, the "agreement-like" qualities of some Security Council resolutions, such as resolution 1244, may warrant meaningful consideration.

32. The Court's interpretation of Security Council resolution 1244 surprised Serbia, which has been a most important stakeholder in the peace plan in Kosovo. It accepted that peace plan and should have a legitimate expectation regarding what that plan should mean. Security Council resolution 1244 notes the acceptance of Serbia.[56] A permanent member of the Security Council also relied on this acceptance as one of the reasons for not vetoing the proposed resolution.[57] Now Serbia finds that its expectation means nothing. How would this affect future peace-keeping efforts of the Security Council? Will stakeholders be discouraged by the Court's interpretation of Security Council resolutions? At least in the future they will no doubt have to insist, through [their] own persuasion or a protector in the Security Council, on clearer language for any guarantees, rather than hoping that a brief preambular paragraph would come to their aid. This will surely toughen and lengthen the negotiations in the future. Hopefully in that process human tragedies will not be aggravated. As interpreted by the Court, the deal here is lopsided against Serbia: on the one hand, its hands are tied by ceding authority to govern Kosovo to the international administration, while, on the other hand, nothing prevents a declaration of independence. One is tempted to say, if such a declaration is to

---

56 S/RES/1244 (1999), para.2.

57 Statement of China, as quoted in para.5 of China's Oral Statement, CR 2009/29, 30.

be made, it should only be made, fair and square, when authority to govern is given back to Serbia.

33. Secondly, the Court treated the Constitutional Framework as international law, which formally may be correct. This may be a controversial point. It has been argued that the effects of acts done under this framework may not necessarily be "international".[58] It may be possible to treat this Constitutional Framework as only "national" law. When the international administration was established, Kosovo was supposed to enjoy "substantial autonomy within the Federal Republic of Yugoslavia",[59] now Serbia. As a result, the international administration simply assumed the powers and responsibilities of Serbia. As such, the acts of the administration can have no greater formal authority than the acts of Serbia. The Constitutional Framework issued for the governance of Kosovo by a power assuming the powers of Serbia therefore has no greater force than the constitutional law of Serbia. If so, whether the declaration of independence violated the Constitutional Framework could be considered an issue that general international law is silent on, as discussed above. This may be a reasonable position that does not elevate the status of the Constitutional Framework to a level that may lead to unforeseen consequences in the future.

34. Thirdly, during the proceedings it has been argued that the international administration of Kosovo somehow has made Kosovo a unique case or that this reality somehow has given Kosovo residents the right to stay separate. For example, the Ahtisaari Report of 2007 says:

> For the past eight years, Kosovo and Serbia have been governed in complete separation. The establishment of the United Nations Mission in Kosovo (UNMIK) pursuant to resolution 1244 (1999), and its assumption of all legislative, executive and judicial authority throughout Kosovo, has created a situation in which Serbia has not exercised any governing authority over Kosovo. This is a reality one cannot deny; it is irreversible. A return of Serbian rule over Kosovo would not be acceptable to the overwhelming majority of the people of Kosovo. Belgrade could not regain its authority without provoking violent opposition. Autonomy of Kosovo within the borders of Serbia—

58 See CR 2009/32, 47–48, paras.6–7 (Crawford, arguing for the UK).

59 S/RES/1244 (1999), para.10.

however notional such autonomy may be—is simply not tenable.[60]

35. This is an argument that finds no support in law. If the international administration would have any effect on Serbia's sovereignty over Kosovo, it would seem to be a kind of standstill effect, freezing the situation to the time when the international administration started in 1999. More importantly, this uniqueness argument is most pernicious to the UN's future peace-keeping efforts. If this argument prevails, who would allow international administration in the future? To some extent, it is a good thing that this argument has been aired in the Kosovo crisis, providing education to other State actors who should no doubt take preventative action against any resort to such an argument in the future. One just hopes that this argument will not cause the relevant actors to try to cling to the use of force rather than to agree to peace-keeping by the UN.[61]

IV.C. Self-determination or remedial secession

36. The Court decided not to address the argument that "the population of Kosovo has the right to create an independent State either as a manifestation of a right to self-determination or pursuant to what they described as a right of 'remedial secession' in the face of the situation in Kosovo".[62] Although not

---

60 S/2007/168, Report of the Special Envoy, para.7.

61 Indeed, the Kosovo crisis may move a fair-minded person to consider whether Mr. Ahtisaari's conduct is still that of an even-handed moderator or facilitator in the Kosovo status process or that of an active promoter of independence. This question may be asked about the entire international civil presence. It would be interesting also to consider whether the UN and/or UN members should be held responsible for any misbehaviour, although the prevailing political reality may make this inquiry difficult if not impossible. When the UN organization is actively promoting the rule of law at national and international levels, the idea for such an inquiry should not be completely out of its radar screen. For a general analysis on "member responsibility", see Sienho Yee, The Responsibility of States Members of an International Organization for Its Conduct as a result of Membership or Their Normal Conduct Associated with Membership, in: Maurizio Ragazzi (ed.), International Responsibility Today: Essays in Memory of Oscar Schachter (2005), 435–454 [Chapter 16 below].

62 Kosovo AO, para.82, et seq. For a commentary on this issue, see Cedrick Ryngaert and Christine Griffioen, The Relevance of the Right to Self-determination in the Kosovo Matter: In Partial Response to the Agora Papers,

completely clear, the Court seemed to give three reasons for this decision. The first is that the fact that this argument was made "in almost every instance only as a secondary argument".[63] The second is the assessment that this is

> a subject on which radically different views were expressed by those taking part in the proceedings and expressing a position on the question. Similar differences existed regarding whether international law provides for a right of "remedial secession" and, if so, in what circumstances. There was also a sharp difference of views as to whether the circumstances which some participants maintained would give rise to a right of "remedial secession" were actually present in Kosovo.[64]

37. The third is the position that it is not necessary to resolve these issues because the question, re-characterized by the Court, only called upon the Court to "determine whether the declaration of independence violated either general international law or the *lex specialis* created by Security Council resolution 1244 (1999)".[65]

38. Whether or not the third reason is legitimate depends on whether the reformulation of the question is proper or not. The latter issue has been dealt with above in paragraphs 20–27.

39. The first and second reasons given by the Court not only serve as legitimate support for declining to address the argument that outside the defined context of colonial experience and alien subjugation, the international law of self-determination confers upon part of the population of an existing State a right to separate from that State or a right to remedial secession, but also provide a negative answer to that argument, if only implicitly. These reasons for not addressing the argument precisely show that there was no *opinio juris* for it. The fact, as pointed out by the Court, that radically different views were expressed on this question during the proceedings demonstrates the lack of any extensive and uniform *opinio juris* supporting this claimed right. If one is to follow the normal method of finding customary international law as required by Article 38(1)(b) of the ICJ Statute, no custom regarding such a right can be found here. The "secondary argument" fashion in which this claim was made in

---

8 Chinese JIL (2009), 573.

63 Ibid., para.82.

64 Ibid.

65 Ibid., para.83.

these proceedings even by those who supported it testifies to how weak the claim was even in the hearts of the supporters or, rather, promoters. Therefore, although the Court did not say so *expressly*, and although the Court may not have intended to say so *at all*, the Court did manage to give a negative answer co-incidentally or collaterally to the argument for external self-determination or remedial secession. The answer came by necessary implication from the Court's assessment of the state of the divided opinion and the generally accepted customary international law framework.

40. Interestingly, in the *Nuclear Weapons* Advisory Opinion, the Court has relied on the difference of opinion to find no *opinio juris*:

> 66. Some other States, which assert the legality of the threat and use of nuclear weapons in certain circumstances, invoked the doctrine and practice of deterrence in support of their argument. They recall that they have always, in concert with certain other States, reserved the right to use those weapons in the exercise of the right to self-defence against an armed attack threatening their vital security interests. In their view, if nuclear weapons have not been used since 1945, it is not on account of an existing or nascent custom but merely because circumstances that might justify their use have fortunately not arisen.
>
> 67. The Court does not intend to pronounce here upon the practice known as the "policy of deterrence". It notes that it is a fact that a number of States adhered to that practice during the greater part of the Cold War and continue to adhere to it. Furthermore, the members of the international community are profoundly divided on the matter of whether non-recourse to nuclear weapons over the past 50 years constitutes the expression of an *opinio juris*. Under these circumstances the Court does not consider itself able to find that there is such an *opinio juris*.[66]

41. In the *Kosovo* Advisory Opinion, too, the radically different views expressed during the proceedings, the strong oppositions to the claimed right of self-determination or remedial secession put forward by those specially affected States which have to endure any potential fallout, and the half-hearted "secondary argument" of those States little touched by and situated far away

66 Legality of the Threat or Use of Nuclear Weapons, Advisory Opinion, ICJ Reports 1996, 226.

from the claimed right all militate against the finding of an *opinio juris* supporting such a claimed right. As the Court taught in the *North Sea Continental Shelf* cases, the views of the specially affected States are of the utmost importance.[67]

42. Although the Court did not deal with the various arguments made by the participants in the proceedings, two points presented against the finding of such a claimed right are of interest. The first is the way the right to remedial secession allegedly debuted in an official instrument adopted by States, as an *a contrario* argument from the "safeguard clause" in the section on the principle of equal rights and self-determination of peoples in the Friendly Relations Declaration.[68] One wonders whether such an important position, if serious, would ever be put forward in such an *a contrario* way. As pointed out by China, "the so-called right to 'remedial self-determination' clashes with the principle of State sovereignty and territorial integrity. It is obvious that if such a claim were permitted under international law, as it concerns the fundamental interests of States, there should have been positive and explicit legal provisions to that

---

67 North Sea Continental Shelf Cases, Judgment, ICJ Reports 1969, 3, paras.73–74.

68 Declaration on Principles of International Law concerning Friendly Relations and Co-operation among States in accordance with the Charter of the United Nations, GA Res 2625(XXV), 1970, UNYB (1970), 788 ("Nothing in the foregoing paragraphs shall be construed as authorizing or encouraging any action which would dismember or impair, totally or in part, the territorial integrity or political unity of sovereign and independent States conducting themselves in compliance with the principle of equal rights and self-determination of peoples as described above and thus possessed of a government representing the whole people belonging to the territory without distinction as to race, creed, or colour."). Earlier, in the Aaland Islands case, a report submitted to the Council of the League of Nations by the Commission of Rapporteurs (League of Nations, Doc. B.7. 21/68/106, 1921, 28, as quoted in the Oral Statement of Finland (Päivi Kaukoranta), paras.10–11, CR 2009/30 (8 December 2009), 55–56) stated: "The separation of a minority from the State of which it forms a part and its incorporation in another State can only be considered as an altogether exceptional solution, a last resort when the State lacks either the will or the power to enact and apply just and effective guarantees." The Commission was one to make recommendation only and in this matter did not find any justification for separation. This position seemed to have been made not as a matter of law but as a hypothetical matter of good policy.

effect. No such provisions however exist in international law."[69] Indeed, when criticizing the attempt to squeeze an oversized substantive argument into the small container of a simple jurisdictional clause in the *South West Africa (Second Phase)* cases, the ICJ itself pointed out the unreal remarkableness of the argument that an important right, having potentially far-reaching consequences, could have been "created indirectly, and in so casual and almost incidental a fashion".[70] This argument would seem to stand, despite the infamous holding in that case, probably resulting from other aspects of its reasoning.

43. A second point seems to be presented as one showing the conditions for the exercise of remedial secession did not exist in 2008 when the declaration of independence was made, but seems to me to prove that there is no such a claimed right. Some States noted that at the end of the NATO bombing in 1999 no claim of remedial secession was made, not formally in any event. In 2008, the Kosovo Albanians were much better off under international administration and therefore the conditions for such a claim did not exist, but the claim was made.

---

69 Oral Statement of China, CR 2009/29 (7 December 2009), 36, para.25.

70 South West Africa, Second Phase, ICJ Reports 1966, 6, 38:

> 62. It is next contended that this particular jurisdictional clause has an effect which is more extensive than if it is considered as a simple jurisdictional clause: that it is a clause conferring a substantive right,—that the substantive right it confers is precisely the right to claim from the Mandatory the carrying out of the "conduct of the Mandate" provisions of the instrument of mandate,—and that in consequence, even if the right is derivable from no other source, it is derivable from and implicit in this clause.
>
> 63. Let it be observed first of all that it would be remarkable if this were the case,—that is to say if so important a right, having such potentially far-reaching consequences,—intended, so the Applicants contend, to play such an essential role in the scheme of the Mandate—of all the mandates, and of the system generally—had been created indirectly, and in so casual and almost incidental a fashion, by an ordinary jurisdictional clause, lacking as will shortly be seen in any of the special features that might give it the effect claimed,—and which would certainly be requisite in order to achieve that effect. The Court considers it highly unlikely that, given the far-reaching consequences involved and, according to the Applicants, intended, the framers of the mandates system, had they had any such intention, would have chosen this particular type of jurisdictional clause as the method of carrying it out.

44. This contrast between 1999 and 2008, however, seems to be better proof that there is no such claimed right because there was no *opinio juris* for it. The lack of a claim for remedial secession in the aftermath of the NATO air campaign in 1999 seemed to demonstrate that *either* the situation was not so deplorable for the Albanians so as to present no conditions for remedial secession *or* no such right to remedial secession ever existed. One would agree that if such a right existed, the severity of the humanitarian crisis would have presented the conditions for its exercise. Yet no claim for it was made in 1999. Thus, the notorious humanitarian crisis and the lack of a claim in 1999 for remedial secession can only lead one to the conclusion that no *opinio juris* existed for such a right to remedial secession. In 2001, I happened to have taken notice of this situation and observed that the *a contario* argument presented earlier by Antonio Cassese [71] "did not receive the endorsement of the international community in the Kosovo crisis. There the ethnic Albanians' situation which was so dire as to provoke military intervention has not caused the international community to support their call for independence. Rather, the international community seems to be content with ensuring internal autonomy for the residents in Kosovo, mainly the ethnic Albanians."[72] There is no reason for one to change this assessment at present.

IV.D. Unlawful use of force by the NATO in 1999

45. One issue that has not been presented directly or not meaningfully[73] is how the use of force by the NATO in 1999 should affect the answer to the question presented by the UNGA. A student of international relations and international law may reasonably observe that the current situation in Kosovo is very much a direct result of the unlawful use of force by the NATO in 1999, in addition to some other factors. While the legality of the NATO's campaign is a question to be decided definitely, very few participating States have claimed it to be lawful; they prefer the phrase "morally legitimate". Given this situation, one would

---

71 Antonio Cassese, Self-determination of Peoples: A Legal Reappraisal (1995), 101–133.

72 Sienho Yee, Towards an International Law of Co-progressiveness, in: Sienho Yee and Wang Tieya (eds.), International Law in the Post-Cold War World: Essays in Memory of Li Haopei (2001), 32.

73 Some States have mentioned the topic, notably Cyprus (Oral Statement of Cyprus, CR 2009/29, 41, paras.28–29) and China (Oral Statement of China, CR 2009/29, 29–30, paras.4–6).

think that any solution to the current problem would probably require one to revisit the origin of that problem for guidance. For whatever reason, strategic or otherwise, Serbia did not make any argument from this angle. This, in my view, is unfortunate for both Serbia and the international community. This shows that the world is quite a distance from one under the rule of law. As the issue of use of force was not dealt with in the Advisory Opinion, I will not deal with the substantive content of it, but will highlight briefly how it could have affected the proceedings.

46. We all know that the prohibition of the illegal use of force, as reflected in Article 2(4) of the UN Charter, is one of the most fundamental rules of the current international legal system. This prohibition is a clear case of peremptory norm. As a corollary of that rule, the creation of a claimed State entity as a result of that unlawful use of force is illegal and without effect. One could reason that any attempts to create such an entity including a declaration of independence, by persons connected with or enabled by the violation, would be illegal. As has been noted, "The international community has with considerable consistency refused to accept the legal validity of acts done or situations achieved by the illegal use of force."[74] So viewed, one may argue that the declaration of independence of Kosovo would be both "not in accordance with international law" and "adopted in violation of international law", in whichever reformulation of the question presented to the Court.

47. Interestingly in this case the Court did take note of the illegality of some declarations of independence as a result of violations of the *jus cogens* norm prohibiting the use of force, but in a slightly different context:

> 81. Several participants have invoked resolutions of the Security Council condemning particular declarations of independence: see, *inter alia*, Security Council resolutions 216 (1965) and 217 (1965), concerning Southern Rhodesia; Security Council resolution 541 (1983), concerning northern Cyprus; and Security Council resolution 787 (1992), concerning the Republika Srpska.
>
> The Court notes, however, that in all of those instances the Security Council was making a determination as regards the concrete situation existing at the time that those declarations of independence were made; the illegality attached to the declarations of independence

---

74 James Crawford, The Creation of States in International Law (2d edn., 2006), 132.

> thus stemmed not from the unilateral character of these declarations as such, but from the fact that they were, or would have been, connected with the unlawful use of force or other egregious violations of norms of general international law, in particular those of a peremptory character (*jus cogens*). In the context of Kosovo, the Security Council has never taken this position. The exceptional character of the resolutions enumerated above appears to the Court to confirm that no general prohibition against unilateral declarations of independence may be inferred from the practice of the Security Council.[75]

48. So all the Court found to be important is the condemnation by the Security Council, and the lack of such a condemnation in the Kosovo case somehow distinguishes it from all others.

49. Although this approach is not necessarily incorrect in the context of finding no general prohibition of declarations of independence, one wonders whether it is at all proper to give such importance to the condemnation by the Security Council, as if the consequence of a violation of the *jus cogens* norm is dependent upon such a condemnation. In fact, such a position is incorrect; the consequence is self-executory.[76] The condemnation by the Security Council is at best evidence regarding the unlawful nature of the condemned act. One hopes that if the issue is properly before it, the Court would decide on its own whether a violation of the prohibition of the use of force occurred.

50. To the extent that this is not a contentious case, it would be difficult to argue that the Court had to rely on the claims made, in the same fashion as in a contentious case, by the participants. So would it be proper to argue that the Court should decide a point, such as the one relating to the unlawful use of force, essential to giving a proper reply to the question presented? I am not sure on this point and I am thinking aloud, so to speak.

51. To the extent that such a point is really not a "claim" but a question of law only, the Court may be duty-bound to decide it, once it has taken jurisdiction. As the Court said in a contentious case (this should apply, *mutatis mutandis*, to Advisory Opinion proceedings if applicable),

> It being the duty of the Court itself to ascertain and apply the relevant

---

75 Kosovo AO, para.81.

76 See, in a slightly different context, Judge Skubiszewski, Diss. Op., East Timor (Portugal v. Australia), Judgment, ICJ Reports 1995, 224, 263, para.125.

> law in the given circumstances of the case, the burden of establishing or proving rules of international law cannot be imposed upon any of the Parties, for the law lies within the judicial knowledge of the Court.[77]

52. To the extent that the axiom "the Court knows its own law" has force in a contentious case, its force is greater in an advisory opinion proceeding.

V. Conclusion

53. Despite its anti-climatic appearance, the *Kosovo* Advisory Opinion does give us a great deal to digest. It is too early to assess its impact on the reality on the ground in Kosovo or on the international legal system. However, to some, this Advisory Opinion may give the occasion for reconsidering whether the Advisory Opinion facility is a good forum for settling international disputes.[78]

---

77 Fisheries Jurisdiction Case (F.R. Germany v. Iceland), ICJ Reports 1974, 174, 181, para.18.

78 Poscript: Of course, the point here is not that the advisory opinion facility is strictly speaking a forum for dispute settlement, but that it has been used as such in practice. The wisdom of so doing needs to be reassessed.

Chapter 4

The International Law of Co-progressiveness and the Co-progressiveness of Civilizations*

I. Introduction

At the end of his 1996 book, *The Clash of Civilizations and the Remaking of World Order*, Samuel Huntington said: "The futures of both peace and Civilization depend on understanding and cooperation among the political, spiritual, and intellectual leaders of the world's major civilizations."[1] I have a hunch that understanding and co-operation alone may not be enough to ensure a good future for us all. It is possible that we do understand each other quite well, and we do co-operate, but our different perspectives remain, get entrenched, and become irreconcilable. The step taken from irreconcilable differences is pivotal. It can help us to assure a good future for ourselves, if that step is taken with a bent for progressiveness, within the framework of the international law of co-progressiveness,[2] which is summarized and elaborated in Chapter 1 of this

---

* Revised from a paper under the same title first published at: 12 Chinese JIL (2013), 9-17. That was a revised version of my remarks delivered at the tenth anniversary session of the Rhodes Forum—Dialogue of Civilizations on 4 October 2012, in Rhodes, Greece, organized by World Public Forum. The preparation of this comment forms part of the work of Research Project No. 08&ZD055 of the China Social Sciences Foundation. Part II of the original version of this paper is a summary of the international law of co-progressiveness, in a discrete section, and has been deleted from this version in order to avoid repetition with Chapter I of this book which is a more comprehensive summary. Appropriate adjustments have been made and paragraph numbering has been removed.

1 Samuel Huntington, The Clash of Civilizations and the Remaking of World Order (1996), 321.

2 This Comment draws heavily upon my own previous publications: Sienho Yee,

volume. Here I will briefly explore the role of civilizations within this framework.

II. Role of civilizations

Where can we fit civilizations with this frameowork? What role can civilizations play?

One possibility would be for a civilization[3] to occupy the same place as a State and plays the same role. However, this possibility probably will not work. As we know, as the main subjects of international law States are special because they are the organizing units of the world. The world is too big. In order to make sense of it and to manage it, we have to divide it up into some manageable units. By historical accident if nothing else, States are now those units. Civilizations, as we can observe currently, cannot be those units. First of all, civilizations usually imagine themselves as being a kind of universality or capable of being universal. As such, a civilization is not an organizing unit, but is the whole world in itself. Secondly, a civilization does not have a spatial dimension, which is necessary for its becoming an organizing unit of the world. Now, if a civilization does have such a dimension, it covers too large an area for it to be such a unit in the general sense. Thirdly, the existing example of the Holy See acting as a subject of international law shows how difficult it is for a "civilization" to be such a subject. When the Holy See was taken to court in the USA as such a subject, one argument that the Holy See made in order to avoid liability was that the local churches and priests were responsible, not the Holy See itself.

A second possibility would be for a civilization to take the place as a special subject or participant in the system, similar to that of a non-

---

Towards an International Law of Co-progressiveness, in: Sienho Yee and Wang Tieya (eds.), International Law in the Post-Cold War World: Essays in Memory of Li Haopei (2001), 18–39; Sienho Yee, Sovereign Equality of States and the Legitimacy of "Leader States", in: Ronald St John Macdonald and Douglas M. Johnston (eds.), Towards World Constitutionalism (2005), 737–772 [reprinted as Chapter 8 below]; Sienho Yee, Towards a Harmonious World: The Roles of the International Law of Co-progressiveness and Leader States, 7 Chinese JIL (2008), 99–105 [reprinted as Chapter 9 below].

3 I am using this term as what is commonly understood and used in Samuel Huntington, n.1 above. There he divided the world into several major civilizations.

governmental organization (NGO), and to play a special role so as to promote certain positions, hoping to influence the decision-making of the main subjects of international law. In this promoter role, a civilization may have a strong impact in many fields and may become a strong special promoter of the co-progressiveness of international society and human flourishing. Hopefully this will lead to more perspectives shared by all civilizations. Probably it is in this sense that the idea of trans-civilizational perspectives of international law has meaning and is of use.

III. Making the promoter role effective

As a special promoter of the co-progressiveness of international society, a civilization will have to struggle with some problems in order for that role to be effective.

First of all, a civilization itself has to be a progressive one. If not, that civilization may run the risk of being considered not practicing what it preaches and its effectiveness will suffer substantially. If each civilization is progressive separately, co-progressiveness of all civilizations would naturally result. How does a civilization become progressive? Usually, progress is internally driven. Internally driven progress retains the richness of diversity and also lasts long. Ideally, a civilization should have a built-in engine for self-propelled progressiveness. Absent such a built-in engine, conscious efforts may be mounted to establish internal mechanisms for promoting a tendency for self-propelled progressiveness. There are many internal mechanisms now in the various civilizations, some working to ensure doctrinal purity, others to serve a variety of other purposes. It would not be difficult for us to imagine a mechanism for the promotion of self-propelled progressiveness. If a civilization does have, on its own initiative, an urge to pursue progressiveness, even if it decides what constitutes progressiveness and at what pace it would like to pursue it, this will ultimately lead to overall progressiveness among all civilizations and in the world.

Of course, progressiveness in a civilization can also be externally induced, just as personal liberty can be. Such inducement may come from exchange of ideas between a civilization and outsiders including States, other civilizations and organizations as well as individuals. Further inducement may be implemented more consciously as part of development programs but not as conditions for such programs. For example, State A may provide development assistance to a certain civilization or a State primarily under the influence of that civilization, and include a program of seminars or discussions of rule of law or gender equality issues—randomly picked for illustration—as part of that development program, but may not impose as conditions for the development any measures on the rule of law or gender equality. Such further action will be left to the wisdom of the particular civilization or State concerned. Having such discussions, hopefully, will ultimately lead to beneficial developments within that civilization or State.

Within our framework of the international law of co-progressiveness there is no room for external coercion of a civilization even if the purpose of the coercion is for co-progressiveness. In short, outsiders may provide inducement but not coercion.

In the light of the inevitable intercourse between and among civilizations and States, a civilization must be able to manage its external relations with other sister civilizations, with States and other participants in international society in a satisfactory manner, so that all civilizations become co-progressive. Of course, how to achieve this is the most difficult question, and there is no silver bullet to solve this. Assuming that between civilizations there should never be any malice or intentional harm and that inclusiveness is a virtue, I offer three additional tools here: (1) a "two-men mindedness" attitude when taking action; (2) a Thomas Henry Sanderson lens when perceiving a challenge; and (3) benign competition. I will explain these one by one.

III.A. The "two-men mindedness" attitude

This attitude was given a chance to find a place in the Universal Declaration on Human Rights, but did not make it there, probably because of the Tower of Babel. Mary Ann Glendon related this to us in her book on the drafting of the Universal Declaration. During the drafting process, the working group added to René Cassin's draft preamble the sentence that "All men are brothers. Being endowed with reason and members of one family, they are free and equal in dignity and rights." Then, the Confucianist that participated in the drafting, Mr. P.C. Chang,

> suggested that besides naming "reason" as an essential human attribute, the article ought to include another concept. What he had in mind, he said, was a Chinese word that in literal translation meant "two-man mindedness" but which might be expressed in English as "sympathy", or "consciousness of one's fellow men". The word was *ren* (仁), a composite

> of the characters for "man" (人) and "two" (二).
>
> A word emblematic of an entire worldview and way of life, *ren* has no precise counterpart in English. To Cassin, it would surely have evoked Rousseau's notion of compassion, but that word, too, fell short of the mark. Chang's suggestion was accepted, but his idea was rendered awkwardly by adding the words "and conscience" after "reason". (That unhappy word choice not only obscured Chang's meaning, but gave "conscience" a far from obvious sense, quite different from its normal usage in phrases such as "freedom of conscience.").[4]

The essence of this "two-men-mindedness" attitude is that whenever one takes any action, one should take account of the presence or existence of one's fellow inhabitants in the community and act accordingly. Probably this does not lead to "love thy neighbour", but it does counsel some self-restraint in the exercise of one's rights. Indeed, this attitude may move one to strike a proper balance between respecting other people's sensibility and dignity on the one hand and enjoying one's maximum freedom, on the other.

If individuals adopted such an attitude, probably there would not have been those insulting cartoons or movies. Nor their aftermath. If a civilization adopted such an attitude, there would be fewer occasions for tension or worse. The world community missed the opportunity to capitalize on this piece of wisdom during the drafting of the Universal Declaration on Human Rights; it is important that we should not miss it again in the future.

III.B. The Thomas Henry Sanderson lens

From time to time, one civilization may feel that another is presenting a challenge or a threat to its interests or even its existence itself. This ultimately leads to tension and conflict. In such a situation, any minor irritation is often magnified to the extreme. It is important for civilizations to put a particular situation in perspective.

One may learn a lesson from a piece of advice that was probably not heeded in history. When the British Empire was presented with Germany as its challenger, any advantage for the challenger was considered a disadvantage for the Empire. Mr. Crowe, a career Foreign Office official, wrote the famous

---

4 Mary Ann Glendon, A World Made New: Eleanor Roosevelt and the Universal Declaration of Human Rights (2001), 67–68.

Crowe memorandum, perceiving a "titanic struggle"[5] between the two, and counselling hard-nosed containment.[6] However, that view was challenged by Mr. Thomas Henry Sanderson, another Foreign Office official. He wrote:

> It has sometimes seemed to me, to a foreigner reading our press the British Empire must appear in the light of some huge giant sprawling over the globe, with gouty fingers and toes stretching in every direction, which cannot be approached without eliciting a scream.[7]

Crowe's lens no doubt resulted in the image of the Empire that Sanderson was making fun of. Sanderson's lens differs from that. The essence of that lens is that things are not necessarily so bad. Taking a more relaxed attitude may help to put things in perspective and promote cool-headed reactions to perceived disadvantages, challenges or even threats.

III.C. Benign competition

The clash of civilizations is something we should try our hardest to avoid; benign competition, however, may be something beneficial to all civilizations. This may serve as an external inducement towards co-progressiveness. In real life, such benign competition is also unavoidable, as much as we may try not to see it.

How such competition can be done or even promoted is a tough question, particularly if we accept that each civilization is of equal worth. From such a point of departure, civilizations probably should not compete on any alleged criteria of intrinsic worth, unless they can agree on those criteria.

Previously I considered the issue of inter-State competition.[8] I argued that from the starting point of equality of States—the irreducible minimum is equal juridical status in terms of dignity and position and territorial integrity and

---

5 To borrow a phrase used in another context in Henry Kissinger, On China (2011), 110.

6 Ibid., 514–530.

7 As quoted in the website of the Foreign and Commonwealth Office of the United Kingdom (http://www.fco.gov.uk/en/about-us/our-history/historical-publications/research-projects/history-pus/the-last-super-clerk-1894-1906 (accessed 27 September 2011)).

8 Sienho Yee, Sovereign Equality of States and the Legitimacy of "Leader States", n.2 above, 737–772.

political independence—and under the basic condition of respecting the irreducible minimum of sovereign equality of States, a State that has legitimately managed to become strong on a set of difference arguments is a strong State. A State is a great State if it has legitimately become a strong State and has achieved big power status, and has paid due respect to the value of, and shouldered, with substantial success, the hefty responsibility towards, the international system. A State is a "leader State" if it has respected the value of, and shouldered, with success, substantial responsibility toward, the international system, and has not only been making good faith efforts or even exemplary efforts to comply with the existing legitimate rules, but also, more importantly, has helped to formulate or refine a proper vision of the international system and to build it up so that the flourishing of humanity can be achieved to the greatest extent possible.

Obviously, this framework cannot be applied straightforwardly to inter-civilizational competition, but probably we can do a dépeçage by combining (1) the respect for State territorial integrity and political independence and (2) a contribution to the international system and human flourishing as the criteria for benign competition between civilizations. This way, we can avoid passing judgment on the inherent worth of a civilization and still can make an assessment on the basis of what it does in international relations.

By partial analogy to the State competition system, a civilization that has legitimately managed to become strong on a set of difference arguments is a strong civilization, due respect having been paid to State territorial integrity and political independence. A civilization is a great civilization if it has legitimately become a strong civilization and has achieved "big power" civilization status, and has paid due respect to the value of, and shouldered, with substantial success, the hefty responsibility towards, the international system. A civilization is a "leader civilization" if it has respected the value of, and shouldered, with success, substantial responsibility toward, the international system, and has not only been making good faith efforts or even exemplary efforts to comply with the existing legitimate rules, but also, more importantly, has helped to formulate or refine a proper vision of the international system and to build it up so that the flourishing of humanity can be achieved to the greatest extent possible.

In this scheme of benign competition, each civilization would have its role in promoting the co-progressiveness of all civilizations as well as international society as a whole. A strong civilization and a leader civilization obviously will play a stronger role, as appropriate. It is important for international society to have such a competitive drive, so that a future vision of that society would come "from commitment, not resignation to the inevitable".[9]

IV. Final remarks

These thoughts are impressionistic but I hope they can provoke further consideration of the issues dealt with here. The existence of alliances of civilizations and dialogues of civilizations indicates that these issues are on the agenda of international debate. It would be ideal if each civilization and all main civilizations as a whole would improve its organizational apparatus to study and promote the co-progressiveness of civilizations and of international society as a whole, in addition to holding dialogues at various locations. For example, there are so many academies in the world, why not one devoted to civilizations? There is a Security Council for international peace and security, why not a "Civilizational Council" for the progressiveness of international law and relations? Hopefully one of these will emerge in the near future, so that dialogues between civilizations do not stop at dialogues.

---

9 Henry Kissinger, n.5 above, 530.

Chapter 5

The Role of Law in the Formation of Regional Perspectives on Human Rights and Regional Systems for the Protection of Human Rights: The European and Asian Models as Illustrations*

I. Introduction

I propose to say something about the role of law in the formation of regional perspectives on human rights and the regional systems for the protection of human rights, using the European model and the Asian model (or the lack thereof) as illustrations. First, I would like to say that my goal is a modest one. I do not hope to have any last word on the topic; I simply would like to provoke those interested in the topic to consider some of these issues. Secondly, I would like to note that I am speaking from the perspective of someone who is interested in theoretical inquiry, and yet does not consider himself a theoretician. I am afraid what I have to say here will have to be more or less impressionistic, although, I guarantee to you, it does not come easily, and will be difficult to prove to any degree of certainty, whether theoretically or empirically.

---

* First published at 8 Singapore YBIL (2004), 157–164. This short note is based on my remarks presented at a conference on public goods and regional integration organized by the United Nations University Programme on Comparative Regional Integration Studies on 20 November 2003 at Bruges, Belgium. Thanks go to Dr. Lim Chin Leng and his colleagues at the Singapore Year Book of International Law and Chris Gray at Colorado for their comments and assistance.

II. The Role of Law and the Formation of Community Order in General[1]

I will first speculate on the role of law and the formation of community order in general. Of course, for one to consider the role or rule of law, one must have a certain understanding of what law is. This is a question that has been with us for a long time, but has yet to induce a single right answer. Here I will simply adopt a particular answer, without attempting to defend it, although this is the version that I believe to be correct.

In its concrete manifestations, law means the legal rules and principles that frame and solidify the relationships (or rights and obligations) between and among the different players in society. How we arrive at these rules and principles, and how they are distinguished from other non-legal rules and principles, are very difficult questions to answer.

One answer to these questions is to say that what law is is decided upon through the process by which the actors in society internalise laws so as to treat a certain course of conduct as the standard of conduct and to use it as the basis for critiquing (including self-critiquing) the conduct of the actors and ultimately serves as sufficient reason for voluntary action. Only then does law come into existence. This idea was considered by H.L.A. Hart to be the internal aspect of law.[2]

The internalisation process might result from and be aided by many factors, one of which may be certain rules of recognition. Under such rules (or

---

1 This part draws heavily upon Sienho Yee, Towards an International Law of Co-progressiveness (Martinus Nijhoff Publishers, 2004) ff 42 (Chapter 3, "The Perfect Rule of Law").

2 See H.L.A. Hart, The Concept of Law (Oxford: Clarendon Press, 1961) at 54-57, 79-91 and 102-103. As Hart observed, some people wrongly misrepresented the internal aspect of rules as a "mere matter of 'feelings' in contrast to externally observable physical behavior", after saying that the psychological experiences analogous to those of restriction or compulsion may exist, he gave this response: "But such feelings are neither necessary nor sufficient for the existence of 'binding' rules. There is no contradiction in saying that people accept certain rules but experience no such feelings of compulsion. What is necessary is that there should be a critical reflective attitude to certain patterns of behavior as a common standard, and that this should display itself in criticism (including self-criticism), demands for conformity, and in acknowledgements that such criticism and demands are justified, all of which find their characteristic expression in the normative terminology of 'ought', 'must', and 'should', 'right' and 'wrong'." Hart at 57.

better, normal rules) of recognition, the actors may quickly and easily recognise certain rules as rules of law. Law under such a regime of easy rules of recognition perhaps can be called "law for dummies" (to borrow a phrase from computer literature). There is much virtue in this; law must be easily accessible to ordinary people.

However, the leap from rules in general to rules of law cannot be reached simply through the rules of recognition, although H.L.A. Hart seemed to assume that it could or that the rules of recognition would necessarily lead to the internal aspects of law. Giving the rules of recognition so powerful a role may not be appropriate.[3] Rather, that leap may have to be assisted by many additional factors such as morality.

The rules of recognition, in my view, only let us reach the "marks" of rules of law, but not *necessarily* the rules of law themselves.[4] Certain rules that might have passed as rules of law according to the rules of recognition may be subsequently invalidated as against certain fundamental norms. Furthermore, the rules of recognition seem to have validity only within a certain defined regime and cannot take account of revolutions. For example, under normal rules of recognition, the decrees issued by a legislature and/or constituent assembly are to be complied with as law. During the French Revolution, however, neither such decrees nor such rules of recognition had any teeth. As

---

3 The confidence that H.L.A. Hart has in his rule of recognition may result from his own experience with the British legal system where Parliament is supreme. Under such a system, a rule of law considered as such—under a rule of recognition that an act of Parliament is a rule of law—will always be so. This is only peculiar to the British system or something like it. For his own treatment of "pathology" of the legal system, see ibid., 117-23. He seemed to have only some particular forms of revolutions in mind, but not others.

4 I do not challenge the existences of such rules of recognition, although I am not sure whether they are necessarily "legal rules" or can be moral rules. All I am trying to say is that such rules of recognition are part, but not all, of the factors that would lead to the internalisation of law in the minds of players in society. O.A. Elias & C.L. Lim, The Paradox of Consensualism (The Hague/ Boston/New York: Kluwer Law International, 1998) at 255-277, have argued that various state actors may perceive the rules of recognition differently, but none would disagree that there are such rules. In such a situation, all one can say is that the internalisation process becomes much easier. Indeed, in most situations such a state of affairs exists, and that is the reason, to a large extent, why generally there is order and stability. Still, one may wonder whether the content of such rules of recognition is "law", or simply morality or tradition.

Madame de Staël powerfully explained:

> The Constituent Assembly ever believed, erroneously, that there was some magic in its decrees, and that all would stop in every way at the line it traced. But its pronouncements can be compared to the ribbon which had been drawn through the garden of the palace (Tuileries) to keep the people at some distance from the palace; while opinion remained favourable to those who had drawn the ribbon, no one dreamed of trespassing; but as soon as the people wanted no more of this barrier, it became meaningless.[5]

Obviously, many social factors contribute to the "internalisation" of law in the actors, leading to the phenomenon of law serving as the sufficient reason for voluntary action. No doubt there should be at least a general voluntary compliance with law; otherwise such a view of the law would appear ridiculous, which in turn would prevent any internalisation from taking place. Other factors may include certain substantive justness and procedural fairness,[6] the "internal morality of law",[7] the certainty and clarity of the rules or a good judiciary that is characterized by independence, integrity and competence.[8] Additional factors may include a relatively good educational level (particularly when society is getting more and more complex everyday), a tolerable standard of living, a general atmosphere of happiness or being content with the realities of life, and a strong-enough sense of belonging to the community. The cross-fertilization of ideas and virtue will also be important.

If we adopt this version of the concept of law, we may make several inferences regarding the role of law in the formation of community value. We first of all can discern a constitutive role of law. That is to say, law, the common standard of conduct, represents or constitutes the essence or spirit of the

---

5 Mme Baronne de Staël, 1 Considérations sur les Principaux Evénements de la Révolution Française (Liege: J. Latour, 1918) at 416 (English translation taken from Bertrand de Jouvenel, The Pure Theory of Politics (Cambridge: University Press, 1963) at 47).

6 See Mireille Delmas-Marty, "Present-day China and the Rule of Law: Progress and Resistance", (2003) 2 Chinese J.I.L. 12.

7 See generally, Lon L. Fuller, The Morality of Law (New Haven, Yale University Press, 1963).

8 Sandra Day O'Connor, "Vindicating the Rule of Law: The Role of the Judiciary", (2003) 2 Chinese J.I.L. 1.

community. This happens when the internalisation process has been completed. This general observation would apply to both primary rules of conduct and the secondary rules regarding the making, changing and enforcing of the primary rules of conduct, as both may embody a certain spirit of the community. From this perspective, law has a passive quality; it can be no better than what the community is. The community's tradition and morality finally concretize and solidify in what we call law.

Next, we may also discern an instrumental role of law which may manifest in several ways. First, some members of the community may agree to a certain course of conduct, and the rest of the members somehow see the value of that course of conduct and agree to it as the standard of behavior. In this instance, law performs the function of transforming the attitude of some of the members in the community.

Second, the secondary rules on enforcing the primary rules of conduct—such as bringing the policemen to help us, or asking the judge for an order—play a predominantly instrumental role. These rules ensure that the primary rules of conduct are adhered to.

Third, the instrumental role of the rules on enforcing the primary rules of conduct also manifests in the fact that, almost always, the enforcement of the primary rules of conduct leads to the further elaboration and improvement of the primary rules of conduct themselves.

Of course, you can see that in the above analysis I have been speaking about a community. The presumed prototype of that community is that of a more or less self-contained and more or less homogeneous community. As the community expands to cover greater space both geographically and socially, the quantity of the common course of conduct that is accepted as law may be reduced, in general and as a natural development. That is to say, the constitutive role of law diminishes naturally. In such a situation, if one were to reverse this, one could perhaps strengthen the instrumental role of law by beefing up enforcement.

This is an observation that would be helpful when one examines the formation of regional perspectives of law or human rights. Generally, one can see that a regional setting is well-placed for the deepening of certain norms. Regions are neither too big nor too small, and can still be more or less self-contained. As a result, regions make such deepening more likely. As one commentator has observed, "shared legal, political, socioeconomic, intellectual, and cultural traditions and aspirations within a regional setting are more likely and do serve as cardinal bases for particularized and effective human rights protections at the regional level."[9]

Finally, as a general observation, one can see from history that there can be a certain "over-riding factor" that may "make or break", so to speak, the formation of a regional system, but always "makes" the regional perspective, of which the over-riding factor may form a part. Thus, this over-riding factor no doubt plays a constitutive role, but sometimes its instrumental role may predominate. This will become clearer later on in my discussion.

III. The European Perspectives on Human Rights and the European System for the Protection of Human Rights

The above general observations can find some proof in the formation of the European perspectives on human rights and the European system for human rights protection. As has been told time and time again, several factors are important in the emergence of the European system.

First of all, the most important factor is the European humanist culture. As the main drafter of the European Convention on Human Rights, P.-H. Teitgen, observed:

> The nations of western Europe as a community are co-heirs to an inheritance, a common heritage which they have to join forces to protect. This is their humanist culture, according to which right is pre-eminent over might and the purpose of the State, as of any other societal structure, is not its own greatness, power or riches but the individual self-fulfilment of everyone subject to its rule with due respect for his or her dignity and freedom. In short, in our humanist culture all persons, by reason of their origin, their nature and their destiny, have certain indefeasible rights, against which no reason of State may prevail.[10]

Against the background of such a tradition and such a culture, it is no wonder that the modern European perspectives on human rights and the system for their protection would have emerged, sooner or later. The reason why it

9 George William Mugwanya, "Realizing Universal Human Rights Norms through Regional Human Rights Mechanisms: Reinvigorating the African System", (1999) 10 Ind.Int'l & Comp.L.Rev. 35 at 41.

10 P.-H. Teitgen, "Introduction to the European Convention on Human Rights" in R. St. J. Macdonald et al. eds., The European System for the Protection of Human Rights (Boston: Kluwer, 1993) at 3.

emerged shortly after the Second World War has to do with what I described as the over-riding factor above. The horrible experience that the Europeans went through during the Second World War and the fear of the Soviet Union served as the over-riding factor in a positive way to bring about the European system of human rights protection. In so doing, the system builders hoped that the humanist culture would be further strengthened and would become the citadel against any possible future suppression. They had high expectations for the instrumental role of the law. To a large extent their attempt has been successful, as has been generally recognised. In an ironic way, one can find in this success at least one beneficial function of Communism!

The humanist culture is now reflected in the content of the European human rights law. This part of the law plays the constitutive role. The crowning achievement of this system is the European Convention on Human Rights and its effective enforcement. The Convention generally reflects a particular vision of the nature of human beings and of what the European region or societies believe to be most important for the self-fulfillment of individuals. This is not the place to go into the details but suffice it to say that this vision has the individual as the sacred being, more or less atomised, and most in love with civil and political rights. Painting the picture with a broad brush has its perils but sketches also serve the function of capturing the essential features of the object. This picture may have a point if you ask why the European Social Charter does not enjoy much success, not yet anyway.

As a system of enforcement mechanism, the Convention obliges each State party to ensure that the human rights of every person within its jurisdiction be respected, in a legally and, one should add, judicially, enforceable manner. Now every State party to the Convention also agrees to be sued by a person within its jurisdiction and by another State party before the Europe Court of Human Rights. It is well recognised that this system is most effective not only in enforcing the rights enumerated in the European Convention, but also, as has been noted, in helping to "accelerate" the harmonious evolution of human-rights standards in Europe. [11] The law plays a most effective instrumental role in the European system.

---

11 Catherine Lalumière, "Human Rights in Europe: Challenges for the Next Millennium" in R. St. J. Macdonald et al. eds., The European System for the Protection of Human Rights (Boston: Kluwer, 1993) xv-xvi.

IV. The Asian Perspectives on Human Rights and the Lack of an Asian System for the Protection of Human Rights[12]

On the other hand, the vast area of Asia as a whole has not witnessed any homogenised culture or tradition that covers the entire geographical span of Asia, other than their common experience of being under colonial control, to a large extent if not completely.

The nature of this situation naturally leads to a diminishing constitutive role of law. However, one must take note that the Bangkok Declaration, adopted in 1993 by the Asian States in preparation for the Vienna Conference on Human Rights, does reflect some broad principles that can be considered to constitute the Asian perspectives of human rights. These may be summarized as follows:

First of all, the Asian States do not disagree with the sacred nature of the human being. However, many of them do not agree with the atomized image of the individual. They believe that the individual stands in a balanced relationship with society. Particularly in areas where Confucianism holds sway, the individual is cultivated to possess a certain sense of being conscious of the existence of other fellow individuals or "two-men-mindedness", to use the literal translation of the corresponding Chinese character 仁 (ren), a composite of the characters for "man" (人) and "two" (二),[13] and with a sense of responsibility to him- or herself and the world other than him- or herself. This is succinctly stated in the Confucianist maxim: Cultivating oneself, regulating the family, ordering the State and bringing peace to the world.[14] I believe it was in this spirit that Hu Jintao, when introducing President Bush to students at Tsinghua University, said, from a slightly different angle, that China and the United States had many

---

12 This section draws heavily upon Sienho Yee, Towards an International Law of Co-progressiveness (Martinus Nijhoff Publishers, 2004) at 289-300 (Chapter 14, "The Concept of Human Rights in Asia").

13 During the drafting of the Universal Declaration of Human Rights, P.C. Chang attempted to enshrine this in the Declaration, but the idea was only "imperfectly" included. See Mary Ann Glendon, A World Made New: Eleanor Roosevelt and the Universal Declaration of Human Rights (New York: Random House, 2001) at 67-68.

14 The maxim is from Daxue (大学, The Great Learning), and appears in Chinese as "修身齐家治国平天下", pronounced as "xiushen qijia zhiguo pingtianxia". I have translated the maxim slightly differently than the translation commonly found.

things in common, among which was their common responsibility to the world.[15]

Asian States generally have stressed the need for taking account of the historical, cultural, and national background of the different States in human rights discourse.[16] While such an emphasis can be (and normally has been) considered one regarding the implementation of human rights, it can also be rationalized as implying that one's personhood is inherently tied to one's cultural, historical and national background. Few would say history, culture and nationality would not inform and enrich their personality. Their sense of belonging to a particular history, culture, and State can be significant. The common argument asserting the decay of State and State sovereignty ignores this aspect.

Many Asian States have also emphasized equality between States, and the evenhandedness required for the treatment of human rights issues. This, while outwardly assuming the appearance of an argument from State sovereignty, can be seen as a manifestation of the fight for dignity and equality, which is part of any personhood.

In the context of most Asian States, the emphasis on history, culture, sovereignty and national identity, and equality also takes on a dimension of self-determination. For those who have been through the troubled history of Asia, their personality must have been imprinted with deep scars that have resulted from oppression and with great pride that has resulted from achieving self-determination.[17] The fact that the Asians were willing to take such a more or less confrontational attitude on these issues show that they took self-determination seriously, and their history of being under colonial domination

---

15 "Chinese Vice-President Welcomes US President at Tsinghua University", Xinhua News Agency (22 February 2002) online: China Internet Information Centre <http://www.china.org.cn/english/27348.htm>.

16 Bangkok Declaration, reprinted in (2002) 1 Chinese J.I.L. 730; Liu Huaqiu Statement at Vienna Conference, ibid., 735; Statements by Indonesian authorities, as related by Christina M. Cerna, "East Asian Approaches to Human Rights", (1995-1996) 2 Buff.J.Int'l L. 201. See also Ming Wan, Human Rights in Chinese Foreign Relations (Philadelphia: University of Pennsylvania Press, 2000).

17 State Council Information Office of the Peoples' Republic of China, "White Paper, Fifty Years of Progress in China's Human Rights (June 2000)" reprinted in (2002) 1 Chinese J.I.L. 741 at 744; Statements by General Carlos Romulo, in Mary Ann Glendon supra note 13 at 215-16.

may have a great deal to do with it.

Regarding the particular rights, many Asian States tend to argue for an integrated approach,[18] while, at the same time, they often—if not always—list economic, social and cultural rights (and sometimes the right to development) first,[19] thus implicitly emphasizing them. The statements by officials make the emphasis much clearer.[20] They stress the economic, social and cultural rights, both as a separate category of rights, and as a condition for the realization of other rights. Such emphasis sometimes is characterized as a manifestation of Marxist and Third World approaches taking root, and, therefore, not very "Asian". Whatever label one might prefer, the logic for this emphasis is apparent: it is an argument from necessity as well as from history. Necessity tells these statesmen that the people must be fed reasonably well first before other human rights can be implemented. One cannot demand the impossible. History tells them that "they have been there" and other approaches have been tried and they did not work.*

The emphasis on economic, social and cultural rights has a concomitant emphasis on stability—whose most prominent champions include Mr. Lee Kuan Yew[21]—which serves as the precondition for economic, social, and

---

18 See Bangkok Declaration, preamble, supra note 16.

19 Ibid. See also Fifty Years of Progress in China's Human Rights (June 2000), supra note 17.

20 See, e.g., Liu Huaqiu Statement, ibid., 737; Wang Guangya Statement, ibid., 782.

* Postscript: Ten years after the first publication of this paper, President Xi Jinping of China made a speech at the College of Europe on 1 April 2014. He said (http://www.china.org.cn/world/2014-04/04/content_32004856.htm):

> In 1911, the revolution led by Dr. Sun Yat-sen overthrew the autocratic monarchy that had ruled China for several thousand years. But once the old system was gone, where China would go became the question. The Chinese people then started exploring long and hard for a path that would suit China's national conditions. They experimented with constitutional monarchy, imperial restoration, parliamentarism, multi-party system and presidential government, yet nothing really worked. Finally, China took on the path of socialism.

21 See, e.g., Richard Klein, "Cultural Relativism, Economic Development and International Human Rights in the Asian Content" (2001) 9 Touro Int'l L.Rev. 1 at 31 fn. 69 and Jacques deLisle & Kevin P. Lane, "Hong Kong's Endgame and the Rule of Law (II): The Battle over 'the People' and the Business Community in the Transition to Chinese Rule", (1997) 18 U.Pa.J.Int'l Econ.L.

cultural development, and a concomitant non-implementation of direct democracy at the national level anyway. There is merit to such a way of seeing the world. The difficulty is in finding the right mix.

As an Asian, I might indulge myself in thinking that these perspectives on human rights are quite rich. And yet, there is no Asian system for the protection of human rights similar to that which prevails in Europe. One naturally would ask why. I venture to give you the following reasons for this absence.

First of all, although these perspectives of human rights are rich, they consist of mostly broad principles and philosophical ideas on the nature of the individual and the community that are not susceptible of being concretized as enforceable rules and principles of law.

Then one may ask why a system has not been established for the part of the perspectives that can be concretized as enforceable rules and principles of law. There is merit to this question, as the Asian States do not mount any frontal attack, in general, against civil and political rights as such; in fact, they agree to the universal character of human rights, if one can trust the official declarations such as the Vienna Declaration and Programme of Action.[22] So in principle a collective system like that of the European system can be established in Asia, and yet none exists there *so far*.

One reason for this absence may be that the current economic development in Asia generally is such that the States may not believe they are capable of fulfilling their obligations yet. This may explain why they are willing to make a political declaration like that of the Bangkok Declaration, but not willing to adopt a legal convention about human rights.

One may wonder whether Asia's favorite mode of getting things done in a conciliatory nature may prevent a system like that of the European system from being established. Litigating may go against the Asian style, so to speak. This explains, at least in part, the Asian—particularly the Chinese—penchant for quiet dialogues and negotiations regarding human rights issues.[23] However, if this is the obstacle, then a more conciliatory system can be created to achieve the same goal, if not to the same extent of success.

The most important reason, I speculate, is what I consider to be the

---

811 at 880-881.

22 A/CONF.157/23.

23 Bangkok Declaration, supra note 16 at 734 para.25. Also, Liu Huaqiu Statement, supra note 16 at 739.

over-riding factor in the Asian context: their staunch adherence to the principle of non-interference in the domestic affairs of another State[24] as a reaction to their experience of being under colonial control. This principle is ingrained in the Asian psyche and constitutes an essential part of it at the present anyway. While Asian States may now agree that in principle human rights issues are not purely domestic issues anymore, they still seem to believe the *enforcement* of human rights is still essentially a domestic issue. Having suffered dearly when they were under colonial control, Asian States now zealously guard against any encroachment on their sovereignty. The effect of this attitude is often unelaborated in writing but can hardly be underestimated. Building a system of human rights protection that would allow a citizen to haul his or her government before an *international* court is contrary to the principle of non-interference. At least that is the appearance. The recent Western enlisting of human rights as an aid in ideological and political struggles or the demonstration of moral superiority does not help to alleviate the concerns of Asian States.

For the reasons mentioned above, law has not been able to play a more effective instrumental role in improving the systematic enforcement of human rights in Asia, at least not as effective as it has been in Europe. However, one must not be blind to the fact that the vast majority of the people in Asia are not in any dire straits at the moment. So law may be playing an instrumental role in the national systems. Of course the visible incidents have always had a strong hold on our imagination, and rightly so. Yet we must put the phenomenon and the causes for it in perspective. Perhaps this part of the world is *generally* doing better than some other parts of the world that have established systems of

---

24 For example, the Bangkok Declaration, supra note 16 at 731-32 para.5, emphasizes "the principles of respect for national sovereignty and territorial integrity as well as non-interference in the internal affairs of States, and the non-use of human rights as an instrument of political pressure." See also State Council Information Office of the Peoples' Republic of China, "White Paper on Human Rights Record of the United States in 2001", (2002) 1 Chinese J.I.L. 767 at 776-780 and Statement of Sha Zhu Kang, the Head of Chinese Delegation to the United Nations Human Rights Commission at the 58th Session of the Commission on Human Rights (8 April 2003 in (2004) 3 Chinese J.I.L. 342 at 343. On these questions, literature abounds. See generally, e.g., Richard Klein, supra note 21 and Michael C. Davis, "Constitutionalism and Political Culture: The Debate over Human Rights and Asian Values", (1998) 11 Harv.Hum.Rts.J. 109.

human rights protection. Moreover, with regard to particular rights, one must not forget that different people may value different rights differently. Some particular rights that do not fare well in Asia may have a stronger hold on the imagination of the Westerners than that of the Asians. For example, freedom of speech may not be enjoyed in Asia as in the West, yet one can walk at night in the streets of a big part of Asia feeling safer than in many parts of the United States. So it might be a mistake if one judges the human rights situation in Asia simply by reading the sensational news reports in the mass media.

Perhaps there will be no collective system for the protection of human rights in Asia until Asian States have changed their attitude toward this overriding factor—the principle of non-interference. I do not know when this may happen. However, the reports from Asia are positive. Recent developments in ASEAN show that changes may be on the way. For example, the governments decided at a meeting in Cambodia in June 2003 that they would speak with the Myanmar government about the plight of the Nobel Peace Prize laureate Daw Aung San Suu Kyi.[25] We may take this as cause for optimism. When the Asian States feel more secure about themselves, they will naturally give greater consideration to the possibility of establishing a regional system for the protection of human rights.[26]

Postscript

The paper as originally published contains this abstract:

> Adopting the concept of "internal aspect of law", the comment explains that law has a constitutive function (primary rules of conduct may embody the spirit of the community) and an instrumental function (secondary rules help to enforce the primary rules of conduct). Regions are well placed for

---

25 See "ASEAN calls for Suu Kyi release", CNN (17 June 2003) online: Cable News Network <http://www.cnn.com/2003/WORLD/asiapcf/southeast/06/17/myanmar.asean/>.

26 Postscript: Since the first publication of this paper, there have been many developments in this part of the world that give us cause for greater optimism, for example, the ASEAN Charter entered into force in 2008, and an ASEAN Intergovernmental Commission on Human Rights has been established. See <http://www.asean.org/asean/asean-charter>; <http://www.asean.org/communities/asean-political-security-community/category/asean-intergovernmental-commission-on-human-rights-aichr>.

the two functions to help to form regional perspectives and regional systems, but sometimes an "over-riding factor" plays a special role. There exist certain regional perspectives in Europe and Asia. However, the over-riding factor in Europe (fighting communism and preventing another World War II) helps to promote the formation of a strong regional system, whereas in Asia the staunch adherence to the principle of non-interference helps to prevent its formation.

Chapter 6

The Intrinsic and Instrumental Values of Diversity and the Settlement of the Conflicts between Them: Some Philosophical and Legal Considerations*

In this paper I shall try to highlight two basic values—intrinsic and instrumental values—that exist in the world and illustrate, in a more or less impressionistic way, how these values may manifest themselves in matters relating to diversity and how conflicts in general and conflicts specifically relating to diversity can be seen as conflicts of these values. This is a tentative attempt, meant to bring out into the open some implicit ways of or framework for seeing and rationalizing the world, and to generalize the issues to a certain level so as to order our examination, analysis and rationalization in a better way. In so doing, I hope to help deepen our understanding of diversity, improve the quality of relevant decision-making, and ultimately promote it in however small a way.

I. Intrinsic and Instrumental Values as Two Basic Values

Probably one would agree that I do not need any footnotes to talk about this idea. Probably one may even say that the very talk of it is cliché. The idea is basically this. For almost everything or every phenomenon in the world, one can find in it or assign to it two values: intrinsic value and instrumental value. This is also true with human beings. As we will see, each value is virtuous in a different way. Often "inherent" is used as synonymous with "intrinsic". The latter will be primarily used here, because "inherent" sometimes is too protean a term.

---

* Revised from: The Intrinsic and Instrumental Values of Diversity: Some Philosophical and Legal Considerations, in: Sienho Yee & Jacques-Yvan Morin (eds), Multiculturalism and International Law: Essays in Honour of Edward McWhinney (Martinus Nijhoff 2009), 207-226.

As is also cliché, an instrumental value is that which is good only as an instrument for something else. I want one US Dollar not to keep it for good, but to use it to buy a cup of coffee. The dollar bill is an instrument for me to obtain my coffee. On the other hand, an intrinsic value is an end value in itself. For example, my experience is an intrinsic value to me: it is unique and it forms part of me, my personhood, and that's it. Period. Without insisting on particular wording to define these terms, one can generally agree: "That which is intrinsically good is nonderivatively good; it is good for its own sake. That which is not intrinsically good but extrinsically good is derivatively good; it is good, not (insofar as its extrinsic value is concerned) for its own sake, but for the sake of something else that is good and to which it is related in some way."[1]

Generally speaking, the two values may exist in the same thing at once: a value, independently evaluated, can be an intrinsic value; yet it may be an instrument for another intrinsic value. To this extent, these two values signify ways of seeing values and the world. One may see one value or another, depending on one's world view and orientation.

As is obvious, what follows from being treated as an instrumental value may be vastly different from what follows from being treated as an intrinsic value. For example, if indeed we are so special as an end in itself or as ends in ourselves, as Kant taught us,[2] we (or humanity) would reign supreme as end units, and not as instrumental units for the glory of the community, nation, society, or even God. If we were only instrumental members in a community, nation, society, or fellowship in Christ, we would have to sacrifice us for the benefit of the community, nation, society, or God. Of course, closer to the truth is the position that both values may co-exist in us; and one may inform or promote the other. When they do come into conflict, which one should prevail is a perennial question.

An instrumental value will expire when the end for which the instrumental value is an instrument has been achieved. That is to say, the *raison d'être* of the instrumental value no longer exists and the instrumental value should not exist any further. In contrast, an intrinsic value, or an end in itself, may not expire as a value, although I am not sure whether it is wise to say

---

1 See Intrinsic vs. Extrinsic Value, in: Stanford Encyclopedia of Philosophy (http://plato.stanford.edu/entries/value-intrinsic-extrinsic/#WhaIntVal).

2 See generally Kant, The Groundwork of the Metaphysics of Morals (1785); for an analysis of the humanity formula, see the entry on this in Stanford Encyclopedia of Philosophy (http://plato.stanford.edu/entries/kant-moral/#HumFor).

never. Therefore, if we can find an intrinsic value in a thing or a phenomenon, there can be better and longer life for that thing or phenomenon.

Perhaps for these and for other reasons, it has been observed that "Intrinsic value [...] has a certain priority over extrinsic value. The latter is derivative from or reflective of the former and is to be explained in terms of the former. It is for this reason that philosophers have tended to focus on intrinsic value in particular."[3] In this short paper I hope to show that political leaders and legal decision-makers, too, have seen the world this way. At least in the international arena, they have given priority, to some extent, to intrinsic value, although not yet in an ideal way.

II. The Intrinsic and Instrumental Values of Diversity

Diversity is a phenomenon in the world. It possesses both intrinsic and instrumental values and we can identify them. In a conscious and perhaps incomplete way, the analysis in the broadest outline may run as follows. On the one hand, generally speaking, diversity can serve as an intrinsic value in itself. In itself it is so beautiful. It is so glorious. It is so enriching.[*] It is so special. We just like it. It is part of us. It is constitutive of society. On the other hand, diversity can serve also as an instrument to promote the betterment of society, with the understanding that such betterment can come in an infinite variety. Sometimes diversity is recognized as having both values in the same instrument in international law.

This analysis figures in any debate regarding diversity and its associated regimes. Sometimes it is consciously and expressly done. Sometimes it is not, but the analysis can still be rationalized this way by an objective observer. Most of the time decision-makers do not present a clear analysis, for whatever reason. Illustrations can be found in both national and international law.

---

3 See Stanford Encyclopedia of Philosophy, above n.1; see also text to n.27 below.

* Postscript: After the first appearance of this paper, I have received a comment regarding this aspect, particularly whether "enriching" is an instrumental matter. While at the vanishing line degree and kind may intersect, "enriching", when signifying a sensation, is, or can be deemed, an intrinsic value.

II.A. A National Law Illustration: the Affirmative Action Controversy

Normally a general analysis in national law will not proceed from an explicit analysis of intrinsic and instrumental values. Every issue, ultimately, may have to be evaluated under a constitutional lens. As Rehnquist observed, when a democratic society

> adopts a constitution and incorporates in that constitution safeguards for individual liberty, these safeguards indeed do take on a generalized moral rightness or goodness. They assume a general social acceptance neither because of any intrinsic worth nor because of any unique origins in someone's idea of natural justice but instead simply because they have been incorporated in a constitution by the people.[4]

This approach is no less true in the specific context of diversity. This would seem to explain why any *express* attempt to assert simple diversity as an intrinsic value and to pursue it as such seems to have been precluded from the constitutional discourse in the United States. However, the instrumental value analysis done in an implicit fashion where such an analysis is not mentioned by name is unmistakable in the cases.

An illuminating example is the treatment of affirmative action policies applied by the US universities in favor of the "disadvantaged" minority applicants. Normally such an applicant would be given some favorable weight so that he or she stands a better chance getting admitted into a particular program than a normal applicant. This would amount to applying racial classification and would give rise to claims of racial discrimination or "reverse discrimination", as some have called. The university would normally present a variety of purposes or interests to justify the policy. Under US constitutional law, a university is said to have a "compelling interest in attaining a diverse student body", [5] or, as sometimes described alternatively but probably synonymously, a "compelling interest in securing the educational benefits of a diverse student body".[6] As a result, the university may apply a narrowly tailored

---

4 William H. Rehnquist, The Notion of a Living Constitution, 29 Harvard J. of Law and Public Policy (2006) (reprinting an earliest article), 401, 412.

5 Grutter v. Bollinger, 539 U.S. 306 (2003), 328.

6 Ibid., 333.

affirmative action policy to serve that compelling interest.[7]

There is no *express* attempt to assert simple diversity as an intrinsic value. To pursue it as such is precluded by the current US case law—under *Bakke* and *Grutter*.[8] These cases hold that a simple attempt to assure within a student body some specified percentage of a particular group merely because of its race or ethnic origin is against the Equal Protection Clause and therefore unconstitutional.[9]

The cases, however, did do an instrumental value analysis without labeling it as such. The very characterization of the "compelling interest" alternatively as in "attaining a diverse student body",[10] or "securing the educational benefits of a diverse student body"[11] betrays this instrumental outlook of the Court. Some language of Justice Powell's opinion in *Bakke* (not necessarily representing that of the Court) touched upon diversity as part of academic freedom grounded in the First Amendment. Such language is susceptible of being stretched as "intrinsic value" talk,[12] as First Amendment values are often or at least sometimes considered intrinsic values. But Justice

7 See Regents of the University of California v. Bakke, 438 U.S. 265 (1978); Grutter v. Bollinger, 539 U.S. 306 (2003).

8 Grutter, 539 US, 330.

9 I reserve for the future the question whether a "diversity as an intrinsic value" argument may have any force under US constitutional law, despite current case law, or under the International Convention on the Elimination of All Forms of Racial Discrimination (http://www.unhchr.ch/html/menu3/b/d _icerd.htm; GA Res 2106 (XX), 21 Dec. 1965).

10 Grutter v. Bollinger, 539 U.S. 306 (2003), 328.

11 Ibid., 333.

12 One commentator seemed to be doing this, and yet he quickly also turned to the instrumental part of the analysis:

> Powell conceptualized diversity as a value intrinsic to the educational process itself. He regarded diversity as essential to "the quality of higher education," because education was a practice of enlightenment, "of 'speculation, experiment and creation'" that thrived on the "robust exchange of ideas" characteristically provoked by confrontation between persons of distinct life experiences. Powell understood diversity as necessary to facilitate this process of education.

Robert C. Post, Foreword: Fashioning the Legal Constitution: Culture, Courts and Law, 117 Harvard LR (2003), 4, at 59-60 (internal citations omitted). From this, one is not clear whether the commentator was doing an intrinsic/instrumental analysis.

Powell seemed to have instrumental values in mind: his was an instrumental First Amendment. It was the "robust exchange of ideas", the "quality of higher education", the better "future of the nation" that he was after, which diversity was thought to promote.[13]

This instrumental analysis was amplified in the *Grutter* case in 2003[14] in the US Supreme Court. In that case, the University of Michigan Law School applies a nuanced affirmative action policy in order to attain a critical mass of disadvantaged minority students in its student body. The Court endorsed Justice Powell's earlier analysis and upheld this policy. The Court held that the Law School has a compelling interest in attaining a diverse student body and in obtaining the educational benefits that flow from such a student body. If Justice Powell primarily had First Amendment values in mind, the *Grutter* Court cast the net of "educational benefits" much more widely and thus made much clearer the instrumental calculus:

> These benefits are substantial. As the District Court emphasized, the Law School's admissions policy promotes "cross-racial understanding," helps to break down racial stereotypes, and "enables [students] to better understand persons of different races." [...] These benefits are "important and laudable," because "classroom discussion is livelier, more spirited, and simply more enlightening and interesting" when the students have "the greatest possible variety of backgrounds." [...]
>
> The Law School's claim of a compelling interest is further bolstered by its amici, who point to the educational benefits that flow from student body diversity. In addition to the expert studies and reports entered into evidence at trial, numerous studies show that student body diversity promotes learning outcomes, and "better prepares students for an increasingly diverse workforce and society, and better prepares them as professionals." [...] These benefits are not theoretical but real, as major American businesses have made clear that the skills needed in today's increasingly global marketplace can only be developed through exposure to widely diverse people, cultures, ideas, and viewpoints. [...] What is more, high-ranking retired officers and civilian leaders of the United States military assert that, "[b]ased on [their] decades of experience," a "highly qualified, racially diverse officer corps ... is

13 Bakke, 312-313.

14 Grutter v. Bollinger, 539 U.S. 306 (2003).

essential to the military's ability to fulfill its principal mission to provide national security."[15]

As is clear from this discussion, the Court's justification for the affirmative action policy in issue is instrumental. As such, the Court's analysis will encounter the normal problems associated with an instrumental value analysis. For example, when the educational benefits (not including just having a diverse student body) have been obtained, there would be no place for the policy. Indeed, the Court itself declared: "We expect that 25 years from now, the use of racial preferences will no longer be necessary to further the interest approved today."[16] This of course is a wishful thinking now. One wonders: (1) what may happen if 25 years is not enough; and (2) if, when the benefits listed have been obtained, but still no diversity has in fact resulted, will what the Court "expects" now become what the law mandates then?[17]

II.B. Some International Law Illustrations

Perhaps in some contrast to the situation in national law, *explicit* assertions and/or arguments based on an analysis of intrinsic and instrumental values can be found in various international instruments. This may have resulted from the fact that since the very beginning of modern international law, philosophers and philosophical considerations have been exerting a stronger impact on international law. Grotius was both a philosopher and a practitioner of international law. The modern human rights movement started with several philosophers hammering out the Universal Declaration of Human Rights.[18]

---

15 Ibid., 330-331 (internal citations omitted).

16 Ibid., 343.

17 Apparently there is a "best 10%" experiment going on to achieve the same goal as does an affirmative action policy. That experiment takes the best 10% of the graduates from every high school in a particular state, which appears fairer. Because the high school student population is not evenly distributed racially, leaving some high schools with a certain concentration of students of a particular minority. Taking the best 10% from each high school might result in getting the best 10% of various concentrations of racial groups.

18 See generally Mary Ann Glendon, A World Made New: Eleanor Roosevelt and the Universal Declaration of Human Rights (2001). See also Christopher McCrudden, Human Dignity and Judicial Interpretation of Huamn Rights, 19 EJIL (2008), 655.

Apparently as a result of this, philosophical phrases sprinkle around in international law debates.

Philosophical influence is especially pronounced in the international law on human rights. The Universal Declaration of Human Rights[19] declares in its preamble that "recognition of the inherent dignity and of the equal and inalienable rights of all members of the human family is the foundation of freedom, justice and peace in the world". This is repeated in both the International Covenant on Civil and Political Rights (ICCPR) [20] and the International Covenant on Economic, Social and Cultural Rights (ICESCR).[21] The latter two further recognize, in the preamble of each, that "these rights derive from the inherent dignity of the human person". Furthermore, they contain particular provisions on certain inherent rights such as Article 6(1) of the ICCPR (the right to life) and Article 25 of the ICESCR (the right to enjoy and utilize natural resources). Finally, the Vienna Declaration and Programme of Action[22] recognizes and reaffirms that "all human rights derive from the dignity and worth inherent in the human person". By resorting to the concept and the express term of "worth inherent", this latter position brings out into the open what is implicit in the earlier human rights instruments recognizing the inherent dignity of the human person. Instrumental analyses are even easier to find, and one can see various examples in the ICCPR (e.g. Article 4(1)) and the ICESCR (e.g., Article 13).

In the context of diversity, several instruments have shown their recognition of the intrinsic and instrumental values of a thing or phenomenon and the distinction between them. Three instruments that specifically deal with diversity illustrate this point very well.

The UNESCO Universal Declaration on Cultural Diversity (the UNESCO Declaration)[23] and the UNESCO Convention on the Protection and Promotion of the Diversity of Cultural Expressions (the UNESCO Convention)[24] contain in each an article declaring that cultural diversity is a common heritage of mankind. The UNESCO Declaration in Article 1 recognizes that:

---

19 Http://www.un.org/Overview/rights.html.

20 Http://www.unhchr.ch/html/menu3/b/a_ccpr.htm.

21 Http://www.unhchr.ch/html/menu3/b/a_cescr.htm.

22 Http://www2.ohchr.org/english/law/vienna.htm.

23 Http://www2.ohchr.org/english/law/diversity.htm.

24 Http://portal.unesco.org/culture/en/ev.php-URL_ID=33232&URL_DO=DO_TOPIC&URL_ SECTION=201.html.

> Culture takes diverse forms across time and space. This diversity is embodied in the uniqueness and plurality of the identities of the groups and societies making up humankind. As a source of exchange, innovation and creativity, cultural diversity is as necessary for humankind as biodiversity is for nature. In this sense, it is the common heritage of humanity and should be recognized and affirmed for the benefit of present and future generations.

This is a recognition of the intrinsic or inherent value of cultural diversity, although such terms are not employed.

The Declaration in Article 3 further recognizes the instrumental value of cultural diversity as a factor in development: "Cultural diversity widens the range of options open to everyone; it is one of the roots of development, understood not simply in terms of economic growth, but also as a means to achieve a more satisfactory intellectual, emotional, moral and spiritual existence". Furthermore, the Declaration in Article 7 recognizes "cultural rights as the wellspring of creativity".

Similarly, the UNESCO Convention in its preamble affirms that "cultural diversity is a defining characteristic of humanity" and recognizes that "cultural diversity forms a common heritage of humanity and should be cherished and preserved for the benefit of all". The Convention further describes in its preamble the instrumental value of cultural diversity as "a mainspring for sustainable development for communities, peoples and nations" and "indispensable for peace and security at the local, national and international levels" and celebrates "the importance of cultural diversity for the full realization of human rights and fundamental freedoms proclaimed in the Universal Declaration of Human Rights and other universally recognized instruments".

Another instrument that has deployed such an analysis is the Convention on Biological Diversity.[25] The contracting parties to the Convention declare that they are "[c]onscious of the intrinsic value of biological diversity and of the ecological, genetic, social, economic, scientific, educational, cultural, recreational and aesthetic values of biological diversity and its components" and of "the importance of biological diversity for evolution and for maintaining life sustaining systems of the biosphere", and note "that, ultimately, the

25 Http://www.cbd.int/convention/convention.shtml.

conservation and sustainable use of biological diversity will strengthen friendly relations among States and contribute to peace for humankind". Expressly employing the term "intrinsic value" and terms such as "importance for" and "will strengthen", the Convention unmistakably follows an intrinsic/instrumental value framework of analysis.

Unmistakable though it may be, the framework of analysis deployed in these instruments is not perfect, as discussed below.[26] While components of the framework are visible, there does not seem to be a clear spine that would connect them into a proper order. The implications of recognizing an intrinsic value are not clearly laid down. Policy-making will be fraught with uncertainties and conflicting demands.

III. "Conflicts of Values": Some Tentative Observations

As can be gleaned from the above discussion, the world can be seen through such a lens so that intrinsic and instrumental values can be observed in every thing and every phenomenon including diversity. The lens so far is very hazy, however, with many of the issues addressed in an incomplete manner or not addressed explicitly at all.

Still, if the world can be seen through such a lens, many disputes in society can be cast as conflicts or clashes of these values. The resolution of such disputes is then a choice between such values within the same category (an intrinsic value vs. another intrinsic value, or an instrumental value vs. another instrumental value) or between two values from different categories (an intrinsic value vs. an instrumental value). Roughly speaking,[27] a reasonable person under normal circumstances would probably choose the more efficient one between two instrumental values and the more important one between two intrinsic values or between an intrinsic value and an instrumental value. Furthermore, one would give priority to an intrinsic value in the last scenario, if the intrinsic value is as important as or perhaps slightly less so than the instrumental value.[28]

---

26 One would hope that the recently adopted UN Declaration on the Rights of the Indigenous Peoples (A/RES/61/295, http://www.un.org/esa/socdev/unpfii/en/drip.html) would give us another ideal example of an analysis of intrinsic and instrumental values. The text of the Declaration is not such a model.

27 A workable, comprehensive compass for resolving such disputes cannot be attempted in this paper and will be left for another day or other thinkers.

28 See the entry in Stanford Encyclopedia of Philosophy, text to above n.3.

A society as a whole, however, most likely would opt for the value perceived to be more important, often in a most un-nuanced fashion and without the benefit of an explicit intrinsic vs. instrumental value analysis. Such a choice may exhibit itself in law. In the following observations, I shall attempt to bring into the open such an analysis, by readily found examples, in more general and non-diversity situations and then in diversity matters.

III.A. Non-Diversity Illustrations

A real life example in a non-diversity context is Mr. Diallo's case[29] in the Bronx, New York. This case is probably affected by diversity considerations (at least in the background) but can be analyzed as a general case because there has been no challenge to jury impartiality on grounds of racial bias in a specific way. Mr. Diallo was a young African immigrant who had returned to his building on the night of 4 February 1999. About 12:40 a.m. on that night, four New York police officers, all in street clothes, approached Mr. Diallo on the stoop of his building and fired 41 shots, striking him 19 times, as he retreated inside. The officers, who are white, said they had thought he had a gun. It turned out to be a wallet. The police perpetrators were acquitted in a subsequent prosecution by a jury consisting of four blacks and eight whites, because in its view what the officers were doing was considered not unreasonable so as to persuade it to convict them. So, the police perpetrators were reasonably conducting self-defence. In the jury's mind, then, although what the perpetrators did was *in fact* wrong, it was considered to be legitimate *in belief*, for the good of society.

We do not see any express explanation of its action by the jury, but what it did can be rationalized this way: while the mistaken self-defence cost the life of Mr. Diallo, it was legitimate and necessary for society (at least the particular version of it in the Bronx) to survive. That is to say, it was all right for Mr. Diallo to die for the good of society. Two versions of the conflict of values are apparent: one between Mr. Diallo's life as an intrinsic value to him and his

---

29 Jane Fritsch, The Overview: 4 Officers in Diallo Shooting Are Acquitted of All Charges, NY Times, 26 Feb. 2000 (http://partners.nytimes.com/library/national/regional/022600ny-diallo.html). Postscript: Recently the USA witnessed the shooting of Trayvon Martin, a case weirdly similar to the Diallo case. In Martin's case, the law of the state in issue, Florida, is more favorable to the defendant (see http://en.wikipedia.org/wiki/Shooting_of_Trayvon_Martin), and Mr. Michael Brown (http://www.reuters.com/search?blob=ferguson).

death as an instrumental value to society and one between his life as an intrinsic value and the survival of society (ultimately) as an intrinsic value. The intrinsic value of Mr. Diallo's life was apparently considered not as important as his death's instrumental value to society *or* as the intrinsic value of the survival of society. This shows that at a critical moment even a capitalistic or liberal society (New York), which champions human rights, freedom or liberalism, ultimately sacrifices individuals for its own good,[30] although one might not like to see the events in this light.

There is no shortage of conflicts of such values and their resolution in international law. In human rights law one can find the resolution of many conflicts of values as well as compromises between them. In several articles of the ICCPR (e.g., Articles 12, 18, 19, 21, and 22), there are several exceptions embedded in the articles delineating the rights. We may call these "in-article exceptions". If the rights at issue can be considered intrinsic values, such values are nevertheless no match to their limitations which serve as instrumental values to society. One example is the exception in Article 18(3): "Freedom to manifest one's religion or beliefs may be subject only to such limitations as are prescribed by law and are necessary to protect public safety, order, health, or morals or the fundamental rights and freedoms of others."

Then there is also the "general exception" under Article 4 of the ICCPR.

---

30 This was in fact put in starker terms by Justice Oliver Wendell Holmes in Buck v. Bell, 274 U.S. 200, 207 (1927), a case affirming a state policy of sterilizing mentally retarded people of third generation of such a condition: "We have seen more than once that the public welfare may call upon the best citizens for their lives. It would be strange if it could not call upon those who already sap the strength of the State for these lesser sacrifices, often not felt to be such by those concerned, in order to prevent our being swamped with incompetence. It is better for all the world, if instead of waiting to execute degenerate offspring for crime, or to let them starve for their imbecility, society can prevent those who are manifestly unfit from continuing their kind. The principle that sustains compulsory vaccination is broad enough to cover cutting the Fallopian tubes. [...] Three generations of imbeciles are enough." 274 US 200 (1927), 207 (internal citation omitted). Mr. Justice Butler dissented, without opinion, ibid., 208. While such a case may be decided differently these days, the reasoning given by Holmes may still have sway. A subsequent out of court settlement for $3 million by the City with the Diallo family (see http://www.nytimes.com/2004/01/06/nyregion/06CND-DIAL.html) does not in any way change the analysis in the criminal law context. Furthermore, no admission of mistake was made.

Under paragraph 1 of that article, either the "life of the nation" is considered a value more important than the intrinsic value of many of the human rights; or the instrumental value of the forfeiture of many of these rights is more important than the intrinsic value of these rights. That provision states:

> In time of public emergency which threatens the life of the nation and the existence of which is officially proclaimed, the States Parties to the present Covenant may take measures derogating from their obligations under the present Covenant to the extent strictly required by the exigencies of the situation, provided that such measures are not inconsistent with their other obligations under international law and do not involve discrimination solely on the ground of race, colour, sex, language, religion or social origin.

That calculation does not work with respect to some rights. Under paragraph 2 of Article 4, "No derogation from articles 6, 7, 8 (paragraphs 1 and 2), 11, 15, 16 and 18 may be made under this provision". The rights delineated under these enumerated articles, and the intrinsic value thereof, are considered more important than the instrumental value of the forfeiture of them. Probably one cannot say that a conscious decision has been made to prioritize the intrinsic value of these rights over that of the "life of the nation". Rather, the decision is probably that the enjoyment of the rights under the enumerated articles would not threaten the "life of the nation"; or that the forfeiture of these rights would not lessen or eliminate such a threat if it exists.

III.B. Diversity Illustrations

Similarly, many disputes relating to diversity can also be seen as conflicts between intrinsic and instrumental values. The resulting choices may be rationalized as one value being given priority over another. However, decision-makers may not have seen things through such a lens. Or, if they have, the pictures they have seen are incomplete or even garbled.

In national law, an obvious example is again the *Grutter* case in the US Supreme Court. As demonstrated above, the Court clearly recognized the instrumental value of diversity and its ultimate decision could be rationalized as one championing one value—the instrumental value according to the Court—over another, the intrinsic value of Grutter's right not to be discriminated against. In whatever manner the Court would like to explain its decision, by necessary implication, it must have decided this way.

However, the *modus operandi* in the Court's decision-making in this and similar cases appears not to pit these two values against each other expressly, but to ask: "Whether diversity is a compelling interest that can justify the narrowly tailored use of race in selecting applicants for admission to public universities".[31] This question was analyzed and answered in a way so that the challenger—Grutter—seemed to have disappeared from the picture, as if the compelling interest, which was an instrument to obtain the assorted educational benefits, were some sort of *force majeur* making it futile to address other rights and interests. Still, by necessary implication, the Court gave priority to an instrumental value—diversity as a means of securing the educational benefits—over an intrinsic value associated with not being discriminated against.

Such a governmental interest and/or educational benefits as an overriding "trump" over equal protection rights seem not to be based on some textual home in the Constitution but on the Court's own constitutional doctrine-making. Neither can one find such a home for "diversity" as such. As has been noted by Rehnquist, the received wisdom is that constitutional rights, not intrinsic worth, prevail in constitutional decision-making.[32] One thus is left with only the option of locating diversity in an established constitutional right in order to endow it with the fair power to override equal protection rights. It seems to be such a reasoning that was at work in Justice Powell's opinion in *Bakke*, where he did notice in his analysis a conflict of values—or, he may call it a conflict of interests, as can be inferred from his choice of word "interest". But he did not pursue such a line of reasoning till the end. He said:

> in arguing that its universities must be accorded the right to select those students who will contribute the most to the "robust exchange of ideas," petitioner [the Regents of the University of California] invokes a countervailing constitutional interest, that of the First Amendment. In this light, petitioner must be viewed as seeking to achieve a goal that is of paramount importance in the fulfillment of its mission.[33]

Pitting a First Amendment interest against an equal protection right, an eminently intrinsic value, would seem to be presenting a better fight than pitting

---

31 Grutter, 539 US, 321.

32 See text to n.4 above.

33 Bakke, 438 US, 313.

the assorted educational benefits against an equal protection right. Letting a First Amendment interest prevail over an equal protection right would seem to be more reasonable than letting the assorted educational benefits prevail over an equal protection right. It would seem that the triumph of one intrinsic value over another intrinsic value would make one feel better than the triumph of an instrumental value over an intrinsic value. If the First Amendment interest can be considered to have intrinsic value (probably not the version that Justice Powell had in mind), the conflict will then be between two intrinsic values. One wonders whether, under US law, there can be a plausible analysis that would treat diversity as an intrinsic value without going through the avenue of the First Amendment and would tackle the conflict between diversity and equal protection rights or other rights directly as a conflict between two intrinsic values.

There may be a better chance to see many diversity disputes being analyzed as conflicts of values, whether intrinsic or instrumental, in international law. This is so because many international law instruments, as discussed above, expressly recognize the intrinsic and instrumental values of the subject matters being dealt with. Such an express recognition is the point of departure of any analysis conscious of the values involved. This is particularly true with the above discussed two international conventions directly dealing with diversity. However, one must not exaggerate such a chance. While international law may have a good point of departure, it is not clear to what extent such an analysis already has been conducted or can be conducted in the future.

The situation seems to be better with the Convention on Biological Diversity.[34] First of all, the Convention expressly recognizes in the preamble the intrinsic value of biodiversity. Naturally then, its operative provisions aim to achieve "the conservation of biological diversity, the sustainable use of its components and the fair and equitable sharing of the benefits arising out of the utilization of genetic resources", as stated in Article 1. Still, the operative provisions do not seem to give biodiversity a very strong position. The objectives of the Convention have to be mostly entrusted to national efforts, and subject to national sovereign rights (Article 3). Most of the provisions (for example, Articles 5-11) spelling out the obligations of a State contain phrases such as "in accordance with its particular conditions and capabilities" or "as far as possible and as appropriate". This shows that a decision has been made to

---

34 Http://www.cbd.int/convention/convention.shtml.

accommodate national capability, thus giving priority to various other values over the intrinsic value of biodiversity when there is a conflict between them in the internal context. This is apparently a resignation to the inevitable: international law cannot demand the impossible from the participants in the system.

However, in the international context the Convention prioritizes biodiversity in the most critical situation when biodiversity is faced with serious damage or threat thereto. Article 22(1) of the Convention states: "The provisions of this Convention shall not affect the rights and obligations of any Contracting Party deriving from any existing international agreement, except where the exercise of those rights and obligations would cause a serious damage or threat to biological diversity." The Convention thus seems to be saying that some damage is fine but no serious damage is permitted. Here biodiversity as an intrinsic value prevails. The basis for triumph is the possible severity of damage. So prevail the intrinsic value does, with difficulty.

The situation seems to be less clear with the UNESCO Convention on the Diversity of Cultural Expressions. As discussed above, the Convention clearly recognizes the intrinsic value of cultural diversity in its preamble, and aims to protect and promote such a value. Article 1 of the Convention declares that "The objectives of this Convention are: (a) to protect and promote the diversity of cultural expressions; [...] (b) to create the conditions for cultures to flourish and to freely interact in a mutually beneficial manner", among others. Under Article 5, "The Parties, in conformity with the Charter of the United Nations, the principles of international law and universally recognized human rights instruments, reaffirm their sovereign right to formulate and implement their cultural policies and to adopt measures to protect and promote the diversity of cultural expressions and to strengthen international cooperation to achieve the purposes of this Convention." Under certain circumstances a State party may take special measures to protect cultural expressions under Article 8.

Thus, the general framework of the Convention appears to be "strong national measures, diverse cultures", again primarily relying on the efforts of the States parties to achieve the aims of the Convention. Of course "strong national measures" will most likely come into tension, if not in conflict, with the rights and obligations arising under other species of international law. Most obvious among them will be the treaties promoting free trade and free market in general.

On a generalized level, this would present a conflict of the intrinsic value of cultural diversity and other values such as the instrumental value of free trade. The States parties to the Convention are conscious of this conflict and have determined to give priority to cultural diversity *to some extent*. Thus, the preamble states that the parties were "convinced that cultural activities, goods and services have both an economic and a cultural nature, because they convey identities, values and meanings, and must therefore not be treated as solely having commercial value" and notes that "while the processes of globalization, which have been facilitated by the rapid development of information and communication technologies, afford unprecedented conditions for enhanced interaction between cultures, they also represent a challenge for cultural diversity, namely in view of risks of imbalances between rich and poor countries".

Implementing this disposition, Article 20 of the Convention, whose heading reads "Relationship to other treaties: mutual supportiveness, complementarity and non-subordination", stipulates:

> 1. Parties recognize that they shall perform in good faith their obligations under this Convention and all other treaties to which they are parties. Accordingly, without subordinating this Convention to any other treaty,
>   (a) they shall foster mutual supportiveness between this Convention and the other treaties to which they are parties; and
>   (b) when interpreting and applying the other treaties to which they are parties or when entering into other international obligations, Parties shall take into account the relevant provisions of this Convention.
>
> 2. Nothing in this Convention shall be interpreted as modifying rights and obligations of the Parties under any other treaties to which they are parties.

The extent to which the intrinsic value of cultural diversity has been given priority over other values is not clear from this provision. This provision will present a Herculean task of interpretation, which must await further development. Paragraphs 1 and 2 separately seem to be pulling us into different directions, seemingly resulting in an equality between this Convention and other relevant treaties and agreements. The only thing in favor of cultural diversity would be the duty of the States parties to foster mutual supportiveness and take into account of the relevant provisions of this Convention, which does not mandate any particular result of course.[35] One hopes that this "obligation of process" will culminate in a result favorable to cultural diversity.

A more cultural diversity friendly argument may be made. The issue first has a dimension as one of conflict of treaties. Coupled with the rule restated in Article 30 of the Vienna Convention on the Law of Treaties,[36] Article 20 of the UNESCO Convention would not clearly give priority to the UNESCO Convention or to the other treaty that might be in tension with it. The issue also has a dimension as one of treaty interpretation. Article 20 of the UNESCO Convention and its entire scheme (with the clear purpose of the Convention favoring the intrinsic value of cultural diversity and its preamble as part of the context to be interpreted and applied), when coupled with provisions in another treaty that directs the parties to take account of other international law rules and principles, and with the rules restated in Articles 30 and 31-32 of the Vienna Convention, may give a decision-maker sufficient ammunition to reach a plausible conclusion that cultural diversity as an intrinsic value prevails over other values such as free trade. If indeed these factors only present a scenario with various values hanging on a balance, any leaning towards intrinsic value in general or that of cultural diversity in particular, as has already been expressed in the UNESCO Convention itself, would help tip the balance in its favor.

Such a dispute could present itself to the WTO Dispute Settlement Body soon. The WTO agreements appear to be elastic enough to permit a cultural diversity triumph. This can be done (1) by treating WTO law as having incorporated such rules and principles in favor of cultural diversity, (2) by treating cultural diversity as an exemption from free trade, or (3) by giving cultural diversity priority over free trade. It seems that there is cause for cautious optimism for a triumph of cultural diversity over free trade as a result of interpreting the WTO Agreement and other relevant instruments. Indeed, the Dispute Settlement Understanding directs that the clarification of the WTO agreements should be "in accordance with customary rules of interpretation of public international law".[37] The Appellate Body of the WTO appears to have

---

35 For details, see Ivan Bernier, The UNESCO Convention on the Protection and Promotion of the Diversity of Cultural Expressions: A Cultural Instrument at the Junction of Law and Politics (http://www.diversite-culturelle.qc.ca/fileadmin/ documents/pdf/carrefour-du-droit_eng.pdf) (May 2008), 21-23.

36 1155 U.N.T.S. 331; http://untreaty.un.org/ilc/texts/instruments/english/conventions/1_1_1969.pdf.

37 WTO Dispute Settlement Understanding, Art. 3(2).

given some further elasticity to the WTO agreements in a case involving environmental law. In the *United States-Shrimp* case it adopted a dynamic interpretation of treaty terms "in the light of contemporary concerns of the community of nations".[38] Although the force of that decision is not clear, one cannot but notice the movement from "in accordance with customary rules of interpretation of public international law" to "in the light of contemporary concerns of the community of nations". One cannot but agree that one of the most important contemporary concerns of the community of nations is cultural diversity, as is made clear in the UNESCO Convention and other international rules and principles such as the UNESCO Declaration and human rights law.[39] Accordingly, there is not much a distance between the *United States-Shrimp* approach and a conclusion that would favor cultural diversity.[40]

IV. Conclusions

Society has taken cognition of the intrinsic and instrumental values of diversity. In conflicts of values relating to diversity, society often has put diversity on the pedestal. Yet it is not always conscious of whether it is the intrinsic value or instrumental value of diversity that it is championing. Clearer and better analyses that tackle such conflicts in a more direct way seem to be in demand. Such clearer and more direct analyses will help to concentrate the mind so as to allow conscious and perhaps tough decision-making. Diversity as a pure intrinsic value and its effects from such a status appear to be a territory awaiting exploration and development. Such further work will inform society's efforts to prioritize the more important value over others.[41] This will improve the quality

---

38 WTO Appellate Body, United States – Import Prohibition of Certain Shrimp and Shrimp Products, WT/DS58/AB/R, 12 October 1998, para. 129.

39 For an inspiring rendition of the right to cultural identity, see Antônio Augusto Cançado Trindade, The Right to Cultural Identity in the Evolving Jurisprudential Construction of the Inter-American Court of Human Rights, in Sienho Yee & Jacques-Yvan Morin (eds.), Multiculturalism and International Law: Essays in Honour of Edward McWhinney (2008), 477-499.

40 Of course I am only attempting to highlight some directions for further analysis.

41 Similarly such work will also illuminate other questions such as whether it is permissible to prioritize the rights of some individuals such as the right to self-determination over the right of others to cling to their land and their perception of nationhood (e.g., in Kosovo).

of the exercise of decision-making power and, of course, the ultimate result of that exercise.

Chapter 7

Public Opinion*

A. Concept

1. Without attempting to precisely define the term, public opinion is the prevailing opinion of the public of a particular community or segment of that community about a particular topic. In the political sphere, the 'will of the people' is generally used to express the same idea. Sometimes public opinion has been considered as something in contrast to the views of the government, or representing the conscience or the more progressive tendencies of society. That is to say, public opinion seems to present the image of some dichotomy between the government and the people. Of course, there have been times during which public opinion may reflect the not so progressive or the unenlightened sentiments of the times.

2. Depending on how the prevailing opinion of the public is arrived at, one can see two versions of the concept: the aggregative or intersubjective (see generally Jaeger [2008]). The aggregative version essentially emphasizes the 'aggregate of the individual views, attitudes, and beliefs about a particular topic, expressed by a significant proportion of a community' (Encyclopaedia Britannica). The intersubjective version essentially emphasizes the result of the public deliberative or intersubjective dialogue process.

3. Theorists may differ in many respects regarding public opinion. They generally agree that four conditions are essential to the formation of public

---

* First published online in Max Planck Encyclopedia of Public International Law (January 2013). This piece follows the style of the Encyclopedia, with many periods omitted. The individual names or publication names in the parentheses refer to works as listed in the Select Bibliography at the end. The subject names (except abbreviations or acronyms) in the parentheses refer to the other entries in the Max Planck Encyclopedia of Public International Law.

opinion: the existence of: (i) an issue; (ii) a significant number of individuals expressing opinions on the issue; (iii) some kind of consensus among the opinions; and (iv) the influence of this consensus (Encyclopaedia Britannica).

4. Public opinion has been a force to reckon with since antiquity. It has been observed that the structure of the public sphere and its transformation determine the nature and quality of the public opinion that prevails in a particular public sphere and/or at a particular time. It has been claimed that during the Enlightenment period, public opinion of a high-quality emerged in the bourgeois public sphere, characterized by a spirit of rational-critical debate and the recognition of the authority of the good argument. As society moved into modernity, the public sphere became more passive and culture-consuming, with the concomitant deterioration of the quality of the public opinion, now characterized more by a display of preferences and tastes in a consumerist fashion (see generally Habermas).

5. Still, public opinion exerts great influence in government, culture, and many other aspects of the public life. The influence of public opinion may vary with the cultural and political tradition of the particular community. However, its effect has not always been consistent or benign; nor has its sphere of influence covered all areas of human activities or the entire world. Its influence is at its greatest in the truly democratic States and at its weakest in the undemocratic States, although even in the latter usually there are mechanisms for canvassing the views of the ordinary people and considering them in decision-making. Important factors that affect the formation and the impact of public opinion include social environmental factors (such as family and educational background), the strength of the mass media (see also Mass Media, Influence on International Relations), the role of interest groups (pressure groups; lobby groups), and the existence of opinion leaders on a particular topic. Sometimes the general public may be under some improper influence, so much so that the tyranny of the majority has been an issue that has bothered philosophers and sociologists alike. The need to combat such tyranny played a role in the drafting of some constitutions such as the Constitution of the United States. Sometimes the influence of pressure groups is so powerful that these groups are considered to have captured the public opinion. Modern consumerism to some extent has accentuated the undesirable side of public opinion.

6. Despite various complications, public opinion has also played an important and substantial role in international affairs since at least the 18th century. This influence has been on ascendancy. The early glimpse of this

influence is found in the allusion to 'a decent respect to the opinions of mankind' in the very first paragraph of the Declaration of Independence of the United States of America. The movement to promote peace and humanitarian considerations since at least the 19th century has benefited greatly from public opinion (see generally Toyoda; Jaeger [2005], [2007], [2008]; Herberichs). Illustrations of this ongoing movement include the peace movement of the 19th century, the Russell Tribunal on Palestine, and the mass demonstrations against the Vietnam War as well as against the Iraq War in 2003 (Iraq, Invasion of [2003]). Even the Nobel Peace Prizes have in recent years been awarded possibly with a view to influencing public opinion, with controversial effects.

7. As a result of the dramatic increase in globalization (including telecommunication, trade, and transportation) and a growing trend toward international solidarity among peoples (Solidarity, Principle of) and co-progressiveness in the world (Yee 1–26), the influence of public opinion on world affairs is ever more prevalent, so much so that terms such as 'world opinion', 'world public opinion', and 'international opinion' have become part of our vernacular. Another, perhaps the most important, reason for the stronger role of public opinion in international affairs is the conscious efforts spearheaded by Woodrow Wilson to apply to external affairs the ideas and practices considered essential to liberal democracy in the internal arena (Nicolson 84). This, as has been claimed, has led to a transition from the 'old diplomacy' characterized by an emphasis on confidential, continuous, dignified, and rational negotiations between States often in a bilateral context to the 'new diplomacy' characterized by an emphasis on the equality of States and diplomacy proceeding frankly and in the public view often in a multilateral context, paving the way for public opinion to play a greater role in international affairs, especially in 'diplomacy by conference', as well as for the abuse of that role (ibid 84–93; Diplomacy; States, Sovereign Equality). To some extent, there is certain parallel between the transition from the old diplomacy to the new and the structural transformation of the public sphere that Habermas observed, with all the attendant pitfalls.

B. Functions and Legal Significance in General

8. Public opinion is generally considered to be an influence on the decision-makers, moving them to make their decisions one way or another. A more detailed analysis can reveal that public opinion can serve as: (i) an anterior basis for decision-making; (ii) the decision itself; or (iii) a posterior approval of or

sanction for a decision.

9. In the context of law and government, one can identify several functions of public opinion in similar terms. Of course one can observe that public opinion in a general way influences, informs or promotes decision-making, law-making or the development of the law or the interpretation of the law, as well as law-enforcement, whether judicial or political. In more concrete and nuanced terms, however, one can see the role of public opinion in several possible formulations.

10. Firstly, public opinion can be considered the basis for the entire framework of government. This finds support in the general expression that the will of the people shall be the basis of the authority of government. It is inconceivable that a system of government or law can be sustainable if it does not command the support of public opinion at least in a general way over a longer period of time. This is powerfully proved in the events generally called the Arab Spring and their aftermath.

11. Secondly, in a narrower way, public opinion can be considered an anterior basis for political decision-making or law-making, or as an aid to such political decision-making, law-making or the interpretation of law. In some countries such as the United States, their highest judicial authority may make a constitutional decision in part, though the extent of which is extremely uncertain given the vociferous internal debate as exhibited in the majority as well as the concurring and dissenting opinions, on the basis of the prevailing public opinion or even world opinion (see Atkins v Virginia; Roper v Simmons). The fear of public opinion may cause a political or judicial decision-maker to make a decision in a certain way.

12. Thirdly, public opinion as expressed in the resolutions passed in a referendum or plebiscite constitutes the political decision or the law in itself. This often takes place in well organized and well-to-do democracies such as Switzerland. Of course referenda or plebiscites on particular issues are not often conducted. However, they are utilized more and more when matters that substantially concern the public present themselves.

13. Fourthly, public opinion plays a very important role in promoting enforcement of the law. Certain violations may or may not be enforced, and certain enforcement actions may be pursued more forcefully than others. Public opinion often may be the factor that makes the difference. Sometimes, public opinion may be employed as the sanction for the violation of the law. The stigma that results from the conviction of a crime and the publication of the crime has always been an important factor in penology. Furthermore, in some

national legal systems, some crimes carry very light punishment; others are not enforced meaningfully. In these instances, the disapproval from public opinion may be the only punishment that a violator of the law endures.

14. While the various roles of public opinion can be identified as described, it is not possible to conclude that these represent some kind of general situation in the various domestic systems. Different systems may provide for all or some of these functions. Even within the same system, the situation may change over time, without any necessary consistency. But the general tendency is that public opinion is playing an ever stronger role.

C. Functions and Legal Significance in the International Legal Context

15. As is the general situation discussed above, the force of public opinion has been substantial in international law, although probably not as strong as in the domestic field. This influence is getting stronger as a result of the advances in mass communication technology and of the emergence of the non-governmental organizations ('NGOs') and the so-called international civil society in general, and the ever stronger efforts by some governments and many NGOs in applying to external affairs the ideas and practices considered essential to liberal democracy in the internal arena (Nicolson 84).

16. As is in the general context of law and government, one can identify several functions of public opinion in the international legal context. Public opinion in a general way influences, informs or promotes decision-making with international implications, international law-making or the development of international law or the interpretation of international law, as well as its enforcement, whether judicial or political. To the extent that consent is the essential basis of international law, public opinion influences the formation and quality of that consent and thus can be considered to be of fundamental importance.

17. In a general way, the contemporary framework of international relations and international law as embodied in the United Nations (UN) system both institutionally and normatively has received the general support of public opinion in the world (see generally Jaeger [2005]; Herberichs). To some extent, the formation of this framework had been promoted by public opinion for a long time. Furthermore, there seem to be some efforts or even a trend in promoting basing international or national governmental frameworks on democracy or public opinion (Art. 25, International Covenant on Civil and Political Rights [1966]; Pmbl and Art. 21, Universal Declaration of Human

Rights [1948]; see generally Crawford; Doehring), but the status of these efforts or this trend is uncertain, despite the important role that public opinion has played in national as well as international affairs. This may have to do with the particular preferences of the main players involved in a particular matter as well as the possible double standards being applied from time to time.

18. Public opinion has also been incorporated to some extent as international law or has informed international law-making. The *locus classicus* is the Martens Clause, under which the requirements or 'dictates of the public conscience' are declared to be a basis from which the principles of the law of nations result. Public opinion and the participation of the 'public' via NGOs or the so-called international civil society in the law-making process, especially at the UN forums as well as the diplomatic conferences for treaty drafting, have become a strong force in recent years. They appear to have begun to have an effect on even the judicial decision-making process. Thus, the International Court of Justice (ICJ) recently in its Practice Direction XII provides for a method to take account of statements and documents submitted by NGOs in an advisory opinion case.

19. Sometimes it is argued that the public opinion of the local residents, expressed through a plebiscite or referendum, should be taken as the direct basis for decision, in the cession of territory or the final settlement of the status over disputed territories. This does not appear to have become a rule of customary international law (Brownlie 161–62).

20. Public opinion has also been exerting an ever greater role in the enforcement of international law. Against the background of a lack of compulsory and forcible enforcement of international law in general, a State's concern about its reputation and the role of public opinion is even more prominent (see generally Mushkat [2011]). This was already well appreciated in 1908 by none other than Elihu Root who had been a strong promoter of international law. The fear of adverse public opinion may force decision-makers in an action under consideration to internalize international law requirements in their decisions. If not, then public opinion can be galvanized to impact on the morale of the participants and the consent of the population at large, which furthermore may cause the decision-makers to change their decisions. Additionally, public opinion can also cause the early bystanders or the international community at large as regards a situation or a conflict to attempt to contain, and even to join in, that situation or conflict so as to remedy the situation or to bring the conflict to an end. Finally, it appears that international judges also consider the possible reaction of public opinion in their decision-

making (Biddle 452).

21. As public opinion can be effective in the enforcement of international law, there are efforts to promote the formation of public opinion and its influence. The normal approach is to publicize the violations. Given the advancement in mass media technology, the publication of serious violations of international law usually becomes instantaneously an international affair. Another approach is to condemn violations of international law in UN forums such as the UN General Assembly or the United Nations Commission on Human Rights/United Nations Human Rights Council. These can be generally described as 'public shaming'. It has also been described as 'image sanction', to the extent that much of the criticism and condemnation is without binding effect (Yee 20–21).

22. The role of public opinion in promoting the enforcement of international law is even stronger in the context of human rights and international humanitarian and human rights law (Human Rights, Role of Non-Governmental Organizations). Image sanction or public shaming was probably an instrument that States were keen to deploy when they attempted to condemn various States at the former Human Rights Commission, as the resolutions of that body were only symbolic and non-binding. The interesting phenomenon is that the addressees of those efforts also cared a great deal about the prospect of being condemned, despite the non-binding nature of the statements from the Commission. The public airing of the crimes committed in Bosnia and Herzegovina and subsequently in Kosovo apparently was an important factor in moving the world community into action. The same also occurred in Darfur, Sudan, although it had taken longer for public opinion to take effect there. The role of public opinion has been similarly strong, if not stronger, in the promotion of humanitarian law and its enforcement (Humanitarian Law, International). Indeed, the birth of the so-called Geneva law owed a great deal to public opinion, capably promoted by Henri Dunant (see generally Veuthey). In more contemporary international life, there is no lack of examples in which public opinion has exerted a strong impact on decision-makers. For example, it is believed that during the Vietnam War, President Lyndon Johnson and his secretary of defence micro-managed air force bombing operations because 'the politicians did not want to piss people off' (Bush 195). A general summary has been given by Wolfrum and Fleck as follows:

> In the present days of mass media, the role which public opinion plays in humanitarian law enforcement is growing both within states parties to a

conflict and in other countries. There are numerous examples of this. An important one is the US entry into World War II after breaches committed in territories of, and occupied by, the German Reich. The course of the Vietnam conflict was clearly influenced by public opinion both from within the United States and from outside. Pictures broadcast from Iraq, former Yugoslavia, and Somalia contributed substantially to the willingness of the community of states to attempt to contain these conflicts (at para. 1402).

The publishing of a violation of international law may render an essential contribution to enforcing behaviour is in compliance with international law. To this end, considering the global information network, the media (press, broadcasting, television) and their aids (radio, satellites) can be employed today in an incomparably better and thus more efficient manner than has been the case in previous armed conflicts. When offences against international law become known, each party to the conflict must expect that truthful enemy reports on its violations of international law will impair the fighting morale of its forces and the consent of its own population (at para. 1403).

23. Public opinion has also played a very important role in international environmental law (see also Environment, Role of NGOs). Public opinion and public participation in environmental matters have promoted the adoption of various treaties and the formation of various customary international law norms on the environment as well as the enforcement of these norms. Indeed, the role of public participation has been enshrined in Principle 10 Rio Declaration on Environment and Development (Stockholm Declaration [1972] and Rio Declaration [1992]). Public outcry and demonstration have no doubt caused governments to reconsider and modify many projects with a view to providing better protection for the environment.

24. In summary, public opinion has played a very important role in several ways in the making and enforcement of international law in every field. This role is becoming stronger for a variety of reasons such as the advancement in mass communication, increasing globalization, the resultant growing trend toward international solidarity and co-progressiveness and the push to apply domestic democratic principles to international affairs.

D. Special Problems

25. As powerful and salutary as it may be, public opinion is shrouded in controversy or even fraught with problems. These relate to several aspects of the phenomenon of public opinion.

26. The first problem with public opinion is the difficulty in identifying the community and ascertaining its prevailing or representative opinion. Difficult enough in the national context, this task becomes a herculean one in the international context. How one characterizes the international community and how its prevailing opinion can be ascertained are questions that have not been answered properly. In the light of this situation, one can only resort to the proxy or proxies to the international community, such as the UN or the international civil society as represented by the international NGOs. While the UN may have the virtue of being representative of the world, sometimes it has been claimed that it is only representative of governments, not ordinary people. While so-called international civil society attempts to present or even represent the views of ordinary people, the lack of resources, frameworks and accountability relating to how this can be done has given many a great deal of qualms and reservations. It has sometimes been asked, 'who elects the NGOs?'. All these issues chip away at the legitimacy of the claimed 'public opinion' on a particular issue in the international context (see generally Anderson; Yee 14–15).

27. The second problem, which is related to the difficulty in identifying and representing the community, is that public opinion may be manipulated. Various theories such as public choice theory teach that, at the end of the day, it is not the public opinion that is exerting influence, but the opinion of the most powerful groups or the various opinion leaders. In the international arena, this possibility becomes greater as only the powerful groups will have the resources to channel public opinion across a wide area such as the international community.

28. The third problem is that the mass media, one of the structural pillars on which public opinion can be galvanized and projected to a larger geographical area, may be biased or one-sided. If so, the resultant public opinion can only be biased or one-sided. Or, if the mass media is slow in identifying a potential problem, public opinion about that problem cannot emerge so as to influence decision-making (see generally Grzyb).

29. The fourth problem relates to the method that public opinion is being employed—the so-called image sanction or public shaming. To the extent

that such public shaming exerts some positive influence in policymaking, it is a valuable tool; to the extent that it is merely a means of demonization, it can do a disservice to the enforcement of international law by breeding cynicism in some and hatred in others, or even entrenching negative views and decision-making (Yee 21). As a result, image sanction or public shaming is a tool that should not be lightly triggered.

30. Finally, sometimes it is believed that public opinion may have some inherent weaknesses when applied to international affairs, probably as a result of the problems arising from distance and scale as well as the general difficulty and lack of sophistication in dealing with international affairs. These weaknesses were pointed out many years ago. In 1954 Harold Nicolson criticized Woodrow Wilson for arguing that 'the reign of law, based upon the consent of the governed and sustained by the organized opinion of mankind' this way:

> He failed to realize that the public is bored by foreign affairs until a crisis arises; and that then it is guided by feelings rather than by thoughts. Nor did he foresee that it would be impossible to organize the same opinion in every country simultaneously, or that the conscience of mankind, as a means of sustenance, might prove inadequate when faced by a dictator controlling all means of information (Nicolson 86–87).

Nicolson proceeded further:

> He believed that the misfortunes of mankind were due to the faults of statesmen and experts and that 'the people' were always right: he did not realize that, although it may be difficult to fool all the people all the time, it is easy to fool them for a sufficient period of time to compass their destruction (ibid 91).

In a similar vein, Walter Lippmann famously said, on the situation in democracies:

> The unhappy truth is that the prevailing public opinion has been destructively wrong at the critical junctures. The people have impressed a critical veto upon the judgments of informed and responsible officials. They have compelled the governments, which usually knew what would have been wiser, or was necessary, or what was more expedient, to be too late with too little, or too long with too much, too pacifist in peace

> and too bellicose in war, too neutralist or appeasing in negotiation or too intransigent. Mass opinion has acquired mounting power in this country. It has shown itself to be a dangerous master of decision when the stakes are life and death (Lippmann [1955] 20).

While it is difficult to assess the correctness of this view, the problem pointed out in it deserves serious consideration and strong efforts should be made to counteract such weaknesses. Given the general progress in education and in the quality of the general populace around the world, one hopes that Lippmann's judgment on public opinion in international affairs can be revised now or soon.

31. These problems with public opinion are serious enough to cause a relevant decision-maker to pause for reflection before relying on it. How to properly evaluate public opinion and how to harness it in the service of international peace and justice are questions deserving serious consideration.

Select Bibliography

- E Root, 'The Sanction of International Law', (1908) 2 AJIL 451–57.
- W Lippmann, Public Opinion (Macmillan New York 1927).
- H Nicolson, The Evolution of Diplomatic Method (Constable London 1954).
- W Lippmann, Essays in the Public Philosophy (Little, Brown and Company Boston 1955).
- F Biddle, In Brief Authority (Doubleday Garden City 1962).
- Q Wright, A Study of War (2nd ed University of Chicago Press Chicago 1965) 1079–1117.
- G Herberichs, 'On Theories of Public Opinion and International Organization' (1966) 30 Public Opinion Quarterly 624–36.
- A Kiss and D Shelton, 'Systems Analysis of International Law: A Methodological Inquiry', (1986) 17 NYIL 45–74.
- J Habermas, The Structural Transformation of the Public Sphere: An Inquiry into a Category of Bourgeois Society (5th ed MIT Press Cambridge 1993).
- O Niedermayer and R Sinnott (eds), Public Opinion and Internationalized Governance (OUP Oxford 1995).
- FL Rusciano and others (eds), World Opinion and the Emerging

International Order (Praeger Westport 1998).

- WR Pace and M Thieroff, 'Participation of Non-Governmental Organizations', in RS Lee (ed), The International Criminal Court: The Making of the Rome Statute: Issues, Negotiations, Results (Kluwer The Hague 1999) 391–98.
- S Splichal, Public Opinion: Developments and Controversies in the Twentieth Century (Rowman & Littlefield Lanham 1999).
- K Anderson, 'The Ottawa Convention Banning Landmines: The Role of International Non-Governmental Organizations and the Idea of International Civil Society', (2000) 11 EJIL 91–120.
- J Crawford, 'Democracy and the Body of International Law' in GH Fox and BR Roth (eds) Democratic Governance and International Law (CUP Cambridge 2000) 91–120.
- P Everts, 'War without Bloodshed: Public Opinion and the Conflict over Kosovo' in P Everts and P Isernia (eds) Public Opinion and the International Use of Force (Routledge London 2001) 222–52.
- R Mushkat, 'Public Participation in Environmental Law Making: A Comment on the International Legal Framework and the Asia-Pacific Perspective', (2002) 1 Chinese Journal of International Law 185–224.
- A Chua, World on Fire: How Exporting Free Market Democracy Breeds Ethnic Hatred and Global Instability (Doubleday New York 2003).
- H-M Jaeger, '"World Opinion" and the Turn to Post-Sovereign International Governance', in M Albert and L Hilkermeier (eds), Observing International Relations: Niklas Luhmann and World Politics (Routledge London 2004) 142–56.
- A Kiss and D Shelton, International Environmental Law (3rd ed Transnational Ardsley 2004).
- M Veuthey, 'Public Conscience in International Humanitarian Law Today', in H Fischer and others (eds), Krisensicherung und Humanitärer Schutz - Crisis Management and Humanitarian Protection: Festschrift für Dieter Fleck (Berliner Wissenschafts-Verlag Berlin 2004) 611–42.
- S Yee, Towards an International Law of Co-progressiveness (Nijhoff Leiden 2004).
- M Iovane, 'The Role of Public Opinion and Non-Governmental

Organisations in the Reconstruction of General International Norms on the Use of Force', in E Cannizzaro and P Palchetti (eds) Customary International Law on the Use of Force: A Methodological Approach (Nijhoff Leiden 2005) 219–31.

- H-M Jaeger, 'World Opinion' and World Organization: Governmentality, System Differentiation, and the International Public Sphere (PhD thesis Columbia University New York 2005).
- D Mepham and A Ramsbotham (eds), Darfur: The Responsibility to Protect (Institute for Public Policy Research London 2006).
- S Gopalan, 'Alternative Sanctions and Social Norms in International Law: The Case of Abu Ghraib', (2007) 4 Michigan State Law Review 785–839.
- H-M Jaeger, '"Global Civil Society" and the Political Depoliticization of Global Governance', (2007) 1 International Political Sociology 257–77.
- I Brownlie, Principles of Public International Law (7th edn OUP Oxford 2008).
- M Castells, 'The New Public Sphere: Global Civil Society, Communication Networks, and Global Governance', (2008) 616 Annals of the American Academy of Political and Social Science 78–93.
- CE Foster, 'Public Opinion and the Interpretation of the World Trade Organisation's Agreement on Sanitary and Phytosanitary Measures', (2008) 11 JIEL 427–58.
- H-M Jaeger, '"World Opinion" and the Founding of the UN: Governmentalizing International Politics', (2008) 14 European Journal of International Relations 589–618.
- R Wolfrum and D Fleck, 'Enforcement of International Humanitarian Law', in D Fleck (ed) The Handbook of International Humanitarian Law (2nd ed OUP Oxford 2008) 675–722.
- K Doehring, 'Democracy and International Law', in S Yee and J-Y Morin (eds), Multiculturalism and International Law: Essays in Honour of Edward McWhinney (Nijjhoff Leiden 2009) 199–205.
- L Galenskaya, 'The International Institutional System and International Non-Governmental Organizations', in S Yee and J-Y Morin (eds), Multiculturalism and International Law: Essays in Honour of Edward McWhinney (Nijjhoff Leiden 2009) 415–28.

- S Kull and C Ramsay, 'American Public Opinion on International Courts', in CPR Romano (ed), The Sword and the Scales: The United States and International Courts and Tribunals (CUP Cambridge 2009) 12–29.
- T Toyoda, 'Influence of Public Opinion on International Law in the Nineteenth Century', (2009) 46 AltaLRev 1100–13.
- GW Bush Decision Points (Crown New York 2010).
- AF Grzyb, 'Media Coverage, Activism and Creating Public Will for Intervention in Rwanda and Darfur', in AF Grzyb (ed), The World and Darfur: International Response to Crimes against Humanity in Western Sudan (2nd edn McGill-Queen's University Press Montreal 2010) 61–91.
- D Listoe, 'Rhetoric, Rights and the Boundaries of Recognition: Making Darfur Public', in AF Grzyb (ed), The World and Darfur: International Response to Crimes against Humanity in Western Sudan (2nd ed McGill-Queen's University Press Montreal 2010) 254–79.
- R Mushkat, 'State Reputation and Compliance with International Law: Looking through a Chinese Lens', (2011) 10 Chinese Journal of International Law 703–37.
- —— 'Public Opinion' in Encyclopaedia Britannica Online Academic Edition 2012, http://www.britannica.com/EBchecked/topic/482436/public-opinion (10 August 2012).
- AWM Gerrits, 'Exploring Democracy in the Russian Federation: Political Regime, Public Opinion and International Assistance', in P Burnell and O Schlumberger (eds), International Politics and National Political Regimes: Promoting Democracy - Promoting Autocracy (Routledge London 2012) 33–48.

Select Documents

- Atkins v Virginia, United States Supreme Court (20 June 2002), 536 US 304.
- The Chicago Council on Global Affairs (ed), 'Public Opinion Surveys' http://www.thechicagocouncil.org/Files/Studies_and_Publications/All_Publications/Files/Studies_Publications/Public_Opinion.aspx (10 August 2012).
- Convention with Respect to the Laws and Customs of War by Land

and its Annex: Regulations Respecting the Laws and Customs of War on Land (signed 29 July 1899, entered into force 4 September 1900) (1898–99), 187 CTS 429.

- Practice Directions of the International Court of Justice (as amended on 20 January 2009), http://www.icj-cij.org (10 August 2012).
- Roper v Simmons, United States Supreme Court (1 March 2005), 543 US 551.
- UN Conference on Environment and Development, 'Rio Declaration on Environment and Development', (14 June 1992) UN Doc A/CONF.151/26/Rev.1 (Vol. I), 3.
- WorldPublicOpinion.org, http://www.worldpublicopinion.org (10 August 2012).

Part II

Leadership

Chapter 8

Sovereign Equality of States and the Legitimacy of Leader States[*]

One can easily agree that the principle of sovereign equality of States and the role and place of the "leader States"[1] concern nothing less than the organizing principles for the international community. For example, Brownlie says, "The sovereignty and equality of states represent the basic constitutional doctrine of the law of nations, which governs a community consisting primarily of states having a uniform legal personality."[2] It is thus fitting or even obligatory to address this topic and the related issues when one contemplates world constitutionalism.

---

* First published in: Ronald St. John Macdonald and Douglas M. Johnston (eds.), Towards World Constitutionalism (Martinus Nijhoff 2005), 737-772. I am grateful to the late distinguished Editors for their invitation to participate in this important project and for assigning me this topic, particularly Judge Macdonald with whom I had many conversations on the topic and the project. This assignment forced me to consider the various issues more carefully than I would otherwise have. I was grateful despite the fact that I had to write this paper under considerable pressure and stress. This paper was completed on December 27, 2004.

The paper consists of the following parts: 1. The State and the Equality of States; 2. Current Authoritative Statements on Sovereign Equality of States; 3. Understanding Sovereign Equality of States: Its Maximum, Its Minimum, and the Continuum; 4. Safeguarding the Irreducible Minimum and Promoting Greater Equality while Justifying Differences Fairly: "Difference Arguments"; 5. Leader States' Legitimacy.

1 The term "leader States" is given to me by the Editors. I am using it to denote States that exhibit leader qualities, not in the sense of Führerstaat (a State under the control of the leader). See Part 5 of this paper for further analysis.

2 Ian Brownlie, Principles of Public International Law (6th ed., 2003), 287.

The topic and the related issues have caught the attention of many scholars.[3] The common discussion of the topic normally recounts the history of the development of the doctrine, and comments on its current status. The common analysis involves (1) treating the doctrine of State equality as having two components, equality or equal protection before the law, and equal rights, and (2) emphasizing the former. While such a distinction has contributed to the

---

3 Useful literature includes: Bardo Fassbender & Albert Bleckmann, Article 2(1), in: Bruno Simma (ed.), The Charter of the United Nations: A Commentary (2002), 68; Michael Byers & Georg Nolte (eds.), United States Hegemony and Foundations of International Law (2003); Michael Cosnard, Sovereign equality—"the Wimbledon sails on", ibid., 117; Nico Krisch, More equal than the rest?—Hierarchy, equality and US predominance in international law, ibid., 135; GAO Feng, China and the Principle of Sovereign Equality in the 21st Century, in: Sienho Yee & WANG Tieya (eds.), International Law in the Post-Cold War World: Essays in Memory of Li Haopei (2001), 224; Athena Debbie Efraim, Sovereign (In)equality in International Organizations (2000); Christian Tomuschat, International Law: Ensuring the Survival of Mankind on the Eve of a New Century, General Course on Public International Law, 281 Recueil des cours (1999), 161-202; Thomas Franck, Fairness in International Law and Institutions (1995); Manfred Lachs, Some Thoughts on Equality, in: Ronald St. John Macdonald (ed.), Essays in Honour of Wang Tieya (1994), 483; Alan Branthwaite, The Psychological Basis of Independent Statehood, in: Robert H. Jackson & Alan James (eds.), States in a Changing World: A Contemporary Analysis (1993), 46; R.P. Anand, Sovereign Equality of States in International Law, 197 Recueil des cours (1986-II), 9; Vratislav Pechota, Equality: Political Justice in an Unequal World, in: Ronald St. John Macdonald & Douglas M. Johnston (eds.), The Structure and Process of International Law: Essays in Legal Philosophy Doctrine and Theory (1983), 453; Hans Kelsen, The Principle of Sovereign Equality of States as a Basis for International Organizations, 53 Yale Law Journal (1944), 207; P.J. Baker, The Doctrine of Legal Equality of States, 4 British Year Book of International Law (1923-24), 1.

For an examination of equality regarding individuals, see Amartya Sen, Inequality Reexamined (1992).

I would like to note that the idea of equality was the subject of some stinking trade-off at the Paris Peace Conference. See Robert A. Klein, Sovereign Equality Among States: the History of an Idea (1974), 76-83.

As I was finalizing this paper, the useful document called "A more secure world: our shared responsibility: Report of the High-level Panel on Threats, Challenges and Change" ("High-level Panel Report"), A/59/565 (2004; http://www.un.org/secureworld/) was released on December 2, 2004.

understanding of the doctrine, there is still much to be desired, as was pointed out already in 1944 by Kelsen.[4]

I shall not "reinvent the wheel," so to speak, by repeating the fine work that has already been done, but will only touch upon some aspects that are of particular interest to me. I will take a slightly different course. I will discuss these issues one by one: (1) the phenomenon of the State and equality of States; (2) the current authoritative statements on sovereign equality of States; (3) understanding sovereign equality of States: its maximum, its minimum, and the continuum; (4) safeguarding the irreducible minimum and promoting greater equality while justifying differences fairly, on the basis of a set of "difference arguments"; and (5) leader States' legitimacy. My focus is on conceptual, and, to some extent, philosophical inquiries, and thus I will not deal with all aspects of the topic, particularly those that fall within the sphere of application of the various types of arguments. As it is rather difficult to summarize the arguments made here, I will not attempt to rehash them at the end of my paper, except that in the final paragraph I will summarize what I consider to be the qualifications for the status of the strong State, the great State and the leader State.

One may find some of my arguments disagreeable. I simply would like to say, at the outset, that these arguments are presented here as an earnest effort to participate in the consideration of some tough issues, a venture that could provide fertile ground for mistakes by all participants.

1. The State and the Equality of States

As the concept of sovereign equality of States has the phenomenon of the State at its root, our understanding of the need for and the meaning of the concept of sovereign equality of States must be based on our perception of the value of the State. By now probably we must be content with the fact that the world is organized along State lines, with the State as the primary end unit.[5] Yet, many people probably also would not believe in the existential or mysterious indispensable value of the phenomenon called "State". After all, the world was once not organized this way—witness, for example, the pre-Westphalia world. Some philosophers have also argued that in due course the State would wither away. In addition, many people also believe that in the final analysis, human

4 As already detailed by Kelsen, n.3 above (1944).

5 See High-level Panel Report, n.3 above.

values are the end goal of all societal organizations.[6] Naturally one would ask, consistent with pursuing human values as the end goal of all social organizations and with the historical record of and sensible future projections for the world, why our society has to be organized as it is? If it need not be organized around States as the primary end units, then we do not need to speak of sovereign equality of States at all.

Such a question apparently is not susceptible of any definitive answer. At least we can perhaps say that such is the world as a matter of historical fact or accident, and the fact that it has been so may prove that it is better than what it might have once been historically and, perhaps, better than what philosophers have projected for it in the future. It is difficult to argue with such success.

One can say probably that as a matter of efficiency or instrumental value, the world must be organized in a way so as to assure certain efficiency in social activities in an all-encompassing way, politically, economically and culturally. Organizing the world along State lines, despite its wide variety, has proven to be tolerable for the purposes of efficiency, in its totality; at least we perhaps may conclude that a better arrangement has not been found. The pre-Westphalia world apparently removed the authorities from the realities of life, too far, and blinded them to the pains and suffering of the local denizens. The projected withering away of the State in the future assumes the noble character of all individuals, and thus may never take place.

If the State were just about a matter of economic activities, one perhaps could imagine nicer arrangements for the world, such as regions, blocks, unions, and the like. However, the phenomenon of the State involves more, and other aspects of social activities may have to be premised on the phenomenon of the State. For example, political life and democracy only thrive within a manageable community. We have been told that "all politics is local". One can imagine what a task it would be to organize world democracy without borders, if it is possible at all. Indeed, if Aristotle had to suffer his fate the way he did in the hands of democracy even in a small city republic in ancient Greece, should we have greater confidence in world democracy without borders?

More important, although normally we tend to think of the State as more or less a matter of political function, psychologists have demonstrated that there

---

6 See, e.g., Charles de Visscher, Theory and Reality in Public International Law (3d ed. (1960), P.E. Corbett tran., 1968); Sienho Yee, Towards an International Law of Co-progressiveness (2004), 23-26.

is more to the phenomenon.[7] Certain intrinsic value may be inherent in the phenomenon. There is certain psychological basis for statehood that consists of citizens or nationals identifying themselves with the State, together with the assorted cultural, traditional, and other folklore, which serves as the unifying force connecting citizens and nationals and provides one of the bases for their solidarity. The sense of belonging to the State adds to the personality or personhood of the citizens. In fact, these factors may be the moving forces in the establishment of many States. Thus, the existence of the State furthers the end goal of social organizations by making human values fuller and richer.

Such are the virtues of the phenomenon of the State that it is only natural for the organized entities to strive to become States in the pursuit of self-determination and, ultimately, sovereignty, and equality of dignity—or more formally called equality of States. These further dimensions of statehood afford great value to the world at large. Self-determination means being one's own master. Equality means a State is being its own master in the same way that another is. These two aspects of statehood were felt most strongly in the leaders and citizens of those States which were previously not considered to be equals to the other States. No one has savored this better than the citizens of those States who finally have managed to throw away the colonial yoke and become masters of their destiny.[8] To this extent, the equality of States has intrinsic value; it is a virtue to be pursued in and of itself.

These values of the State should have moved the world to promote strong States and strong cultures. However, the post-Cold War history until now has been largely one of dismantling the big States. And the values of strong States seem to have been appreciated by some only recently, perhaps somewhat unfortunately. Thus, the deadliness of failed or weak States to their own citizens, as well as to the outside world, was pointed out in the National Security Strategy of the United States.[9] It is to the credit of the statesmen that the importance of the State as the primary end unit of the international system was emphasized in December 2004 by the High-level Panel on Threats,

---

7 See Alan Branthwaite, n.3 above (1993); Sienho Yee, n.6 above. See also the insistence on the real and effective nationality in the Nottebohm Case (Liechtenstein v. Guatemala), ICJ Reports 1955, 4.

8 See, e.g., Wang Tieya, The Third World and International Law, in: R. St. J. Macdonald and D.M. Johnston (eds.), The Structure and Process of International Law (1983), 955.

9 See http://www.whitehouse.gov/nsc/nss.html.

Challenges and Change convened by the United Nations Secretary-General.[10] Indeed, the failure of one State is now the national security problem of another. One hopes that such "recent" revelations would move States to stop the practices that were originally intended to prevail over their enemies in the ideological contest between the communist and capitalist systems, which have resulted in the breakup of some States or in serious tension within some States almost to a point of breaking up. These practices include selling arms to secessionist movements or generally fanning the fervency of secessionist sentiments. Such practices go against the need to promote strong States and strong cultures, and can lead to chaos in the affected States and greater national security crises for other States. On the other hand, a tendency or bias in favor of holding States together would be beneficial to all concerned.

Such a view of the world consisting of States as the primary end units would require us to evaluate all sorts of problems, such as the challenges posed by non-State actors,[11] in the framework of States. That is to say, ultimately almost all issues of the world can be dealt with, to a large extent, as issues relating to the State. Such a view of the world would also make it a meaningful exercise for us to consider the topic of sovereign equality of States and the role of the leader States in the present world.

2. Current Authoritative Statements on Sovereign Equality of States

Such are the virtues of the phenomenon of the State and equality of States that we should not be surprised by the strenuous pursuit of sovereignty and equality of States. Many years' efforts have culminated in the current scene of more than 190 sovereign States in the world and in some more or less authoritative statements on the idea of equality of States. By now the idea has become recognized as one of the foundations of the modern international political and legal system.

The Charter of the United Nations, in Article 2(1), declares that "[t]he Organization is based on the principle of sovereign equality of all its Members." That is to say, the new United Nations Organization was built upon this principle. Article 2(4) provides that "All Members shall refrain in their international relations from the threat or use of force against the territorial

---

10 See High-level Panel Report, n.3 above.

11 As my inquiry focus on States, issues relating to non-State actors can only be mentioned in passing.

integrity or political independence of any state, or in any other manner inconsistent with the Purposes of the United Nations." Article 2(7) declares that "Nothing contained in the present Charter shall authorize the United Nations to intervene in matters which are essentially within the domestic jurisdiction of any state or shall require the Members to submit such matters to settlement under the present Charter; but this principle shall not prejudice the application of enforcement measures under Chapter VII."

These provisions are given some concretization in the subsequent elaboration of the term "sovereign equality," in the United Nations Declaration of Principles of International Law Concerning Friendly Relations and Cooperation of States (the "Friendly Relations Declaration"):

> The principle of sovereign equality of States
>
> All States enjoy sovereign equality. They have equal rights and duties and are equal members of the international community, notwithstanding differences of an economic, social, political or other nature.
>
> In particular, sovereign equality includes the following elements:
>
> (a) States are juridically equal;
> (b) Each State enjoys the rights inherent in full sovereignty;
> (c) Each State has the duty to respect the personality of other States;
> (d) The territorial integrity and political independence of the State are inviolable;
> (e) Each State has the right freely to choose and develop its political, social, economic and cultural systems;
> (f) Each State has the duty to comply fully and in good faith with its international obligations and to live in peace with other States.[12]

This elaboration no doubt has gone a long way in giving meaning to the concept of "sovereign equality of States". Still different readers may see different things in this elaboration. In the next section, I shall present a reading of the concept, more or less according to me, without taking account of all

---

12 UNGA Res. 2625 (SSV) (1970). See Aleksandar Magaršević, The Sovereign Equality of Sates, in Milan Šahović (ed.), Principles of International Law concerning Friendly Relations and Cooperation (1972), 171.

views because of the abundance of literature on point.

3. Understanding Sovereign Equality of States: Its Maximum, Its Minimum, and the Continuum

The normal discussion of the issue speaks of "the equality of States." Immediately the term "sovereign equality of States" presents something of an enigma. According to researchers, the term first appeared in the Moscow Declaration of October 13, 1943,[13] in which the United States, the United Kingdom, the Soviet Union and China declared that "they recognize the necessity of establishing at the earliest practicable date a general international organization, based on the principle of sovereign equality of all peace-loving States, and open to membership by all such States, large and small, for the maintenance of international peace and security." The term has ever since been shrouded in mystery. Efforts have been made to understand it in different ways.[14] It is not clear whether such efforts have been successful, or whether the term is really meant to be rhetorical—meaning no more than "equality of states"—and was used to better galvanize the support of all States to participate in the new world organization.

To some extent, putting "sovereign" and "equality" together appears to be awkward at least, if not oxymoronic. Two kinds of difficulty may present themselves when we try to understand the phrase in its ordinary meaning. The first is that "equality" may be meaningless. "Sovereign" appears to refer to certain "supreme quality". If so, what does "equality" add? This is the normal difficulty in understanding the term "equality" in general: the term may often be tautological; nothing that it conveys seldom cannot be ascertained through another substantive criterion. For example, if legality is assured, equality is simply its resulting corollary.[15] A second difficulty is that equality may mean "equally supreme" or "equally minimal", and if the latter version of "equality" is adopted, the juxtaposition of "sovereign" and "equality" together would lead to a logical difficulty: something of "supreme quality" may yet be a minimal equal to others.

The prevailing international realities, however, may reduce the difficulty to some extent, so that we can find some meaning in the phrase "sovereign

---

13 UNYB 1946-47, 3.

14 See Fassbender & Bleckmann, n.3 above (2002); Kelsen, n.3 (1944).

15 See Kelsen, n.3 above (1944).

equality of States". Following the understanding of the phrase sketched above, I think we can find evidence that the phenomenon has been understood as having a maximum, an irreducible minimum and a vast continuum from the minimum to the maximum.

A. The Flawed Vision of the Maximum

It seems that when the equality of States idea first came into the picture, it was envisioned as having a maximum: each State has the same rights and obligations in every respect and is entitled to participate in international life equally. Championing this view were theoreticians as well as politicians. The basis for this view was apparently the attempt to analogize the phenomenon of the State to the individual and to resort to the principle that one individual is equal to another.

This approach crumbled immediately when it got into contact with two important objections. The first objection was put forward by none other than Elihu Root, a very international-law-friendly United States statesman, in the context of discussing the necessity for some kind of permanent representation of the big powers in the new Permanent Court of International Justice that was being proposed in 1920. He said that every individual in a democracy would like to have his or her vote carry the same weight as that of the citizen of another State. Therefore:

> [I]t would be impossible to put forward a plan in which, for instance, the hundred million inhabitants of the United States would have to consent to have the sovereign rights of their country limited by a Court on which the vote of the half-million inhabitants of Honduras might decide a case against the United States.[16]

While this understanding of the judicial character of the Court might not be perfect, the message against the absolute equality of States is powerfully devastating to any attempt to base that equality on an analogy of the State to the individual.

The mistake in such an analogy is explicable this way: while the individual

16 Permanent Court of International Justice Advisory Committee, Procès-verbaux of the Proceedings of the Committee, June 16th–July 24th, 1920 (1920), 134-35.

is the end unit for many things, or almost everything, the State is not necessarily such an end unit for so many things. An attempt to build perfect equality of States by analogizing the State to the individual, with the ostensible goal of promoting democracy, would simply turn democracy on its head: it would treat individuals differently simply on the basis of which State he or she belongs to.

The second objection was epitomized by that given by one of the main drafters of the Covenant of the League of Nations, Mr. David Hunter Miller. After paraphrasing a statement on equality of States as "The rights and obligations of Albania as a member of the League are no more and no less than those of the British Empire", he proceeded:

> As to such a statement my view is that what it suggests is nothing but a form of words having no meaning whatever in the actual world in which human beings live. Of course the doctrine of equality of states means that a small and insignificant and feeble state is entitled to fair and just treatment on a footing of equality before the law with larger neighbors; but to say that in any international organization or in international affairs however conducted or in international relations either of the present or of any past whatever, the influence or moral or political authority in the world of a few thousand backward people organized as an independent unit or state entity has been or should be the same as that of a country like the United States, for example, is simply to shut one's eyes to everything except a few words of print.[17]

This objection speaks from experience and reality. And there is logic to this argument, although the coldness of that logic is not appetizing. However, the insistence on equality in the face of such realities will quickly yield if the equal obligations are also imposed on the small States which would have trouble fulfilling them.

Perhaps for these reasons, one can find only a grand statement on this point in the "chapeau" of the section on the principle of sovereign equality of States in the Friendly Relations Declaration, which states, in part, that all States "have equal rights and duties and are equal members of the international community".[18] The elaboration of the detailed content of this concept seems to

---

17 David Hunter Miller, 1 The Drafting of the Covenant (1928, reprinted 1969), 23 (footnote omitted).

18 Text to n.12 above.

have a different emphasis. One might have reason to think, then, the maxim of sovereign equality is a slogan, a catchphrase, an ideal that we put on the pedestal to look at, to look to, or even to be drawn to, yet unrealizable.

B. The Irreducible Minimum of Sovereign Equality of States

If one cannot find concrete elaboration on the maximum of sovereign equality of States in the Friendly Relations Declaration, one can find one on the minimum of it. After the grand statement in the chapeau of that section, the Declaration proceeds to spell out what States consider to be most important elements by prefacing them with the phrase "In particular". These elements have been considered to be essential to the concept so as to warrant such a treatment of being singled out for elaboration. They can be distilled into two concretizable points: (1) juridical equality and (2) inviolable territorial integrity and political independence.

The first guarantees the equal juridical status to each State. This formulation of equality is a slightly narrower and more precise than "equality before the law", as commonly used. Juridical equality, to my mind, only means the status that a State enjoys before the law, probably only in the sense of capacity, procedure, and pomp and appearance. As such, it has a dignity dimension that many States care about, particularly before international courts and tribunals. On the other hand, "equality before the law" may have a broader scope in the minds of the ordinary people. Still, this aspect of the concept is not that useful in practical terms.

The second element is the core of sovereignty/independence, as time and again affirmed by States and international judges, and as embodied in Article 2(4) of the United Nations Charter. As Judge Huber explained in *Island of Palmas*, "Sovereignty in the relations between States signifies independence. Independence in regard to a portion of the globe is the right to exercise therein, to the exclusion of any other State, the functions of a State."[19] As recognized by Judge Anzilotti, sovereignty/independence is the "normal condition of States according to international law",[20] meaning that "the State has over it no other authority than that of international law".[21] As a result, one can clearly tell that its

---

19 2 RIAA 829, 838 (decision of 1928).

20 Autro-German Customs Regime, PCIJ, Series A/B, No. 41 (1931), 57 (individual op. Anzilotti).

21 Ibid.

content does not derive from "equality", but from "sovereignty", and in this sense one can see the merits to Kelsen's argument that equality may be really legality.[22] However, precisely because of this one can make sense of the phrase "sovereign equality": "Sovereignty" leads to "equality" in the minimum sense of the latter term in this context.

While limiting and constraining to some extent, sovereign equality in this minimum sense has its beauty: Small though a territory may be, there is no other place like it for the sovereign over it. At least there is one piece of space within which the sovereign people may express themselves and realize their value and virtues to the full, without outside interference. For this reason, if this minimum of sovereign equality can be safeguarded, the world would still be in a good shape.

C. The Continuum from the Irreducible Minimum to the Maximum

Beautiful though the minimum of sovereign equality may be, it seems to fit the isolated co-existence of States best. This irreducible minimum can be said to be the crowning achievement of the international law of co-existence. As soon as States interact with each other, as soon as they start to jointly conduct international activities, they will have to go out of their "castles", so to speak, realizing that such a way of seeing the world will not be adequate to the tasks of taking account of different issues and situations.

Unreachable though the maximum of sovereign equality may be, it is an ideal that holds certain attraction for many. It makes people—generally, and particularly those in smaller countries—feel that their dignity is respected, that their worth is being appreciated and recognized. As a result, it would be easier to obtain their support for any views and projects under such a condition of maximum equality.

Since the early 1960s, the world has moved into the sphere of co-operation, where solidarity of peoples and interactions between and among them are the highlight of the day. It has now entered the sphere of co-progressiveness after the end of the Cold War, where international law has become all encompassing (hence "co"), preoccupied with advancements at an appropriate speed in moral and ethical terms more than in other respects and, in my view, having human flourishing as its ultimate goal (hence "progressive-ness"). The advancements in international law continue unabated, despite the

---

22 See Kelsen, n.3 above.

aberrations such as those that manifested as the September 11 attack and its aftermath.[23]

In order for co-operation and co-progressiveness to be realized to the fullest, States must, while preserving the irreducible minimum of sovereign equality, go beyond it. The need to galvanize as many people as possible from around the world to promote peace, security, prosperity and progressiveness would militate in favor of moving towards the maximum scope of sovereign equality, to the extent possible, though we know that we will never reach that point. As explained, that maximum point is not necessarily a good point to reach, but the movement towards it is of value. Accordingly, the best scope of sovereign equality under current conditions and in anticipation of a better future has to be a continuum from the irreducible minimum to the maximum. Within the continuum, there is an infinite variety of diverse States, and rights and obligations. Thus, differences and inequalities are inevitable, and we must be content with the fact that it is not possible to please everyone in the world.

4. Safeguarding the Irreducible Minimum and Promoting Greater Equality while Justifying Differences Fairly: "Difference Arguments"

A. Background Considerations

Given the essential importance of the irreducible minimum of sovereign equality and the central place that it holds in the hearts and minds of the people around the world, it requires no stressing that the most important task of international law is to safeguard the irreducible minimum of equality from being eroded. In my view, this is taken as granted and axiomatic, without any further need for justification. Thus, when there are breaches of this cardinal principle, such breaches present themselves not as the result of a direct attack on this principle; rather, other creative, though not necessarily successful, arguments were presented to justify such breaches. For example, the United States had to attempt to justify its use of force against Nicaragua as an exercise of the right of collective self-defense, rather than saying that there was no rule on point or that there was a rule but it did not care about it.[24] So there is no need for me to defend the need to safeguard the irreducible minimum of sovereignty equality.

---

23 See Sienho Yee, Towards, n.6 above, 1-26.

24 See Case concerning Military and Paramilitary Activities in and against Nicaragua (Nicaragua v. United States), ICJ Reports 1986, 14.

The appeal that the vision of the maximum of sovereign equality has to the world, its value as a slogan and as something to put on the pedestal, is the reason why we may want to realize it. The inevitable differences and inequalities convince us that we simply cannot achieve it; they do not, however, prevent us from moving in that direction. Naturally, our task is how to promote equality to the greatest extent and to deal with or manage such differences and inequalities in a way that is satisfactory to the greatest number of States and people possible.

Accordingly, one can see the task of international law as threefold: to safeguard the irreducible minimum of sovereignty equality, to promote greater equality to the extent possible, and to try our best do so, while justifying the differences and inequalities in a fair way.

To a great extent, the idea of a rule of law itself has a certain equalizing effect: at least consistency is achieved in the application of a rule. As human behavior almost always is oriented around certain rules or customs—whether moral, social or legal, a certain minimum level of equality in the form of consistency in their application obtains. Consistency applies horizontally to all subjects of law (i.e., the same law applies to everyone unless valid exceptions apply—famously described by Anatole France as "the majestic equality of the laws, which forbid rich and poor alike to sleep under bridges, to beg in the streets, and to steal their bread"[25]) and vertically to the conduct of one subject of law over a period of time. We shall refer to this as the "minimal consistency" condition.

Because of this minimal consistency, often both equality and differences are present in one and the same argument: equality is usually equality according to one criterion, while differences often result from the application of some criteria equally. As a result, it is not easy for one to separate equality and differences in a discussion, and I will touch upon both issues often. However, as we often agree on the attractiveness of equality, I will focus on the tougher task of justifying differences and inequalities.

Without going into all the details, there can be two kinds of differences: (1) the law provides for the same treatment for each State, but that law is applied differently; or (2) the law provides for different treatment for different States, and it is applied consistently. Many arguments can be considered to be relevant to our inquiry as to how each kind of differences can be justifiable or legitimate. In this section, I will attempt to provide a list of the main arguments and critique them only briefly. These arguments may apply only to *some* players

---

25 Anatole France, The Red Lily (Winifred Stephens trans., 1930), 95.

in the world and only to *some* circumstances, rather than to all and for all seasons. For the sake of simplicity, I will refer to these arguments as "difference arguments". I choose this phrase rather than the more grandiose "difference principles" because I am not sure about the validity of, nor do I agree with, some, or even many, of these arguments. I will simply present them here for the appreciation of the readers.

B. *Meta-arguments*

There are several arguments that can be categorized as "meta-arguments" attempting to justify differences generally. Ordinarily these meta-arguments appear to operate at the law-making stage. At the law-application stage their relevance is not clear, although a rule of law that does not pass muster under these arguments can potentially be considered invalid. As such, these arguments may have a corrective function in favor of equality. Probably they do not, however, function in a way at the law-application stage so as to require different applications of the same law.

These meta-arguments include the age-old "treat like cases alike" principle which touches upon both kinds of differences as described above. Obviously this principle has a strong equality component, and it acts as a meta-principle so that, whatever happens, this principle may still be applied. To this extent, it is part of minimal consistency. However, embedded in this principle is a fundamental difference principle: the corollary of "treat like cases alike" is "treat different cases differently". While "treat like cases alike" is not difficult to apply, "treat different cases differently" may prove difficult to struggle with: one still needs to find criteria for defining what cases are different and how differently to treat them. So in the final analysis, this principle may help to justify or explain the need for different treatment of different cases, it does not provide further guidance.

Another meta-argument is Thomas Franck's formulation of the criteria for the legitimacy of a rule of international law, which I shall call "the secondary rule meta-argument". To his mind, a primary rule of conduct's legitimacy can be measured through several criteria that relate to the secondary rules (such as law-making) showing the "associative" nature of the community. These criteria include: determinacy, symbolic validation, coherence, and adherence.[26] One can accept these criteria in general, so that if these criteria have been met and if

---

26 Thomas Franck, Fairness in International Law and Institutions (1995), 30 ff.

differences still exist, then they will be considered fair to some extent.

One wonders, however, whether this approach—focusing on the secondary rules—is sufficient. To some, no matter how fair the process may be, how determinate the rules may be, what matters at the end of the day is whether the substantive content of the rules is fair and acceptable. That is to say, any differences must pass the test of substantive fairness. Although the "coherence" criterion in Franck's sketch could include an element of substantive fairness, his discussion seems to focus on the even-handed or uniform application of the law such as the "treat like cases a like" principle.[27] In any event, the unmistakable focus of Franck's formulation is on the "associative" secondary rules, not the primary rules of conduct. As a result, Franck's sketch of legitimation is incomplete.

One meta-argument that clearly has primary rule fairness in mind comes from a social scientist in an attempt to formulate a rule to justify power. Power in this sense can be generalized as the ability to assert a role that overwhelms others in a way that does not include the use of force. On this view:

> Power can be said to be legitimate to the extent that:
> i) it conforms to established rules,
> ii) the rules can be justified by reference to beliefs shared by both dominant and subordinate, and
> iii) there is evidence of consent by the subordinate to the particular power relation.[28]

Such a justification would thus be all encompassing, drawing upon established rules, shared beliefs and consent. If all these obtain, the justification can be almost perfect. However, such conditions are often difficult to establish. As a result such a perfect justification may be impossible most of the time. While this argument applies *prima facie* to both primary and secondary rules, its emphasis is on primary rules, and I shall call it the "primary rule meta-argument".

As can be seen, each of these meta-arguments would serve to promote equality and to help to justify differences and inequalities, to a great extent. However, meta-arguments often work well in terms of general direction; they cannot take account of many micro-issues. Nevertheless, perhaps one may say that an equality that satisfies the primary rule and secondary rule meta-

---

27 Ibid., 38-41.

28 David Beetham, The Legitimation of Power (1991), 16.

arguments would probably be a virtue, and a difference that satisfies both would probably be fair.

C. *Specific Arguments*

In addition to meta-arguments, human intelligence has also produced many specific arguments targeting particular issues, although they do not work well once taken out of the particular contexts. In this section, I will briefly describe and critique some of these specific arguments, in an illustrative manner only. I will put them in two broad categories: (1) arguments for exceptions to a rule of law and (2) arguments for differing rights and/or obligations. While I will explain the reasons for this categorization, I do not attempt here to provide any systemic rationalization for them, as that would be a difficult task, though a very interesting one. Nor will I attempt to evaluate the potential success of each argument, although I will comment on its merits, and will mention, where appropriate, their compatibility with the meta-arguments discussed above.

i. Arguments for Exceptions to a Rule of Law

Arguments sometimes are made for a general exception to a rule of law or an *ad hoc* exception to a rule of law "just this once", for the benefit of one or more, but not all, subjects of law, while affirming the force of the existing rule itself. As such, the arguments for exceptions to rules of law address the scope of application of the rules of law. They deal with issues surrounding "equality" or "inequality" before the law.

These arguments are not the same as those for exceptions to a rule of law that are available to any subject of law. For example, the right to self-defense is an exception to the prohibition against the use of force. These exceptions are not for some subjects of law only, but for all. They serve to delimit the content of the general rule, not the scope of its application only.

These arguments for exceptions do not include, of course, the attempts to make a new rule of customary international law. As the perennial debates on this issue show us, sometimes when a new customary international law rule is being made, the very first attempts to do so may not be consistent with existing rules of law.[29] Before a new rule formally solidifies, there is a period of time

---

29 See Sienho Yee, The News that Opinio Juris "Is Not a Necessary Element of Customary [International] Law" Is Greatly Exaggerated, 43 German Yearbook

during which there is uncertainty as to whether a certain course of conduct is lawful or not. This situation differs from attempts to claim an exception to a rule of law: the attempt to make a new rule does not recognize the existing rule as proper (as regards all), while the attempts to claim exceptions recognize as proper the existing rule of law, but claim that it does not apply to the claimant only. If the attempts to make a new rule succeed, then the new rule would apply to all.

(a) Arguments for a general exception to a rule of law. Such an argument proceeds this way: We agree that there is a rule of law (such as each coastal State is entitled to a territorial sea of 12 miles from the baseline), but it does not apply to us at all. In the law of treaties, a State can achieve this result by making a valid reservation to a treaty.

In customary international law, currently a State can achieve this result by attempting to establish its status as a persistent objector to an emerging rule of customary international law. The persistent objector rule is probably a widely accepted rule of law. The International Court of Justice in the *Fisheries Jurisdiction (United Kingdom v. Norway)* case[30] seemed to support this concept and this approach.

However, sometimes one encounters an argument that proceeds from a simple assertion of national interest: because this rule harms our national interest, therefore, we will not follow it. We shall call this a "national interest argument". To some extent such an argument constitutes the original foundation of the persistent objector rule. The difference between this argument and the persistent objector rule is that the persistent objector rule has been accepted generally by the international community, and is available to a State that has met the requirement of having made objections to a rule when it emerges and has persisted in objecting to it. The national interest argument ignores these requirements, and uses national interest as the sole criterion for behavior.

In addition, while it is difficult to require a State to forego its national interest for the sake of complying with international law, several difficulties may

---

of International Law (2000), 227, reprinted in: Sienho Yee, Towards, n.6 above, 27.

30 ICJ Reports 1951, 116, 131 ("In any event the ten-mile rule would appear to be inapplicable as against Norway inasmuch as she has always opposed any attempt to apply it to the Norwegian coast."). See also Asylum, ICJ Reports 1950, 277-278.

arise from such a way of justifying exceptions from the law. Because of the need for minimal consistency, the predominantly national interest argument would lead to undesirable consequences both vertically—within one State—and horizontally, across the world. One serious problem with this argument is the difficulty in defining national interest. Vertically within one State, different sectors may each have a different definition and the same sector may have different definitions at different times. Then there are different versions of how national interest yearnings can be satisfied: Morgenthau may think that a nation is an extension of a relentlessly power-hungry individual; Mearsheimer may think that nations are under the spell of "offensive realism" so that their survival mandates aggressive behavior, without any stopping until the State becomes "the hegemon in the system".[31] So painted, every State is a scary, insecure creature constantly fearing being cornered.

No doubt horizontally different States, if allowed the same national interest argument, may have an equal or greater number of different definitions of national interest. There is simply an infinite variety of the argument, defying any meaningful response to it. The only way out seems to be to build up one's own military force. Certainly an enlightened leader would appreciate that a peaceful and stable world is in the best interest of any State in the long term at least, yet history has shown time and again that a short-sighted assessment of the immediate national interest has driven leaders down the ugly path.

Because of these difficulties, the national interest argument normally is not compatible with the primary rule and secondary rule meta-arguments discussed. However, in the extreme circumstance, this argument may still have some value, particularly in the extreme circumstance of self-defence where the very survival of the State is at stake. This has been recognized by the International Court of Justice in the *Nuclear Weapons* advisory opinion.[32]

Sometimes one can see an even more blatant form of the argument: this rule does not apply to us because we have the power to prevent it from being applied to us. As this argument does not even attempt to find justification in any principle other than the proponent's perceived overwhelming power to get its way, we shall called this argument "raw power argument". While this argument is seldom made in plain language, it may have been the basis for military action many times. Recently there is a streak of this argument in the

---

31 John J. Mearsheimer, The Tragedy of Great Power Politics (2001), 21 and generally.

32 ICJ Reports 1996 (Generally Assembly request), 226.

debate regarding the justification for the use of force against Iraq in March and April of 2003. This argument was described in the media as this: because the United States was the only remaining superpower, and because the United States could use force to defeat Saddam Hussein, it might just as well put that power to use.[33] This argument has the beauty of simplicity, and an appeal from its straightforwardness. These qualities of this argument become more obvious when this argument is compared to the other strained justifications such as previous authorization by the Security Council or Iraq presenting a threat to the United States or even its neighbors, often contorted to such an extent that they show either disingenuousness or an inability to understand the world.

However, by giving up all pretense to legitimacy based on principle and by basing its conduct on the perceived ability or raw power to get its way, the sole superpower will return the world to its state of nature where, as the ancients have told us, "the strong do what they can and the weak suffer what they must."[34] In such a world, one cannot be sure whether the status of power will be immutable and what the consequences will be when there is a change in that status.

Second and more important, such an argument with express resort to raw power and overwhelming force normally breeds resentment and provokes strong reaction against it. Normally the overwhelming power that the superpower enjoys would make it suicidal for any State to attempt to put up a fight with the superpower, and, therefore, the superpower almost always gets its way. However, there may be some objectors, normally non-State actors, who may internalize their objection to this form of exercise of raw power as their cause to pursue, and persist in pursuing, their objection despite sacrifices. Such "internalization", according to social scientists, is the strongest form of motivational force.[35] It can lead to strong compliance with norms, or, one may

---

33 See, e.g., William Bunch, Invading Iraq Not a New Idea for Bush Clique, http://www.philly.com/mld/dailynews/2003/01/27/news/local/5025024.htm?1c.

34 Thucydides, The Peloponnesian War (Modern Library ed., 1951), 331.

35 Alan Branthwaite, The Psychological Basis of Independent Statehood, in: Robert H. Jackson & Alan James, n.3 above, at 62, said that there were three levels of motivation for compliance with norms: (1) Compliance, produced by social pressure, and maintained by rewards and punishments; (2) Identification, conformity out of a desire to be like other people whom they admire (inwardly and personally motivated; also maintained by social incentives); and (3) Internalization, strongest personal commitment to group norms and

add, to horrendous devastation on the scale of the September 11 attacks. So the world may be that on the one hand, the superpower may exert its overwhelming power on sovereign States, but, on the other hand, it may have to face retaliation by determined non-State actors who take up the cause of the "oppressed" State or group as their own. Whether this is a good price to pay is better left to the appreciation of the decision-makers.

(b) Arguments for an ad hoc exception to a rule of law. Such an argument proceeds this way: We agree that there is a rule of law and it applies to us, too, generally but not in this instance. Such an argument does not appear to be supportable under general international law as we know it today. Therefore the proponent normally would resort to morality or other considerations. Such arguments can hardly meet the "legitimacy" conditions laid down in the primary rule and secondary rule meta-arguments described above

One prime example of this is the attempt to deal with the aftermath of the Kosovo war waged by the NATO. The resort to morality was made by some of the NATO members when attempting to justify the alleged humanitarian intervention in Kosovo in 1999. At least officials from Germany and the United States have said that the Kosovo approach does not apply elsewhere and that others should not try it either.[36]

One can imagine that the different formulations of "national interest argument" and the "raw power argument", as described above, would be made even more often or with stronger voice when arguing for an *ad hoc* exception than for a general exception. As the evaluation of national interest varies, so does the need for exceptions. As a result, *ad hoc* exceptions may be of greater value to those who would resort to this argument.

ii. Arguments for Differing Rights and Obligations

The arguments for exceptions to rules of law deal with equality or inequality before the law, focusing on the application of the existing rules and principles. They do not argue with the content of the rules and principles themselves

---

standards—conformity to norms because they make sense, and are believed by the individual to be right and worthy.

36 See the analysis on this point in Vaughan Lowe, International Legal Issues Arising in the Kosovo Crisis, in: Sienho Yee & Wang Tieya (eds.), n.3 above (2001), 278, 282 (quoting statements by the German Foreign Minister and the US Secretary of State).

directly, although the disagreement with the content of these rules and principle may have motivated some of the arguments. If indeed disagreement with the content of the rules and principles is of the essence, the rules and principles may themselves be under pressure for a reformulation so that they provide for differing rights and obligations, leading to the result that, while these rules and principles apply equally to all the subjects of law, the outcome varies with each of them.

The arguments for differing rights and obligations seem to succeed more often in treaties and conventions than in general customary international law. The reason for this discrepancy is probably thus: treaty making depends on consent and the parties may make compromises and delimit their rights and obligations in any way they deem fit, while in general customary international law the ideal of equality of all subjects of law exerts greater influence. Still we can find instances of differing treatments that have been provided in customary international law. Examples can be found in the law of the sea where some States are allowed a straight baseline system, and some States are given the archipelagic State regime. In my discussion here, I will not make a distinction between the two categories in a strict fashion, but will address these arguments in a more or less general way. This is reasonable because, although we have the impression that differing treatments in customary international law are based on generalizable reasons, while those in treaties are based on ad hoc horse-trading consent, we often can see that even consent in treaty-making is further based on generalizable reasons or is informed by them to a large extent.

Some of the varied arguments for differing rights and obligations are as follows:

(a) Argument from retribution. This is an argument to tie responsibility to past behavior as, for example, those who polluted more in the past must now contribute more to clean up the environment. This in fact is one strand of the justification for the commonly accepted "common but different responsibility" in international environmental law.[37] This argument has moral appeal and, perhaps for this reason, has led to the general acceptance of the "different but common responsibility" principle, although its concretization is still to be found.

---

37 For an analysis, see Sienho Yee, Towards, n.6 above, 16-17.

(b) Argument from capability. This is an argument that attempts to tie responsibility to capability. It is simply this: We will contribute what we can. It is not that easy to justify such argument, but we know that it is impossible to demand more of a State than it can give. Perhaps this is more a resignation to the inevitable than anything else. This is also a strand of the justification for commonly accepted "different but common responsibility" in international environmental law.[38]

Another form of this argument can be made to tie right to capacity: because we are able to do this, therefore we have the right to do it. The right to over-flight in outer space may have received support from this argument, and *vice versa.* Originally, the *usque ad coelum* ("all the way up to heaven") rule provides for State sovereignty over territorial airspace to an unlimited extent. The launch of the satellites and other spacecraft by the Soviet Union and the United States in 1950-60s immediately brought a modification to this rule, with the acquiescence of other States, so that the sovereignty of States over their airspace is now limited in height to the point where airspace and outer space meet.[39] This is perhaps the best example of the assertion by some States of a right based on capability and the resignation of other States because of inability.

Tying right to capacity can often be abused. For example, a State may make an argument for a right in a neutral way, knowing that only itself or a small number of powerful States similarly situated may be able to avail themselves of the right. For example, in the *Corfu Channel* case the United Kingdom argued that it had the right to intervene in the territory of another State to "secure possession of evidence in the territory of another State, in order to submit it to an international tribunal and thus facilitate its task".[40] The International Court of Justice resoundingly rejected this argument:

> The Court cannot accept such a line of defence. The Court can only regard the alleged right of intervention as the manifestation of a policy of force, such as has, in the past, given rise to most serious abuses and such as

38 For an analysis, see ibid.; Michael Weisslitz, Rethinking the Equitable Principle of Common but Differentiated Responsibility: Differential versus Absolute Norms of Compliance and Contribution in the Global Climate Change Context, 13 Colorado Journal of International Environmental Law and Policy (2002), 473.

39 See, e.g., Malcolm N. Shaw, International Law (4th ed., 1997), 381-82; Bin Cheng, United Nations Resolutions on Outer Space: "Instant" International Customary Law?, 5 Indian Journal of International Law (1965), 23.

40 ICJ Reports 1949, 4, 34.

> cannot, whatever be the present defects in international organization, find a place in international law. Intervention is perhaps still less admissible in the particular form it would take here; for, from the nature of things, it would be reserved for the most powerful States, and might easily lead to perverting the administration of international justice itself.[41]

As is clear, the argument criticized by the Court is really an argument based on power or raw power, but under camouflage. The same kind of logic may be present in the arguments for making a new rule of law or for making a general exception to a rule of law, and should be rejected for the same reasons.

(c) Argument from need. This is an argument that ties right to need. Its logic is simple: we should have this right simply because we need it. This is even harder to justify, but traces of it can be found in Kant's concept of an "imperfect duty" on the part of us to help those in need.[42] Of course, the ideal distribution of goods in communism would be done on this principle. At this moment the arguments for foreign aid are closer to Kant's imperfect duty than to the ideal distribution of goods.

(d) Argument from democracy. This argument can take two forms. One is that, because we are a democracy, we should have more rights. This idea at this moment is not yet generally accepted, although democracies may grant to each other more rights than to non-democratic States.

Another form of the argument from democracy is based on the "one man, one vote" ideal, so that we will have "one man, one right", leading to a greater collective sum of rights for a State with a bigger population than for a State with a smaller population. In international relations this argument would favor a State with a large population.

The importance of this principle is obvious. The world has generally agreed that the will of the people is the basis of government.[43] The emphasis on the "human ends" of power and international order goes to the very root of the

---

41 Ibid., 35.

42 See I. Kant, The Metaphysics of Morals (1797, M. Gregor tran. 1991), 241-42.

43 See Univ. Declaration of Human Rights, UNGA Res. 217(A) (1948), art. 21 ("The will of the people shall be the basis of the authority of government"); Int'l Covenant on Civil & Political Rights, 999 UNTS 171, art. 25. See also James Crawford, Democracy and International Law, 64 British Year Book of International Law (1993), 113.

principle.[44] Its importance is becoming greater still day by day as the bugle of democracy has been sounding very loudly and the bandwagon of democracy has promised to leave no one behind. If one is to be faithful to what one preaches, this principle must be given serious effect.

On the other hand, giving this argument unfettered effect would lead to a situation where a big State such as China or a small number of the big States would control the decision-making in the world. While such an outcome is not necessarily unfair in itself (indeed, if the argument from democracy is a fair one, such an outcome is a corollary of it), it would still be unseemly, so to speak, and it would impede the efforts to promote greater sovereign equality. So some form of compromise is in order.

(e) Argument from economic power or GNP. This argument is simply that the rights and obligations of a State should be decided upon its economic power or GNP. Needless to say, there is some logic to this argument, and it can be grounded generally on capacity, need, or retribution/reward. But such argument can only be good up to a point, and cannot be carried to its extreme, just as the argument from democracy. In addition, there can be some controversy as to whether economic power in itself should be given such weight. Even if so, it is not certain that GNP should be the proper measure for economic power.

(f) Argument from comprehensive national strength. This argument would base a State's rights and obligations on that State's comprehensive national strength, including population, national economic power, military power, possession of nuclear weapons, etc. This argument would operate in a way similar to the argument from economic power or GNP, and is supported by the same reasoning and open to similar challenges. However, comprehensive national strength would seem to be a better basis upon which rights and obligations are grounded. In the customary international law-making process, the special weight that the big powers possess has long been recognized. Charles de Visscher noted long ago that the more powerful an actor was the heavier its footprint would be in the development of customary international law.[45] One may characterize these States as the "heavy footprint" States. The smaller States were not well-

44 Charles de Visscher, n.6 above, 124-34.

45 See Charles de Visscher, n.6 above, 155. See also generally M. Byers, Custom, Power and the Power of Rules (1999); contra, M. Chemillier-Gendreau, Humanité et souverainetés: Essai sur la fonction du droit international (1995).

endowed enough to be contenders in this process.

The argument from economic power or comprehensive national strength may be perceived as a resort to raw power. Yet power cannot be ignored. For this reason, neither argument is easily accepted; each is usually swallowed with a sense of resignation.

(g) Argument from efficiency. This argument would base a State's rights and obligations on some index of efficiency. Such an argument has great appeal, which takes on a greater dimension in some particular areas such as the utilization of resources. The argument is that since we are faced with scarcity of resources in the world, we must let the most efficient user of resources take the best advantage of the limited supply. However, whether efficiency is a virtue itself, so that greater efficiency is our pursuit, is not a settled question; if one were to be able to find a formula to produce a balanced mix of happiness and a lower level of efficiency, I suppose that formula should be the basis for decision-making, not the pursuit for the greatest efficiency. Such a possibility would counsel against resorting to efficiency in a strong manner.

(h) Argument from the nature of the function at issue. This argument attempts to base rights and obligations on the particular function at issue: (1) the distribution is made on a function-by-function basis rather than across the board, and (2) the rights and obligations are closely tailored to the particular function at issue so that those who are better in performing the function will be in a privileged position. Such a distribution of rights and obligations can be grounded on moral reward as well as efficiency—in fact, sophisticated efficiency. Thus, those who are peace-loving and strongly interested in safeguarding peace and security of the world are normally placed in some privileged position in the performance of such a function such as permanent membership in the United Nations Security Council, an organ entrusted with the primary responsibility to maintain peace and security in the world. Conversely, one who aspires to permanent membership in the United Nations Security Council should have the qualities for performing that function—being peace-loving themselves and being capable of performing the tasks entrusted to them. So when Japan—whose leaders annually go to worship at a shrine where former Class A war criminals convicted of most heinous international crimes including war of aggression and crimes against humanity were buried—pleads for permanent membership in the United Nations Security Council, one wonders whether such a plea for privilege was intended as a mockery of the very function of the United Nations Security

Council.

(i) Argument from potential effects on certain States. This is the argument that the rights and obligations may be determined, to a large extent, on the effects that a State may have to shoulder. Reasonably enough, this reasoning would apply to States big or small. While not directly dealing with this issue, the International Court of Justice appeared to give special weight to the practices of "specially affected"[46] States in the search for the trajectory of customary international law formation. While its import is not completely clear, this concept of "specially affected State" stands in contrast to what may be termed the "heavy footprint State" concept as intimated by de Visscher,[47] because even a diminutive State can be specially affected under some circumstances.

However, it has been accepted that the big powers would be affected most by the disturbances in the world, although this point does not appear to have been perfectly explained. And the big powers relied upon this for their privileged status in the League of Nations and then United Nations. As related by David Miller, a chief drafter of the Covenant of the League of Nations, Woodrow Wilson supported the primacy of the great powers on the ground that:

> [T]he chief physical burdens of the League will fall on the great powers whether these burdens are military or economic… It is desirable to make the plan acceptable that the powers should be in Executive Council. … The general idea is that the Executive Council will consist of those other powers whose interests are affected. The scheme is to have the Executive Council consist of the interested parties. The great powers are always interested.[48]

Subsequently this logic was affirmed by the Permanent Court of International Justice:

> [I]t is hardly conceivable that resolutions on questions affecting the peace of the world could be adopted against the will of those amongst the Members of the Council who, although in a minority, would, by reason of their political position, have to bear the larger share of the responsibilities

46 North Sea Continental Shelf, ICJ Reports 1969, 3, paras. 73-74.

47 Text to n.45 above (idea of "heavy footprint" States).

48 David Miller, n.17 above, 146.

> and consequences ensuing therefrom.[49]

Similarly, the Joint Statement of the big powers stated eloquently at San Francisco:

> In view of the primary responsibilities of the permanent members, they could not be expected, in the present condition of the world, to assume the obligation to act in so serious a matter as the maintenance of international peace and security in consequence of a decision in which they had not concurred. Therefore, if a majority voting in the Security Council is to be made possible, the only practicable method is to provide, in respect of non-procedural decisions, for unanimity of the permanent members plus the concurring votes of at least two of the non-permanent members.[50]

Accordingly, it seems that it is generally accepted that being affected gives one the right to participate in decision-making; being affected substantially entitles one to substantial weight in the decision-making. Big powers are always affected most and therefore they are always entitled to special privilege in the decision-making, so goes the argument. That is to say, big powers have big powers' burdens, big powers' perils and, therefore, should have big powers' privileges.

(j) Argument from contribution. This is a general argument formulated as follows: the rights a State enjoys in the international community are to be determined by the contribution it makes to that community. Thus formulated, there is a ring of reasonableness to it, as a general consideration. It can be grounded on retribution or reward. As they say, one who pays the piper calls the tune. However, the specific formulations of this argument can encounter several problems such as the difficulty in comparing different types of contribution, the frequent mismatches between the function at issue and the contribution, and the possible over-privileging of contribution to an extent well above the proportion of the contribution. The difficulty in comparing different types of contribution is easy to appreciate and needs no elaboration.

---

49 Interpretation of Article 3, paragraph 2 of the Treaty of Lausanne, Advisory Opinion, PCIJ, Series B, No. 12 (1925), 29.

50 As quoted in: Report to the President on the Results of the San Francisco Conference by the Chairman of the US Delegation (Dept of State, pub. No. 2349, 1945), 76.

The mismatches between the function at issue and the contribution are illustrated by the recent debate on whether Japan should be given permanent membership with veto power at the United Nations Security Council because Japan is among the biggest financial contributors to the United Nations. One response was that the Security Council was not a "board of directors".[51] The High-level Panel on Threats, Challenges and Change convened by the United Nations Secretary-General seemed to believe that increased involvement in the decision-making of the United Nations Security Council should be based on contributions to the United Nations, "financially, militarily and diplomatically",[52] a position that appears to be reasonable, at least better than focusing on financial contributions alone.

The over-privileging of contribution can occur when the biggest contributor or contributors manage to exact a veto over the decision-making of an organization, at least on some issues, although the contribution is not necessarily very big in absolute terms. For example, at the International Monetary Fund and the World Bank this phenomenon may exist at the moment because the voting is weighted so that a *de facto* veto obtains.

5. Leader States' Legitimacy

Given the inevitable differences and the great variety of arguments justifying such differences, it is easy for one to imagine that there is inevitably a great spectrum of differing positions in the world for different States to occupy. At what point does a State achieve the leader State position, and what constitutes the basis for its legitimacy?

As neither the term "leader States" nor "legitimacy" has received official definition, I shall take these as encompassing several possible understandings.[53] Before we examine these possibilities, let me state my assumptions and explain, in general, how I will address these two issues.

As I set out in the beginning of this paper (Parts 1 & 2), I stress the intrinsic and instrumental value of the phenomenon of the State and territorial integrity and political independence as the irreducible minimum for sovereign

---

51 See news report at: http://www.chinadaily.com.cn/english/doc/2004-09/22/content _376639.htm (financial contribution).

52 High-level Panel Report, n.3 above, 66-67.

53 It is clear that we are not here dealing with the domestic order, and we will exclude from the term the sense of Führerstaat (a State under the control of the leader).

equality. These two positions will serve as the starting point for our analysis, and they are treated as axiomatic without any need for legitimatizing.

As a State moves from this starting point of "equal State" to another place, it may achieve another position in the spectrum of States, and there is an index of legitimacy that accompanies this movement. This index will be deemed to have included the respect for the irreducible minimum of sovereign equality. Any violation of this minimum would make the changed position of a State illegitimate.

A. The Strong State

One obvious possibility would be to treat a State that has managed to move from an equal State to achieve a privileged position or a strong position in the spectrum as a "leader State". Such a State would be in the part of the spectrum that would indicate that it is stronger or better than many other States. The index of legitimacy for such a position would include, in addition to respect for the irreducible minimum of sovereign equality, all the difference arguments[54] that result in a privileged position if these arguments can be applied in a way that does not offend the minimum consistency condition and can meet, to the best, the conditions of fairness either in the meta-arguments or in each individual arguments. Of course, as the above analysis shows, this can be a Herculean exercise, and, at the end of the day, one can only achieve an approximate assessment. Such an assessment may be a virtue in itself, and may exert an influence on State behavior.

In my view, however, if a State manages to move from an equal State to achieve a privileged or strong position legitimately, it is only a "strong State", not yet a "leader State". This is so because *most* of the difference arguments, as described in Part 4 above, all proceed from the perspective of the particular State itself; they are self-centered arguments. Several arguments have the potential of being more, such as the argument from the potential effects on particular States, but they are asserted from a self-centered perspective. Viewed this way, such a State is simply one that is fending for itself; it is acting like an individual elbowing to make a living, not to make a difference. For a strong State to secure a better status, it must adopt a course of action and an outlook that are "other-regarded", and must also reason from the perspective of other

---

54 As described in Part 4 above.

States.[55]

B. The Great State

Another possibility would be to treat the big powers, such as the permanent members of the United Nations Security Council or States with almost the same power (other than the veto) in international governance, as the leader States. The claim to such a status can be based on the fact that they are big powers, sufficient to move mountains, and on their index of legitimacy, including all the components as included in the index of legitimacy for a "strong State". To this extent, the big powers in the United Nations Security Council and their influence serve as a proxy, not a perfect reflection, of a fair result if most of the "difference agreements" including the argument from democracy are given effect in as fair a way as possible.

In my view, however, if a State manages to achieve the big power status legitimately, it is only a "great State", not necessarily a "leader State". The big powers are "great States" for the reasons given here; they are not necessarily "leader States" for the reasons to be given below. As Phillip Jessup noted, "Great powers have power because they are great".[56] I can say that great powers are great not simply because they have power. Their greatness comes from their respect for the value of, and their responsibility toward, the international system as a whole—maintaining peace and security and generally contributing to the health of the system—and their success in fulfilling this responsibility. The responsibility and success are both necessary components of the "great State" status. No doubt a State that shoulders a hefty responsibility toward the international system as a whole can be said to have paid the dues for that status. However, responsibility alone would not suffice; a State which bears such a responsibility but frequently leaves a mess behind in any venture would be simply doing a disservice to the international system. Substantial success in acquitting oneself of the responsibility is a necessary condition for greatness, as one can infer from the fact that international law has always placed great weight

55 This is similar to the Confucianist understanding of human nature as "being conscious of others". See Sienho Yee, Towards, n.6 above, 293 (chapter 14, The Concept of Human Rights in Asia).

56 See P.C. Jessup, Introduction to the Equality of States as Dogma and Reality, LX Political Science Quarterly (No. 4, Dec. 1945), 530 ("Great powers have power because they are great and not because a skillful draftsman has invented an ingenious formula"), as quoted in Lachs, n.3 above, 486.

on the idea of effectivity.[57] Success is, perhaps, the ultimate qualification for the great State status: one simply cannot argue with victory. Of course, a single State will not be able to fulfill such a responsibility; collective action is required.

Such a way of seeing the world is reasonable. The international system is a public good whose benevolence is available to all. More than that, the international system is a public infrastructure on which the welfare of all depends. Systemic value and the responsibility toward the system as a whole have always weighed heavily on the hearts and minds of great statesmen and great States in history. For example, the Confucianist ideal includes several stages of achievement: cultivating oneself, regulating the family, ordering the State and bringing peace to the world.[58] The United States participated in both World Wars, which were fought far away from its own shores, because the international system could not survive the victory of the other side.

At the end of World War II, the great States took upon themselves the "primary responsibility for the maintenance of international peace and security" under Article 24 of the United Nations Charter.[59] The word choice of "maintenance" was deliberate; it was meant to convey the systemic nature of world peace and security and the nature of the responsibility of the big powers. The Chairman of the United States Delegation to the San Francisco Conference put it elegantly this way: "We realize, in short, that peace is a world-wide problem and that the *maintenance* of peace, and not merely its *restoration*, depends primarily upon the unity of the great powers".[60] As a result, the "provisions for the Security Council recognize the special responsibilities of the great powers for maintaining the peace and the fact that the maintenance of their unity is the crucial political problem of our time".[61]

Even in times of peace, statesmen often remind themselves of the great

---

57 This seems to inform the ICJ's view on the so-called objective personality of the United Nations vs. non-members. See Reparation for Injuries Suffered in the Service of the United Nations, Advisory Opinion, ICJ Reports 1949, 174, especially 185. For a succinct general analysis on effectivity, see de Visscher, n.6 above, 318-32.

58 The maxim is from Daxue (大学, The Great Learning), and appears in Chinese as "修身齐家治国平天下", pronounced as "xiushen qijia zhiguo pingtianxia". I have translated the maxim slightly differently than the normal translation.

59 See also Hans Kelsen, The Law of the United Nations: A Critical Analysis of Its Fundamental Problems, with Supplement (1964), 272-73.

60 Report to the President, n.50 above, 66.

61 Ibid., 67.

States' responsibility toward the international system. For example, Hu Jintao, when introducing President Bush to students at Tsinghua University, said that China and the United States had many things in common, among which was their common responsibility to the world.[62] I am sure the list of examples is very long, and I shall not attempt to complete it.

Such a responsibility sometimes entails selfless self-sacrifice, at least if an accounting is done for the *immediate* cost and benefit arising from a certain course of action, although in the long term a properly functioning international system always redounds to the benefit of all, including the self-sacrificing great States. To a great extent, this self-sacrifice was exhibited to its best by the United States' participation in the two World Wars.

It was also illustrated by the Chinese government's decision to refrain from devaluating the Chinese Yuan during the height of the Asian financial crisis back in the late 1990s in order to make Chinese products competitive with those from the other Asian States whose currencies had devalued dramatically. A devaluation of the Chinese Yuan then, so it was commonly thought, would have sent the already distressed Asian economies into a tailspin, which possibly could send the entire world into a depression, and would definitely have delayed the possible Asian recovery, if ever. Currently, in the debate as to whether the Chinese Yuan should be appreciated in value, the Chinese leaders again have been acting very cautiously. In the face of the dropping dollar, the Chinese leaders are calling upon the United States to fulfill its historic responsibility toward the international system, by adopting the same attitude that China did during the Asian crisis, which would mean beefing up the dollar.[63] It remains to be seen how this battle of currencies will play out in the future.

So far the record of the great States in acquitting themselves of their responsibility toward the international system has been good overall. Since World War II, there has been no worldwide or systemic war. While the Cold War created tension and separation between the socialist and capitalist camps, systemic peace was assured, perhaps as result of that tension, ironically enough. In addition, overall economic development and the improvement of livelihood have been remarkable. For these reasons, perhaps the great State status that the

---

62 "Chinese Vice-President Welcomes US President at Tsinghua University", Xinhua News Agency (22 February 2002) online: China Internet Information Centre <http://www.china.org.cn/english/27348.htm>.

63 See news report on the dispute: www.forbes.com/home_asia/currencies /2004/12/02/ cz_rm_1202chinadollar.html.

big powers enjoy has been earned.

However, the international system is faced with serious challenges at present. The High-level Panel on Threats, Challenges and Change convened by the United Nations Secretary-General is of the view that

> [T]he biggest security threats we face now, and in the decades ahead, go far beyond States waging aggressive war. They extend to poverty, infectious disease and environmental degradation; war and violence within States; the spread and possible use of nuclear, radiological, chemical and biological weapons; terrorism; and transnational organized crime. The threats are from non-State actors as well as States, and to human security as well as State security.[64]

Serious indeed are these challenges, and hefty is the responsibility of the great States toward the international system. As to how the great States may fulfill their responsibility, the High-level Panel has a great deal to say, and it is not my intent to deal with the details here.

However, I would like to say that the alleged right of humanitarian intervention and the exaggerated right to self-defense have the potential of disturbing the existing system, if the minimal consistency condition were to apply to these alleged rights. The chaos created in the world system, as a whole, by the alleged right of humanitarian intervention and the almost inevitable result of causing greater sudden and dramatic sufferings than non-intervention (which could result in more slow sufferings), would seem to make such an alleged right suspect, to say the least, if not outright unlawful and immoral.[65] An exaggerated right to self-defense of one State against another or of one State against non-State groups in another State can also lead to inroads into the current regime of sovereign equality. It would seem that, at least in the long term, the best antidote to the problems created by non-State groups is to promote strong States around the world and the cooperation between and among them.

C. The Leader State

A further possibility would be to identify a "leader State" by identifying what is the function at issue and assessing how a particular State is carrying out that

---

64 High-level Panel Report, n.3 above, 11.

65 See Sienho Yee, Towards, n.6 above, 21-22.

function, with a view to ascertaining whether certain "leader qualities" are exhibited or not. In the context of our inquiry here and in order to make the inquiry manageable, I have in mind only the function that the great States perform in the international system—maintaining peace and security in the world and generally contributing to the health of the system as a whole.[66] Obviously, in order to be a contender as a "leader State", a State must be a big power or something close to it; otherwise, it would not have the wherewithal to perform this important function.

With this in mind, let us inquire into what would constitute the index of legitimacy for a "leader State". This index must include the entire index of legitimacy for "great States", although the measure of success need not be as substantial as that for a great State. Slightly weaker States too can be leaders if they have also contributed, to a significant extent, to maintaining international peace and security and to meeting the interconnected, serious challenges that the world is facing.

Second, and more importantly, this index must include a component dealing with how such a contribution is made. Current understanding of "leadership" seems to be saying that leadership is based on a position of authority, the ability to receive deference from the followers.[67] Different philosophers and sociologists have given us different formulations of leadership. Its essence has remained the same: Leaders are not leaders because they manage to get ahead of the pack, but because they lead the pack, and are followed by the pack.

Several factors may help one earn deference from others. First of all, the existence of a body of legitimate rules and the leader's own good faith efforts to follow them are among the most important factors that give rise to authority and leadership in modern societies.[68] The international community is no different and those big powers that make good faith efforts to follow the existing legitimate rules will no doubt receive deference from other States.

---

66 No doubt there is an infinite variety of functions and of the ways and means of performing those functions. Limiting our inquiry this way does not mean slighting other important functions; it is simply a resignation to the inability to deal with all of them here.

67 See generally, Thomas Carlyle, On Heroes, Hero-Worship, and the Heroic in History (1900); From Max Weber: Essays in Sociology (H.H. Gerth & C. Wright Mills eds., 1991), Part II.

68 Max Weber, ibid.

Thus, it would seem that the prevailing of the general state of the rule of law[69] and the potential leaders' good faith efforts in contributing to that general state of affairs are important minimal bases for the leader State status.

Second, in addition to good faith efforts, sometimes potential leader States may have to make exemplary efforts to comply with the existing rules, in order to induce deference from others or voluntary compliance with the rules by others. Dissenting in a case on a point of domestic law, Justice Louis D. Brandeis of the United States Supreme Court put it this way:

> Decency, security and liberty alike demand that government officials shall be subjected to the same rules of conduct that are commands to the citizen. In a government of laws, existence of the government will be imperilled if it fails to observe the law scrupulously. Our Government is the potent, the omnipresent teacher. For good or for ill, it teaches the whole people by its example. Crime is contagious. If the Government becomes a lawbreaker, it breeds contempt for law; it invites every man to become a law unto himself; it invites anarchy. To declare that in the administration of the criminal law the end justifies the means—to declare that the Government may commit crimes in order to secure the conviction of a private criminal—would bring terrible retribution. Against that pernicious doctrine this Court should resolutely set its face.[70]

What Brandeis said about the "teacher" role of the United States Government can also be said about any State in a potential leadership position. Such a State too is an "omnipresent teacher" to the world. The need to induce deference by exemplary efforts applies with greater force to the international community because of its existing disorganized and semi-anarchical nature. Otherwise, the anarchy that Brandeis feared would be visited upon the world. Brandeis thus painted a vivid picture of constructivism with leadership at the center.

Sadly enough, some major powers are still sticking to their mentality held over from a beyond era called the Cold War and attempt to produce "deference" or compliance through deterrence and coercion. Needless to say, such an approach has not produced any deference or good results.

---

69 For a formulation of such a state of affairs, see Sienho Yee, Towards, n.6 above, 41-58.

70 Olmstead v. United States, 277 U.S. 438 (USSC 1928), 485, 48 S.Ct. 564, 575 (Brandeis, J., dissenting).

In no other area than in the non-proliferation and elimination of nuclear weapons have the pitfalls of this approach been shown clearly. Without going into the details and without attempting to be meticulous in details, one can say that the reality of the current regime of non-proliferation and elimination of nuclear weapons consists of basically two points: (1) the "haves" shall keep what they have for now, and the "have-nots" shall wash their hands of them; and (2) the "haves" shall in due course eliminate what they have. Obviously this regime is born of a concession to reality. It also serves, however, to magnify the injustice that inheres in a world consisting of haves and have-nots. Exacerbating this feeling is the lack of genuine efforts on the part of the haves to move towards eventual elimination, the nice promise notwithstanding, because without complete elimination, the injustice becomes permanent, rather than only temporary. Thus, the commentator David Scofield reported that when South Korean President Roh Moo-hyun visited California, he "stunned many in the audience of foreign-policy experts with his assertion that the central argument underpinning North Korea's nuclear-weapons program—that it is a necessary defense in the face of hostility and threat—is not entirely illogical."[71] Appropriate inducement in the form of promises of reward sometimes may work wonders, such as in the case of Libya's elimination of its program of weapons of mass destruction. But, in the nature of things, such wonders will be limited if minimal logic or fairness is not assured.

Furthermore, the policy of nuclear deterrence or coercion is still a tool that has been resorted to by some nuclear powers. For example, some nuclear powers, such as the United States, have not made the "no first strike" pledge. Some are making efforts to neutralize the nuclear capability of others, in the name of building a "National Missile Defense" system. While dressed up in the garb of self-defence, such a system becomes an offensive system especially when coupled with the failure of some nuclear powers to make the "no first strike" pledge. Such efforts obviously can only lead to an arms race, and the recent Russian pronouncement[72] that it is working on a new nuclear system is prime proof of that.

So it would seem that unless the nuclear powers start to make genuine

---

71 David Scofield, Seoul rows against the US tide, Asia Times, 24 Nov. 2004, http://www.atimes.com/atimes/Korea/FK24Dg03.html.

72 Putin Says Russia Working on New Nuclear Systems, Reuters News, Moscow, 17 November 2004, http://www.washingtonpost.com/wp-dyn/articles/A56417-2004Nov17.html.

and exemplary efforts to move towards eventual elimination of nuclear weapons, one can understand why there would be dogged and clandestine attempts to obtain the forbidden fruit. For the sake of the world, any State that aspires to the leader State status should act like a leader in the non-proliferation effort.

One wonders whether the possibility that that non-State groups may attempt to obtain nuclear weapons would serve as the saving grace for the nuclear deterrence policy propounded by some States. I do not believe so. First of all, the victims of the execution of the deterrence policy will probably be innocent bystanders, not the culprit groups. Second, so far the lowest-tech, not high-tech, has been used by such groups, and evidence shows that it is difficult for such groups to obtain nuclear weapons without the assistance of States. Accordingly, the possibility that non-State groups may manage to obtain nuclear weapons should be cause for the world to promote strong States capable of controlling such non-State groups, and, more important, for the nuclear powers to move as soon as possible to complete elimination of nuclear weapons so that it would be impossible for non-State groups to obtain them.

In other areas, the behavior of some potential leader States seems to paint a picture of strong States elbowing for their own advantages only or even simply for the sake of throwing their weight around, demonstrating who is the boss, showing pride or moral superiority, punishing others for spite, or simply ensuring that one can have his or her way. Clearly such behavior is no leader's style. It epitomizes the kind of behavior that starts with a self-regarded perspective, without regard to others,[73] a tendency that can lead to untold misery in the future. Clearly such behavior will not induce any positive results for the world. It serves only as a source for bad examples.

Against the background of use of force or deploying force to settle disputes, an exemplary effort to settle disputes by peaceful means was made by France and the Republic of Congo. On December 9, 2002, the Republic of the Congo (the Congo) filed an application against France, alleging that in attempting to prosecute a Congolese Minister and to seek to examine the Congolese President as a witness, France violated the principle of sovereign equality and the criminal immunity of a foreign Head of State. The Congo sought to found the jurisdiction of the International Court of Justice (ICJ), pursuant to Article 38, paragraph 5,[74] of the Rules of Court, "on the consent of

---

73 See paragraph accompanying n. 52 above ("other-regardedness").

74 Article 38(5) of the 1978 Rules of Court states:

the French Republic, which will certainly be given".[75] This is normally considered an attempt by the Congo to employ the doctrine of *forum prorogatum*.[76] Such an attempt can be described as a "naked attempt" for the reason that when the application was filed there was *plainly* no basis for jurisdiction over the other State. And yet it can be successful, sometimes. By a letter dated April 8, 2003 and received on April 11, 2003 in the Registry, the French Republic stated that it "consent[ed] to the jurisdiction of the Court to entertain the Application pursuant to Article 38, paragraph 5".[77] This marks "the first instance since the adoption in 1978 of Article 38, paragraph 5, of the Rules of Court in which a State has thus accepted another State's invitation to recognize the jurisdiction of the International Court of Justice to deal with a case against it",[78] and thus the return of the doctrine of *forum prorogatum* to the International Court of Justice since probably the *Haya de la Torre* case.[79] The ICJ has now entered this case in the General List as "the case concerning *Certain Criminal Proceedings in France (Republic of Congo v. France)*".[80]

By any standards, the French acceptance of the Congo's invitation, which it need not accept, is exemplary. The Agent for France made clear before the Court that France had done so because of the following reasons: the importance of the good faith search for peaceful settlement of international disputes in international relations; the confidence France has in and the respect it has for the Court; and its belief that neither its laws nor the acts of its

---

> When the applicant State proposes to found the jurisdiction of the Court upon a consent thereto yet to be given or manifested by the State against which such application is made, the application shall be transmitted to that State. It shall not however be entered in the General List, nor any action be taken in the proceedings, unless and until the State against which such application is made consents to the Court's jurisdiction for the purposes of the case.

75 ICJ Press Release 2002/37 (9 December 2002).

76 See Sienho Yee, Forum Prorogatum Returns to the International Court, in: Yee, Towards, n.6 above, 85.

77 ICJ Press Release 2003/14 (11 April 2003). [Since the publication of this paper, France has accepted the Court's jurisdiction in the same way over another case, see Certain Questions of Mutual Assistance in Criminal Matters (Djibouti v. France), Judgment, I.C.J. Reports 2008, 177, 118, para.4.]

78 Ibid.

79 ICJ Reports 1951, 71.

80 ICJ Press Release 2003/15 (23 April 2003). See also ICJ CR 2003/20 (28 April 2003), 1.

judiciary in this particular case violated any rules of international law.[81] Not directly addressed by the French Agent is the question whether, at the particular moment when the Iraq War was going on, France intended to provide a counter-example to the unilateral use of force by the United States. Yet this question might be on the minds of many. One wishes that the exemplary urge would move France soon to re-accept the Court's "compulsory jurisdiction" by filing a declaration under Article 36(2) of the ICJ Statute. That would be the ultimate example for France to set and for other States to follow. Judicial settlement of disputes no doubt will redound to benefit of the parties to a dispute and the world at large; it is far better to go to court than to go to war.

The ultimate leader State is, however, a leader State that has not only been making good faith or even exemplary efforts to comply with the existing legitimate rules, but, more importantly, has helped to formulate or refine substantially a good vision of the international system and to help build it up. That is to say, the ultimate leader State is not only a vision purveyor and promoter or a system maintainer and promoter, but also a vision originator or refiner and a system builder. The ultimate leader State helps to mold the world. While some might believe that the destiny of history has already been predetermined, great leaders and great leader States have never given up their efforts to formulate better visions for the international system and to build up the system according to their visions.

The United States has been a most powerful leader in this regard. In the aftermath of both World Wars, the United States devoted considerable time and energy to formulating better visions for the world system and building it up. This great story has been told many times, and need not be repeated here.[82] This leadership role may be changing. One can see evidence of this, for example, in the recent brouhaha surrounding the International Criminal Court (ICC), such as the "unsigning" of the Rome Statute and making the weak and meek States sign the so-called "Article 98 agreements". These agreements were thought to be capable of ensuring that United States nationals would not end up as defendants before the ICC, after the proposed control of the United Nations Security Council over the ICC's activities (under Article 23 in the draft

---

81 ICJ CR 2003/21 (28 April 2003, un-corrected version), 6-7.

82 See, e.g., David Miller, n.17 above; Report to the President, n.50 above; Ruth B. Russell, A history of the United Nations Charter : the role of the United States 1940-1945 (1958); Mary Ann Glendon, A World Made New: Eleanor Roosevelt and the Universal Declaration of Human Rights (2001).

statute proposed by the International Law Commission) was overridden by subsequent developments.[83] I can see that the erstwhile moral leader has now become the persistent objector in the progressive development of international law. I can only sigh: what a reversal of roles. I also see something unseemly in asking the weak and meek States to be the henchmen in one's own fight. If I were to coax anyone, I would choose the big and strong as my targets. Even a neighborhood bully will get bored with bullying the little ones, and will pick on the stronger and stronger for a fight.[84]

Of course, the vision that a leader State helps to formulate must be a good and fair one. There can be many such visions, all focusing on international peace and security, friendly relations and economic development. This can be seen in the Friendly Relations Declaration, which embodies a vision that has commanded the general support of the world community, and in the "Five Principles of Peaceful Coexistence" championed by China and India.[85] The High-level Panel convened by the United Nations Secretary-General has also presented in its report a vision of a solidly multilateral system for the world for decades to come, focusing on security challenges.[86] Such an emphasis is of course appropriate, as peace is the foundation for all, whether it is human rights or development. Without peace and security, one will only see a mirage of idealism.

In the National Security Strategy of the United States,[87] a vision of the

---

83 See my paper, A Proposal to Reformulate Article 23 of the ILC Draft Statute for an International Criminal Court, 19 Hastings Int'l & Comp. Law Review (1996), 523, reprinted in Sienho Yee, Towards, n.6 above, 105.

84 It is not my goal here to give an assessment of the US arguments against the ICC; other scholars have done so. Nevertheless, I would like to mention that the normal commentaries published in the US media regarding the expansive jurisdiction of the ICC or the possible loss of US sovereignty do not seem to have been well-informed. The Rome Statute in fact implements a version of the jurisdictional principle that is narrower than is permissible under international law, and the complementarity principle and other safeguards more than protect the sovereignty of any reasonable State.

85 See generally the 50th Anniversary celebration symposium in 3 Chinese Journal of International Law (2004), 363 et seq.

86 High-level Panel Report, n.3 above.

87 See http://www.whitehouse.gov/nsc/nss.html. For commentaries, see Edward McWhinney, President Bush and the New U.S. National Security Strategy: The Continuing Relevance of the Legal Adviser and International Law, 2 Chinese Journal of International Law (2002), 421; Christine Gray, The

proper world order was also presented. The interconnected nature of the world and the importance of eliminating poverty and promoting economic development were appreciated. To this extent, the National Security Strategy embodies an integrated approach, and there is much to commend it. However, a strong unilateral approach to security has also been asserted. This is commonly called the Bush doctrine of preemption. It would seem that one generally has sympathy for the perception of threat, particularly after the threat came true on September 11, 2001. Yet, a proper response in a pre-emptive manner must answer the question "how much in advance can the response be" in a balanced and proper fashion. If this question is dealt with improperly, the world may return to the state of nature. Another question to consider is how to distribute State responsibility for any mistakes in conducting pre-emptive strikes, on a post-facto examination of the situation, although the mistakes appear reasonable immediately before such strikes occur.

It remains to be seen how the Bush vision may affect the world both externally and internally, and whether this vision may become the vision for the world. The recent events that have resulted from the execution of this vision have led to hardship and reduced liberty for many, although my assessment may be wrong. One only hopes that if justice in the world can only be an ideal, life would be at least bearable—not too much a comedy for those who think, and not too much a tragedy for those who feel.

The wide variety of visions for the world would seem to make it fruitless for one to evaluate them one by one. Still I cannot resist presenting what I consider to be the best one in general and abstract terms.

In my view, any proper vision would have to take human flourishing as the ultimate goal. Any proper international system must be one that would provide the playground for the flowering of individuals, keeping in mind that the personhood of any individual may include belonging to a particular community and a particular State. Under such a vision, life cannot simply be bearable; life must be beautiful. It should include making firecrackers out of gunpowder, and not gunpowder out of firecrackers. Under such a vision, leadership does not mean the power to use bows to shoot, guns to destroy, or lasers to fry, but the intelligence to lead, the strategy to guide, and the prowess

---

US National Security Strategy and the New "Bush Doctrine" on Pre-emptive Self-defence, ibid., 437. [For further discussions, see the editorial comments in the September 2014 issue of the Chinese Journal of International Law.]

to inspire all to achieve the flourishing of humanity.[88]

This would require the world, particularly the leader States, to place an emphasis on winning the minds and souls of all players in the world to move towards that goal. My assessment, which can be wrong, is that currently there is a strong tendency, at least in some quarters, in idolizing overwhelming force, or superiority, or the appearance thereof. Such a culture normally leads to over-moralization of, and antagonism in, international relations. This needs to be changed, and it can be changed only by immersing everyone in the world in an atmosphere of idolizing refinement and the pursuit of excellence in airing differences orally rather than violently, in arts and sciences, and in culture generally. Or, as Montesquieu would have it, everyone should be immersed in a culture of "soft manners and morals".[89] He said that such "softness" would

---

88 Commenting on historical Chinese figures, Chairman Mao Zedong muses in a poem that many of them knew only power and force; they lack "literary inspiration". Mao Zedong, Qinyuan Chun, Snow (1936), in: Selected Poems of Mao Zedong (Lao Chi, ed., 1993), 143. The poem is in a classic form of Chinese poetry, and reads in part as follows: "江山如此多骄，引无数英雄竞折腰。惜秦皇汉武，略输文采；唐宗宋祖，稍逊风骚。一代天骄，成吉思汗，只识弯弓射大雕.俱往矣，数风流人物，还看今朝。" (Here is my own English rendition of this: "Motherland, you are so beautiful; you move countless heroes to compete to serve you selflessly. Pity Qin Emperor the First and Han Emperor Wudi: they lacked the literary inspiration for civilian governance; Pity Tang Emperor Tangzong and Song Emperor Taizu: they lacked the poetic prowess for civilian success. Too bad too, the chosen Son of Heaven, of one time, Ghenghis Khan, only knew how to shoot the big birds with his magic bow. All this is now passé; if one is to count outstanding figures, one must take a look at those living today.") From this one can see the Chinese ideal of "literary king" and the Chinese dislike of use of force. In fact, if one were to substitute "The world" for "Motherland", the poem could similarly apply to the world. One might wonder how much this had been put into practice by Mao Zedong, particularly in the Cultural Revolution. First of all, such an inquiry is beyond the scope of my paper; as mentioned earlier, my goal is not to survey practice, but to focus on conceptual and philosophical inquiries, perhaps in an idealist fashion. In any event, the very name of "Cultural Revolution" itself reflects Mao's philosophy—a revolution of culture—and the actual events that took place during the course of the Cultural Revolution no doubt diverged, for whatever reason, from the original intent. In any event, one may simply consider the Cultural Revolution an aberration from the general course of the unfolding of the normal Chinese philosophy or pursuits.

89 Montesquieu, The Spirit of Laws, XX.i (T. Nugent tran. 1823).

naturally help to promote commerce and elevate humanity.[90] Perhaps he was right; he could find support in the earlier teachings of Confucius on the "middle way" as the ideal way of managing things,[91] as well as of those of many others following him.

Previously,[92] I have explained that having human flourishing as the ultimate goal of any society is nothing new, and that freedom or liberty in its negative and/or positive form might not be enough for this purpose, and that a third form of "induced liberty" may be important. The web of relations and responsibility serves as an important force to induce liberty. Furthermore, general achievements in human rights and a properly functioning democracy will also promote human flourishing. Diversity to the widest extent possible will serve to produce richness that would form the basis for human flourishing.

To some extent, the High-level Panel Report[93] can be faulted for only focusing on security challenges and peace-building, and not paying sufficient attention to the need for better education, cultural and spiritual enrichment and a general atmosphere conducive to human flourishing and conducive to inducing human flourishing, which in the long term will be more important. A glance at the table of contents of the Report reveals this. Perhaps a second report focusing on the ways and means of inducing human flourishing will be of value. Leader States have a substantial responsibility in providing such ways and means and generally in building up the international system that would support and promote human flourishing. I hope in due course the work of UNESCO will be recognized as important in this regard, although the term "UNESCO" was reported by my computer as "not found" in this High-level Panel Report.[94]

Such a vision of human flourishing, in the final analysis, would present the best strategy for eliminating terror and threat to security, by inducing the various players into performing tasks that would enrich their lives, thus

---

90 Ibid. See also T. Pangle & P. Ahrensdorf, Justice among Nations (1999), 160.

91 See Confucius, The Analects, especially Bk. VI, Chp. XXVII (William E. Soothill tran. Dover ed. 1995), 32.

92 See generally Sienho Yee, Towards, n.6 above, 24-26.

93 High-level Panel Report, n.3 above.

94 I must say that I do not vouch for my computer search skills. The absence of UNESCO from the Report may have resulted from the fact that the Report had a narrow scope in mind: only the UN agencies themselves are examined, not the specialized agencies. Then one can disagree with such a narrow scope, given the title of the Panel.

eradicating the roots for terrorism. One fully understands that it will take time to achieve this. The States feeling threatened now may believe that they would not have the luxury to wait for that to happen, and may resort to high-pressure tactics in order to prevent terrorism, which may then turn the world into a spiral of horribles. An alternative view can be that precisely because of this situation and this possibility, the leader States shall feel a greater urgency to make stronger efforts to win the minds and souls of everyone.

In conclusion, let me say to the States:

(1) When you (a) have respected the irreducible minimum of sovereign equality and (b) have managed to move from an equal State to reach a privileged or strong position legitimately under the difference arguments, you are merely a strong State;

(2) When you (a) have respected the irreducible minimum of sovereign equality, (b) have moved from an equal State to become a strong State legitimately and have achieved the big power status, and (c) have paid respect to the value of, and shouldered, with substantial success, the hefty responsibility toward, the international system, you are merely a great State;

(3) When you (a) have respected the irreducible minimum of sovereign equality, (b) have respected the value of, and shouldered, with success, substantial responsibility toward, the international system, (c) have not only been making good faith efforts or even exemplary efforts to comply with the existing legitimate rules, but also, more important, (d) have helped to formulate or refine a proper vision of the international system and to build it up so that the flourishing of humanity can be achieved to the greatest extent, you are a leader State.

Chapter 9

Towards a Harmonious World: The Roles of the International Law of Co-progressiveness and Leader States*

I. The Harmonious World as the next destination

1. The next destination on the road to a better world will take us all to a new vista. That is called the Harmonious World by our leaders. President Hu Jintao mentioned this idea in April 2005 at the Asian-African Summit in Jakarta.[1] Before this, the Chinese Communist Party had propounded the idea of a Harmonious Society,[2] and the idea of the Harmonious World apparently appeared as a sister concept to the former. In July 2005 the Harmonious World idea made its way into a joint statement by China and Russia during Hu's visit to Moscow.[3] Hu Jintao then sketched it out further in September 2005 at the

---

* First published at 7 Chinese JIL (2008), 99-105. The original paper contains this abstract: "This paper briefly summarizes the tenets of the idea of a Harmonious World as proposed by China, compares them with those of a Co-progressive World as proposed by the author and highlights the important roles of the international law of co-progressiveness and leader States in realizing the vision of the Harmonious World or Co-progressive World."

1 For a brief summary of the process of the debut of this concept, see: http://news.xinhuanet.com/ziliao/2006-08/24/content_5000866.htm; http://news.xinhuanet.com/politics/2006-08/23/content_4999294.htm; see also Yang Jiemian, Tentative comments on interaction between the concept of the Harmonious World and the transformation of the international system, Mao Zedong Deng Xiaoping Lilun Yanjiu [Studies on the Theories of Mao Zedong and Deng Xiaoping], 2007, No. 1, 61.

2 See background materials on the idea of a Harmonious Society (http://politics.people.com.cn/GB/8198/70195/70201/4757608.html).

3 See http://news.xinhuanet.com/ziliao/2006-08/24/content_5000866.htm.

United Nations. He placed emphasis on, first, multilateralism and collective efforts to safeguard peace and security; second, mutually beneficial cooperation and development for common prosperity; third, tolerance; and, fourth, strengthening the UN.[4]

2. In August 2006, the Central Committee of the Chinese Communist Party held an important meeting on foreign affairs. Many important figures of the Party and the government participated in that conference. According to the Xinhua News Agency, the meeting further elaborated the idea of the Harmonious World as follows:

> To promote the building of the Harmonious World is a natural component of our following the path of peaceful development, and is a natural condition for us to realize the goal of peaceful development. We shall work hard to promote mutual respect, consensus building, and harmonious co-existence, and respect the right of the peoples of each State to freely choose their social system and their path of development, adhere to the right of each State to participate in the management of international affairs, and to promote the democratization of international relations; we shall also work hard to deepen cooperation, achieve shared development, mutual benefit and win-win results, and to promote the sharing of economic globalization and technological progress, so as to bring about the world's general prosperity; we shall also work hard to strengthen interactions between diverse civilizations, mutual understanding, and cross-fertilization of progress, so as to champion diversity in the world and to promote the development and progress of human civilization; and we shall work hard to deepen mutual trust, strengthen dialogues, increase cooperation, to confront together the various global issues that humanity is faced with, to promote the peaceful settlement of international disputes, and to safeguard international as well as regional peace.[5]

---

4 Build Towards a Harmonious World of Lasting Peace and Common Prosperity, Speech by H.E. Hu Jintao, President of the People's Republic of China, at the United Nations Summit, New York, September 15, 2005 (http://www.china-un.org/eng/zt/shnh60/t212915.htm).

5 The translation is mine. The original from Xinhua News Agency is: "坚持推动建设和谐世界。推动建设和谐世界，是我们坚持走和平发展道路的必然要求，也是我们实现和平发展的重要条件。要致力于同各国相互尊重、扩大共识、和谐相处，尊重各国人民自主选择社会制度和发展道路的权利，坚持各国平等参与国际

3. Then in his Report to the Seventeenth National Congress of the Communist Party of China on 15 October 2007, Hu Jintao first said in one section that we must "develop a global and strategic perspective"[6] and then said in another section:

> Sharing opportunities for development and rising to challenges together so as to further the noble cause of peace and development of humanity bear on the fundamental interests of the people of all countries and meet their common aspirations. We maintain that the people of all countries should join hands and strive to build a harmonious world of lasting peace and common prosperity. To this end, all countries should uphold the purposes and principles of the United Nations Charter, observe international law and universally recognized norms of international relations, and promote democracy, harmony, collaboration and win-win solutions in international relations. Politically, all countries should respect each other and conduct consultations on an equal footing in a common endeavour to promote democracy in international relations. Economically, they should cooperate with each other, draw on each other's strengths and work together to advance economic globalization in the direction of balanced development, shared benefits and win-win progress. Culturally, they should learn from each other in the spirit of seeking common ground while shelving differences, respect the diversity of the world, and make joint efforts to advance human civilization. In the area of security, they should trust each other, strengthen cooperation, settle international disputes by peaceful means rather than by war, and work together to safeguard peace and stability in the world. On environmental issues, they should assist and cooperate with each other in

事务，促进国际关系民主化；致力于同各国深化合作、共同发展、互利共赢，推动共享经济全球化和科技进步的成果，促进世界普遍繁荣；致力于促进不同文明加强交流、增进了解、相互促进，倡导世界多样性，推动人类文明发展进步；致力于同各国加深互信、加强对话、增强合作，共同应对人类面临的各种全球性问题，促进和平解决国际争端，维护世界和地区安全稳定。" (中央外事工作会议在京举行，胡锦涛作重要讲话，http://news.xinhuanet.com/politics/2006-08/23/content_499929 4.htm).

6 See http://www.china.org.cn/english/congress/229611.htm (part III) ("树立世界眼光, 加强战略思维").

> conservation efforts to take good care of the Earth, the only home of human beings.[7]

4. This statement more or less repeated the earlier elaboration, with additional or more explicit language on environmental protection.

5. Without these words before my eyes, I imagined a similar world and published a paper in April 2001 entitled *Towards an International Law of Co-progressiveness*.[8] I observed that the primary concern of international society was co-existence at the height of the Cold War, co-operation during the period of détente and is now co-progressiveness in the post-Cold War era. As there was no pre-existing word that followed perfectly from co-existence and co-operation, I coined the phrase "co-progressiveness". By the world of co-progressiveness is meant a society that is all encompassing (hence "co"), preoccupied with advancements at an appropriate speed in moral and ethical terms more than in other respects and having human flourishing as its ultimate goal (hence "progressiveness"). Of course, the leitmotiv in each period is not the only theme audible to us: in co-existence there was co-operation; co-existence was the background note to co-operation; and co-existence and co-operation are the background notes to co-progressiveness.

6. We can see that the concept of the Harmonious World is anchored by a preoccupation with harmony, although the skeletal description of the concept by the Communist Party does show concern for the progress of human civilization.[9] The beauty of the concept is that it is at once characteristic of Chinese culture and consistent with the purposes and principles of the United

---

7 Ibid., part XI (The Chinese original (http://www.china.com.cn/17da/2007-10/24/content_9119449_11.htm) reads: "共同分享发展机遇，共同应对各种挑战，推进人类和平与发展的崇高事业，事关各国人民的根本利益，也是各国人民的共同心愿。我们主张，各国人民携手努力，推动建设持久和平、共同繁荣的和谐世界。为此，应该遵循联合国宪章宗旨和原则，恪守国际法和公认的国际关系准则，在国际关系中弘扬民主、和睦、协作、共赢精神。政治上相互尊重、平等协商，共同推进国际关系民主化；经济上相互合作、优势互补，共同推动经济全球化朝着均衡、普惠、共赢方向发展；文化上相互借鉴、求同存异，尊重世界多样性，共同促进人类文明繁荣进步；安全上相互信任、加强合作，坚持用和平方式而不是战争手段解决国际争端，共同维护世界和平稳定；环保上相互帮助、协力推进，共同呵护人类赖以生存的地球家园。").

8 Sienho Yee, Towards an International Law of Co-progressiveness, in: Sienho Yee and Wang Tieya (eds.), International Law in the Post-Cold War World: Essays in Memory of Li Haopei (April 2001), 18-39.

Nations and the common urge for peace as exhibited in the main forms of civilization.[10]

7. The Co-progressive World, however, is anchored by a preoccupation with all-inclusiveness and advancements at an appropriate speed in moral and ethical terms more than in other respects and has human flourishing as its ultimate goal. This preoccupation seems somewhat different from that with harmony. The recent official emphasis on "human centrality", as part of the Harmonious Society, appears to be one on servicing the people.[11] However, one may argue that true or perfect harmony must be based on or spearheaded by co-progressiveness—all-inclusiveness and advancements in moral and ethical terms. Such co-progressiveness is all inclusive and, more importantly, dynamic and uplifting. Just the oft-recited mutual respect, mutual tolerance, and cooperation will not lead to perfect harmony, if it exists at all. Accordingly, whatever name one may like to give to any future society, it is imperative to recognize co-progressiveness as an essential component of it. Still, one may argue as to whether it is better to describe such a world as a "Harmonious World" or "Co-progressive World".

8. In our march to the next destination, many factors may play an important role. Two of these factors are the international law of co-progressiveness and leader States.

II. The international law of co-progressiveness

9. International law exhibits a certain spirit of the times in its subjects, its formation, its content and its enforcement and other aspects. The leitmotiv of international law was co-existence at the height of the Cold War, co-operation during the period of détente and is now co-progressiveness in the post-Cold War era.

10. Briefly, the international law of co-existence primarily treats States as its subjects. Its formation depends primarily on the customary international law formation process. Its content concerns itself mostly with the separate existence—and the resulting co-existence—of States. Its enforcement depends on the separate, uncoordinated action by the States such as counter-measures.

11. The international law of co-operation begins to include more subjects

---

9 Above nn.5-7 and accompanying texts.

10 Yang Jiemian, above n.1, at 64.

11 See http://news.xinhuanet.com/politics/2006-08/23/content_4999294.htm.

and/or participants such as individuals, at least for some purposes. Its formation is also helped by a great variety of non-traditional forms of law such as gentlemen's agreements and declarations, or soft law, etc. Its content concerns itself primarily with promoting détente and cooperation between States and with mutual benefit. The cooperative spirit made it possible for several grand concepts to be formulated during the period of détente. Its enforcement is often characterized by a sort of "membership" sanction so that the community simply excludes a non-performing State from the community and therefore also the benefits deriving from membership.

12. The international law of co-progressiveness is even more inclusive. It is all encompassing as far as its subjects and/or participants are concerned, so that individuals and even non-governmental organizations have become such subjects and/or participants, if not yet to the full extent. Its formation is improved by the participation of these new players and the innovative resort to the resolutions of the UN Security Council for the establishment of international criminal tribunals, etc. Its content is preoccupied with advancements at an appropriate speed in moral and ethical terms more than in other respects and having, as its ultimate goal, human flourishing to the fullest extent, so that each individual is able and willing to realize his or her own worthwhile pursuit. This is reflected in further concretization of the grand norms and conclusion of the large numbers of agreements. The enforcement of the law takes center-stage and is characterized more and more by a sort of "image sanction" by which the States and the international community resort to the public shaming of a violator of the law, in order to induce it to come back to the path of law compliance.

13. It is easy for one to see that the international law of co-progressiveness would reflect a world of true harmony or the world of co-progressiveness as I have described. It will be a powerful tool to help realize such visions too.

III. Leader States

14. Equally important will be the role of leader States. In a paper completed in 2004, I presented one formulation of the concept of leader States.[12] I argued

[12] Sienho Yee, Sovereign Equality of States and the Legitimacy of "Leader States", in: Ronald St. John Macdonald and Douglas M. Johnston (eds.), Towards World Constitutionalism (Martinus Nijhoff 2005), 737-772 (A

that from the starting point of equality of States—the irreducible minimum being equal juridical status in terms of dignity and position and territorial integrity and political independence—and under the basic condition of respecting the irreducible minimum of sovereign equality of States, a State that has managed to move from the position of an "equal State" to become strong legitimately is a strong State. A State is a great State if it has legitimately become a strong State, has achieved big power status, and has paid due respect to the values of, and shouldered, with substantial success, the hefty responsibility towards, the international system. A State is a "leader State" if it has respected the value of, and shouldered, with success, substantial responsibility toward, the international system, and if it has not only been making good faith efforts or even exemplary efforts to comply with the existing legitimate rules, but also, more importantly, has helped to formulate or refine a proper vision of the international system and to build it up so that the flourishing of humanity can be achieved to the greatest extent possible.

15. Leader States, defined this way, will take on an important role in our effort to reach the next destination, or to realize the vision of either the Harmonious World or the Co-progressive World. The three essential characteristics of a leader State—dedication to and shouldering substantial responsibility toward the international system, exemplary efforts to promote the rule of law, and the formulation and championing of proper future visions of the international system—will be essential indeed to any vision of the future world. These are issues that no international system can escape from. Whether a leader State is important to a particular vision of the world is then an issue of whether it would champion that particular vision.

16. China has not sought to be called a leader State. So far China has just said that it is a "responsible big power", which can be deemed a reformulation of "great State" in my typology of States. Perhaps this is a reflection of the fear that putting itself up as a potential leader State will be fanning the fervor of those who conjure up a frightening image of some sort of "China threat". Or, this perhaps is a reflection of the genuine Confucianist middle-way. But, in my view, China cannot escape from its leader State role in the world. It has no choice but to be a leader State. This is so because China comprises too big a proportion of the world, both in terms of population and economic activities. It

---

Chinese translation of this paper has appeared at Xi'an Jiaotong Daxue Xuebao (Shehui Kexue Ban) (Journal of Xi'an Jiaotong University (Social Sciences)), 2007, No. 5, pp.54-71.

has almost a quarter of the population of the world. China has often been ranked second in world GDP in terms of PPP (purchasing power parity) by various accounts. According to one commentator, China contributed 20.6% of global economic growth in 2006, more than double the contribution of the US, which was 8.7%.[13] The international system cannot function well without China being in a leader State role. Not being in such a role will prevent China from realizing the traditional ideal of "pingtianxia"—bringing peace to the world. From this perspective, China should simply recognize the need for its leader State role, take up the responsibility of a leader State, not just that of a big power, and try to take some other measures to alleviate the fears on the part of other States of an imaginary "China threat", even if unfounded. Indeed, proposing ideas such as the Harmonious World is a good start, as such an idea is not threatening to any intelligent person.

17. Is China a leader State now under the above definition of "leader State"? In my view, China is no doubt a great State by virtue of its importance and its contributions to the international system. But it is only an emergent leader State. Of the three important characteristics, China has definitely fulfilled one: it has respected the value of, and shouldered, with success, substantial responsibility towards, the international system. As to the second—exemplary efforts to comply with existing rules and to promote the rule of law, China's record can be a mixed one. One can give China credit for its strong efforts to promote the rule of law at both the international and domestic levels. One can also give China credit for its existing record, which is good and is probably the best it can achieve now, given its economic and social conditions. Still, one may question whether China's efforts are already exemplary. One may say probably that China's efforts are so in the international arena. However, one may say that there is room for China to do better in the domestic sphere. For example, bureaucracy and narrow-mindedness still present substantial obstacles to progress and efficiency. Corruption is serious. There is not enough respect for good quality in many fields. These are all manifestations of the lack of the rule

---

13 Victor Fung-shuen Sit, Hong Kong's Role in China's Strategy in Central Asia in the Multicentric yet Increasingly Globalising World, in: Proceedings of Symposium on "China-Central Asia Relations in the Changing World Order", 21 July 2007 (Hong Kong Policy Research Institute and Xi'an Jiaotong University), 24. Recently the World Bank recalculated various relevant data, still ranking China second. See http://siteresources.worldbank.org/ICPINT/Resources/ICPreportprelim.pdf (permanent: http://go.worldbank.org/VMCB80AB40).

of law in the domestic sphere. China has yet to ratify the International Covenant on Civil and Political Rights, indicating that there is some distance between the rights that its citizens and residents enjoy and the international standard. Probably one may say that if a State is not a leader State domestically, it can hardly be a leader State internationally. China will not be a leader State until it treats its own citizens the same way as it treats foreigners. The connection between domestic behavior and the international role of a State has long been recognized.[14]

18. Regarding the third criterion, China has put forward the Harmonious World as a vision of the future. It is no doubt a most promising vision, but it remains to be seen whether it is a proper one and whether it is capable of commanding a strong following from around the world. At this moment, the formulation of the Harmonious World is too broadly-worded. To be impolite, the current formulation seems to be formulaic and slogan-like. Further elaboration and concretization of the concept will be needed for it to have greater influence in the world. For the concept to have maximum impact, its elaboration and concretization must be neither too macro so as to be too vague to give directions to others, nor too micro so as to disorient them.

IV. Conclusion

19. China has put forward the idea of the Harmonious World as a vision of the future. Its reputation is on the line. It will just have to try its best to help realize that vision. To do that, it may have to resort to the role of the international law of co-progressiveness and that of a leader State. How and at what cost China may do that is the task for another day.

---

14 See Rein Müllerson, Central Asia: A Chessboard and Player in the New Great Game (2007), 284-93, on Friedrich F. Martens. While Martens may be wrong on several points, his view on the relationship between a State's domestic behaviour and its international role deserves careful study.

Chapter 10

Military Activities in the EEZ: Moving the Debate to Article 59 of the UNCLOS*

1. Military activities in the Exclusive Economic Zone (EEZ) have been an important and controversial topic. Not too long after the USNS *Impeccable* incident, the *Chinese Journal of International Law* presents in the March 2010 issue an Agora on this topic, with an article by Raul (Pete) Pedrozo[1] from the United States and a commentary on that article by ZHANG Haiwen from China.[2]

2. In an editorial comment published in the same issue, I introduce the Agora and highlighted some arguments on pivotal issues in a more or less summary fashion, so as to provide some background considerations.[3] These include: (1) whether the existing framework of Part V of the United Nations Convention on the Law of the Sea of 1982 (the UNCLOS or Convention), as a result of the existence of Article 59 on residual rights, favours the finding of a security interest of the coastal States to which others acting in the exclusive economic zone (EEZ) must pay due regard; and (2) whether the need to ensure the safety of the freedom of navigation favours the existence of the right to conduct "pure" oceanographic sea lane mapping by other States in the EEZ of a coastal State that is not prejudicial to the security interest of the coastal State. I also telegraph some particular points of view, without attempting to resolve

---

* Revised from my editorial comment at: 9 Chinese JIL (2010), 1-7. Thanks go to Kapinga Ntumba for research assistance. Completed on 5 Feb. 2010.

1 Raul (Pete) Pedrozo, Preserving Navigational Rights and Freedoms: The Right to Conduct Military Activities in China's Exclusive Economic Zone, 9 Chinese JIL (2010), 9.

2 ZHANG Haiwen, Is It Safeguarding the Freedom of Navigation or Maritime Hegemony of the United States?—Comments on Raul (Pete) Pedrozo's Article on Military Activities in the EEZ, 9 Chinese JIL (2010), 31.

3 For a review of this topic, see R.R. Churchill and A.V. Lowe, The Law of the

many of the issues, but unmistakably I hope that the debate would be moved to Article 59 of the Convention and that this article—especially the balancing framework embodied in it—would be given some teeth. This would often lead to an outcome more favourable to the coastal State.

3. First of all, we should note that although the United States is not yet a party to the Convention, the arguments made by Pedrozo track it, obviously taking it as codifying customary international law on point, as far as the issues under discussion are concerned.

4. The controversy surrounding the issue of military activities in the EEZ has been with us from the beginning of the drafting process that has led to the conclusion of the Convention. The intensity of the controversy was such that the ultimate result is: the Convention contains no specific express language dealing with the issue in Part V on the EEZ. This, however, does not necessarily mean that the Convention is completely silent on the topic; the structure, context and the drafting history apparently embody a compromised position. As Tommy Koh has noted, the strongly held initial views on either end did not succeed; it is the middle ground that has carried the day.[4] The real task is then to find out the meaning of this middle ground position.

5. The debate seems to centre on several questions:

(1) The first is whether or not the military activities in question constitute, under Article 58(1) of the Convention, (a) freedom of navigation or another lawful use of the seas or (b) an adjunct to (a) so that there is an implied right (flowing from (a)) to conduct the activities. In the latter situation, the freedom of navigation may imply the right to map out the sea lanes so as to ensure safety in navigation or in the exercise of another right. This latter interpretation may lead to different results for oceanographic surveys, military surveys, or air surveillance.

(2) The second is whether the relevant military activities, whether they constitute navigation or another lawful use of the sea or its adjunct, are of a peaceful nature so that the "peaceful purposes" limitation on the freedom of navigation, etc., incorporated under Article 58(2) of the Convention, is respected.

(3) The third is (a) whether "rights and duties of the coastal State" that

---

Sea (3d ed. 1999), 421-432.

4 See comments by Tommy T.B. Koh and others, quoted and described in Zhang, n.2 above, para.6.

States, in exercising their rights and performing their duties in the EEZ, shall have "due regard" to, under Article 58(3), refer to only the so-called "EEZ resource rights and duties" or also other applicable rights and duties such as the security interest, in particular, of the costal State, and (b) how this "due regard" limitation on the activities of the States other than the coastal State can be respected.

(4) The fourth is how the existence and application of the balancing framework dealing with residual rights under Article 59 of the Convention may affect the debate.

(5) The fifth question is whether the military activities in question constitute marine scientific research, which is subject to a clear regime under the Convention.

6. These issues are addressed in the two articles presented in the above-mentioned issue of the *Journal*. In the following discussion, I will touch upon only some issues, not all of them.

7. As there is uncertainty in the text of the Convention, we have a tough task of interpretation. Taking account of the entirety of the text, context, object and purpose as well as the drafting history of the relevant provisions, we may be drawn to the conclusion that the existence of the balancing framework regarding residual rights in Article 59[5] seems to favour the view that, in addition to resource rights, some other rights are envisioned. According to Satya N. Nandan and Shabtai Rosenne, during the drafting process, Singapore proposed deleting the draft language providing for this framework, describing it as "unnecessary if the Convention clearly gives only resource jurisdiction to coastal States".[6] The fact that the diplomatic conference thought it necessary to retain

---

5 LOS Convention, art. 59, Basis for the Resolution of Conflicts regarding the Attribution of Rights and Jurisdiction in the Exclusive Economic Zone, states: "In cases where this Convention does not attribute rights or jurisdiction to the coastal State or to other States within the exclusive economic zone, and a conflict arises between the interests of the coastal State and any other State or States, the conflict should be resolved on the basis of equity and in the light of all the relevant circumstances, taking into account the respective importance of the interests involved to the parties as well as to the international community as a whole."

6 As quoted in Satya N. Nandan and Shabtai Rosenne (vol. eds), 2 United Nations Convention on the Law of the Sea 1982: A Commentary (2002), 568, para.59.3.

this framework in the Convention shows that other rights may be envisioned. To the extent that the drafters could not agree on any specific language to deal with a particular right, that right may be envisioned as a residual right, and Article 59 is probably what the drafters could muster to tip the balance in favour of the possibility of finding such a right, although the application of the framework may be informed by a consideration of other factors such as equity and the relative importance of the rights involved to the parties.

8. As a result, this framework appears to favour the view that the security interest of the coastal State is envisioned under the provisions on the EEZ. If the fight since the beginning of the drafting process between the maritime powers and the group of developing States regarding the security interest of the coastal State did not result in any specific express language on the point, the framework as interpreted above seems to contain the wherewithal to deal with such an interest and militate in favour of the coastal State, because of the importance of security interest in the light of the proximity of the zone of activities to the coastal State.

9. Indeed, if the security interest of the coastal State cannot be guaranteed, so that the life of that State cannot be maintained, what is the point of having all the rights to the resources in the EEZ anyway? Accordingly, the security interest of the coastal State is an issue of inherent primal importance and must be given paramount consideration. The EEZ resource rights presume the existence of the coastal State and its ability to safeguard its security interest. Perhaps this reasoning alone justifies the finding of a security interest on the part of the coastal State.

10. The factual and operational nature or characteristics of the military activities in question are of great importance to the debate. These activities have been described in various ways. To some, such activities are oceanographic survey; to others, they are spying activities. In our high-tech age, one man's survey may be another's war preparation.[*]

11. Often the United States claims that its military activities are non-threatening. However, as pointed out in Zhang's paper, veterans in military services have recognized that some of such activities are not always so.[7] This

---

[*] Postscript: after this paper was published, Paragraph 10 was quoted in James W. Houck (USN Vice Admiral), Alone on a Wide Wide Sea: A National Security Rationale for Joining the Law of the Sea Convention, 1 Penn State Journal of Law & International Affairs (2012), 1, 9-10 n.50.

[7] See comments by Sam Bateman, as quoted in Zhang, n.2 above, para.40.

point may have a whole host of implications on the debate. Sometimes whether such activities are "hostile" may be an issue but of course hostile acts as a trigger for self-defense or similar response seems to be a different matter.

12. The Convention does not define "peaceful purposes". One may then resort to perhaps an analogy, as an inspiration from the context, to the innocent passage regime detailed in other parts of the Convention[8] or to customary international law. If the military activities in question are "threatening" to the coastal State, it would be impossible for the State conducting the military activities to respect the "peaceful purposes" limitation. The same impossibility would obtain regarding the "due regard" limitation.

13. Even if there are "non-threatening" intelligence activities surrounding and against a coastal State, or specifically targeting it, as claimed, such activities still may be unlawful. The question is whether such intelligence activities can be deemed inherently hostile to the security interest of the coastal State, so as to make it impossible or difficult for the State conducting the intelligence activities to respect either the "peaceful purposes" limitation or the "due regard" limitation.

14. In the light of the uncertainty, if any, in this area, and of the need for a major maritime power to project itself in the world, as far as possible, it may be in the best interest of that power to be assured of the safety of the unobstructed "great highway" that the oceans are,[9] so as to ensure the strategic advantages that only navies may bring because of their local availability and local readiness while uncommitted.[10] Such advantages are important for both the maritime power and the world at large, whether that power assumes the role of a normal State pursuing self-interest or that of a world leader in helping to secure the international system as a whole.[11] Such advantages are necessary, for

---

8 Professor Liu Nanlai has made this argument in various seminars.

9 Alfred Thayer Mahan, The Influence of Sea Power upon History: 1660-1783 (1890), 25.

10 See D.P. O'Connell, The Influence of Law on Sea Power (1975), 3 ("Navies alone afford governments the means of exerting pressures more vigorous than diplomacy and less dangerous and unpredictable in its results than other forms of force, because the freedom of the seas makes them locally available while leaving them uncommitted.").

11 On the roles of a State, see Sienho Yee, Towards a Harmonious World: The Roles of the International Law of Co-progressiveness and Leader States, 7 Chinese JIL (2008), 99-105; Richard Zoellick, "Whither China: From Membership to Responsibility?": Remarks to National Committee on U.S.-

example, for fighting piracy and terrorism and safeguarding peace and security.

15. In order for the major maritime powers to reap the benefits of such advantages, their navies must be able to ensure that the great highway be safe for travel. This may require that the necessary oceanographic mapping be done in advance. If such mapping is considered subject to the unilateral consent, which necessarily includes the possibility of disapproval, of the coastal State, this goal may not be achieved. So it seems that the pure form of oceanographic sea lane mapping that is not prejudicial to the security interest of the coastal State may have to be given a unique consideration, if necessary. For lack of technical expertise, I am not certain whether this type of mapping can be done without sending ships to the area in issue, although it seems that "sea lane mapping by air" is not necessary. Nor am I certain whether a distinction between different kinds of survey can be made or observed technically and honestly. Finally, one can imagine that the "pure" mapping can be done by a military for profit. In that case, a resource is being exploited and such mapping should be subject to the approval of the coastal State.

16. China at the moment is busy with its surrounding areas and thus may not necessarily wish to have the local availability and local readiness of its navy at various places in the world. The difficulty in coordinating its activities in rescuing its nationals around Somalia recently should be a good warning on this point. If at present it does not promote the formation of the rules of law in the right direction, China may find itself in a straightjacket that it has helped to make but from which it cannot free itself, when it finally needs and wants the local availability and readiness of its navy around the world to protect its own national interest or to promote international peace and security.

17. In fact the changing world situation may require both China and the United States to have their navies locally available and locally ready around the globe, separately and/or together. Even together they might have difficulty dealing with the adversities in the world. It is therefore in the best interest of them both to work out an agreement on the ways and means of securing unobstructed freedom of navigation.

18. The existing 1998 agreement between China and the United States

---

China Relations, New York City, September 21, 2005 (www.ncuscr.org/files/2005Gala_RobertZoellick_Whither_China1.pdf); Sienho Yee, Sovereign Equality of States and the Legitimacy of "Leader States", in: Ronald St. John Macdonald and Douglas M. Johnston (eds.), Towards World Constitutionalism (2005), 737-772.

mentioned by Pedrozo does not contain anything specific on the issue under discussion, while providing for a general consultation framework.[12]

19. Pedrozo's comments do not seem to augur well for any formal agreement between the United States and China on this particular topic. The inability to conclude an agreement may lead to a vigorous and contentious, if only of low intensity militarily, customary international law formation process.[13] Such a process may result in some rules that may put both China and the United States in some kind of unenviable position in the future, to the extent that credibility is of value.

20. For the good of both parties, one should consider the earlier practice of "low-level notification" of the passage of warships through the territorial sea, before the 1982 Convention was adopted, as a way to deal with the ambiguity surrounding the need for previous authorization for such passage under the 1958 Geneva Convention on the Territorial Sea and the Contiguous Zone.[14] D.P. O'Connell related this practice to us as follows:

> The Western naval Powers have met the demands for previous authorisation for passage in the coolest possible manner. Where it was unnecessary to transit the territorial sea they have not bothered to do so, therefore preventing the issue from arising. Where they have found it necessary, mainly in the sea lanes of Indonesia and the Philippines, they handled the matter by diplomatic modalities, which again have kept the problem confined to the theoretical. Whereas previous authorisation has been required in principle, the demand has in practice been satisfied by

---

12 Pedrozo, n.1 above, para.35 (Agreement between the Department of Defense of the United States of America and the Ministry of National Defense of the People's Republic of China on Establishing a Consultation Mechanism to Strengthen Military Maritime Safety).

13 On this and related issues, see Bing Bing Jia, The Relations between Treaties and Custom, 9 Chinese JIL (2010), 81-109; Y. St-Fleur, Aerial Belligerency within a Humanitarian Rhetoric: Exploring the Theorizing of the Law of War/Terrorizing of Civilians' Rights Nexus, 8 Chinese JIL (2009) 347, 356-358.

14 The dispute seems to be whether the power to regulate the passage of warships means the power to *completely* exclude warships. Art. 23 of the 1958 Convention states: "If any warship does not comply with the regulations of the coastal State concerning passage through the territorial sea and disregards any request for compliance which is made to it, the coastal State may require the warship to leave the territorial sea."

> notification 'at a low level', which means the naval attaché telephoning a lieutenant-commander at the local Navy Office to say, 'Oh, by the way, H.M.S. So-and-so will be passing ...' and giving details. On the whole, most coastal states have been cautious about striking attitudes on the question, and those that have, [...] have been loftily ignored by others. After all, even a half a dozen swallows do not make a summer.[15]

21. Perhaps the United States and China can draw inspiration from this practice arising from activities in the territorial sea and perhaps straits for dealing with their disputes regarding activities in the EEZ at present and await a propitious time for the making of the proper rules for the EEZ that would be favourable to both of them and to the freedom of navigation throughout the oceans.

Postscript

23. The mass media reported recently that during the 2014 RIMPAC naval exercises China provided "participation plus". The "plus" has been variously described or understood as sending vessels for *general surveillance purposes* together with normal exercise vessels or sending them just to monitor *the exercises* only. This was even welcome by some United States military leaders. Furthermore, China said that it asked the United States to reduce or, better yet, to halt its surveillance of China, without demanding complete elimination of surveillance. It was also reported that the United States claimed that China's lack of transparency on military matters justifies its surveillance activities. This is an admission that its surveillance has not been conducted as an adjunct to the exercise of navigational freedom. In any event, these materials[16] would provide fertile ground for further research and reformulation of the various positions.

---

15 D.P. O'Connell, n.10 above, 140.

16 See generally reports in Global Times, 21 Jul. 2014; Star & Stripe, 29 Jul. 2014; news conf. at the Chinese Ministry of Defense, Jul.31, 2014; China's military secrecy justifies surveillance flights: U.S. official, Reuters, 12 Sept. 2014, http://www.reuters.com/assets/print?aid=USKBN0H72KN20140912; Erik Slavin, Chinese ship spies on Valiant Shield—and that's OK with US, Star and Stripe, 22 Sept. 2014, http://www.stripes.com/news/pacific/chinese-ship-spies-on-valiant-shield-and-that-s-ok-with-us-1.304288.

Chapter 11

Sustainable Development, International Law and China*

It is a pleasure to be invited to give a lunch presentation on The Hague Day at the Dutch Pavilion at the Shanghai World Expo. The topic given to me for my speech today is: "Sustainable development, international law, and the People's Republic of China". I understand that this would require me to outline the idea of sustainable development, its status in international law or the role of international law in promoting it, and relationship between China and sustainable development.

Let me first briefly outline what I consider to be the idea of sustainable development. The Brundtland Commission probably has given the most often-quoted definition of that idea. It defines sustainable development as development that "meets the needs of the present without compromising the ability of future generations to meet their own needs."[1] In the *Gabčíkovo-Nagymaros* case, the International Court of Justice (ICJ) stated "[t]his need to reconcile economic development with protection of the environment is aptly expressed in the concept of sustainable development".[2] In the *Pulp Mills* case, the ICJ had the occasion to comment on "the balance between economic development and environmental protection that is the essence of sustainable

---

* This is more or less the text of the keynote speech delivered on 1 June 2010 at the seminar entitled "The Hague International City of Peace and Justice: International Law and Sustainable Development", hosted by The Hague and other entities at the Dutch Pavilion at the Shanghai World Expo. The websites were last accessed shortly before 1 June 2010 unless otherwise noted.

1 World Commission on Environment and Development, Our Common Future (1987), 43. The chair was Gro Harlem Brundtland, and the Commission is normally known as the Brundtland Commission.

2 Gabčíkovo-Nagymaros Project (Hungary/Slovakia), Judgment, ICJ Reports

development".[3]

The broader debate, however, envisions sustainable development as covering three or four policy areas. They are sometimes called "pillars" of sustainable development. The United Nations 2005 World Summit Outcome Document, in paragraph 48, speaks of the "integration of the three components of sustainable development—economic development, social development and environmental protection—as interdependent and mutually reinforcing pillars". Similarly, in 2002 the International Law Association at New Delhi:

> EXPRESSES the view that the objective of sustainable development involves a comprehensive and integrated approach to economic, social and political processes, which aims at the sustainable use of natural resources of the Earth and the protection of the environment on which nature and human life as well as social and economic development depend and which seeks to realize the right of all human beings to an adequate living standard on the basis of their active, free and meaningful participation in development and in the fair distribution of benefits resulting therefrom, with due regard to the needs and interests of future generations.[4]

However, the UNESCO Universal Declaration on Cultural Diversity[5] posits a fourth pillar or root of development, declaring in Article 3 that "Cultural diversity widens the range of options open to everyone; it is one of the roots of development, understood not simply in terms of economic growth, but also as a means to achieve a more satisfactory intellectual, emotional, moral and spiritual existence".

The International Law Association was of the opinion that the application, consolidation or further development of the following "principles of international law" would be instrumental in pursuing the objective of sustainable development in an effective way:

1997, 78, paras. 140-141.

3 Argentina v. Uruguay, ICJ Reports 2010, para. 177.

4 ILA Resolution 3/2002, ILA New Delhi Declaration on Principles of International Law Relating to Sustainable Development, preamble (third to the last para.), http://www.ila-hq.org/download.cfm/docid/65DD8DEF-E74D-4ED5-925EBC6D73F19C97.

5 http://unesdoc.unesco.org/images/0012/001271/127160m.pdf.

1. The duty of States to ensure sustainable use of natural resources;
2. The principle of equity and eradication of poverty;
3. The principle of common but differentiated responsibilities;
4. The principle of the precautionary approach to human health, natural resources and ecosystems;
5. The principle of public participation and access to information and justice;
6. The principle of good governance; and
7. The principle of integration and interrelationship, in particular in relation to human rights and social, economic and environmental objectives.

The status in international law of the concept of sustainable development and of these principles has been examined thoroughly by Nico Schrijver in his Hague Lectures,[6] which have been published separately as a book.[7] I will not go into the details on this issue. Suffice it to say that the concept of sustainable development has been widely recognized as part of customary international law and so have some of the principles described above, although the detailed operation of the concept and these associated principles may not be of a "hard and fast" nature but subject to flexible adaptation.

The detractors of the concept, however, point to its vagueness, its "softness", and its lack of practical utility. One may say these detractors may have been confused themselves about a need for absolute certainty and strict and uniform density in legal norms. For many years the International Court of Justice in maritime delimitation cases applied, without any difficulty, "equity principles", which can be considered similarly vague. And despite the beautiful essay by Prosper Weil decrying the relative normativity in international law,[8] relative density in such norms has been and will be a fact of life in international law and relations.[9] Last I heard, France has been reported to have changed its opposition to the concept of *jus cogens,* although it is not clear whether it would now support that concept. The story of this change of heart, when told, may be

---

6 Nico Schrijver, The evolution of sustainable development in international law: inception, meaning and status, 329 Recueil des cours (2008), 217-412.

7 Nico Schrijver, The evolution of sustainable development in international law: inception, meaning and status (Martinus Nijhoff, 2008, pocket book edn).

8 P. Weil, Towards Relative Normativity in International Law, 77 American JIL (1983), 413.

9 Sienho Yee, Towards an International Law of Co-progressiveness (2004), 8-9.

illuminating. As to the practical utility of the concept, the detractors are even more mistaken: they need only open their eyes and see the wind power turbines and the solar energy panels all over the world.

The critics of the concept of sustainable development are apparently oblivious to the substantial effect that it has wrought in our lives. Generally one can identify three possible effects (or kinds of effect; "effects" is used for convenience) that the idea of sustainable development and the associated principles may have.

The first effect can be called the "orientational effect". The concept of sustainable development is like a destination beacon for the night travelers. All our activities gravitate towards it. It orients our lives. The concerns for sustainable development are embedded in our psyche or our mindset. This no doubt generally influences us all in big as well as small ways. In mega project planning, sustainable development is part of the consideration. In small daily life situation, we are accustomed to the need for being environment-friendly. This effect is definitely not insignificant.

The second effect can be called the "concretizational effect", for want of a better phrase. The concept and its associated principles may be given more concrete expression and qualification in international law sources such as treaties and customary international law and, according to Judge Cançado Trindade,[10] general principles of law. More importantly, the concept and its associated principles are also given more concrete expression and qualification in national law, the field marshal of international law, as has been called by some scholars. Though not necessarily the concept of sustainable development as a whole, its concrete tenets are detailed as various requirements in international law and national law. These concrete expressions and qualifications are enforceable and are affecting our lives every day if not every minute. The effect of the national implementation of this concept and the associated principles should be similar to that of the implementation across the world of the law of the International Criminal Court under the principle complementarity and to that of the implantation across the world of the WTO law.

The third effect is what has been called "action forcing effect". Some principles relating to sustainable development, such as the principles of prevention and the requirement of environmental assessment, are important because they force decision-makers to take actions, before undertaking projects

---

10 See his separate opinion in Pulp Mills, ICJ Reports 2010, 135.

with significant potential impacts, to ensure that the optimal course of action will be taken. They can be considered mechanisms to ensure the best quality in decision-making. The "mother" of these mechanisms, which has now been followed around the world one way or another, is the "environmental impact statement", an idea originated by Lynton Caldwell, an Indiana University professor. That occurred during the debate that preceded the enactment of the National Environmental Policy Act (NEPA). What federal agencies should do before authorizing a project was a key component in that debate. One requirement would be for the federal agencies to make a statement on the findings of environmental impact of a significant project. Daniel R. Mandelker observed[11]:

> The suggestion for including a "findings" requirement came from Professor Lynton Caldwell, an Indiana University professor, in testimony in the Senate hearings. Caldwell viewed the findings requirement as the "action-forcing" component of NEPA, a phrase which has survived in NEPA terminology. Caldwell stated:
>
>> I would urge that in the shaping of such a policy, it have an action-forcing, operational aspect. When we think of policy we ought to think of a statement which is so written that it is capable of implementation; that it is not merely a statement of undesirable goals or objectives; but that it is a statement which will compel or reinforce or assist … the kind of action which will protect and reinforce what I have called the life support system of the country.[12]

Such action forcing mechanisms may not lead us to our goals in one scoop; they at least force us to deliberate to our best and to improve the decision-making at least in an incremental way. This is important as it happens before a project is finally authorized.

Of course, despite these good effects that sustainable development and its associated principles may have, sustainable development has not been

---

11 Daniel R. Mandelker, NEPA Law and Litig., §2:2 (2009; 2d ed. 2013)(on Westlaw).

12 Ibid., quoting Hearings on S. 1075, S. 237 & S. 1752 before the Senate Committee on Interior & Insular Affairs, 91st Cong., 1st Sess. (1969), 116.

achieved yet. The reasons for this state of affairs are manifold. I cannot detail them here now, but I believe these are important:

1. The irrational use of resources has not been tamed—for example, the World Expo here in Shanghai, with many buildings to be torn down shortly after the close of the Expo, is not necessarily a model of rational use of resources.
2. The accumulated problems have been too overwhelming.
3. Those responsible for the accumulated problems have not had the courage to own up to their deeds and discharge their responsibility.
4. The aid promised for the developing countries in terms of direct aid or technology transfer is too slow in coming to fruition, and may be considered "too little, too late".

Given the limited time allowed for my speech, I cannot go into the details of these issues, but allow me to give you some observations on the characterization of the responsibility for the accumulated problems. In my view, the term "historical responsibility" is not accurate and is not conducive to promoting sustainable development. The better phrase is "accumulated responsibility".

So what is in the name? As already noted,[13] *pace* Shakespeare, a proper term is important. As Confucius cautions us that,[14] an improper name confuses the ear and confounds the eye, particularly those who are at their first exposure to international law. A proper characterization of the responsibility involved may help to persuade those responsible to own up to their conduct and their responsibility. "Historical responsibility" is static. It appears so distant. It may signal that the current generation has nothing to do with it. They may say, our grandfathers, and great grandfathers may have done it but that's not our fault. We are our own moral agents, not our forebears'. On the other hand, "accumulated responsibility" is dynamic. It is in both past and present tenses. It more accurately describes the current and existing responsibility of the responsible emitters of pollution since the very first act. It will reveal the close connection between the activities of responsible States and the current and existing pollution that they have generated, not something in the distant past. A State or entity with a continuing life obviously cannot escape from accumulated

---

13 See Chapter 2 above, 34.

14 Confucius, Lunyu, Zilu.

responsibility. A State or an entity or even a natural person currently in existence, but not having been in continuing existence since the very first act resulting in damage, could not escape from the accumulated responsibility resulting from the line of succession because the current State, entity or person cannot benefit unjustly from the damaging acts of the predecessor in the relevant line of succession. This formulation thus may have a better chance to persuade these States to appreciate their responsibility and to acknowledge and discharge it.

One would hope that such a distinction is more significant to the lay person than to the professionals including the scientists who are supposed to go through the surface to get to the essence of things. However, according to several leading scientists, this distinction is also lost to some extent on the Climate Change Negotiators who may have a static calculation of the situation in a future point of time. They argued for a dynamic calculation, saying that "current emission trends are incompatible with the goal of limiting cumulative emissions to a level that provides an acceptably low risk of dangerous climate change" and that "in devising emission targets for 2020 and 2050, governments need to be aware of their implications for cumulative emissions".[15]

If the idea of accumulated responsibility is accepted, the common but differentiated responsibility principle may appear more reasonable to us. This principle recognizes that those who can may be required to do more and those developed countries that have taken advantage of natural resources in the past may be required to refrain from certain acts to a greater extent than are the less developed States. "Historical responsibility" is usually said to underlie that principle. However, "accumulated responsibility" would seem to be a better foundation for it. Recognized and demanded is not just moral retribution for the sake of making amends to past wrongs but also concrete, direct and proportionate remedial action to cure past and existing wrongs. The "doing a good deed" part of that principle would be reduced; direct responsibility will receive its due airing. After all, it is common knowledge that the total accumulated emissions of CO_2 from the developing countries are small compared to those from the developed countries.

---

15 Oxford news item, Scientists call for limits on cumulative emissions of carbon dioxide, 10 June 2009 (http://www.ox.ac.uk/media/news_releases_for_journalists/090610_1.html), attaching their Open Letter to the Negotiators of the UNFCCC: The need to limit cumulative carbon dioxide emissions to avoid dangerous climate change.

Now I come to the relationship between sustainable development and China.

It is fair to say that China has placed great emphasis on sustainable development. We sent our premier to attend the Rio Earth Summit. Pursuant to China's views and positions expressed in Rio in 1992 and elsewhere, China adopted in 1994 China's Agenda 21[16] and subsequently a document titled China's Agenda 21 Priority Projects.[17] In 2003, another instrument called China's Action Plan for Sustainable Development at the Beginning of the 21st Century[18] was adopted. In July 2003, the Secretary-General of the Communist Party and President of China, Mr. Hu Jintao, propounded in a speech the idea of "scientific outlook on development" (科学发展观), which is a view of "comprehensively coordinated sustainable development" based on "human-centrality". The English rendition of the concept—"scientific outlook on development"—is borrowed from others, although in my view it can be put more simply as "rational development". This subsequently has been incorporated into the Constitution of the Communist Party of China at the 17th Plenum of the Party.[19] Various government white papers have been issued on sustainable development. A national legislation on environmental impact assessment has been adopted. The Ministry of Environmental Protection has been given teeth. Recently the government has been strongly promoting the development of clean energy in China, an area in which China shows the promise of becoming a leader. China is also actively seeking international cooperation in promoting sustainable development and its weight is being felt most strongly in Copenhagen last year.

As with other issues, it is not possible for me to review in any detail all these documents or instruments as well as China's conduct here. Allow me however to offer some generalized comments. As usual, generalized comments are to be considered with the usual perils of such comments in mind. From the above mentioned materials one can observe the following:

1. China takes a broader vision of sustainable development.

---

16 中国21世纪议程(http://www.acca21.org.cn/english/index.html).

17 中国21世纪议程优先项目计划(http://www.acca21.org.cn/english/index. html).

18 中国21世纪初可持续发展行动纲要 (http://www.acca21.org.cn/english/index.html).

19 Constitution of the Communist Party of China, General Principles (http://www.gov.cn/jrzg/2007-10/25/content_786434.htm), partially revised at the 17th Plenum, adopted on 21 Oct. 2007.

2. China takes seriously its responsibility towards its own large population.
3. China prioritizes development, ahead of sustainable development, that is to say, as stated in China's Agenda 21, "without development, there cannot be sustainable development to talk about".
4. China places social development or a harmonious society at the core of its development.
5. China is reluctant to accept any strict quota or limitations on its right to development.
6. China is banking on the development of technology to give a boost to sustainable development.
7. China supports the common and but differentiated responsibility principle.
8. China actively seeks international cooperation on sustainable development including issues relating to climate change.

While these positions are generally unchallengeable, except putting development ahead of sustainable development, the current situation in China is not yet a happy one. It is normal for one to see: people walking shoulder to shoulder in the streets, traffic jam lasting for a long time, heavy smoke from the chimneys, and dust raining down on Beijing. Above all, clear sky, not to mention blue sky, is a rare commodity.

This is not surprising when we take a look at the numbers. According to Zhang Hui,[20] since 1949, China's GDP has increased by 10 times, but its consumption of mineral sources has by 40 times. In 2003, China consumed resources of the world in several categories to the tune of 7.4%, 31%, 27%, 25%, and 40%, but the GDP took up only 4% of that of the world. These numbers say it all.

This result is probably no surprise when for many years our guiding doctrine is "fast and good quality development" ("you kuai you hao de fazhan", with the implication that speed may trump quality), which has only recently been changed to "good quality and fast development" ("you hao you kuai de fazhan", with the implication that quality takes priority over speed).[21] I hope

20 ZHANG Hui, Kechixu fazhanguan, Zhongguo de SEA jinzhan ji anli, 2 (Lecture posted at a World Bank site: info.worldbank.org/etools/docs/library/211095/ZhangHuiSEA.pdf) (documented created 2006; visited 20100601).

21 About the move from "又快又好的发展" to "又好又快的发展", see

that such a change of our doctrine will in fact change the orientation of our activities and help to improve the situation, not to prove again that we are good at cooking up slogans for propaganda only.

Clearly there are many challenges for China in the area of sustainable development. Let me offer a few points for consideration:

First of all, China must improve the enforcement of its laws and policies relating to sustainable development. China does not lack nice laws and policies, on the books at least. But its record of enforcement is very poor.

Second, China must wage a movement for sophistication and for efficiency in the use of resources. In the rough and tumble world of fast development, a lot of things are done without any concern for quality. Worse yet, they may be done with a view to drumming up the GDP data. People simply want to get the task finished. This situation results in serious irrational use of resources. For example, the houses built in China have only an average expected life of about 35 years, according to the widely reported views. Soon the same construction boom and the consumption of resources will have to restart, threatening to become an unending cycle. This situation is disastrous as far as sustainable development is concerned. I understand that there is some urgency to build as many houses for as many people as possible, but I wonder whether other formulation of the policy can be hammered out so as to assure an optimal balance between quantity and quality as well as sustainable development.

Third, China's push for better technology for clean energy and for development generally is laudable and should be sped up. However, a comprehensive and integral approach to development should be adopted, including paying attention to small step solutions, rather than completely banking on big technology. For example, it is mind-boggling to see that whenever people think of a square, they think of a square paved with concrete blocks, and they build it up that way. As a result, the temperature around the square will be observably higher than elsewhere; the baking sun gets more unrelenting there, of course. This may also have some impact on local dust formation. If one such square does not matter, if every square in China is built that way, one can imagine what effect squares will have on the cities in China. In environment-friendly places, people think of a square as a place covered with grass and trees and they build them up that way. One need only take a look at Boston Commons or the Mall in Washington, DC. One wonders whether this

---

http://bkso.baidu.com/view/3153709.htm.

is really an issue of habit of the mind. Is it possible that local city planners are simply not aware of such matters and design squares with a closed mind? How nice it would be if architectural or city planning agencies simply could be told that no more squares can be built with concrete blocks! Of course, it will take more time and great costs to build such environment-friendly squares, which a political leader anxious for promotion and thus needing visible records of fast achievement cannot afford. We are then back to the issue of what constitutes the optimal balance between sustainable development and other things.

Fourth, China must pay more attention to social problems. According to the mass media, there are serious social problems facing China, including suicides, mental illnesses, and other issues. The recent spate of violent attacks on schools and the various violent protests may be signs of spiraling violence yet to come. The rough and tumble world of development apparently has eroded the fabric of the family and the society to a substantial extent. The disparity between the rich and the poor has led to anger among the latter. If this trend is not reversed or at least arrested, the society may become unsustainable.

Fifth, in the international area, as a result of size and bulk, in terms of population and economy, China must take up the responsibility of a leader on the world stage. Currently our leaders have said, "We will discharge our responsibility" and we will be a responsible big State. In my view, that is not yet sufficient. China must do more to help shape the direction of the world, and not stop at the receiving end of responsibility. Although we can understand that China may not want to advertise itself as a leader State, it must think and act as a leader State. Previously I have proposed the idea of leader States and I shall not repeat that effort here, but the idea is that in addition to making substantial contribution to the international system, a leader State helps formulate a better vision of the future and leads, by exemplary conduct, the world in the direction of realizing that vision.[22] In several areas including in international negotiations on climate change, China may have its weight felt, but the bigger challenge is to secure agreement for sustainable development, not to forestall consensus. China of course is leading the charge in promoting the concept of differentiated responsibility. Now it has made a specific promise for voluntary reduction in carbon density. The beauty of this measurement is that it would require, in the opposite direction, an increase in the density of and, more importantly,

---

22 See Sienho Yee, Sovereign Equality of States and the Legitimacy of "Leader States", in: Ronald St. John Macdonald and Douglas M. Johnston (eds.), Towards World Constitutionalism (2005), 737-772 (Chapter 8 above).

efficiency in the efforts to combat carbon emission, without necessarily arresting development. If such voluntary action example can be followed by everyone in the world, the impact will be dramatic too. Perhaps in this way China can be a leader.

Recently China has put forward the idea of a Harmonious World. We shall see whether that concept will help to improve the world and to put it on a course for sustainable development.[23]

Postscript

Not long after the speech was delivered, the data that became publicly available show that China's contribution to the recent growth of the world economy had been greater than the figure given earlier,[24] and the cost to China had also been much greater. Soon after that the smog that engulfed a big part of China now and then and the PM2.5 meters going off in Beijing again and again became regular news items in China. Ultimately the government decided to earmark a huge amount of funding for fighting against the smog and air pollution generally in China. Had the development not been carried out at such a breakneck pace, the cost probably would not have been so huge.[25] Yet one does see a ray of hope, as it seems that the balance between sustainable development and other things is now being recalibrated. Thus, one can see optimistic headlines such as this one from Reuters on 15 March 2014: "China set to elevate environment over development in new law".[26] Whether or not we have found, or can find at all, the *optimal* balance, however, is another matter. Maybe it is and will be just our perpetual pursuit.

---

23 See Sienho Yee, Towards a Harmonious World: The Roles of the International Law of Co-progressiveness and Leader States, 7 Chinese JIL (2008), 99-105 (Chapter 9 above).

24 See above n.20 and accompanying paragraph.

25 Glimpses of this are here: Beijing plans to spend CNY 760 billions to fight smog (http://news.sciencenet.cn/htmlnews/2014/3/290113.shtm); China vows to clean up 60 percent of cities by 2020 (http://www.reuters.com/article/2014/03/17/us-china-pollution-idUSBREA 2G06V20140317).

26 Reuters news report (http://www.reuters.com/article/2014/04/15/us-china-environment-idUSBREA3E02H20140415).

Chapter 12

The Dynamic Interplay between the Interpreters of Security Council Resolutions*

1. In the advisory opinion on *Accordance with International Law of the Unilateral Declaration of Independence in Respect of Kosovo* (the "*Kosovo* advisory opinion"), the International Court of Justice described in general terms its approach to the interpretation of UN Security Council resolutions as follows:

> 94. Before continuing further, the Court must recall several factors relevant in the interpretation of resolutions of the Security Council. While the rules on treaty interpretation embodied in Articles 31 and 32 of the Vienna Convention on the Law of Treaties may provide guidance, differences between Security Council resolutions and treaties mean that the interpretation of Security Council resolutions also require that other factors be taken into account. Security Council resolutions are issued by a single, collective body and are drafted through a very different process than that used for the conclusion of a treaty. Security Council resolutions

---

* First published in 11 Chinese Journal of International Law (2012), 613-622. I realize that it might be better to limit the consideration here to only the major interpreters of Security Council resolutions but that classification can be difficult. I am content that the readers will understand that we are dealing with interpreters of some importance. This comment was completed on 15 December 2012 and the websites cited were current as of this date.

The original version contains this abstract: "This editorial comment calls for (1) greater attention to the dynamic interplay between the interpreters of a Security Council resolution and those of a possible future resolution and its negative effect on the ground in peacekeeping operations, (2) abandoning the expansionist interpretation of Security Council resolutions, and (3) putting on hold any political or ideological differences and favoring the inclusion in a resolution of language that would tend to promote the protection of civilians."

> are the product of a voting process as provided for in Article 27 of the Charter, and the final text of such resolutions represents the view of the Security Council as a body. Moreover, Security Council resolutions can be binding on all Member States (*Legal Consequences for States of the Continued Presence of South Africa in Namibia (South West Africa) notwithstanding Security Council Resolution 276 (1970), Advisory Opinion, I.C.J. Reports 1971*, p. 54, para. 116), irrespective of whether they played any part in their formulation. The interpretation of Security Council resolutions may require the Court to analyse statements by representatives of members of the Security Council made at the time of their adoption, other resolutions of the Security Council on the same issue, as well as the subsequent practice of relevant United Nations organs and of States affected by those given resolutions.[1]

2. In an earlier commentary in December 2010 on the *Kosovo* advisory opinion,[2] I observed that the Court's approach was propounded in majestic generality and is destined to be cited frequently but argued that the interpretive operation in that advisory opinion itself may have over-played the autonomous or self-contained nature of the resolution and paid insufficient attention to its context and the understandings of the other parties which may have informed the intent of the Council. I claimed that these factors were particularly important when a resolution also may function as a sort of agreement or incorporate one, settling a dispute or bringing peace with a party involved, which in my view was the case with resolution 1244. In the *Kosovo* advisory opinion, the intent of the Federal Republic of Yugoslavia ("FRY"), now Serbia, whose acceptance of the

---

1 Accordance with International Law of the Unilateral Declaration of Independence in Respect of Kosovo, Advisory Opinion, ICJ Reports 2010, 404, 442. The Court further recalled its previous statement in Namibia: "The language of a resolution of the Security Council should be carefully analysed before a conclusion can be made as to its binding effect. In view of the nature of the powers under Article 25, the question whether they have been in fact exercised is to be determined in each case, having regard to the terms of the resolution to be interpreted, the discussions leading to it, the Charter provisions invoked and, in general, all circumstances that might assist in determining the legal consequences of the resolution of the Security Council." Ibid., para. 117, quoting from ICJ Reports 1971, 53, para. 114.

2 Sienho Yee, Notes on the International Court of Justice (Part 4): The *Kosovo* Advisory Opinion, 9 Chinese JIL (2010), 763, 772-773 (Chapter 3 above).

peace plan regarding Kosovo was noted by the Security Council in the resolution, and of some members of the Council including veto-wielding permanent members, was not given much consideration; neither was FRY's understanding of the famous 10th preambular paragraph. Nor were the understandings of two permanent members of the Council[3] given meaningful attention. Rather, the famous 10th preambular paragraph which stated "[r]eaffirming the commitment of all Member States to the sovereignty and territorial integrity of the Federal Republic of Yugoslavia"[4] was paraphrased by the Court as simply "recalled the sovereignty and the territorial integrity of the Federal Republic of Yugoslavia".[5] Thus, "reaffirming the commitment of all Member States to" was treated as simply "recalled". After being so recalled, the famous preambular paragraph then seemed to have dropped out of sight in the rest of the Court's analysis. In an earlier part of the advisory opinion, the Court said "the principle of territorial integrity is confined to the sphere of relations between States".[6] One wonders whether that necessarily excludes a special meaning that may have accrued in the treatment of the experiences of internal strife since World War II. Without trying to get to the right answer because I am here only to lament at the lack of attention to the factors not meaningfully dealt with by the Court,[7] I believe it may be worth asking whether, against the background of the Kosovo matter, which presented itself as a case of *internal*

---

3 See CR 2009/29, 30 (Statement of China, para. 5); CR 2009/30, 44-50 (Statement of the Russian Federation, paras.26-54).

4 S/Res/1244 (1999), preamble, para.10.

5 Kosovo Advisory Opinion, n.1 above, 443, para.95.

6 Ibid., 437, para.80.

7 The implications of the appearance of the term "unity" or "national unity" in some resolutions before resolution 1244 (e.g., S/RES/498 (1981), para.2, on Lebanon; S/RES/1076 (1996), preamble, on Afghanistan), and some subsequent to the resolution but before the Kosovo advisory opinion was delivered (e.g., S/RES/1559 (2004), para.1, on Lebanon; S/RES/1595 (2005), preamble, on the assassination of Hariri), are not clear. The Court did not seem to deal with this issue in its advisory opinion. Since that time, the term "unity" has appeared, apparently with some added frequency, in the resolutions on Libya (e.g., S/RES/1973 (2011), preamble; S/RES/2009 (2011), preamble; S/RES/2016 (2011), preamble; S/RES/2017 (2011), preamble; S/RES/2022 (2011), preamble; S/RES/2040 (2012), preamble), Mali (e.g., S/RES/2056 (2012), S/RES/ 2071 (2012), preamble) and Syria (S/RES/2042 (2012), preamble; S/RES/2043 (2012), preamble). Does this added frequency reflect lessons learned from the Kosovo advisory opinion?

struggle and separatist secession, it was natural for the Security Council in this preambular paragraph to have in mind the need to guarantee or protect the FRY from *external* aggression, and whether it might be more reasonable to consider the famous preambular paragraph as envisioning territorial integrity as a "result commitment", irrespective of who would be attempting to ruin that integrity. If one were to answer these questions conscientiously, the view that resolution 1244 does not apply to the authors of the declaration of independence—whoever they may be—was not so persuasive.

3. Fearing unfavorable consequences from what I perceived to be the weakness in the Court's reasoning, I wondered:

> How would this affect future peacekeeping efforts of the Security Council? Will stakeholders be discouraged by the Court's interpretation of Security Council resolutions? At least in the future they will no doubt have to insist, through [their] own persuasion or a protector in the Security Council, on clearer language for any guarantees, rather than hoping that a brief preambular paragraph would come to their aid.[8]

4. This phenomenon can be called the dynamic interplay between the interpreters of Security Council resolutions, for want of a better phrase. Of course there is always an interplay between the interpreters of a particular resolution. What I have in mind here is the interplay between the interpreters of one resolution and those of another resolution or a possible or draft resolution in the future, as well as the interplay between (1) the interplay between interpreters of one resolution and (2) the interplay between the interpreters of another resolution or a possible or draft resolution in the future. In any event, the interpretation of a resolution by an authoritative or just important interpreter will have an impact on the future drafting and adoption of another resolution. The dynamic impact may have a dramatic negative effect on the ground in peace-keeping matters.

5. Unfortunately this fear seemed to have come true, all too soon, in the dynamic interplay between the interpreters of Security Council resolution 1973 (2011) on Libya and those of a possible resolution on the Syrian crisis. The excessively expansive interpretation of resolution 1973 championed by NATO members has the effect of preventing the Security Council from taking what many have considered desirable measures.

---

8 Yee, n.2 above, 775, para.32.

6. Setting up a regime of civilian protection in Libya, resolution 1973, adopted on 11 March 2011, in paragraph 4:

> *Authorizes* Member States that have notified the Secretary-General, acting nationally or through regional organizations or arrangements, and acting in cooperation with the Secretary-General, to take all necessary measures, notwithstanding paragraph 9 of resolution 1970 (2011), to protect civilians and civilian populated areas under threat of attack in the Libyan Arab Jamahiriya, including Benghazi, while excluding a foreign occupation force of any form on any part of Libyan territory, and *requests* the Member States concerned to inform the Secretary-General immediately of the measures they take pursuant to the authorization conferred by this paragraph which shall be immediately reported to the Security Council.[9]

Paragraphs 6-12 also set up a no-fly zone and paragraph 8 authorized "all necessary means" to enforce compliance.

7. Majestic phrases such as "take all necessary measures" obviously are susceptible of various interpretations.[10] According to the Institut de droit international[11] and some serious scholars,[12] resolutions on the authorization of use of force shall be interpreted strictly, with the implication that any ambiguity shall be resolved in favor of a narrow construction. This view is in some

---

9 S/RES/1973 (2011), para. 4.

10 Using such vague and undefined terms have been roundly condemned by a political philosopher in these terms: "To 'authorize' states to use 'all necessary measures' in the enforcement of a legally binding resolution is an invitation to an arbitrary and arrogant exercise of power, and makes the commitment of the United Nations Organization to the international rule of law void of any meaning." Memorandum by Hans Köchler, President of the International Progress Organization, on Security Council resolution 1973, http://i-p-o.org/IPO-Memorandum-UN-Libya-26Mar11.pdf. See also Edward McWhinney, A New, Multicultural World Community and an Emerging New, Pluralistic World Order System, 11 Chinese JIL (2012), 469, 482-485.

11 Institut de droit international, Resolution on the Authorization of the Use of Force by the United Nations (2011), Article 9, http://idi-iil.org/idiE/resolutionsE/2011_rhodes_10_%20D_en.pdf.

12 See, e.g., J.A. Frowein, Unilateral Interpretations of Security Council Resolutions: a Threat to Collective Security, in: V Götz et al, Liber Amicorum Günter Jaenicke zum 85. Geburtstag (1998), 97, 112.

contrast to the position on treaty interpretation taken in the Vienna Convention on the Law of Treaties. As is generally recognized, under the Convention the starting point is the intent of the parties and the best evidence of common intent is the specific language of a treaty, which is an instrument bearing the consensus of the parties. However, Frowein argued:

> It is quite different with Security Council resolutions, particularly from the point of view of the state against whom enforcement measures are being taken. Such a resolution is the legal basis for the most severe encroachment upon the sovereignty of a member of the United Nations. It is submitted, therefore, that for the interpretation of such a resolution the old rule according to which limitations of sovereignty may not be lightly assumed is fully justified. Only where the use of force against a sovereign state is clearly authorized by a resolution this is in fact lawful under United Nations law.[13]

Scholars also have noted the importance of building a majority in the Security Council including the permanent members.[14]

8. According to others, as recounted in a UK House of Commons briefing paper, however, this phrase was considered to have given "clearly a broad authorization"[15] and the paragraph was "a very broad provision". It thus may be given a broad interpretation so that the coalition forces were considered authorized to attack Libyan air defences right away, although the Qaddafi regime had immediately announced a ceasefire:

> It is possible that Qaddafi might have complied with the no-fly zone, but coalition planners may have come to the conclusion that he probably would not, and that the regime would prefer to bring down one coalition aircraft and then have its air defences destroyed than to have them destroyed immediately. The coalition therefore decided to act against Libyan air defences immediately, following the line suggested by the US defence secretary, Robert Gates.[16]

---

13 Ibid.

14 Ibid.

15 See, e.g., Ben Smith and Arabella Thorp, Interpretation of Security Council Resolution 1973 on Libya, UK House of Commons Library Briefing Paper SN/IA/5916, www.parliament.uk/briefing-papers/sn05916.pdf.

16 Ibid., 3.

Furthermore, the resolution was considered to have permitted attacking Libyan military assets even if they were not attacking civilians.[17] Some officials even did not exclude the possibility of targeting Gaddafi personally.[18] So on and so forth.

9. Such cavalier interpretation of resolution 1973 was of course surprising to some other members of the Security Council, including some permanent members. One can only wonder how the coalition leaders and their lawyers may be feeling when they saw their "ingenious" interpretation of resolution 1973 prevailed. The disappointment or even anger of the unhappy members of the Security Council was, however, evident in their public reactions to the coalition campaign. The coalition "military action interpretation" of the resolution, however, did not have a button for "reset" or re-interpretation. Nor is it subject to any review, judicial[19] or otherwise. The unhappy members of the Council were thus relegated to likening the action to a "medieval call for a crusade";[20] arguing that "[t]he U.N. resolution on the no-fly zone over Libya aimed to protect civilians. We oppose abuse of force causing more civilian casualties";[21] refusing to send soldiers to take part in the action;[22] or opposing a stronger role for the NATO in the action.[23] China subsequently also declared in an open Security Council meeting on Libya that it was "not in favor of arbitrary interpretation of UN resolutions".[24] Meanwhile, the "coalition" action went on and the rest is now history.

10. And the Libyan situation at present, one year and three quarters after the coalition campaign, is by no means satisfactory to the civilians—those that

---

17 Ibid., 3-4.

18 Ibid., 5.

19 On how potential judicial review, direct or indirect, may have a role to play in influencing the consideration of issues inside and outside the Security Council, see Dire Tladi and Gillian Taylor, On the Al Qaida/Taliban Sanctions Regime: Due Process and Sunsetting, 10 Chinese JIL (2011), 771.

20 Russian Prime Minister Vladimir Putin, as quoted in Smith and Thorp, n.15 above, 9.

21 Chinese Foreign Ministry spokeswoman, as quoted in ibid.

22 Ibid., describing German reaction.

23 Ibid., describing German, French and Turkish views.

24 China not in favor of arbitrary interpretation of UN resolutions on Libya: envoy (5 May 2011), http://news.xinhuanet.com/english2010/china/2011-05/05/c_13859189.htm.

Security Council resolution 1973 was adopted at the outset to protect—despite the formal end of military operations and the civil war.

11. The lessons learned by the unhappy members of the Security Council from the interplay between the interpreters of resolution 1973 on Libya then was promptly applied to the Security Council's consideration of the situation in Syria which has similarly been embroiled in turmoil since March 2011 as a result of the Arab Spring. This time some of the members that were angered by the cavalier interpretation of resolution 1973 were determined to ensure that no resolution with any troubling wording susceptible of similarly cavalier interpretation would be adopted. Thus, a draft resolution on Syria, submitted by France, Germany, Portugal and the United Kingdom of Great Britain and Northern Ireland was vetoed on 4 October 2011. After the vote, the representative of the Russian Federation said:

> Our proposals for wording on the non-acceptability of foreign military intervention were not taken into account, and, based on the well-known events in North Africa, that can only put us on our guard. Equally alarming is the weak wording in connection with the opposition and the lack of an appeal to them to distance themselves from extremists. Given the basis of statements by some Western politicians on President Al-Assad's loss of legitimacy, such an approach could trigger a full-fledged conflict in Syria and destabilization in the region as a whole. The collapse of Syria as a result of a civil war would have a very destructive impact on the situation in the entire Middle East.
>
> The situation in Syria cannot be considered in the Council separately from the Libyan experience. The international community is alarmed by statements that compliance with Security Council resolutions on Libya in the NATO interpretation is a model for the future actions of NATO in implementing the responsibility to protect. It is easy to see that today's "Unified Protector" model could happen in Syria. All present should understand that the Russian position regarding the conflict in Libya is in no way based on any kind of special ties with the Al-Qadhafi regime, especially since a number of States represented at this table had warmer relations with the Libyan Arab Jamahiriya.
>
> The people of Libya have spoken regarding Al-Qadhafi, and they have determined his fate. For us, Members of the United Nations, including in terms of a precedent, it is very important to know how the resolution was implemented and how a Security Council resolution

turned into its opposite.[25]

Subsequently Prime Minister Vladimir Putin similarly declared that "Learning from that bitter experience, we are against any U.N. Security Council resolutions that could be interpreted as a signal for military interference in domestic processes in Syria".[26]

12. The exercise of the veto power and these statements by the Russian representatives clearly drove the point home to us all. The interplay between the interpreters of resolution 1973 had a dramatic impact on the interplay between the interpreters of the draft resolution, or simply put, on the consideration of the draft resolution on Syria, so much so that it was vetoed. Playing fast and loose with the language of a Security Council resolution has its perils. The experience with resolution 1973 left so deep a scar that in April 2012, on adoption of resolution 2043 (2012), the representative of the Russian Federation returned to this theme again: "We now believe the main aim to be the unwavering and clear respect by all parties for the provisions of the resolution. Any deviation, whether from the resolution's provisions or in their interpretation, will be unacceptable. The Libyan model should remain forever in the past."[27]

---

25 S/PV.6627 (4 Oct. 2011), 4.

26 Putin Warns West Over Syria, Iran, AP News (27 Feb. 2012). Russia was not alone in expressing such concerns. In the General Assembly, Cuba criticized the "position assumed in recent months by some members of NATO on the Middle East, the unjustifiable bombings resulting from a manipulative interpretation of Security Council resolution 1973 (2011)" (A/66/PV.96 (13 Feb. 2012), 4). On another occasion, Grenada also made the same point: "Regarding draft resolution A/66/L.36, entitled 'The situation in the Syrian Arab Republic', Grenada places on record that it is our understanding that the draft resolution will do only what it says, namely, to provide diplomatic support to Syria, the Arab League and the Secretary-General in order to help the Government and people of Syria end all bloodshed and find an agreed solution to the internal situation. [...] Grenada understands that in and with this draft resolution, the General Assembly is not voting on or for a resolution that directly or indirectly or through interpretation or reinterpretation can be used as the basis for the removal of a Government, military intervention or other acts against the Charter of the United Nations in letter or in spirit. With that understanding, and naturally with a prayer and a hope, Grenada will vote for the draft resolution." A/66/PV.97 (16 Feb. 2012), 7.

27 S/PV.6756 (21 April 2012), 2.

13. If a different interpretation of resolution 1973 has been adopted by the relevant actors, would it have made a difference? As far as the protection of civilians was concerned, would it have made a *positive* difference? The fact that resolution 2043 was adopted in April 2012 seems to show that some kind of positive difference was possible. Whether stronger protection for civilians than that provided for in resolution 2043 (in, e.g., paragraph 2 could have been authorized), if a proper interpretation of resolution 1973 was applied, is not too difficult a question to answer. From this perspective, one cannot but call for abandoning the expansionist interpretation of Security Council resolutions.

14. One may say that the veto of the draft resolution on 4 October 2011 was the work of political and philosophical differences in the Security Council, primarily between the big powers. A closer examination of the records debunks this view. It is true that on the veto of the draft resolution, the French representative claimed that "This is not a matter of language, it is a political choice. It is a veto on principle, which means that it is a refusal of all Council resolutions against Syria. It shows disdain for the legitimate aspirations that have been so bravely expressed in Syria for the past five months. It is a rejection of this tremendous movement for freedom and democracy that is the Arab Spring."[28] The representative of the Russian Federation also recognized that "[i]t is clear that the result of today's vote reflects not so much a question of acceptability of wording as a conflict of political approaches", but he also made clear that "[t]hat is the only part of what was said by my French colleague with which I agree".[29] He recounted how Russia, together with China, drafted a resolution, which commanded the support of the BRICS countries, that reflected "the logic of respect for the national sovereignty and territorial integrity of Syria as well as the principle of non-intervention, including military, in its affairs; the principle of the unity of the Syrian people; refraining from confrontation; and inviting all to an even-handed and comprehensive dialogue aimed at achieving civil peace and national agreement by reforming the socioeconomic and political life of the country."[30] On the other hand, the draft resolution that was vetoed reflected the philosophy of "confrontation".[31] Most importantly he proceeded to point out, as quoted above, that "Our proposals for wording on the non-acceptability of foreign military intervention were not

---

28 S/PV.6627 (4 October 2011), 3.

29 Ibid.

30 Ibid.

31 Ibid.

taken into account, and, based on the well-known events in North Africa, that can only put us on our guard."[32] This shows that any clash of political or ideologies may have been subordinate to the reaction to the expansionist interpretation of resolution 1973.

15. To the extent that indeed there was a gulf between different political approaches or ideologies at the Security Council, one may ask why any such differences should not put on hold for the purposes of protecting civilians in internal strife. Furthermore, in this day and age when non-use-of-force, territorial integrity and political independence have been put on the pedestal called Article 2(4) of the UN Charter, why was it so difficult for some States to accept in a resolution language "on the non-acceptability of foreign military intervention"? The difficulty in accepting such language is even more difficult to understand against the background of an urgent need to take measures to protect civilians. If such language were considered unnecessary, it would not hurt the protection of civilians, either, and therefore could have been included, to err on the side of being over-innocuous. If one's goal was to provide protection for civilians, the cost of including some innocuous language would be a cost that one would gladly bear. Does this failure to include such language give one ground for putting one on one's guard, as the Russian representative said,[33] thus questioning the genuineness of the professed intent of those who refused such language to protect civilians and searching for any ulterior motive behind the draft resolution? In any event, faced with a humanitarian catastrophe and thus an urgent need to protect civilians, the relevant players in the international system must put on hold any political or ideological differences and favor the inclusion in a resolution of language that would tend to promote the protection of civilians.

---

32 Ibid., 4.

33 Ibid.

Chapter 13

En Route to the Final Shape of the UNCLOS Dispute Settlement System: Some Pivotal Negotiating Procedural Steps Worthy of Consideration by Future Treaty-makers and Leaders in Treaty-making*

I. Introduction

1. It is a great pleasure for me to contribute this paper on the birth of the dispute settlement system under the 1982 United Nations Convention on the Law of the Sea (UNCLOS or the Convention)[1] to the collection in honor of Professor Budislav Vukas, former Judge and Vice-President at the International Tribunal for the Law of the Sea (ITLOS) at the beginning of its life.

2. Described as a "constitution for the oceans"[2] by none other than Tommy Koh (Singapore) who, as President of the Third United Nations Conference on the Law of the Sea (UNCLOS III or the Conference) after the

---

* First published 13 Chinese JIL (2014), 185 and intended for inclusion in: Rüdiger Wolfrum, Maja Seršić and Trpimir M. Šošić (eds), Liber Amicorum Vukas (Martinus Nijhoff Publishers: Leiden, forthcoming 2014). The preparation of this paper benefited from the support from the Fundamental Research Funds for the Central Universities in China as well as Research Project No. 08&ZD055 of the China Social Sciences Foundation, all conducted at Wuhan University. This paper was completed on 30 November 2013. The websites cited were current as of that date.

1 For text and other materials, see http://www.un.org/Depts/los/convention_agreements/convention_overview_convention.htm.

2 Tommy T.B. Koh, A Constitution for the Oceans, in Myron H. Nordquist (ed.), 1 United Nations Convention on the Law of the Sea 1982: A Commentary (2002) ("Virginia Commentary"), 11-16.

presidency of H.S. Amerasinghe, skillfully brought the negotiations to a close, the UNCLOS contains 17 parts with 320 articles and 9 annexes, covering almost all important law of the sea issues. It is perilous for one to attempt to summarize the UNCLOS in short space. Perhaps we can say that the UNCLOS reflects (1) the reconciliation between seaward claims by the coastal States for resources and the landward claims by the international community for preserving as much as possible the international seabed for common benefit as the "common heritage of mankind"; (2) the associated impact on or attempt at the definition and delineation as well as delimitation if necessary, of the various maritime zones and activities within these zones, with navigational freedom considered the most important for the major maritime powers; and (3) the commitment that rights and benefits are to be enjoyed with the corresponding duties and obligations. Obviously disputes relating to all these issues are bound to arise and a system for the settlement of disputes is necessary for the UNCLOS to work and for the hard-won compromises to hold up.

3. As we know, the successful negotiation of the UNCLOS was no small feat. The successful negotiation of the UNCLOS dispute settlement system was probably a more important part of that achievement. One can imagine how difficult the negotiating process could be. That obviously cannot be treated in full here in limited space. Nor is a full treatment necessary, as there are a number of such works already published, including that by President Tommy Koh himself with his colleague Shanmugam Jayakumar.[3] What I intend to do here is to first outline the UNCLOS dispute settlement system and then summarize and comment on several of what I consider to be pivotal negotiating

---

3 On the UNCLOS negotiations generally, see Third UN Conf. on the Law of the Sea, 1973-82, Official Documents (UNCLOS III Official Documents) (http://legal.un.org/diplomaticconferences/lawofthesea-1982/lawofthesea-1982.html); Alan Beesley, The Negotiating Strategy of UNCLOS III: Developing and Developed Countries as Partners—A Pattern for Future Multilateral International Conferences?, 46 Law and Contemporary Problems (1983), 183-194; Myron H. Nordquist (ed.), 1 Virginia Commentary, n.2 above; Constantin A. Stavropoulos, Procedural Problems of the Third Conference on the Law of the Sea, ibid., lvii-lxv; Bernardo Zuleta, Introduction to the United Nations Convention on the Law of the Sea, ibid., 17; Tommy T.B. Koh and Shanmugam Jayakumar, Negotiating Process of the Third United Nations Conference on the Law of the Sea, ibid., 29-134; L.D.M. Nelson, The Work of the Drafting Committee, ibid., 135-152.

procedural steps en route to the final shape of the dispute settlement system.[4] These no doubt can offer inspiration to future negotiators, but they are usually scattered in various places; as Adede pointed out, "most of the substantive negotiations of the Convention were undertaken in informal meetings of the Conference Committees and special Negotiating Groups of which no formal records were produced".[5] My limited ambition here is to sweep all these together with some comments where appropriate so as to provide convenience to future treaty makers, especially those aspiring to be leaders in treaty-making, so that they will be able to quickly get a glimpse of what may help to pave the way for success in complicated negotiations even if not as difficult as those during the monumental UNCLOS III. Of course, what I consider pivotal will inevitably show my own reflection on this matter, albeit as an outsider. In doing so, I do not hope to be comprehensive because, not being present during the negotiations, I am handicapped to some extent.

4. These pivotal negotiating procedural steps include, for want of better phrasing, the following: (1) the package deal decision; (2) the consensus approach; (3) building consensus by privileging the best second choice; (4) building consensus by privileging the existing negotiating text through the rule of silence; and (5) failing consensus in the Negotiating Group, the Chairman presenting his own proposals as suggestions to the plenary. As we can see, the first set the overall goal of the Conference. The second specified the general method to achieve that goal. The last three were concrete steps to implement that method. I am calling these "procedural steps" rather than "decisions", because not all of them were formal decisions and because I am not certain about the provenance of some of them.

---

[4] On the negotiation of the UNCLOS dispute settlement system, see, e.g., 5 Virginia Commentary, n.2 above; 2 Virginia Commentary, n.2 above, 796-816; 945-985; 1000-1018; 6 Virginia Commentary, n.2 above, 595-644; Eero J. Manner, Settlement of Sea-Boundary Delimitation Disputes according to the Provisions of the 1982 Law of the Sea Convention, in Jerzy Makarczyk (ed.), Essays in International Law in Honour of Judge Manfred Lachs (1984), 625-643; A.O. Adede, The System for Settlement of Disputes under the United Nations Convention on the Law of the Sea: A Drafting History and a Commentary (1987); Shabtai Rosenne, UNCLOS III: The Montreux (Riphagen) Compromise, in Shabtai Rosenne, An International Law Miscellany (1993), 495-506; Louis Sohn, Settlement of Law of the Sea Disputes, 10 Int'l J. Marine & Coastal L. 205 (1995).

[5] Adede, n.4 above, 4.

II. The UNCLOS dispute settlement system in a nutshell

5. The UNCLOS dispute settlement system that the States parties managed to persuade themselves to accept is a comprehensive and "non-reservable" one, embodied primarily in Part XV. It covers all disputes relating to the interpretation or application of the UNCLOS. It respects free choice of means of dispute settlement (Part XV, section 1), but has a compulsory component in terms of binding decision-making (Part XV, section 2), which still allows a choice of procedures under article 287 including the International Tribunal for the Law of the Sea (ITLOS or Tribunal), the International Court of Justice (ICJ), arbitration under Annex VII or special arbitration under Annex VIII. This compulsory component is subject to some automatic exceptions under article 297 (exclusive economic zone (EEZ) disputes) and optional exceptions under article 298 (delimitation, military or enforcement activities or UN Security Council action), where "compulsory reconciliation" is used as some kind of substitute for compulsory binding decision-making in some but not all of the excepted areas. Article 299 then reminds the States parties that they can still agree afresh to submit the excepted matters to a section 2 court or tribunal.

6. Articles 15, 74 and 83 provide for "criteria" for delimitation of sea boundaries. Obviously these may serve as a sort of applicable law provisions, essential to the settlement of disputes and thus can be considered part of the dispute settlement system in the broad sense, but one must remember that articles 74(1) and 83(1) deal with "delimitation by agreement", not otherwise. However, the principles employed in these provisions may have a broader application.

7. Furthermore, a special regime with very broad jurisdiction is also created under Part XI, section 5 for settlement of disputes relating to the international seabed area (the Area), including the advisory opinion jurisdiction of the Seabed Disputes Chamber of the ITLOS, which was not envisioned for the full Tribunal.[6] This was considered necessary to meet the novel challenges coming from the exploration and exploitation of the Area.

8. Finally, the Commission on the Limits of the Continental Shelf is established under article 76(8) and Annex II to examine the claims of a State party for outer continental shelf beyond 200 nautical miles. The Commission

---

6 See Adede, n.4 above, 196, 275; 5 Virginia Commentary, n.2 above, 416, para.A.VI.204.

can be considered a quasi-dispute settlement body.

III. Pivotal negotiating procedural steps

9. Needless to say, many factors contributed to the emergence of the final shape of the dispute settlement system under the UNCLOS. Among these were some "negotiating procedural steps", as explained and listed above in paragraph 4. Let us briefly examine these one by one in the order given there.

III.1. The package deal decision

10. The final emergence of the dispute settlement system as an integral part of the UNCLOS as a whole, which is not reservable or optional (i.e., presented as a separate system in a separate treaty or an optional protocol) owes a great deal to the common understanding very early on that "the problems of ocean space are closely interrelated"[7] and that a comprehensive regime for the law of the sea is required for building a just and equitable international economic order governing ocean space. Otherwise, raw calculation of national interest would lead to States cherry-picking the parts most favorable to them to accept, resulting in several treaties on the law of the sea with limited participation, as had happened in the past. Thus, the idea of one big package deal for all aspects of law of the sea issues was conceived. In due course, the General Assembly (GA) specified the mandate for the Conference as "to adopt a convention dealing with all matters relating to the law of the sea".[8] This decision predetermines to a great extent the final shape of the UNCLOS, including the dispute settlement system as an integral, non-reservable part.

11. The magnitude of this undertaking was of course not lost on the leaders in the negotiations. Constantin A. Stavropoulos, Under-Secretary-General and Special Representative of the Secretary-General to the Conference described this "gigantic package deal" this way: "The 1958 Conference accepted four separate conventions and a protocol, and thus to a certain extent problems could be isolated and settled one by one. The work of the Third Conference, however, is to adopt, by consensus if possible, one gigantic 'package deal' covering the whole area under discussion, which will have sufficient support to

---

7 Report of the First Committee, A/9278, as quoted in 1 Virginia Commentary, n.2 above, 190 n.1.

8 A/Res/3067, para.5.

be ratified and come into force on a substantially world-wide basis."[9]

12. Obviously, a gigantic package deal requires tough compromises and it cannot be negotiated like a big banquet with all participants making decisions all at once. The task was further complicated by the fact that there was no single negotiating text agreed upon when the Conference started. With unprecedented interest from States and an unprecedented number of participants, the Conference appreciated at the beginning that it would be impossible to conduct all the negotiations all at once in plenary. As a result, three main Committees were established, but none for dispute settlement, which was considered to be within the province of each Committee when relevant. In addition, many working groups or negotiating groups were established, formally or informally, to hammer out the decisions and then to refer them to the larger and/or formal bodies for further decision. Among the most important working/negotiating groups for the dispute settlement system was the Informal Working Group on the Settlement of Disputes, with Galindo Pohl (El Salvador), Ralph Harry (Australia) and A.O. Adede (Kenya), as co-chairmen, and Louis Sohn (USA) as the rapporteur of the Group.[10] Shabtai Rosenne, another very influential person in the negotiating process, described Sohn as also the *de facto* "scientific director".[11] Subsequently, President Amerasinghe took personal interest in the topic and was authorized to produce a set of draft articles which were included in the Informal Single Negotiating Text as a basis for negotiation. But resistance remained. Subsequently Negotiating Groups 5 and 7 were formally established by the Conference[12] to wrestle with various "hard core" issues in dispute settlement relating to EEZ disputes and delimitation. All these groups and individuals worked heroically and contributed substantially to the final agreement on the dispute settlement system.

13. Just as the big package deal could not be negotiated with all participants working together all at once, it did not arrive in one scoop. In fact, the big package deal was made up of a series of "partial package deal",[13] or "mini-package" deals or conditional mini-package deals reached as the necessary

---

9 Stavropoulos, in 1 Virginia Commentary, n.2 above, lxv.

10 Tommy T.B. Koh and Shanmugam Jayakumar, n.3 above, 110.

11 Rosenne, n.4 above, 497.

12 10 UNCLOS III Official Documents, 7-8 (Organization of Work: Decisions taken by the Conference at its 90th meeting on the report of the General Committee, A/CONF.62/62 (1978), para.5); Tommy T.B. Koh and Shanmugam Jayakumar, n.3 above, 94.

13 Stavropoulos, in 1 Virginia Commentary, n.2 above, lxv.

compromises were struck on a particular sector, segregated from the rest. When such a mini-package solution to such sectorial issues consisting of various compromises received "widespread and substantial support", it would be considered amounting to a "conditional consensus": the mini-package is one conditional upon an overall package deal.[14] One can find many illustrations in the UNCLOS. A prime example in the dispute settlement system is article 297, "Limitations on applicability of section 2".[15] This complicated article with about 750 words embodies a series of compromises relating to the settlement of EEZ disputes, on very tough issues relating to sovereign rights and discretion. The *Virginia Commentary* summarized them as follows:

> Disputes relating to marine scientific research and fisheries were divided into three categories: those that would remain subject to adjudication (namely all those that do not fall into the other two categories), those that would be completely excluded from adjudication (and, like all other disputes, would remain only subject to section 1 of Part XV), and those that would be subject to compulsory resort to conciliation. To the second group belong primarily disputes relating to the exercise by a coastal State of those powers with respect to which the substantive provisions of the Convention granted such State complete discretion. The third group includes disputes involving clear cases of abuse of discretion, where a State manifestly or arbitrarily has failed to comply with some basic obligations under the Convention. In a case relating to such an abuse of discretion, the conciliation commission shall, in accordance with Annex V, section 2, examine the claims and obligations of the parties and make recommendations to the parties for an amicable settlement, provided that the conciliation commission shall not substitute its discretion for that of the coastal State. The report of the conciliation commission is to be communicated to the appropriate international organization.[16]

This "mini-package deal" helped to move the negotiators closer to the big package deal. Furthermore, it apparently served as a model for the yet to be

14 Adede, n.4 above, 174.

15 Adede, n.4 above, 166, 174.

16 Rosenne and Sohn, 5 Virginia Commentary, n.2 above, 105.

resolved dispute settlement issues, notably delimitation questions,[17] to which we will come shortly.

III.2. The consensus approach

14. As a most important instrument to assure the success of the big package deal, a gentlemen's agreement was reached early on to apply the "consensus approach" to decision-making during the Conference. This was ultimately approved by the General Assembly in a decision as follows:

> Recognizing that the Third United Nations Conference on the Law of the Sea at its inaugural session will adopt its procedures, including its rules regarding methods of voting, and bearing in mind that the problems of ocean space are closely interrelated and need to be considered as a whole and the desirability of adopting a Convention on the Law of the Sea which will secure the widest possible acceptance, the General Assembly expresses the view that the Conference should make every effort to reach agreement on substantive matters by way of consensus, that there should be no voting on such matters until all efforts at consensus have been exhausted, and, further, that the Conference at its inaugural session will consider devising appropriate means to that end.[18]

15. This approach reflected the general understanding that agreements reached by a favorable vote of the majority or a super-majority may not last, but agreements reached by consensus most of the time stick. Furthermore, it was well understood that the Conference's mandate would include changing existing rules and making new ones on the law of the sea. In such a situation, it would be essential to have the widest agreement among the States since, if a significant segment of the community of States were to pursue a different path, anarchy would result. With 149 States having been invited to the Conference, in the words of Constantin A. Stavropoulos, Special Representative of the Secretary-General to the Conference,

---

17 Adede, n.4 above, 183.

18 Decision made by the GA at the 2169th meeting in 1973, 28 GAOR, 24 (Item 40), on the proposal of the First Committee, in A/9278, para.16.

> The two-thirds majority voting rule followed in plenary by almost every previous United Nations conference, including all the codification conferences, would obviously not be satisfactory if any alternative to it were available, since to adopt a rule over the opposition of as many as 50 States might be only a dangerous mockery.[19]

The cogency of this argument strengthens as the number of States in the international community gets bigger and bigger, now over 190.

16. Of course, the consensus approach was not a pact for the Conference participants to go to the dead end together. Thus, after "all efforts at consensus have been exhausted", recourse may be had to voting. Stavropoulos was of the view: "That moment will presumably come if a substantial majority of delegations are convinced that further efforts at reconciling viewpoints are futile."[20]

17. In due course, this was translated into detailed rules of procedure by the Conference. The effect of this approach apparently resulted in more compromises struck, and struck at the sharpest point where no further yielding by either side would be possible. Glimpses of this can be found already in article 297, as discussed above in paragraph 13. In the following discussion one will see that this effect pervaded the entire negotiation process on the dispute settlement system.

III.3. Building consensus by privileging the best second choice

18. The single most distinct feature of the UNCLOS dispute settlement system is probably its assurance of maximum respect for States parties' freedom of choice of peaceful means and/or forum of settlement. Section 1 of Part XV of course can be considered as expressing only one point, and that is freedom of choice of peaceful means of settlement of disputes. Even section 2, which provides for compulsory procedures entailing binding decisions, makes the best attempt at assuring such respect, within the framework of binding settlement. Of course, complete respect is not always possible.

19. As usual, there were a variety of existing procedures or forums for

---

19 Stavropoulos, in 1 Virginia Commentary, n.2 above, lxiii.

20 Ibid., lxiv. For a more general treatment of the consensus approach, see Wang Chen, Issues on Consensus and Quorum at International Conferences, 9 Chinese JIL (2010), 717.

States to choose from for settling disputes relating to the interpretation and application of the Convention. At the beginning the US proposed the establishing of a new law of the sea tribunal on the ground that special expertise—rather than general expertise in international law—may be required. The US explanatory note accompanying its proposal stated that "[t]he new Law of the Sea Convention will contain many technical provisions requiring judges with a special competence in the various fields covered by this Convention".[21] With this proposed addition, the list of available means got even longer. Thus a question arose as to whether any particular means should be selected or given preference at least. The Informal Working Group on the Settlement of Disputes held an inter-sessional meeting in Montreux, Switzerland in 1975. The report of that meeting stated that:

> A participant stated that the choice of tribunals would follow the defendant. The convention would also make provision for the situation where the defendant failed to act.[22]

20. According to Rosenne, this proposal was made by Willem Riphagen, Chairman of The Netherlands delegation, and would come "to constitute the kernel of the so-called Montreux Compromise, now embodied in article 287"[23] of the Convention. Probably Rosenne's assessment goes to the general framework providing for a list of choices and a default forum in that article. Perhaps it was in this sense that Tommy Koh and Shanmugam Jayakumar stated that "Willem Riphagen of the Netherlands outlined an approach to dispute settlement which found general favor in the group and which later was embodied in the Convention".[24] Adede was of the view that the Montreux formula "became an important aspect of the acceptance of multiplicity of jurisdictions as a permanent feature of the disputes settlement system being established under the Convention".[25]

21. One supposes that the normal consent principle would require the choice to follow not only the defendant but also the plaintiff, as common

---

21 As quoted in Adede, n.4 above, 15.

22 Meeting of the Members of the Working Group Considering the Question of the Settlement of Disputes – Montreaux [sic] – 22-23 March 1975, as quoted in Rosenne, n.4 above (1993), 500.

23 Ibid.

24 Koh and Jayakumar, n.3 above, 110.

25 Adede, n.4 above, 54.

choice is required. So the first part of Riphagen's proposal could be only accepted on the condition that the defendant's choice is also that of the plaintiff. It was apparently not too difficult to accept this point. Greater difficulty remained in (1) implementing the second part of Riphagen's statement, because apparently no particular forum should be privileged, as article 33 of the UN Charter does not do so, and (2) settling on a forum when the defendant's choice is not that of the plaintiff, a possibility not mentioned in the summary just quoted above. On this matter, it seemed that Riphagen himself had no key to offer.

22. This issue did not get settled until later. The solution that solved the problem is what I would like to call "building consensus by privileging the best second choice". According to Louis Sohn:

> When an informal working group, on which all regional and functional groups of states were represented, discussed this issue during the Conference, the informal rapporteur of the working group suggested a non-binding secret ballot, on which each participant would list both a first choice and a second one. The result was that while the first choice listed all four dispute settlement methods, almost all of those who did not list arbitration as their first choice selected it as their second choice. It was agreed, therefore, that where the parties do not agree on a first choice, the parties would have to resort to arbitration. A complex issue was solved by a simple procedural devise, and the full meeting accepted it by consensus.[26]

This idea would ultimately find expression in article 287(3) and (4), essentially stating that if the choices of the parties in a case made in advance by declaration do not overlap or, if one of the parties did not make any choice at all, arbitration under Annex VII would be the residual forum. The beauty of this approach is that each party is given the chance to name its best choice and thus can have no complaint, or is less likely to have any, when it has to take the best second choice selected in advance by consensus at the Conference because the best choices of the parties are not the same.

23. There was another issue relating to whether preference should be given to some form of an expert body to decide matters of a special technical nature such as those relating to seabed mining. Indeed, at the beginning it was

---

26 Sohn, n.4 above, 212.

envisioned that a seabed tribunal would be established separately as an organ of the Seabed Authority. The general idea on the need for special expertise in dispute settlement was well received and did not appear to encounter a great deal of resistance. Ultimately this idea culminated in the establishment of a Seabed Disputes Chamber as part of the ITLOS with its jurisdiction provided for under Part XI, section 5, the availability of special arbitration under article 287(1)(d) and Annex VIII, and, I should like to add, the establishment of the Commission on the Limits of the Continental Shelf, as mentioned above in paragraph 8.

III.4. Building consensus by privileging the existing negotiating text through the rule of silence

24. In a massive conference such as the UNCLOS III, it is usually a herculean task to move the negotiation forward, with many proposals at the table and many delegates raising their hands to speak. After a single negotiating text was presented, one device adopted at the Second Committee to carry out that task was the "rule of silence". According to the Chairman of that Committee:

> Early in its work the Committee agreed to follow "a rule of silence", whereby delegations would refrain from speaking on an article if they were essentially in agreement with the single text. Silence on amendments would be interpreted as lack of support for such amendments. The rule was to be applied flexibly and was not intended to result in any arithmetic calculations or be taken as a form of indicative vote. In my interpretation of the effect of this rule, I took into account the fact that with regard to certain issues, only those delegations most directly involved would normally participate in the discussion. Nevertheless, the rule allowed a general classification of the issues before the Committee.[27]

The rule obviously gives preference to the negotiating text before the Conference, for good or ill.

25. This tool apparently was put to wider use subsequently at the Conference.[28] Thus, a decision was adopted so that:

---

27 5 UNCLOS III Official Documents, 151, 153, para.6. The "single text" refers to the "Informal Single Negotiating Text".

28 See UNCLOS III Official Documents, vol.5, 81, passim; vol.9, 80, para.55 (Iceland), 138-140, passim; vol.13, 27, para.40; vol.14, 144, para.3; and vol.16,

> Any modifications or revisions to be made in the Informal Composite Negotiating Text should emerge from the negotiations themselves and should not be introduced on the initiative of any single person, whether it be the President or a Chairman of a Committee, unless presented to the Plenary and found, from the widespread and substantial support prevailing in Plenary, to offer a substantially improved prospect of a consensus.[29]

26. The President's Collegium adopted something similar, too, in its concrete operation. Bernardo Zuleta, Special Representative of the Secretary-General to the Conference, wrote that after hard-core issues were identified, the formal institution of the President's Collegium was formed as a practice to promote agreement. This body consisted of

> principal officers of the Conference which acted in an advisory capacity to the President. It had been the principal officers who had informally prepared and revised the negotiating texts upon which the work of the Conference had been focused all along. However, the programme of work now established stringent standards to direct the Collegium in its work: it mandated that no revision could be made without prior presentation of the proposed change to the Plenary, wherein it must have received "widespread and substantial support," indicating that it offered a "substantially improved prospect of consensus." By [this device] the Conference was able to ensure that the package remained cohesive until such time as all of the pieces fell into place.[30]

Obviously this device has the same effect as the rule of silence in moving the negotiations forward and in doing so by privileging the existing negotiating text.

27. Although this rule originated not specifically in the context of dealing with dispute settlement but in the Second Committee, it must still have had an impact on the final emergence of the dispute settlement system. This rule was

---

277.

29 10 UNCLOS III Official Documents, 8 (Organization of Work: Decisions taken by the Conference at its 90th meeting on the report of the General Committee, A/CONF.62/62 (1978), para.10).

30 Zuleta, n.3 above, 21-22.

specifically referred to in the debates on dispute settlement.[31] This was only natural, as each Committee also dealt with settlement of the disputes relating to matters within its province. Negotiating Groups 5 and 7 were formed by the Conference to deal with "hard core" delimitation disputes on the agenda of the Second Committee.[32] These groups worked under the framework of this rule and their reports were considered in that Committee.[33] Furthermore, the work of the Collegium would also have a bearing on the final outcome of the entire Convention including the dispute settlement system.

III.5. Failing consensus in the Negotiating Group, the Chairman presenting his proposals as suggestions to the plenary

28. For many States participants in the Conference, the ideal means of dispute settlement would be third party judicial or arbitral settlement. For others, however, the preference was different. With respect to disputes directly relating to the exercise of sovereign rights and jurisdiction in the EEZ or to the integrity of the territorial status such as the delimitation of the territorial sea, EEZ and the continental shelf between States with opposite or adjacent coasts as well as to historic bays and titles, many States did not want to resort to third party binding settlement. As a result, these two matters (settlement of EEZ activity disputes and settlement of delimitation disputes) were considered among the "hard core" issues and special Negotiating Groups 5 (with Ambassador Stavropoulos (Greece) as Chairman) and 7 (with E.J. Manner (Finland) as Chairman) were established by the Conference to deal with these issues respectively. The Chairmen were mandated to "conduct the necessary consultations within their respective spheres of competence in order, to the extent possible, to reach compromise solutions on outstanding issues" during the first three weeks of the ninth session.[34] Of course, as described above, such promise would have to be able to garner the widespread and substantial support so as to offer a substantially improved prospect of a consensus, to paraphrase a decision of the Conference.[35]

---

31 9 UNCLOS III Official Documents, 80, para.55 (Iceland).

32 Tommy T.B. Koh and Shanmugam Jayakumar, n.3 above, 94.

33 See, e.g., 11 UNCLOS III Official Documents, 63; 101; see also 5 Virginia Commentary, n.2 above, 127, para.298.25.

34 13 UNCLOS III Official Documents, 76 (Report of the Chairman of Negotiating Group 7, A/CONF.62/L.47, para.1).

35 See above para.25, text to n.29.

29. Negotiating Group 5 worked hard and achieved this goal. After isolating the issues, the participants managed to strike several compromises, which would ultimately become article 297. These compromises, as described above in paragraph 13, formed a mini-package deal conditional upon an overall package being accepted. This deal[36] was such that, roughly speaking, (1) disputes relating to non-resource uses of the EEZ (e.g., navigational freedom) and environmental protection would be within the jurisdiction of a section 2 court or tribunal, (2) disputes relating to resource uses of the EEZ over which the coastal States have complete discretion would be outside the jurisdiction of any section 2 court or tribunal, and (3) disputes relating to the abuse of the discretion mentioned would be subject to compulsory conciliation. Under the UNCLOS, compulsory conciliation, which sounds awkward, is compulsory only as a process in the sense that a party has earlier accepted it (here, by ratifying UNCLOS) and must accept it when it is invoked by another party, but it does not result in a binding decision. An additional act of acceptance by the parties is necessary to make the resulting proposals from the conciliator(s) binding. Thus, this procedure offers the pomp and formality of a section 2 proceeding but yields only a non-binding report which may contain recommendations.[37] Of course, the process itself may at least allow the parties the opportunity to appreciate, with the help of conciliator(s), each other's positions realistically, which should be conducive to keeping the negotiations going and perhaps, with some luck, settling their disputes. Under such a framework, the coastal States would not be in fear that their newly obtained sovereign rights and jurisdiction would be discounted by baseless and vexatious litigation.

30. Negotiating Group 7 had no such luck, however. The group segregated the delimitation issues into two categories: (1) criteria for delimitation and (2) dispute settlement procedures, but on neither did it reach consensus, except that there was consensus on the criteria for the delimitation of the territorial sea, which can be summed up as "equidistance plus special circumstances". This would later become article 15.

31. On the criteria for delimiting the EEZ and the continental shelf between States with opposite or adjacent coasts, there had been a strong fight

---

36 See Virginia Commentary, as quoted in paragraph 13 above; Adede, n.4 above, 166-174.

37 On this topic, see Sienho Yee, Conciliation and the 1982 U.N. Convention on the Law of the Sea, 44 Ocean Development and International Law (2013), 315-334.

from the very beginning between the "equidistance" States (those in favor of delimitation on the basis of the equidistance principle with consideration for relevant circumstances) and the "equitable principles" States (those in favor of delimitation on the basis of "equitable principles" with consideration for relevant circumstances). Even after years of negotiation and the hard work of Negotiating Group 7, there was no prospect of either side yielding to the other. One solution thus might be that all the criteria would be stated, alternatively and without priority for either, so as to appease both, but that would also offend both at the same time. Furthermore, during the discussions, it was suggested that, in addition to other criteria, a reference to international law would improve the chances of success.[38] The group worked heroically but could not muster sufficient support for any of the formulations that would pave the way for consensus.

32. On the method for settlement of disputes relating to delimitation, there had been also a strong fight since very early on in the Conference, between the groups for and against compulsory third party binding settlement. The division of opinion was considered by the President of the Conference as nearly equal in 1977.[39] When the text of section 2 was taking shape, it was found necessary to craft exceptions to the general obligation stated therein of submitting disputes to third party binding settlement. The States opposing third party binding settlement considered that such settlement of delimitation disputes and the EEZ disputes would infringe upon the integrity of their territory and their sovereign rights and would not agree to a dispute settlement system that would not provide for exceptions of these two kinds of disputes (EEZ disputes would be dealt with by Negotiating Group 5, as described above). The States in favor of third party binding settlement, primarily Western States, stressed the importance and advantages of third party binding settlement, while "pointing out that the more general and indefinite the criteria of delimitation, the greater the need to submit delimitation disputes to the decision of a Court or Tribunal".[40] Negotiating Group 7 went through arduous consultations and negotiations on this point, but no agreement was on the way, as each camp seemed to be entrenching its position.

33. Then the idea of compulsory conciliation was proposed to take the

---

38 13 UNCLOS III Official Documents, 77 (A/CONF.62/L.47, para.4 and annex).

39 Manner, n.4 above, 636.

40 Ibid.

place of compulsory third party binding settlement regarding excepted matters. This was already accepted within Negotiating Group 5 regarding some EEZ disputes. Probably inspired by this idea and its success in the other group, the Chairman of Negotiating Group 7 offered in 1979 as his "suggestion for a basis for further negotiations on article 298, paragraph 1(a)" a formulation that would permit States parties by optional declaration to except from the applicability of section 2:

> Disputes concerning the interpretation or application of articles 15, 74 and 83 relating to sea boundary delimitations, or those involving historic bays or titles, provided that the State having made such a declaration shall, when such a dispute arises subsequent to the entry into force of this Convention and where no agreement within a reasonable period of time is reached in negotiations between the parties, at the request of any party to the dispute, and notwithstanding article 284, paragraph 3, accept submission of the matter to conciliation provided for in annex IV [later V], and provided further that there shall be excluded from such submission any dispute that necessarily involves the concurrent consideration of any unsettled dispute concerning sovereignty or other rights over continental or insular land territory [….][41]

34. The Chairman further stated that the "lengthy discussions on the settlement of delimitation disputes during the eighth session have strengthened [his] understanding that only a proposal based upon the procedure of compulsory conciliation is consistent with a realistic view of the possibilities, if any, to reach a compromise on this controversial issue".[42] Further tough consultations and negotiations were had subsequently, but no consensus was in sight, still, on this article.[43]

35. At this moment, what should the Chairman do? One supposes that, to be true to his or her mandate, the Chairman could or even should simply report to the Conference the fact that no consensus had emerged in the negotiating group and gave up. However, the Chairman of Negotiating Group 7 did not take such a course of action. Here perhaps one may have glimpses of a leader in treaty-making or intellectual leader never yielding to failure. Mr.

---

41 12 UNCLOS III Official Documents, 108 (Report of Chairman, NG 7/45).

42 Ibid.

43 Ibid., 77 (Report of Chairman, NG7/47).

Manner decided that, in addition to reporting the lack of consensus, he would present his proposals as his own suggestions for the Conference to consider. Regarding the unsettled delimitation criteria, he further improved his proposal to read as follows:

> The delimitation of the exclusive economic zone/continental shelf between States with opposite or adjacent coasts shall be effected by agreement in conformity with international law. Such an agreement shall be in accordance with equitable principles, employing the median or equidistance line, where appropriate, and taking account of all circumstances prevailing in the area concerned.[44]

36. Regarding settlement process and optional exceptions, the Chairman reported that no new features were added to the consideration of this item, reproduced his earlier proposal (paragraph 33 above) and repeated his assessment: "Albeit no consensus has as yet materialized, it is still the Chairman's understanding that only a proposal based upon the procedure of compulsory conciliation may prove consistent with a realistic view of the possibilities to reach a final solution on the question."[45]

37. The step taken by the Chairman was, in his *post mortem* assessment, a "well advised"[46] one or, one may say, it was, *ex ante*, a fateful one, because the final outcome on both issues was facilitated to a great extent by his suggestions and, in any event, did not stray too far from them. Regarding delimitation criteria, there was resistance from both the equidistance group and the equitable principles group and President Tommy Koh decided to personally consult with the leaders of both camps. Soon consensus was reached on the proposal by the President that the criteria should jettison all references to either the equidistance principle or the equitable principles, but should specify the goal of achieving an equitable solution or, one may say, impose an obligation of result. In addition, the reference to international law would be elaborated by reference to article 38 of the ICJ Statute. One may wonder why in article 74 or 83, paragraph 1, a provision on delimitation by agreement, it was considered necessary to specify "applicable law" because an agreement could be based on factors other than law. One may also wonder whether it might be more appropriate to put the

---

44 Ibid., NG7/47, Annex. See also Manner, n.4 above, 630-631.

45 12 UNCLOS III Official Documents, 77 (NG7/47) and Annex.

46 Manner, n.4 above, 638.

reference to article 38 of the ICJ Statute in a provision specifically on applicable law, such as article 293. One may further wonder how much this new formulation may have added substantively (perhaps materially),[47] but the fact that it succeeded in commanding consensus shows the masterful skill of the person making the proposal. Perhaps each of the equidistance camp and the equitable principles camp seemed to be happier to see its criteria not mentioned in the text of the article than to see those of the other camp mentioned, even if together with its own, or the hatred engendered in one camp by the sight of the other camp's criteria was stronger than the pride triggered by the sight of its own. Thus the language in the drafts underwent a sea change from mentioning both camps' criteria to mentioning neither, the effect of which remains to be appreciated in the future. So it seems that each camp was content with leaving the fight and its fate to international law, within the generally recognized framework of article 38 of the ICJ Statute, but otherwise unfixed and evolving. What the content of that law may be is a task for future decision-makers, not the drafters, which may favor one or the other camp, or neither. In any event, the final criteria now embodied in articles 74/83, paragraph 1 read as follows:

> The delimitation of the exclusive economic zone/continental shelf between States with opposite or adjacent coasts shall be effected by agreement on the basis of international law, as referred to in Article 38 of the Statute of the International Court of Justice, in order to achieve an equitable solution.

Regarding the limits of the outer continental shelf beyond 200 nautical miles, a special Commission on the Limits of the Continental Shelf would be established to act on the applications of coastal States, as mentioned above in paragraph 8.

38. On his suggestion regarding settlement process and optional exceptions, that is, using compulsory conciliation to replace third party binding settlement, Manner wrote subsequently as commentator that "the States opposing compulsory third party jurisdiction finally approved the proposal, although as their utmost concession, and the Western countries, on the other hand, did not directly work against its adoption."[48] After some discussion, the Collegium decided to incorporate the suggestion of the Chairman of Negotiating Group 7 in the ICNT/Rev.2 (Informal Composite Negotiating

---

47 For a thoughtful analysis, see e.g., Manner, n.4 above, 638-640.

48 Ibid., 638. See also 5 Virginia Commentary, n.2 above, 129-131.

Text, Revision 2), despite some reservations even from the Chairman of the Second Committee. [49] This suggestion would essentially become article 298(1)(a)(i) ("Optional exceptions to applicability of section 2"), which now reads:

> 1. When signing, ratifying or acceding to this Convention or at any time thereafter, a State may, without prejudice to the obligations arising under section 1, declare in writing that it does not accept any one or more of the procedures provided for in section 2 with respect to one or more of the following categories of disputes:
>
> (a) (i) disputes concerning the interpretation or application of articles 15, 74 and 83 relating to sea boundary delimitations, or those involving historic bays or titles, provided that a State having made such a declaration shall, when such a dispute arises subsequent to the entry into force of this Convention and where no agreement within a reasonable period of time is reached in negotiations between the parties, at the request of any party to the dispute, accept submission of the matter to conciliation under Annex V, section 2; and provided further that any dispute that necessarily involves the concurrent consideration of any unsettled dispute concerning sovereignty or other rights over continental or insular land territory shall be excluded from such submission; [...]

39. One of course cannot be sure what would have happened if the Chairman of Negotiating Group 7 did not take the initiative to make his suggestions. Reverse engineering in treaty-making is no easy business. But with what in fact has happened, we should all be grateful for his suggestions.

IV. Conclusion

40. In this paper, I have highlighted and commented on these procedural steps taken during the Conference: (1) the package deal decision; (2) the consensus approach; (3) building consensus by privileging the best second choice; (4) building consensus by privileging the existing negotiating text through the rule of silence; and (5) failing consensus in the Negotiating Group, the Chairman presenting his own proposals as suggestions to the plenary. These steps no

---

49 See 5 Virginia Commentary, n.2 above, 131, end of para.298.27.

doubt contributed to the emergence of the final shape of the dispute settlement system under UNCLOS, and, in my view, in a pivotal way. The package deal decision and the consensus approach pervaded or even framed the entire Conference. The best second choice preference and the rule of silence helped to build consensus or hold consensus together, when preferences and opinions were numerous and divergent. The Chairman's own initiative in attempting to move things forward when no consensus was forthcoming in the Negotiating Group appears to be most innovative or at least courageous, helping to lead the negotiations out of an apparent dead end. The final shape reflects the balance struck between the wish for widest participation in the Convention regime and the need to maintain the integrity and density of the rights and obligations agreed to.

41. From another angle, one can find in these negotiating procedural steps images of leadership in treaty-making, both intellectual and organizational. One can see how the leaders aimed for overall and long term success of the UNCLOS and settled on the goal of one big package deal and on consensus as the method to achieve that goal. One can also see how a good idea started to lead the debate about, or set the agenda for discussion on, choosing forums of dispute settlement, whether or not it survived intact ultimately; how a skillful rapporteur of a working group applied a simple procedural device to work out consensus; and how a negotiating group chairman, having failed to lead his own group to consensus, attempted to lead the entire Conference by his ideas or proposals as "suggestions", with substantial ultimate success.

42. In the light of the contribution that these negotiating procedural steps made to the final shape of the dispute settlement system and of the leadership qualities that they may exhibit, future treaty-makers and leaders in treaty-making have much to learn from these steps and the experience of the Conference. They no doubt should have a place in the toolkit that similarly tasked persons should have on their minds.

Postscript

This paper as originally published contains this abstract:

> This paper highlights several pivotal negotiating procedural steps that ultimately helped to promote the emergence of the final shape of the UNCLOS dispute settlement system. These steps include, for want of better phrasing, the following: (1) the package deal decision; (2) the

consensus approach; (3) building consensus by privileging the best second choice; (4) building consensus by privileging the existing negotiating text through the rule of silence; and (5) failing consensus in the Negotiating Group, the Chairman presenting his own proposals as suggestions to the plenary. Needless to say, these steps are worthy of consideration by future treaty-makers and leaders in treaty-making when they are faced with complicated negotiating tasks, even if not as difficult as those during the monumental UNCLOS III.

Chapter 14

Reform Proposals regarding the International Court of Justice: Final Report for the ILA Study Group on United Nations Reform*

In 2008, I was invited to act as the sub-reporter on matters relating to "ICJ Reform" for the International Law Association (ILA) Study Group on United Nations Reform. In this capacity I submitted this Final Report on ICJ Reform as part of the final Report of the Study Group for the Sofia Conference 2012. This Final Report consists of: (1) The Preliminary Report of 2008 (paragraphs 1-27), which was submitted to the Study Group at the ILA Brazil Conference in 2008; (2) Comments Received (paragraphs 28-31); (3) Subsequent Developments (paragraphs 32-40); and (4) Conclusions and Suggestions (paragraphs 41-44).

---

* This Report first appeared in ILA, Report of the 75th Conference, Sofia (2012), 948-959, with some ILA editing to conform to its house style, which was not notified to me before publication, neither were the records of the debate upon my presentation of the Report at the Sofia conference in 2012. As a result, any infelicities in those pages, such as the deletion of paragraph numbers (which makes the Report appear strange) were beyond my control. After the ILA Sofia Conference, some minor revisions were made on 13 September 2012 in order to take account of the recent developments. I am grateful to the Chair and Rapporteur of the ILA Study Group on UN Reform for having invited me to write the report on ICJ reform. The preparation of this Report was supported by Research Project No. 08&ZD055 of the China Social Sciences Foundation and the Fundamental Research Funds for the Central Universities in China.

1. The Preliminary Report of 2008[**]

1.1. Introduction

1. The 2005 "World Summit Outcome Document" merely calls upon States to honor their obligations to peaceful settlement of disputes and to promote wider acceptance of the jurisdiction of the International Court of Justice (ICJ or the Court), without mentioning any other concrete reform measures regarding the Court.[1] This absence may be interpreted in several ways. It may be deemed to indicate that the world is content with the current state of affairs at and about the Court. Given the recent successes of the Court in terms of its caseload and its work product, this view may well be plausible. This absence may also be deemed to show a resignation that it is impossible to implement any reform proposals that would require amending the Charter and/or the Statute of the Court. If, as has been claimed, the UN Charter is a "finely tuned" instrument,[2] the ICJ Part[3] of the Charter (consisting of Chapter XIV and the Statute) can be

---

** This section reproduces Sienho Yee, Notes on the International Court of Justice (Part 2): Reform Proposals Regarding the International Court of Justice—A Preliminary Report for the International Law Association Study Group on United Nations Reform, 8 Chinese JIL (January 2009), 181-189, which was a slightly edited version of the Preliminary Report completed on 2 August 2008 for the International Law Association Study Group on United Nations Reform. The Preliminary Report was intended to be a survey on the more significant proposals, not a detailed treatment of any of them. Permission of Oxford University Press and the Chinese Journal of International Law for derivative use is gratefully acknowledged. In the preparation of the 2008 Preliminary Report, I am indebted to President Dame Rosalyn Higgins of the ICJ and Dr Ralph Wilde, Rapporteur of the ILA Study Group, for valuable comments and to Ingrid Kost, Curator of the Peace Palace Library for research assistance. All responsibility is mine alone.

1 UN Doc. A/60/L.1, at documents-dds-ny.un.org/doc/UNDOC/LTD/N05/511/30/pdf/N0551130.pdf, paras.73, 134.

2 Case concerning Military and Paramilitary Activities in and Against Nicaragua (Nicaragua v. United States of America), 3 ICJ Pleadings, 244 (argument of Louis Sohn).

3 This term draws inspiration of the "General Part" in criminal codes and civil codes, and is used for brevity and convenience. Here the provisions relating to amendments to the UN Charter are not included, though they are relevant.

considered even more finely tuned, or at least more finely balanced and, therefore, more resistant to amendment. Indeed, as described in paragraph 8 below, proposals for enlarging the membership of the Court were not accepted, while amendments have been made to the Charter in order to enlarge the membership of other UN organs.

2. Yet reform proposals regarding the ICJ abound.[4] They have been made by States, official bodies including the Court itself,[5] learned societies including the International Law Association and *l'Institut de droit international*,[6] and last but not least, individuals.[7]

---

4 For general assessments, see Wolfram Karl, Article 69, in: Andreas Zimmermann, Karin Oellers-Frahm and Christian Tomuschat (eds), The Statute of the International Court of Justice: A Commentary (Oxford University Press, 2006), 1481–1486; idem, Article 70, ibid., 1487–1490; Shabtai Rosenne, Law and Practice of the International Court: 1920–2005 (4th edn, 2006), 93–96.

5 For proposals made by the Court, States and other official bodies, see summaries and evaluations by Wolfram Karl, above n.4.

6 For general discussion, see, e.g., ABILA Committee on Intergovernmental Settlement of Disputes, Reforming the United Nations: What about the International Court of Justice?, 5 Chinese JIL (2006), 39; BIICL Study Group, The International Court of Justice: Efficiency of Procedures and Working Methods—Report of the Study Group established by the British Institute of International and Comparative Law as a contribution to the UN Decade of International Law, 45 (Suppl) ICLQ (1996), republished with comments in Derek W. Bowett et al., The International Court of Justice: Process, Practice and Procedure (1997); ILA, Report of the 46th Conference (1954), 37–192; idem, Report of the 47th Conference (1956), viii, 64–145; 45 Annuaire de l'Institut de droit international (1954–II), 296.

7 See, e.g., ICJ Registry (ed.), A Dialogue at the Court: Proceedings of the ICJ/UNITAR Colloquium held on the occasion of the Sixtieth Anniversary of the International Court of Justice, at the Peace Palace on 10 and 11 April 2006 (2007); Sienho Yee, A Proposal for Formalizing the "No Case Exists" Objections Procedure at the International Court of Justice, 4 Chinese JIL (2005), 393–416; Mohamed Sameh M. Amr, The Role of the International Court of Justice as the Principal Judicial Organ of the United Nations (2003), pp. 380 et seq.; Geoffrey Palmer, International Law and the Reform of the International Court of Justice, in: Antony Anghie and Garry Sturgess (eds), Legal Visions of the 21st Century: Essays in Honor of Judge Christopher Weeramantry (1998), 579–600; Connie Peck and Roy S. Lee (eds), Increasing the Effectiveness of the International Court of Justice (1997); Louis Sohn,

3. Some proposals would require amending the UN Charter and/or the Statute, while others would not. As we know, no amendments have ever been made to the ICJ Part of the Charter, while the Statute of the Permanent Court of International Justice (PCIJ) was amended once by the Protocol of 14 September 1929. In 1998, the General Assembly requested the Special Committee on the Charter of the United Nations and on the Strengthening of the Role of the Organization "To continue to consider, ... practical ways and means of strengthening the Court, while respecting its authority and independence, on the understanding that whatever action may be taken as a result of the consideration will have no implications for any changes in the Charter of the United Nations or in the Statute of the International Court of Justice".[8] This would seem to exclude any possibility of amending the ICJ Part. Barring a change of this policy, any reform proposals that would require such amendment would seem to be an academic exercise.

4. Furthermore, proposals have been made to call upon the United Nations General Assembly (UNGA) to take certain measures that could have achieved the same aim without amending the ICJ Part of the Charter. These proposals do not seem to have met with any success.

5. The ICJ, however, has been in a continuing process of interpreting the Statute, adopting, interpreting and revising its procedure and working methods to promote efficiency. By doing this, the Court in fact has been effecting reforms in its day-to-day practice and operation.

6. The purpose of this Preliminary Report is to review some of the more significant reform proposals regarding the ICJ and to make some suggestions for further consideration, with a view to producing a second report before the 2010 meeting of the International Law Association at The Hague.

1.2. Significant existing proposals

7. The number of existing reform proposals regarding the ICJ is large. Here, only those that are considered more significant will be briefly discussed. These

---

Important Improvements in the Functioning of the Principal Organs of the United Nations That Can Be Made Without Charter Revision, 91 AJIL (1997), 660; Lori Damrosch (ed.), The International Court of Justice at a Crossroads (1987); Louis B. Sohn, Broadening the Advisory Jurisdiction of the International Court of Justice, 77 AJIL (1983), 124.

8 A/RES/53/106, para.4(e), at daccessdds.un.org/doc/UNDOC/GEN/N99/762/55/PDF/N9976255.pdf.

proposals can be categorized in different ways such as by their effect.[9] For convenience, they will be discussed in following order by subject matter: (a) composition of the Court; (b) jurisdiction: contentious and advisory; (c) applicable law—Article 38 of the Statute; (d) procedure and working methods; (e) working conditions of the Court; (f) the role of the Court and its current workload and type of cases in hand and (g) measures to be taken at the UNGA.

1.2.1. Composition of the Court

8. Membership. A proposal was made by several States in 1956/57 to enlarge the membership of the Court so that it would correspond, on the basis of equitable representation, to the UN membership at large. This was not pursued subsequently.[10] At present, in anticipation of the possible enlargement of the United Nations Security Council (UNSC), a proposal has been made by a committee of the American Branch of the International Law Association (ILA)[11] to enlarge the membership of the Court so that it would mirror that of the UNSC, more or less on the model of the expansion of the European Court of Human Rights. First of all, we may note that although the Court is supposed to be representative of the main forms of civilization and of the principal legal systems of the world under Article 9 of the ICJ Statute, there is no requirement that it would mirror the membership of the UNGA or the UNSC. Secondly, there is no inherent need to enlarge the membership of the Court in order to achieve the goal within the meaning of Article 9. Of course, Article 9 could be changed in future reforms too, but that would give us an altogether different framework. Thirdly, as a deliberative body, there may be an optimal point where a proper balance may be struck between size and efficiency. The current membership so far seems to have worked well, and may be close to that optimal point. Finally, voting patterns shown in the judgments[12] do not suggest any problems relating to its membership that need alleviating. Accordingly, these proposals for enlarging the membership may not have merit.

---

9 See, e.g., Georg Schwarzenberger, Second Report on the Review of the Charter of the United Nations, in: ILA Report (1956), 119–120.

10 See Karl, Article 69, above n.4, 1483–1484.

11 ABILA Committee on Intergovernmental Settlement of Disputes, above n.6, 40.

12 See, e.g., Edith Brown Weiss, Judicial Independence and Impartiality: A Preliminary Inquiry, in: Lori F. Damrosch (ed.), The International Court of Justice at a Crossroads (1987), 123–134.

9. Re-election and tenure. Proposals have been made to eliminate eligibility for re-election with a corresponding expansion of tenure to 12 years, in order to avoid the possible problems of a Judge coming up for re-elections who, in making judicial decisions, may feel a need to please the future electors. This proposal seems to be a reasonable one, aiming to promote the judicial character of the Court, although, on the one hand, the politics of judging may still exist even if the proposal is accepted, while, on the other hand, the proposal presumes a certain weakness in the Judges. Furthermore, extending the tenure to 12 years may have its downside; it will take longer for a Judge who is not performing well to leave the Court.

10. Female members of the Court. Proposals have been made to elect more female members of the Court. The fact that in the entire history of the PCIJ and the ICJ only one female member (Judge and President Rosalyn Higgins) has been elected and one female Judge *ad hoc* (Mme S. Bastid) appointed by a non-national State of the appointee bespeaks the soundness of this proposal. But this is a delicate issue. Rigidity regarding the gender of the candidates may produce adverse consequences. For example, a form of "quota" method of voting for judges of another international court may have led to a feeling of dissatisfaction with the voting patterns in the elections.

11. Age limit. Proposals have been made to apply an age limit to candidacy or even judgeship on which opinion may differ.

1.2.2. Jurisdiction: contentious and advisory

12. Many proposals have been made to expand the jurisdiction of, and/or access to, the Court. These were made primarily when the Court was perceived to be under-utilized and under the perception that the international organizations do not have adequate forums for settlement of disputes.

13. Some of these proposals would expand the Court's contentious jurisdiction by, for example, reformulating Article 36 of the ICJ Statute, such as adopting an "opt out" clause on jurisdiction similar to the type of reservations in the Law of the Sea Convention.[13] Noting the difficulty in implementing this in the Statute, regional treaties were considered ripe for experiment. Some other proposals would achieve the same or similar result by giving intergovernmental

---

13 See unnamed speaker, in ICJ Registry (ed.), A Dialogue at the Court, above n.7, 12.

organizations or even other "public international law organizations" the capacity to be parties in a case before the Court.

14. To the extent that the Court now enjoys a heavy caseload and that the existing mechanisms for settling disputes between intergovernmental organizations and States are adequate, as was the view of the Charter Committee in 1999, [14] these proposals may now have lost their force. International organizations have a variety of means at their disposal such as the advisory jurisdiction of the Court and its innovative form which some have dubbed "'binding' advisory opinions".[15] In any event, contentious jurisdiction really depends on the political attitude of States, and efforts should be made to promote a "go to Court not war" culture.

15. Some proposals would expand the Court's advisory jurisdiction by allowing more international organizations or by having the UNGA authorized more such organizations to seek advisory opinions from the Court. Some would give the UN Secretary-General (UNSG) the power to do the same. To the extent that these proposals were motivated by a perceived relatively infrequent recourse to Advisory Opinions, it has been noted that such a state of affairs is "not necessarily a matter to be regretted".[16] In addition, granting such a power to the UNSG may upset the delicate political balance at the UN and may offend the cardinal principle of international dispute settlement by consent.

16. Proposals have also been made to permit some sort of "referral advisory jurisdiction" similar to that enjoyed by the European Court of Justice so that international courts and tribunals may, pending decision in a case, seek advice from the ICJ, in order to promote the unity of international law. Proposals have been made to allow States to seek advisory opinions in concrete disputes, which are not new. If these proposals had any attraction at a time when the ICJ was under-utilized, they are now unrealistic. They may lead to an even heavier caseload that the Court will have trouble handling—despite the fact that it has proven its ability to move very fast recently—and may lead to tension with the consent principle and with the need to protect the interests of third parties.

---

14 A/54/33 (May 1999), paras.110–116.

15 Robert Ago, "Binding" Advisory Opinions of the International Court of Justice, 85 AJIL (1991), 439.

16 Dame Rosalyn Higgins, A comment on the Current Health of Advisory Opinions, in: Vaughan Lowe and Malgosia Fitzmaurice (eds), Fifty years of the International Court of Justice (1996), 567, at 581.

1.2.3. Article 38 of the Statute

17. Very few proposals seem to have been made regarding this issue.[17] However, proposals have been made to fix the apparent logical mistake in Article 38(1)(b) (custom "as evidence of a general practice accepted as law") and to remove "civilized" from the inappropriate phrase "civilized nations", which would not affect the substantive meaning of the article.[18] Both proposals are in the nature of bringing the plain meaning of the terms of the Statute into line with the meaning that has been applied in actual operation by the Court, which reflects better the meaning intended by the drafters. This is also evidence that the Statute has been "reformed" in practice by the Court.

1.2.4. Procedure and working methods

18. Since the end of the Cold War, the Court has experienced a change of fortune, with its caseload being kept very heavy. This factor, plus the perceived excessive length of time that it took for the Court to complete a case, caused many to make proposals for improving efficiency at the Court, by streamlining its procedure and working methods. These proposals have argued for a variety of positions, such as formalizing a "no case exists" objections procedure,[19] eliminating or modifying the Note system.[20] As these proposals are detailed themselves[21] and about detailed provisions in the Statute, the Rules of Court and other instruments, it is impossible to enumerate and analyse them here. Also, some of these have already been adopted by the Court.

19. The Court itself has been very active in re-evaluating these matters and has adopted many measures to improve the administration of justice.

---

17 There has been some debate on whether the list of sources in Article 38 of the Statute is exhaustive. See, for example, Alain Pellet, Article 38, in: Andreas Zimmermann et al. (eds), above n.4, 700–714.

18 See Sienho Yee, Arguments for Cleaning up Article 38(1)(b) and (1)(c) of the ICJ Statute, 4 Romanian JIL (2007), 33–43 (in part, Chapter 2 above).

19 See Sienho Yee, A Proposal for Formalizing the "No Case Exists" Objections Procedure at the International Court of Justice, 4 Chinese JIL (2005), 393–416.

20 Dame Rosalyn Higgins, in Bowett et al., above n.6, 102–104.

21 See BIICL Study Group, in Bowett et al., above n.6, 73–75; unnamed speaker in ICJ Registry (ed.), A Dialogue at the Court, above n.7, 24–25.

Probably, the most important of these is the interpretation of provisional measures indicated under Article 41 of the Statute as binding.[22] This decision is no doubt a desirable one, although it may be considered an innovation. Another important innovation is to effectively permit the parties in a case to select members of a Chamber if they decide to request the formation of one.[23] Other important measures include the elimination of the judicial "exchange of notes" for decisions in the preliminary phases of most cases;[24] the promulgation of a new form of instruments called "Practice Directions";[25] the periodic revision of rules so as to streamline procedures including setting out a shorter time limit for presenting preliminary objections,[26] and providing for clearer guidance on counter-claims[27] and for receiving input from international organizations regarding the construction of certain treaties.[28] In addition, the Court or perhaps the President acting alone seems to have been moving the parties forward in the proceedings faster than before and keeping a tighter control of the oral proceedings.[29] These no doubt have helped to improve efficiency to a great extent, and the Court appears to be functioning with relatively great dispatch recently, especially where provisional measures are requested.[30] Of course, the main culprits for delay in the proceedings are really the parties in a case themselves.

20. Outsiders such as the ILA would not have any comparative advantage, vis-à-vis the Court, in dealing with the concrete working out of these issues. Still it is worth considering whether the Court has performed well or has done enough to prepare itself to do so in "complex litigation" cases where intervention is in issue or where a cluster of cases based on the same factual or

---

22 La Grand, ICJ Reports 2001, 466.

23 From available information, one can tell that formally the parties do not choose; the reality is that they do.

24 ICJ Press Release 2002/12, para.5. This mirrors, to a large extent, the proposal made by Dame Rosalyn Higgins, in Bowett et al., above n.6, 102–104.

25 See ICJ Annual Report 2005–2006, para.19. The text of these directions can be found at www.icj-cij.org/documents/index.php?p1=4&p2=4&p3=0.

26 See new Art.79 of the Rules of Court.

27 See new Art.80 of the Rules of Court.

28 See new Art.43 of the Rules of Court.

29 See generally ICJ Press Release 2002/12 and the Comptes Rendus in some of the recent cases.

30 See, e.g, La Grand (Germany v. the United States), provisional measures, ICJ Reports 1999, 9.

legal complex have been filed such as the *Legality of Use of Force* cases. Many issues are involved and it may be worthwhile for the Court to examine this question and perhaps provide further guidance in some form.[31]

21. The success of a judicial system normally results from the contribution of both the bench and the bar. While the Court has been making admirable efforts to promote the administration of justice, it is curious that there is neither an organized ICJ Bar nor a model code of conduct for practice before the Court. Such a bar and such a code would seem to be necessary for the promotion of professionalism in the practice before the Court. First of all, some of the problems if any before the Court have been caused by the poor quality of the practitioners, including agents and lawyers, litigating before the Court. Serious mistakes have been made. Fraudulent documents have been submitted. The President has had to give very clear directions to some advocates during oral proceedings. These problems may have been aggravated by the appearance of more and more lawyers who are not specialists in ICJ jurisprudence. A proper professional code of conduct may have prevented some of these from occurring. Secondly, the legal profession everywhere in the world prides itself on being able to promote professional competence and to apply a certain level of self-discipline and the organized bars around the world are performing this function. Perhaps the ways and means of organizing an ICJ Bar and adopting a Model Code of Conduct for practice before the Court should be considered.

1.2.5. Working conditions of the Court

22. The working conditions of the Court are apparently modest indeed, compared with other significant international courts and tribunals and even the highest national courts. As a result, proposals for improving these conditions have been made since a long time ago. The Court itself proposed in 1969 that the seat of the Court may be removed to another location,[32] apparently when it was engaged in a diplomatic struggle with the host State for the construction of

---

31 See BIICL Study Group, in Bowett et al., above n.6, 65–66; James Crawford, The International Court of Justice, Judicial Administration and the Rule of Law, ibid., 116–122; Lori F. Damrosch, Multilateral Disputes, in: Lori F. Damrosch (ed.), The International Court of Justice at a Crossroads (1987), 376–400.

32 See A/7591 (20 June 1969) and Add. 1 and 2; ICJYB (1968–1969), 108, as cited in Karl, Article 70, above n.4, 1489.

additional premises. Such proposals for a better resourced Court have also been made by others.[33]

23. In recent years, the Court has made many direct requests to the UNGA for improving its working conditions. Against a background of great successes at the Court in recent years, it is ironic to see that the Court has had to be wrestling, at the UNGA, with attempts to reduce judicial salaries and miserly grants of law clerk positions.[34]

1.2.6. The role of the Court and its current workload and type of cases in hand

24. The good news about the Court is that it enjoys a heavy workload. The bad news may also be that it enjoys a heavy workload. Furthermore, the heavy workload includes cases dealing with a variety of legal matters and, recently, cases of complex factual questions. The Court's Annual Report 2006–2007 noted in paragraph 11: "The subject-matter of these cases is extremely varied. As well as 'classic' territorial and maritime delimitation disputes and disputes relating to the treatment of nationals by other States, the Court is seized of cases concerning more 'cutting-edge' issues, such as allegations of massive human rights violations, including genocide, or the management of shared natural resources".

25. This situation may lead one to ask whether there may be tension between the Court's role as the principal judicial organ of the United Nations and the World Court and its workload and whether it might be more appropriate for some matters to be dealt with by other organs including other tribunals and the ICJ's own experts and assessors. The Court seemed to strike a good balance in the *Genocide Convention* case (merits) by seeming to apply a certain measure of the idea of "respect for institutional competence", both in declining to accept the challenge to its case law on a point of general public international law by the International Criminal Tribunal for the former Yugoslavia (ICTY) and in according "highly persuasive" value or "due weight" to the various factual findings and evidentiary decisions of the ICTY.[35] Perhaps,

---

33 BIICL Study Group, in Bowett et al., above n.6, 47–49.

34 See Statement by H.E. President Rosalyn Higgins before the UNGA 2007, 5–7, at www.icj-cij.org/presscom/files/3/14113.pdf; ICJ Annual Report 2006–2007, paras.23–24; ICJ Annual Report 2005–2006, paras.20–21.

35 ICJ, Case concerning the Application of the Convention on the Prevention and Punishment of the Crime of Genocide (Bosnia and Herzegovina v. Serbia and Montenegro), Merits, ICJ Reports 2007, paras.223, 402–407.

other response measures can be considered.

1.2.7. Measures to be taken at the UNGA

26. In recognition of the difficulty to amend the ICJ Part of the Charter, various proposals have been made for the UNGA to take measures to achieve the same aim without having to promote any formal amendments. The proposed measures include passing a resolution indicating its reluctance to elect judges over 70 years of age.[36] The UNGA is not anxious to take any such measures.[37]

27. In the light of this inaction and of the recent successes of the so-called "Like-minded Group of States" in pushing through its agenda in the negotiation of the Landmine Convention and the Rome Statute of the International Criminal Court, it is worth noting that no such "Like-minded Group of States" or "League of ICJ-Friendly States" seems to exist to promote the greater use of the ICJ or certain positions at the UNGA, such as pushing for female candidacies and more funding for the Court. Such a group, if large enough to constitute a critical mass of the UNGA membership, would be a force to reckon with.

2. Comments Received

28. The Preliminary Report was presented (by another member of the Study Group due to my absence) and discussed at the meeting of the UN Reform Study Group at the ILA Conference in Brazil in 2008. Comments were received at the Brazil Conference and also separately from various experienced judges and practitioners in the field. The comments received were generally positive, although there were some comments calling for further work. Given the limited mandate for the Report as a survey, fair differences of opinion as well as the perceived difficulty if not impossibility in changing anything in the ICJ Statute, a decision has been made not to make any changes to the Preliminary Report. Rather, I will respond to some of the comments here and also describe some of the subsequent developments relating to issues dealt with in the Preliminary Report.

---

36 See BIICL Study Group, in Bowett et al., above n.6, 74.

37 The UNGA did take action (A/Res/50/54 (1995)) to remove the review jurisdiction regarding decisions of the UN Administrative Tribunal, but this is not a Statute or Charter amendment question.

29. Some comments received from members of the Study Group address the scope, focus as well as the purpose of the Preliminary Report. These comments would change the mandate for the entire Report. As the mandate has not been changed, these comments cannot be taken account of.

30. Some comments relate to the working method in writing up the Preliminary Report, calling for empirical validation such as interviewing or sending questionnaires to the Judges. While it is always desirable to seek empirical validation where possible, the survey nature, again, of this Report does not render it ripe for such an empirical treatment. Furthermore, given the busy schedule of the Court and the delicate nature of dealing with the Judges, such an effort may not be fruitful. Of course, I have taken cognition of the need for some kind of validation. For this reason I had sought comments from various experienced Judges[38] who had served at the Court for a long time as well as from veteran practitioners. Their comments had already been incorporated in the Preliminary Report.

31. There were some specific comments relating to the optimal size of the Court, which was discussed in paragraph 8 in the Preliminary Report. The view expressed there is that no change should be made. As mentioned, several persons experienced in the affairs of the Court had been consulted previously. Subsequently I have discussed this issue with additional experienced persons.[39] They were all strongly against expanding the Court, saying that a bigger ICJ will make its business more difficult to manage.

32. In response to the view that the current size of the ICJ, with 15 members, is probably the optimal one for a world deliberative body, a counter-argument has been put forward: If the European Court of Human Rights (ECHR) with 47 members can work as a deliberative body, why can't an ICJ with a bigger number of members? This counter-argument however improperly fixates the attention on a comparison of the *number* of judges, while disregarding other more important factors. The size of the ECHR[40] is such that it does not

---

38 These include President Rosalyn Higgins (as she then was), as noted in footnote ** above.

39 These included experienced practitioners and one former Judge who had served as a member of the Court for a long time as well as its Vice-President and President.

40 See European Convention on Human Rights, http://www.echr.coe.int/NR/rdonlyres/D5CC24A7-DC13-4318-B457-5C9014916D7A/0/ENG_CONV.pdf; Rules of Court, http://www.echr.coe.int/ECHR/EN/Header/Basic+Texts/Other+texts/Rules+of+Court/.

adjudicate any case in plenary with all its 47 members, but only in a chamber—a very small slice of the whole court (this is true even of the Grand Chamber)—or an even smaller formation, leading to the result that the court is never representative of the entire "Convention space". On the other hand, the ICJ normally works *in plenary*, with judges representative of the whole world (or "the main forms of civilization and of the principal legal systems of the world", as stated in Article 9 of the Statute), and that is one of the most important reasons why States resort to the ICJ for the settlement of their disputes. They hope that in that composition, the ICJ is more likely to be free of prejudices. If States would like to resort to a small part of the ICJ for the settlement of their disputes, they can already now take advantage of the Chamber facility available under the Statute. Experience has shown that very few States have done that and when they did that, they did so with some special reasons, as can be gleaned from the various materials, and these special reasons (such as assuring the presence or exclusion of certain Judges) are too special to be of general application.

33. Despite its demerit, the counter-argument enjoys some popularity. In the light of this, it may be of some importance to condition any enlargement of the Court on the consent of, or at least thorough consultation with, the Court itself, as the Court is the best institution to evaluate whether its enlargement may be detrimental to its character and effectiveness.

34. A question was asked as to whether express, specific provisions should be added to the Statute to ensure the representation on the ICJ of the "the main forms of civilization and of the principal legal systems of the world". As we know currently there are "unwritten rules" dealing with regional grouping and regional representation at the UN. So far these unwritten rules have worked well, and there is no indication that this will not be the case in the future, although there is some speculation about whether some big States may lose their "traditional representation", so to speak, if only the normal informal regime is relied upon. Furthermore, express, specific provisions may bring rigidity into the system that may be difficult to change in the future when for example there are changes to the regional groupings at the UN. In short, it is not advisable to add express, specific provisions on ensuring the representation on the ICJ of the "the main forms of civilization and of the principal legal systems of the world".

3. Subsequent Developments

35. Since the Preliminary Report was submitted in August 2008, there have been some developments relevant to the issues and proposals discussed above. It will be useful to review these briefly.

36. The Court continues to enjoy a heavy caseload with cases coming all regions of the world,[41] to conduct its business with dispatch and to command the respect and confidence of the world. New cases and requests for advisory opinion keep coming to the Court. Of course, the Court's work product has not gone without criticism,[42] as would be expected. One cannot but say that the Court enjoys general success. There is more or less general satisfaction with the Court. Of course, "general" satisfaction does not mean perfect or 100% satisfaction. It is true, as has been pointed out from time to time, that the big powers (e.g., the Permanent Members of the UNSC) generally have not been anxious to accept the Court's compulsory jurisdiction (only the United Kingdom has accepted the Court's compulsory jurisdiction, with many reservations) or to in fact litigate before the Court. But it would be improper to infer too much from this: this situation may have resulted from either lack of satisfaction with the Court or the improper attitude of the big powers (no matter how good the Court may be), or both, or from the possibility that the big powers generally have found another peaceful means of settling their disputes, or most of them, with other States. In any event, the general satisfaction with the Court is clear, and it should be considered offset significantly by the situation with the big powers, although of course it will be nice to have the big powers litigating before the Court.

37. There is no evidence that the Generally Assembly[43] or the various

---

41 See ICJ Annual Report 2010-2011, paras.9-11.

42 See, e.g., Yehuda Z. Blum, Consistently Inconsistent: The International Court of Justice and the Former Yugoslavia (Croatia v. Serbia), 103 American JIL (2009), 264-271; Sienho Yee, Notes on the International Court of Justice (Part 4): The Kosovo Advisory Opinion, 9 Chinese JIL (2010), 763-782. For a comparison of the presidency of the ICJ and that of the ITLOS, see Sienho Yee, The Presidency of the International Tribunal for the Law of the Sea and the "National State Extension" Concern, 10 Chinese JIL (2011), 739-770.

43 See A/Res/64/115 (2009) (Para.8 recognizes the important role of the ICJ and the importance of recourse to the ICJ, and notes the availability of advisory opinion proceedings); A/Res/65/31 (2010) (para.8, same); A/Res/66/101

UN committees (including the Special Committee on the Charter of the United Nations and on the Strengthening of the Role of the Organization[44]) have meaningfully considered issues relating to ICJ reform since the submission of the Preliminary Report. Apparently no need has been felt for such reform.

38. Regarding female members of the Court, an issue discussed in paragraph 10, Ms. Xue Hanqin of China, Ms. Joan E. Donoghue of the USA and Ms. Julia Sebutinde of Uganda have been elected to the Court since the publication of the Preliminary Report. As far as female membership is concerned, these elections are encouraging developments, considering the fact before these members, Judge Dame Rosalyn Higgins had been the only female member on the Court, although there had been some female Judges *ad hoc*.

39. The Court continues to innovate regarding its procedure and working methods, with the latest revision of its Practice Directions issued on 20 January 2009.[45] This shows that the Court is of course the master of its procedure and management and continuously adapting itself to the evolving needs in this regard.

40. The working conditions of the Court seem to have improved as of 2010. In contrast to the normal urgent tone when requesting further posts and funding, the Court's Annual Report for 2009-2010 noted that "Regarding the budget for the 2010-2011 biennium, the Court was pleased to note that its requests for new posts and for an appropriation for the modernization of the Great Hall of Justice, where it holds its hearings, were largely granted".[46] Of course, the Court continues to need further resources and has requested additional posts.[47]

41. In paragraph 21 of the Preliminary Report, a proposal was made for the consideration of "the ways and means of organizing an ICJ Bar and adopting a Model Code of Conduct for practice before the Court". The implementation of this proposal appears to be outside the purview of our Study Group. In addition, this proposal touches upon the competence of another study group of the ILA, namely, the Study Group on the Practice and Procedure of International Courts and Tribunals, co-chaired by Philippe Sands, Laurence Boisson de Chazournes and Campbell McLachlan. In the light of

---

(2011)(para.7, same).

44 See A/64/33 (2009); A/65/33 (2010); A/66/33 (2011); A/67/33 (2012).

45 See ICJ Press Release No. 2009/8 (http://www.icj-cij.org/presscom/files/3/14983.pdf).

46 ICJ Annual Report 2009-2010, para.291.

47 See ICJ Annual Report 2010-2011, paras.27-28.

these factors and at the suggestion of various persons, I contacted Philippe Sands on 17 August 2008 by email to inquire into the possibility of working with that study group on these proposals. Subsequently the Preliminary Report was also sent to him. In 2009, the Study Group on the Practice and Procedure of International Courts and Tribunals started to draft a set of "The Hague Principles on Ethical Standards for Counsel appearing before International Courts and Tribunals". This set of principles was been adopted at the ILA Conference at The Hague in August 2010.[48] These principles are formulated in a general fashion to apply to all international courts and tribunals including the ICJ.

42. No effort however appears to have been made to organize an ICJ Bar, although the comments received indicate some interest in this proposal. Several experienced practitioners have sent comments expressing support for this proposal and for the view that such a Bar and a Code would work only if there are sanctions. It would seem that the inherent power of the Court to regulate practice before it encompasses the power to impose sanctions. This seems however a power that the ICJ has not been anxious to assert. One speculation is that the perceived special status of the agents and lawyers who represent sovereign States before the Court has resulted in the current situation.

43. Nor does any effort appear to have been made by anyone to organize an "ICJ Friends" group at the UNGA to promote the effectiveness and wider use of the Court, as discussed in paragraphs 26-27 in the Preliminary Report. The UN Secretary-General, as well as some member States of the UN (e.g., Norway and Switzerland), has called for the greater acceptance of the Court's jurisdiction and greater resort to the advisory proceedings in the context of promoting the international rule of law.[49] One wonders what has stopped them from channeling their efforts into a more organized endeavor.

---

48 http://www.ila-hq.org/download.cfm/docid/90B50C71-23D6-4366-B5E488 C89D96559A.

49 See generally Report of the Secretary-General, Strengthening and coordinating United Nations rule of law activities, A/63/226 (2008).

4. Conclusions and Suggestions

44. As discussed above, the ICJ currently enjoys general success and there is more or less general satisfaction with the Court.[50] This situation with the Court is such that no urgent reform is necessary. However, there are some desirable practical measures that may improve the effective use and appeal of the Court.

45. In the light of the general state of affairs regarding the Court and the UNGA directive of 1998 to the Special Charter Committee that ICJ issues should be considered "on the understanding that whatever action may be taken as a result of the consideration will have no implications for any changes in the Charter of the United Nations or in the Statute of the International Court of Justice",[51] no measures should be proposed that would require amending the Charter of the United Nations or the Statute of the Court.

46. Several desirable measures proposed in the Preliminary Report have been well received with one having received treatment in another ILA Study Group as mentioned above in paragraph 41. These measures fall under the broad umbrella of ICJ reform but will not necessitate amendment to the Statute, a red line specified by the General Assembly. They are not "over-ambitious", and stand a good chance of being accepted. They may help to promote the effective use and appeal of the Court and to promote a "go to court not war" culture. Indeed, the greater use of the Court depends on the international community's ability to win over the hearts and souls of States. Colleagues may consider calling upon the relevant authorities and persons to study them. These measures are:

a. The adoption of a binding Code of Conduct for practitioners before the Court;[52]
b. The organization of an ICJ Bar that would have disciplinary power;
c. The study of the possible tension between the role of the Court and its current workload and type of cases in hand and any possible solutions;
d. The organization of an "ICJ Friends" group of States at the

---

50 See ICJ Annual Report 2010-2011, paras.9-11.

51 A/RES/53/106, para.4(e), at daccessdds.un.org/doc/UNDOC/GEN/N99/762/55/PDF/N9976255.pdf.

52 As described in paragraph 41 above, another ILA Study Group has produced a draft code, which as such of course has no binding force.

UNGA to promote positions and measures that are favorable to the ICJ such as greater financial support or greater female participation as Judges or staff members.

Chapter 15

The Presidency of the International Tribunal for the Law of the Sea and the "National State Extension" Concern*

1. The mass media and Internet chat rooms in Asia recently have indicated some anxiety[1] that somehow a President of the International Tribunal for the Law of the Sea (ITLOS) might be, and might cause the ITLOS to be, partial towards his national State in a concrete case before the Tribunal or generally. There is no evidence to support such anxiety at all. It is only a concern of a

---

* First published at 10 Chinese JIL (2011), 739-770. The original paper contains a long abstract, which is reproduced at the end of this chapter. This paper was completed on 22 November 2011. The websites cited were current as of this date. The research for this paper received financial support from Research Project No. 09JZD0023 of the Ministry of Education of China and Research Project No. 08&ZD055 of the China Social Sciences Foundation. For valuable comments and questions I am grateful to several reviewers and the participants in a seminar held on 17 November 2011 during which I made a presentation based on a draft of this paper to the Oxford Public International Law Discussion Group. All opinions and errors are personal to me. In the paper, the frequently used abbreviations include: ICJ for International Court of Justice; ITLOS, International Tribunal for the Law of the Sea; PCIJ, Permanent Court of International Justice; UNCLOS, United Nations Convention on the Law of the Sea. "President", "Member" and "Judge", when referring to those at the PCIJ, ICJ or ITLOS, are initial-capped throughout the paper, unless other forms of spelling exist in the original of the quoted materials.

1 See, e.g., http://china.ajnews.co.kr/view_v2.jsp?newsId=20111005000025; http://news.sdchina.com/show/2072263.html; http://v.ifeng.com/news/world/201110/eb49e67f-d7f0-4330-b603-18e9d1b145d5.shtml; http://www.our023.com/bbs/viewthread.php?tid=30685.

general nature. The underlying assumption—a questionable one of course—is that the President of the ITLOS will somehow vote or otherwise make decisions favoring his national State; that is to say, a President or a Judge is an extension of his national State. This assumption may be called the "national State extension assumption"; its milder form may be called the "national State extension concern". This concern may have been accentuated by the various live disputes on law of the sea issues in East Asia and a perception that there exist many uncertainties in the United Nations Conventions on the Law of the Sea (UNCLOS) and the customary international law of the sea.

2. Previously I have criticized such an assumption as being "in tension with the presumed impartiality of the judges and the judicial character of their role",[2] but in an imperfect world such as ours this assumption may be very much present in the minds of officials and the public alike. Accordingly, it is of some value for us to review the essential aspects of the President of the ITLOS, without covering all aspects or being bogged down in details, and to analyze the possible implications of the relationship between these aspects and the national State of the President, as well as any possible antidotes, assuming, *arguendo*, that there is any legitimacy in the flawed "national State extension" assumption. I will first highlight the powers of the President and analyze the existing antidotes to any potential resultant problems. I will then address two issues in the application of the antidotes and make a suggestion for a further antidote.

I. The powerful three-dimensional President

3. The website of the ITLOS gives a brief and general description of the President as follows: "The President and Vice-President are elected by secret ballot by a majority of the members. They serve for a period of three years and may be re-elected. The President directs the work and supervises the administration of the Tribunal and represents the Tribunal in its relations with States and other entities. The President presides at all meetings of the Tribunal. In the event of an equality of votes, the President has a casting vote. The President is also an *ex officio* member of the Chamber of Summary Procedure.

---

2 Sienho Yee, Article 45, in Andreas Zimmermann, Karin Oellers-Frahm & Christian Tomuschat (eds), The Statute of the International Court of Justice: A Commentary (Oxford University Press) (2006), 1054 (MN 17). [After the publication of this paper the publisher produced a second edition of this book in 2012, but the references to the earlier work in this paper are not updated because of the decision not to disturb the original paper.]

The President presides over any Special Chamber of which he is a member."[3] This paragraph paints a very good general picture of the President of the Tribunal.

4. This picture of the President can be considered a three dimensional one: firstly, the President is a normal international judge; secondly, the President is the organizational leader of an international judicial body called the International Tribunal for the Law of the Sea; and thirdly, the President is the judicial leader in a particular case,[4] as the President of the Bench. When a court or tribunal or a chamber thereof finalizes its composition for a particular case, after any disqualifications and/or recusals as well as appointments of Judges *ad hoc*, that final composition is usually called the Bench. In the normal circumstances, the three dimensions are combined in the single person of the President, at which point the President's powers are at their maximum. In some exceptional circumstances, there can be a separation of these dimensions to be given to different persons. Generally speaking, if for some reason the President cannot exercise his or her powers as the organizational leader or judicial leader in a particular case, the vice-president or the senior Judge in precedence will step up to exercise those powers.

5. The functions of the President of the ITLOS find their sources in the various applicable basic instruments including Part XV of the UNCLOS of 1982 (Settlement of Disputes); Annex VI (the Statute of the International Tribunal for the Law of the Sea) and other relevant Annexes to the UNCLOS; the Rules of the Tribunal; and the Resolution on the Internal Judicial Practice of the Tribunal.[5] These instruments to a substantial extent draw upon those that

---

3 http://www.itlos.org/index.php?id=17.

4 The arguments made here about the President's role as a judicial leader in a particular case should also apply to advisory proceedings, to the extent they are applicable. See ITLOS Statute, art. 40(2). However, the issue of advisory jurisdiction before the ITLOS can be somewhat complicated. In order to simplify the analysis, I will leave for the future how my arguments may be relevant, *in concreto*, to advisory matters. The same kind of *mutatis mutandis* application obtains in the ICJ and PCIJ under article 68 of the Statute of each. [After the original publication of this paper, the full ITLOS received a request for advisory opinion and its jurisdiction to do is being contested. See ITLOS, Case No.21, Request for an advisory opinion submitted by the Sub-Regional Fisheries Commission (SRFC), http://www.itlos.org/index.php?id=252.]

5 All these are made available together conveniently at the ITLOS website: http://www.itlos.org/index.php?id=12&L=0. Outside activities of the

set up the system of the International Court of Justice (ICJ) in 1946 and its predecessor the Permanent Court of International Justice (PCIJ) in 1921.[6] The image of the Tribunal is similar, in organization and procedure, to that of the International Court of Justice, and the picture of the President of the ITLOS is similar to that of the President of the ICJ.[7]

6. Here let us first sketch the various functions of the three dimensional

---

President may have a different source. See below, paras.25. For commentaries on aspects of these basic instruments relating to the presidency, see Gudmundur Eiriksson, The International Tribunal for the Law of the Sea (Martinus Nijhoff 2000), especially 51-56; Tullio Treves, The Rules of the International Tribunal for the Law of the Sea, in P. Chandrasekhara Rao & Rahmatullah Khan (eds), The International Tribunal for the Law of the Sea: Law and Practice (Martinus Nijhoff 2001), 135; D.H. Anderson, The Internal Judicial Practice of the International Tribunal for the Law of the Sea, in: P. Chandrasekhara Rao & Rahmatullah Khan (eds), ibid., 197-214; P. Chandrasekhara Rao, ITLOS: The First Six Years, 6 Max Planck Yearbook of UN Law (2002), 183-300; P. Chandrasekhara Rao & Philippe Gautier (eds), The Rules of the International Tribunal for the Law of the Sea: A Commentary (Martinus Nijhoff 2006) ("Commentary on the Rules").

6 The basic documents of the ICJ include the UN Charter, the Statute of the ICJ, the Rules of Court, the Practice Directions, and the Resolution on Internal Judicial Practice, available from its official website: http://www.icj-cij.org/documents/index.php?p1=4. The PCIJ materials are also available at this site (hit the "Permanent Court of International Justice" tab on the left hand column). For commentaries on the ICJ Statute, see, e.g., Andreas Zimmermann et al. (eds.), n.2 above (2006); Shabtai Rosenne, The Law and Practice of the International Court, 1920-2005 (4th edn 2006) (Law and Practice); Geneviève Guyomar, Commentaire du Règlement de la Cour international de Justice adopté le 14 Avril 1978: Interprétation et pratique (1983).

7 See, e.g, Treves, n.5, above, 135; Eiriksson, n.5 above, 51. For commentaries on the President of the ICJ, see, e.g., Sir Percy Spender, The Office of President of the International Court of Justice, 1 Australian Yearbook of International Law (1965), 1–22; M. Bedjaoui, Le Président de la Cour internationale de Justice, in R.-J. Dupuy (ed.), Droit et Justice–Mélanges en l'honneur de Nicolas Valticos: droit et justice (1999), 255–267; Shabtai Rosenne, The President of the International Court of Justice, in A.V. Lowe & M. Fitzmaurice (eds.), Fifty Years of the International Court of Justice: Essays in Honour of Sir Robert Jennings (1996), 406–423; Shabtai Rosenne, Law and Practice, n.6 above, 1109–1116.

President of the ITLOS and then deal with the exceptional circumstances in the next section.

I.A. The normal international Judge

7. The Statute and the Rules of the ITLOS make it clear that the President first and foremost is one of the normal international Judges, as is usual in an international judicial body. The Tribunal elects its President from among its Members, and, upon election, the President continues to act as a normal judge.

In his or her capacity as a normal judge, the President is among equals at the ITLOS. He or she enjoys all the normal judicial powers and shoulders all the judicial obligations. He or she is eligible to participate in a case as a normal judge, including in a case in which his or her national State is a party. He or she is also eligible to serve as a member of any Chamber, sometimes even as an *ex officio* member. The same obtains regarding membership in committees. The President's vote has the same weight as that of another Judge. This is recognized in a summary fashion in article 3 of the Rules of the ITLOS. The only exception is that when the votes are equally divided, the President's leadership role gives him or her a casting vote, as will be discussed below.

I.B. The organizational leader

8. As the organizational leader or head of the ITLOS, the President enjoys under the ITLOS Statute and Rules certain powers to act for the organization as a whole in matters not dealing with a particular case. In so acting, the President deals with matters without targeting a particular State, and the effect of such action is normally on the UNCLOS system or even the world as a whole.

9. The President currently is the only Member that is required to reside permanently at the seat of the Tribunal. As provided for in article 12 of the Rules of the Tribunal, the President presides over all meetings of the Tribunal, directs the work and supervises the administration of the Tribunal. In matters that call for a vote and if the votes are evenly divided, the President has a casting vote. It seems presumed that the casting vote applies to administrative and organizational matters, although there could be a contrary argument from the statutory context, as discussed below in paragraph 21.

10. In the establishment of standing Chambers—the Chamber of Summary Procedures and standing Special Chambers—and committees, the

President has an instrumental role such as proposing candidates.[8] Furthermore, while the Seabed Disputes Chamber elects its own president from among its members, the President of the Tribunal becomes the President of any other Special Chamber if, when formed, it includes the President of the Tribunal, as provided for in article 31 of the Rules. The President is an *ex-officio* member, and therefore the President also, of the Chamber of Summary Procedure.

11. Furthermore, the President also is the face of the Tribunal to the outside world, so to speak. He or she represents the Tribunal in its relations with States and other entities, including delivering the annual report of the Tribunal to the relevant bodies and appearing before UN organs on behalf of the Tribunal.

I.C. The judicial leader in a particular case

12. As the judicial leader in a particular case, the President has extensive powers under the ITLOS Statute and Rules and the Resolution on Internal Judicial Practice. Furthermore, the President also enjoys certain delegated powers from the Tribunal when it is not sitting. The most important of all is of course the right under Article 29(2) of the Statute to exercise the casting vote in decision-making when the votes are evenly divided.

13. These powers come into play only when a particular case presents itself to the Tribunal (or in some instances, the UNCLOS dispute settlement system). They are exercised only in relation to the adjudication of such a case, the process of which can be broadly conceived. In this sense, the role of the President is "judicial" at least in the broad or macro sense of the term.

14. Firstly, the President has a role in the finalization of the constitution or the Bench of the Tribunal, a standing Chamber or an *ad hoc* Special Chamber for a particular case. Article 8(3) of the Statute requires the President to inform a Member of special reasons, if any, that in the President's view should cause the disqualification of the Member. Furthermore, in the use of a standing Special Chamber and *ad hoc* Special Chamber, Article 17(4) of the Statute gives the President extensive powers in consulting with the parties to agree on the finalization of the Bench.

15. Secondly, the President has a case-management role. This entails the

---

8 This may even apply to some situations not expressly regulated under the Statute or the Rules, such as the selection of the members of the Seabed Disputes Chamber. See Eiriksson, n.5 above, 54.

various powers that help to move the case along to bring it to a close. These include ascertaining the views of the parties as to how the case should proceed. When the Tribunal is not sitting, the President has the power to determine the number and order of pleadings, fix deadlines and take a variety of other procedural decisions, often subject to the subsequent decision of the Tribunal. The President also proposes experts under article 289 of UNCLOS. Under article 90(4) of the Rules, pending the meeting of the Tribunal, the President "may call upon the parties to act in such a way as will enable any order the Tribunal may make on the request for provisional measures to have its appropriate effects".

16. The President has control over the oral hearings under article 26 of the Statute, in order to assure these be conducted in a professional manner and in dignity and solemnity. The control involves various procedural measures to ensure good order and decorum in the court room. The Tribunal asks the parties questions through the President. Other Judges who wish to ask questions must first make their intent known to the President. The President's control may also deal with the admissibility of evidence and the questioning of the witnesses, and many other aspects.[9]

17. Under the Resolution on the Internal Judicial Practice of the Tribunal, the President has an extraordinarily strong leadership role, in the Tribunal's deliberations over a case and drafting of any decision. Firstly, the President has a key role in framing the understanding and indeed determination of the case under consideration, by preparing a working paper for circulation, after the closure of the written proceedings and before the deliberation prior to the oral proceedings, outlining the facts and principal contentions of the parties, further explanations and evidence to be sought from them, as well as the issues to be discussed and decided by the Tribunal. After the oral proceedings, the President may circulate a revised list of issues to be examined. During the initial

---

9 On the ICJ experience, see Yee, n.2 above. Neither the ITLOS Statute nor Rules seem to address the question whether one party may put questions to the other party. The same obtains with the ICJ Statute and Rules. However, at the ICJ, at least once, one party attempted to put questions to the other side and the President ruled that: "Il n'est pas d'usage qu'une partie pose des questions à l'autre partie dans une procedure devant la Cour. La Cour a la prérogative de poser des questions aux agents des parties." Haya de la Torre Case (Colombia/Peru), ICJ Pleadings (1951), 151. However, he did proceed to ask whether the other side had any observations to make, to which the answer was "no". Ibid.

deliberation after the oral proceedings, the President may seek to establish a majority opinion as it appears then to exist on each issue and on the reasons to be given.

18. As soon as possible during the deliberations after the oral proceedings the Tribunal will establish a Drafting Committee for the case and elect its members by proposals from the President. If the President belongs to the majority, he or she is a member *ex officio* of the Drafting Committee and becomes its Chairman, unless decided otherwise. When the President is not a member of the Drafting Committee, its chairman keeps him or her informed of the work of the draft judgment and its terms.

19. To crown all presidential powers, the President is given under article 29(2) of the ITLOS Statute a casting vote in the event of an equality of votes whenever the Tribunal takes a decision. The importance of the casting vote is of course in its ability to "create",[10] essentially single-handedly, a decision in a contentious case or a reply in an advisory opinion matter, in some contrast to the situation obtaining in some national legal systems.

20. The decisions reached by the casting vote of the President at the PCIJ and the ICJ include momentous ones such as *S.S. Lotus*,[11] the *Nuclear*

---

10 Rosenne, Law and Practice, n.6 above, 396. [For the contrasting system in the USA, see 2A Federal Procedure, L. Ed. § 3:865, ("The Supreme Court must affirm a judgment if the court is equally divided. In such a case, the Supreme Court can give no opinion on the point raised on appeal. Thus, although the affirmance by an equally divided court is conclusive on the rights of the parties to that appeal, no principle of law is settled by the affirmance, and an unexplained affirmance by an equally divided Supreme Court is a judgment not entitled to precedential weight, no matter what reasoning may have supported the judgment. The Supreme Court will affirm a decision if a majority of the Justices vote in favor of affirmance even though no one opinion commands the concurrence of a majority of the Justices.") (internal footnotes omitted); § 3:880 ("If the Supreme Court is equally divided, it must affirm the judgment below; it has no power to reverse. However, if a majority of the Justices of the Supreme Court vote that a judgment should be reversed, the judgment will be reversed, even though several opinions are presented which state different grounds for reversal, and there is no majority favoring any one of the opinions.") (internal footnotes omitted).]

11 PCIJ, Series A, No.10 (1927), 32. But see the dissenting opinion of Judge Moore, ibid., 65: "In the judgment of the Court that there is no rule of international law by virtue of which the penal cognizance of a collision at sea, resulting in loss of life, belongs exclusively to the country of the ship by or by

Weapons[12] advisory opinion (the UNGA Request) as well as the infamous *South West Africa, Second Phase* cases.[13] Although in these three matters there was no express indication that the President's casting vote was different from his original vote (cast in his capacity as a normal Judge), it seems accepted that the President's casting vote may so differ, in contentious cases and advisory opinion proceedings as well as in administrative matters. This appeared to be the understanding of the PCIJ. Regarding the President's casting votes in the course of the 9th and 10th sessions, the Third Annual Report (1926-1927) of the PCIJ, prepared and issued as usual by the Registry, stated:

> On one occasion, the President for certain reasons exercised his casting vote in a sense contrary to his original vote. On all other occasions he has exercised it in the same sense as his first vote.
>
> It is permissible to conclude from the foregoing practice that the casting vote is a distinct vote which may be exercised at the President's discretion and does not mean merely that a preponderating character is given to the President's original vote.[14]

This conclusion obviously was a general one, making no distinction between contentious cases and advisory opinion matters, on the one hand, and administrative matters, on the other.

21. Interestingly, it seems to be taken by the PCIJ and the commentators[15] for granted that the casting vote applies to all matters. However, the

means of which the wrong was done, I concur, thus making for the judgment on that question, as submitted by the *compromis*, a definitely ascertained majority of seven to five."

12 Legality of the Threat or Use of Nuclear Weapons, Advisory Opinion, ICJ Reports 1996, 226, 266, para. 105(2)(E).

13 South West Africa Cases (Ethiopia v. South Africa; Liberia v. South Africa), Second Phase, ICJ Reports 1966, 3, 51. For commentaries, see V.D. Degan, Reflections on International Judges and Their Decision-making: A Review Essay on Daniel Terris et al. (eds), The International Judge, 8 Chinese JIL (2009), 251, 259-263, paras.48-69.

14 PCIJ, Series E, No. 3, 216. This last sentence appeared to be responding to the controversy as to whether there is a difference between the English version and the French version (voix prépondérante).

15 See Series E, No. 3, 216; No. 14, 158-159; No. 16, 198; Rosenne, Law and Practice, n.6 above, 395-396; Manley O. Hudson, The Permanent Court of International Justice: 1920-1942 (1943), 344.

placement in the PCIJ Statute of article 55, which enabled the casting vote, in the chapter entitled "Procedure" (dealing with contentious cases and, via article 68, advisory matters) and between article 54 on the closure of oral proceedings and deliberations and article 56 on the content of a judgment seems to suggest that it may be reasonable to argue that the casting vote only applies in judicial decision-making in contentious cases or advisory matters. The same statutory context is inherited in the ICJ Statute. A similar context is also found in the ITLOS Statute regarding its own casting vote enabling provision, article 29(2). The same argument should also obtain here. If the casting vote does apply to administrative matters, there is much to commend the practice developed at the PCIJ in this regard. Under that practice, the President would refrain from using his casting vote and to declare lost a motion which failed to obtain a majority of votes. Regarding motions to amend the Rules of Court, the practice was also for the President to give his casting vote for the maintenance of the existing text, regardless of the original vote.[16] Favouring the power of the majority in such administrative matters, this practice jibes with the current understanding of legitimacy in general and it should be followed by the other courts including the ITLOS.

The voting custom of having the President cast his or her vote after all other Judges have cast theirs renders meaningless the issue whether the President's second vote can differ from the first.[17] The issue becomes unfathomable if the voting is done by secret ballot and the President does not disclose the fact that his casting vote is different from his "secret vote". The casting vote may be, of course, used as a tool to induce other Judges to vote a certain way so as to achieve a position with a certain majority. In this situation, there may be an incentive—usually a strategic one at that—for the President to make clear, particularly during some kind of indicative or preliminary voting process, whether the casting vote will be different from the original vote.

22. It is not easy, if not impossible, because of the lack of readily available information, to give a complete and accurate accounting of how the casting votes have been different from the President's original votes in contentious cases and advisory matters as well as administrative matters at the

---

16 See, e.g., Series E, No. 14 and No. 16, ibid. See also Hudson, n.15 above, 344.

17 This custom is in ICJ Resolution concerning Internal Judicial Practice, art. 5(i); ITLOS Resolution on Internal Judicial Practice, art. 9(1). It also renders meaningless the controversy on the difference between the English and French versions. See Rosenne, Law and Practice, n.6 above, 395.

PCIJ.[18] But for the purposes of our discussion focusing on substantive judicial decision-making, it appears that at least in interlocutory voting in contentious cases and advisory matters, the President of the PCIJ had cast his casting votes differently from his first.[19] There is little public data on the casting vote at the ICJ, other than what we can see in the *South West Africa* cases and in the *Nuclear Weapons* advisory opinion, as discussed above in paragraph 20.

23. The record of the casting vote at the ITLOS is not clear, but in 2002 when President Chandrasekhara Rao took stock of the first six years of its existence he gave an interesting summary:

> In practice, so far the President has not had to exercise his casting vote. On one occasion, when there was an equality of votes in indicative voting, the President indicated that he would vote a second time in much the same way as his first vote; the matter was subsequently taken as having been settled without proceeding to a formal vote. However, over the last three years, on each occasion when there was an equality of votes, the voting process was suspended. The President contributed to further elucidation of the issue, both through formal debate and informal consultation. When the vote was subsequently taken, the matter was resolved without the need for the President's casting vote.[20]

The language seems to suggest that it would be possible for the President's casting vote to differ from his first vote.

---

18 According to Rosenne, ibid., 396, "There was no clear-cut practice that the President's second vote had to be the same as the first vote." For further information on the casting vote in the PCIJ, see PCIJ, Series E, No. 3, 216; No. 4, 291; No. 6, 299; No. 7, 298; No. 9, 174; No. 10, 163; No. 11, 150; No. 12, 197; No. 13, 153; No. 14, 158-159; No. 16, 198.

19 See, e.g., PCIJ Series E, No. 6, 299 ("during the discussion of a case, the President exercised his casting vote in a sense contrary to his original vote"); No. 9, 174 (not clear whether "two cases" means "two occasions" or "two judicial cases" in this statement: "During the 26th and 28th Sessions, the President had, on several occasions, to make use of his casting vote. In two cases, he postponed his decision and, finally, gave his casting vote in a sense contrary to his original vote."). Regarding quoting different language versions of texts in the judgments, there was a clear practice for the casting vote to be cast to maintain the status quo. See e.g., PCIJ Series E, No. 14, 158-159; No. 16, 198.

20 P. Chandrasekhara Rao, n.5 above, 6 Max Planck YUNL, 198.

24. As is clear from this discussion, at every step and every turn in the judicial process, there is great room for the President to play a leadership role. Indeed, his or her strong role in the deliberations and the drafting of decisions seems to suggest that the President resembles a permanent "*Juge rapporteur*", with a sharp sword called the casting vote.[21]

I.D. Outside activities

25. As the organizational leader of the ITLOS, the President may be called upon under a variety of instruments to perform functions outside the ITLOS.[22] Sometimes the activities involved, although outside the ITLOS, are not too far away; indeed, they are within the system of dispute settlement established under the UNCLOS. For example, under Annex VII, article 3(e) to the UNCLOS, the President "shall" make certain appointments in order to constitute an arbitral tribunal under certain circumstances.[**] Such activities are a reflection of the esteem the world holds for the ITLOS as well as its President. They may grow as the ITLOS grows in stature.

There are various categorizations of such activities, such as extra-judicial activities or "la fonction gracieuse". However, to the extent that such appointment activities are initiated by the presentation of a concrete, particular dispute before the President, although he or she will not deal with the merits of the matter, these activities take on a judicial dimension, and are similar to the function of the President in establishing a Special Chamber in which he or she would not become a member. Furthermore, the relevant provisions governing such activities may present disputes over interpretation, such as the possible

---

21 The PCIJ did use "*Juge rapporteur*" at the beginning but quickly abandoned this approach in favour of a drafting committee. See PCIJ, Series E, No. 2, 170; Manley O. Hudson, n.15 above, 581. The ITLOS in formulating its Resolution on the Internal Judicial Practice did consult the various approaches. See Anderson, n.5 above, 200-202. The final outcome apparently represents what the ITLOS Judges believed to be the proper balance between a very strong "*Juge rapporteur*" and a "normal" President.

22 For general discussions, see Eiriksson, n.5 above, 56, 23-26; P. Chandrasekhara Rao, n.5 above, 6 Max Planck YUNL, 285-288.

** Poscript: After the original publication of this paper, the President has had occasions to make several appointments under this provision, ITLOS/Press 189 (05.02.2013); ITLOS/Press 191 (25.04.2013); ITLOS/Press 209 (18.03. 2014); and ITLOS/Press 207 (13.01.2014).

interpretation of Annex VII, article 3,[23] which he or she determines by a resolution not differing from a judicial decision. This finds further evidence in the fact that the framers of Annex VII applied the principle of disqualification of the "national President" to this appointment process, as discussed below in paragraphs 42 and 51.

I.E. General comments

26. The three dimensions combined present to us a very strong President of the ITLOS. As has been noted,[24] when the Judges formulated the Resolution on the Internal Judicial Practice, they took note of the prolonged procedures and the inordinate delays that have plagued other courts and tribunals and resolved that "it should attempt to administer justice fairly and efficiently, without unnecessary delay or expense".[25] This and various other factors have persuaded them to decide to promote the more collegial working of the Tribunal and grant the President a prominent leadership role in many respects especially in the deliberations and the drafting of decisions, "with the expectation that he or she would engage in the necessary consultations to assure support for the proposals on which decisions are to be based".[26] As a result, the President of the ITLOS may be in a stronger position than the president of any other international judicial body.

II. Antidotes: short term of office; judicial solemn declaration and the attempt to equalize the parties by ensuring national representation; the principle of separation of the functions and disqualification of the national President

27. As is clear, one can easily tell that the President of the ITLOS is a powerful one. It is possible, however, that the good news is that there is a strong President, but the bad news is also that there is a strong President. If one were to presume the worst for the purpose of argument, these extensive powers and functions could be a very good platform for the "national State extension" vice, if it did exist, to inflict the gravest damage. In a mature system of justice,

---

23 See P. Chandrasekhara Rao, ibid., 286.

24 Treves, n.5 above, 138-139; Anderson, n.5 above, esp. 199-201.

25 Anderson, n.5 above, 199-200.

26 Eiriksson, n.5 above, 51.

antidotes or safeguards would have been instituted to prevent the abuse of office, even if in a minor way. This is true of the ITLOS system. The existing antidotes include imposing a relatively short term of office of three years with eligibility for reelection; requiring the making of a judicial solemn declaration and attempting to equalize the parties by ensuring "national representation"; and separating the functions of the President and disqualifying the President as President, not as Judge, in a case in which his national State is a party. Instituted in the system of the PCIJ, these antidotes have been inherited in that of the ICJ. They have now been adopted into the system of the ITLOS through the Statute and the Rules of the Tribunal.

II.A. Short term of office

28. The importance of the office of the President and the danger that may accompany that importance was immediately clear to the drafters of the PCIJ Statute, the Advisory Committee of Jurists. Therefore, Lord Phillimore expressed the view that "it would be dangerous to make the Presidency of the Court too important a post."[27] The ensuing discussions resulted in a relatively short term of office of three years for the President. According to James Brown Scott, who was present at the drafting conference as a legal advisor to Elihu Root:

> It was felt that, given the immense prestige of the position of president of the court, the power which he might exercise to bear upon his colleagues, it was inadvisable to elect him for the full term of his office, that is, nine years. One year, on the contrary, seemed too short, inasmuch as the president is to reside at the seat of the court. A period of three years was adopted as a compromise [...].[28]

This check on the presidency is a general one. Applied to the national State extension concern (though not specifically discussed in this context by the drafters), or any other concern, this remedy seems to embody the belief that

---

27 PCIJ Advisory Committee of Jurists, Procès Verbaux of the Proceedings of the Committee, June 16th-July 24th, 1920 (1920), 450 (PCIJ ACPV).

28 James Brown Scott, The Project of a Permanent Court of International Justice and Resolutions of the Advisory Committee of Jurists: Report and Commentary (Washington, DC, 1920), 78.

even if the President did act in an improper way, the damage or inconvenience would not last too long.

The drafters did not propose other safeguards specifically against the President. This three-year term of office with the possibility of re-election ultimately was adopted in the PCIJ Statute (article 21), the ICJ Statute (article 21) and, subsequently, in the Statute of the ITLOS (article 12).

II.B. Judicial solemn declaration and the attempt to equalize the parties by ensuring national representation

29. When the "national State extension" concern came to the minds of the framers of the PCIJ Statute, it was the situation of the normal Judge, rather than the President, that preoccupied them. After some discussions, the framers of the PCIJ Statute imposed the requirement of making a judicial oath or solemn declaration and mounted a strong effort to equalize the parties in a case before the Court, leading to the adoption of the system of the national Judges and Judges *ad hoc*. These measures have been followed in the ICJ Statute and that of the ITLOS. These measures are intended to tackle the concern at the basic level of the Judges and, as a result, should also have an impact on the performance of the President.

30. Very early on in the drafting process, the Advisory Committee of Jurists charged with drafting the PCIJ Statute agreed on the need for some form of oath or solemn declaration. M. de Lapradelle was recorded to have spoken of the virtue of such a declaration this way:

> He considered that, if international justice reached a high degree of perfection, it would not be necessary to meddle with the composition of the Court. The oath to be taken or the declaration to be made by the judges should of itself suffice to convey the notion of that complete impartiality on their part, which would induce the States to submit their disputes to the Court as a matter of course, without considering its composition. The judges would be not denationalised but super-nationalised ["supra-nationalisés" in the French original].[29]

The English rendition of de Lapradelle's "supra-nationalisés" as "supernationalised" probably is inaccurate. The "supra-nationalisé" character of

29 PCIJ ACPV, n.27 above, 534.

the international Judge in the mind of de Lapradelle would apparently cause the Judge to transcend any national allegiance. That would be an ideal situation. The PCIJ Statute ultimately provides in article 20: "Every member of the Court shall, before taking up his duties, make a solemn declaration in open Court that he will exercise his powers impartially and conscientiously."

31. To implement this article in more concrete terms, the first formulation in article 5 of the PCIJ Rules of Court in 1922[30] of this solemn declaration by the PCIJ Judges reads: "I solemnly declare that I will exercise all my powers and duties as a judge honourably and faithfully, impartially and conscientiously". The statutory provision has remained the same in the ICJ Statute, but the terms of the declaration have undergone some minor revision. The current formulation of the actual declaration in article 4 of the ICJ Rules reads: "I solemnly declare that I will perform my duties and exercise my powers as judge honourably, faithfully, impartially and conscientiously."

32. All this has been followed in the ITLOS system. Article 11 of the ITLOS Statute provides that "Every member of the Tribunal shall, before taking up his duties, make a solemn declaration in open session that he will exercise his powers impartially and conscientiously." To implement this provision, article 5(1) of the ITLOS Rules stipulates: "The solemn declaration to be made by every Member in accordance with article 11 of the Statute shall be as follows: [...] 'I solemnly declare that I will perform my duties and exercise my powers as judge honourably, faithfully, impartially and conscientiously'."

33. If indeed such a solemn declaration would have the magic power to "supra-nationalize", to follow de Lapradelle's phraseology, then the Judges including the President would not be under any sway of national allegiance. That is to say, the national State extension vice would have been eliminated at the root level. The drafters of the PCIJ Statute, however, were not bleary-eyed idealists so as to believe in such magic power. They proceeded to provide for further safeguards, focusing on the presence on the Bench of the so-called "national Judge" in a case in which his or her national State is a party. Recognizing that although the Judges were to be elected without regard to their nationality, after election they would retain one, the drafters considered several possibilities. One possibility would be to ask all Judges whose national States were parties in a case to abstain from taking part in deciding the case. This approach would reduce the number of available Judges, making it difficult for the Court to operate as a World Court and to win over the confidence of some

---

30 PCIJ, Series D, No. 1 (1992), http://www.icj-cij.org/pcij/serie_D/D_01.pdf.

States who may believe that only when there were Judges of their nationality on the Bench throughout the proceedings, deliberations and decision-making could they be certain that their positions were presented properly and considered thoroughly before a decision was made. Furthermore, the national Judge would also bring local knowledge to assist the Bench's appreciation of the complex factual and legal issues and the drafting of decisions in a way so as to "avoid ruffling national susceptibilities in any way".[31] They also believed that the moral character and professional honor of the Judges would be such that they would not necessarily vote for his or her national State and that if "the opposing views were both represented on the Bench, they would counter-balance one another."[32] Eventually they opted to keep the national Judges on the Bench and to provide for a system of Judges *ad hoc* so that (1) if the Bench includes a Judge of the nationality of one party but not of the other party, then the other party may appoint a Judge *ad hoc* in order to reestablish equality; or (2) if the Bench includes no Judge of the nationality of either party, then each party may appoint a Judge *ad hoc*.[33] The Advisory Committee of Jurists was aware that in the last scenario, the Court "more nearly resembles a Court of Arbitration than a national Court of Justice", but thought that this setup was "necessary" and defended it thus: "Though our Court is a true Court, we must not forget that it is a Court between States. [...] States attach much importance to having one of their subjects on the Bench when they appear before a Court of Justice."[34] This system ultimately was implemented in article 31 of the PCIJ Statute. Article 31 of the ICJ Statute has inherited this system.[35]

34. No doubt this was a strong effort to equalize the parties in a case before the Court. Subsequently a committee of the PCIJ Judges appointed to examine the issue of national Judges and Judges *ad hoc* summarized the system and the motivating factors for it this way:

---

31 PCIJ ACPV, n.27 above, 721.

32 Ibid. High moral character or reputation for integrity subsequently has become part of the qualifications for election as member of the PCIJ, ICJ and also the ITLOS.

33 Ibid., 720-722.

34 Ibid., 722.

35 For further discussions, see Stephen M. Schwebel, National Judges and Judges *ad hoc*, in: René-Jean Dupuy & L.A. Sicilianos (eds), n.7 above, 319-329; Shabtai Rosenne, Article 31 of the Statute of the International Court of Justice Revisited, in: ibid., 301-317.

> In the attempt to establish international courts of justice, the fundamental problem always has been, and probably always will be, that of the representation of the litigants in the constitution of the tribunal. Of all influences to which men are subject, none is more powerful, more pervasive, or more subtle, than the tie of allegiance that binds them to the land of their homes and kindred and to the great sources of the honors and preferments for which they are so ready to spend their fortunes and to risk their lives. This fact, known to all the world, the Statute frankly recognizes and deals with.
>
> It being conceded that equality in the matter was essential, there were two ways of assuring it. These were, either by making allegiance a disqualification, or by placing the parties on an even footing. The Statute (Article 31) chose the latter, by providing (1) that judges of the nationality of each of the parties should retain their right to sit; (2) that, if the bench included a judge of only one of the parties, the others [sic] might name a judge of its nationality; and (3) that, if neither party had on the bench a judge of its own nationality, each might designate such a judge. Thus, the Statute provided for national representation, even where none existed, as well as for equality in such representation.[36]

35. After they agreed on the system of national Judges (only later did States begin to appoint Judges *ad hoc* who are not their nationals), the drafters of the PCIJ Statute seemed to have forgotten about whether there was any need to deal with the situation of the President who is of the nationality of a party in a case before the Court. Following the term "national Judges", let us call the President in such a situation the "national President". Admittedly, the phrase, like the term "national Judge", is not a happy one, but it does convey the idea. No explanation can be readily found in the preparatory work for the silence of the drafters on the national President. Perhaps the force of the judicial solemn

---

36 Report of the Committee, in PCIJ, The Fourth Annual Report (1927-1928), Series E, No. 4, 75-76. It is interesting to see that the PCIJ Judges were so frank in their statement on the force of national allegiance. Of course, at present other forms of allegiance such as ethnic or religious allegiance may be becoming more and more powerful. In this paper I do not deal with these other forms of allegiance and how they can be combatted. The judicial solemn declaration or the presidential solemn declaration suggested below hopefully is a strong enough antidote to those forms of allegiance. Perhaps this issue can be an agenda item for the future.

declaration was thought to be substantial. Perhaps the presence of the national Judge of the other party in the case was considered a powerful check on the conduct of the President. Or, perhaps the two combined were considered sufficient.

36. The same system of national Judges and Judges *ad hoc* has also been implemented in article 17 the ITLOS Statute. The same imperfections if any that may exist under the PCIJ Statute and the ICJ Statute, regarding the situation of the national President or the desire to equalize the parties, would have been carried over into the ITLOS Statute.

II.C. Separation of functions and disqualification of the national President

37. Strong though the efforts made by the framers of the PCIJ to equalize the parties in a case may be, they were an "incomplete revolution", so to speak. As President Huber himself subsequently pointed out, the Statute could not guarantee equality of the parties, when the President is a national of one of the parties who may decide a case by casting vote:

> [L'article 31 du Statut] consacre le principe des juges «nationaux», principe adopté pour mettre les Parties dans une situation d'égalité. Or, ce principe ne peut pas garantir que le résultat visé soit en toutes circonstances attaint. Si, par example, le Président est ressortissant d'un État qui est Partie au litige, il se peut que l'affaire doive être décidée par la voix prépondérante du Président; une pareille situation serait très pénible.[37]

38. He proposed that the Court remedy this situation by rule-making. Obviously—although he did not say so—when the President is a national of

---

[37] PCIJ Series D, No. 2, addendum, 247-248 (1926). The problem that President Huber identified seemed to have been noticed in part earlier. Regarding the control of the discussions or hearing, two earlier documents or draft documents touched upon this issue. See 1907 Convention (XII) Relative to the Creation of an International Prize Court, art. 38 ("The judge appointed by a belligerent Party cannot preside"); 1907 Draft Convention Relative to the Creation of a Judicial Arbitration Court (annex to the first *vœu* of the Second Peace Conference), art. 26 ("The judge appointed by one of the parties cannot preside").

one of the parties to the case, equality of the parties cannot be achieved by adding another President of the nationality of the other party in the case, following what is done regarding the "national Judges". Two Presidents working simultaneously as such in the same case would make the situation untenable. Rather, he proposed two things. The first is to separate the functions of the judicial leader in a particular case—President of the Bench—from the functions of the normal judge and those of the organizational leader. The second is to disqualify the judicial leader from acting as such—that is, the national President would be disqualified as President, but would continue to act as Judge—in a case in which his or her national State is a party, without affecting the other two functions as a normal Judge and as the organizational leader.[38] This can be called the principle of separation of functions and disqualification of the national President. The disqualification here is partial only and applies to his or her functions as President, not those as Judge. If the Bench does not include a national of the other party, it can appoint a Judge *ad hoc*, as usual. The result is to achieve equality of the parties by making sure that no national of any party to a case may act as President in that case. Thus, as regards national Judges, equality of the parties is achieved by adding national Judges or Judges *ad hoc* to the Bench, while as regards the national President, equality is obtained by purging him or her from the presidency, though not the Bench, or by demoting him or her from the presidency to a normal national Judge in the case.

39. President Huber's wisdom was finally adopted as an addition to Article 13 of the Rules of Court in 1926, stipulating:

> Whenever, according to the rules in force, the functions of President should be exercised by a national of one of the parties to the suit, they shall pass, for the purposes of the case in question, in the order of seniority established by the Rules of Court, to the first judge not similarly situated.[39]

40. Then, in 1929, Article 45 of the PCIJ Statute, which previously provided that the oral hearing was under the control of the President, but that if he was absent, then the Vice-President or the senior Judge would preside, was amended essentially by changing "absent" to "unable", in order to take account

38 See PCIJ, ibid.

39 See PCIJ, Series D, No. 1 (1926).

of this rule.[40]

41. The rule proposed by President Huber subsequently became Article 32(1) of the ICJ Rules of Court of 1978:

> If the President of the Court is a national of one of the parties in a case he shall not exercise the functions of the presidency in respect of that case. The same rule applies to the Vice-President, or to the senior judge, when called on to act as President.

42. It is somewhat noteworthy that, in the light of this experience, the framers of the UNCLOS and the Statute of the ITLOS did not feel compelled to incorporate the principle of separation of functions and disqualification of the national President into the ITLOS Statute itself. The non-implementation of this principle in the ITLOS Statute is even more noteworthy when one sees its implementation in part in Annex VII, article 3(e), on the President's obligation to make certain appointments, as touched upon above in paragraph 25. Under this latter article, the President is disqualified from making such appointments if he or she is a national of one of the parties to the dispute.

43. It thus fell upon the Judges of the ITLOS to deal with this issue as a general matter in the formulation of the Rules of the Tribunal. This they did. Currently, Article 16(1) of the Rules provides:

> No Member who is a national of a party in a case, a national of a State member of an international organization which is a party in a case or a national of a sponsoring State of an entity other than a State which is a party in a case, shall exercise the functions of the presidency in respect of the case.

44. The authoritative commentary on this article explains:

> This article is modelled on Article 32 of the Rules of the ICJ. Since the Convention gives access to international organizations and to entities other than States, it was necessary to reflect this in paragraph 1. Hence a Member is barred from exercising the function of the presidency in respect of a case not only when he or she is a national of a party to the case, but also when he or she is a national of a State member of an

40 See below, para.49.

international organization which is a party to the case or a national of a sponsoring State of an entity other than a State.[41]

45. That is to say, Article 16(1) of the ITLOS Rules implements the principle of separation of functions and disqualification of the national President and adapts it to the circumstances of the ITLOS. As the possibility of a Judge *ad hoc* getting elected as the President of an *ad hoc* Special Chamber in the ITLOS has been recognized by some commentators, as discussed below in paragraph 70, one should note that such a possibility would present interesting occasions for the application of article 16(1). One may argue that although the language of article 16(1) limits its application to a "Member" (referring only to an elected Judge, under article 1(e) of the Rules), this article should also apply to all Judges *ad hoc*. A Judge *ad hoc* in a case either is a national of a party in that case, or *can and should be reckoned* as one because of his or her status as the non-national appointee of a party. In case the general argument for applying the article to any Judge *ad hoc* including a non-national Judge *ad hoc* is wrong, this article should at least apply to a national Judge *ad hoc*. In any event, if it is possible for a Judge *ad hoc* to be elected as the President of an *ad hoc* Special Chamber, and if no other provision in the Rules has dealt with the implications of this possibility, article 16(1) may be ripe for amendment or interpretation. It should be noted that the language of article 16(1) is such that a provision for the *mutatis mutandis* application of it to Judges *ad hoc* may not be able to cover non-national Judges *ad hoc*. The application of this provision to all Judges *ad hoc* can be achieved by adding at the end of article 16(1): "Nor shall any Judge *ad hoc*."

III. Two issues in the application of the principle of separation of functions and disqualification of the national President: trigger point and scope of application

46. The above-discussed antidotes are what the existing toolbox affords us in the form of statutory or rule-making endeavors. And they seem to be substantial and reasonable. We do not have sufficient public data on the experience of applying these provisions to tackle the national State extension concern so as to allow us to assess this experience comprehensively. Still, one can imagine that some issues do exist in the application of these antidotes at the

41 P. Chandrasekhara Rao and Ph. Gautier (eds), Commentary on the Rules, n.5 above, 42.

PCIJ and ICJ, and potentially exist at the ITLOS. Here I will highlight two issues regarding the application of the principle of separation of functions and disqualification of the national President at the PCIJ and the ICJ and comment on these issues and their potential implications for the ITLOS.

III.A. The trigger point for the separation of functions and disqualification of the national President

47. Good though a principle may be, if it is applied too late in the process it will not be able to meet the expectation it has generated. This will be true of the principle of separation of functions and disqualification of the national President. Still neither the ITLOS Rules nor the ICJ nor the PCIJ Rules contain a provision in express and specific terms on this point. This situation may give rise to an issue of interpretation. One can imagine that this principle could start to apply at various points: (1) as soon as a particular case is presented to the Court or Tribunal; (2) at the time when any case management function is to be exercised; (3) at the time when the first deliberation is had before the oral hearing; (4) at the time when the President is called upon to preside over the oral hearing; or (5) at the time when deliberation over the merits after the oral hearing is to begin. It is not clear at present which point the ITLOS will choose if such an issue presents itself. At least article 16(1) of its Rules has not spelled this out in clear terms.

48. In the experience of the PCIJ, such a choice was in fact expressly made once in the *Memel* case. There the President (Adatci) was a national of one of the parties to the case. The question whether the President should be replaced by the Vice-President for the purposes of drawing up and signing the Order fixing the time-limits for some pleadings in this case was decided in the negative by the President for the following reasons: (1) "the authors of the provision in Article 13 [of the Rules] had only had in mind the President's functions when the Court was deliberating", (2) "if the President were not to take the requisite administrative decisions in a given case, the work of the Court might be paralyzed, at all events so long as the ordinary members were not bound to reside at the seat of the Court"; and (3) "with regard to the fixing of time-limits, the last paragraph of Article 33 of the Rules afforded the Parties adequate protection".[42] He further observed that "each case should be dealt

[42] PCIJ, Series E, No. 8 (1931-1932), 247-248. Art. 33, last paragraph, of the Rules stated that "If the Court is not sitting, the powers conferred upon it by

with having regard to the circumstances peculiar to it; for it was possible to imagine cases where mere decisions of procedure would entrench upon matters connected with the merits."[43]

49. It is not clear whether, in his first reason, the President was saying that the principle of disqualification of the national President only applied during deliberation over the merits after the oral hearing had been held. If so, he would be taking an overly restrictive and arguably wrong position. In the 1929 amendment of the PCIJ Statute the English version of Article 45 was changed from "The hearing shall be under the control of the President, or in his absence, of the Vice-President; if both are absent, the senior judge shall preside" to "The hearing shall be under the control of the President or, if he is unable to preside, of the Vice-President; if neither is able to preside, the senior judge shall preside", with the intent to take account of the application of the principle of separation of functions and disqualification embodied in article 13 of the Rules (amended in 1926, as discussed above), after this rule was pointed out to the Committee of Jurists which was framing amendments.[44] It was agreed that the original English version did not reflect the intent of the provision, although the French version has remained the same. Therefore, this new English version of the Statute can be deemed to have required the application of the principle at the latest at the time when the oral hearing is held.

50. Furthermore, the President's fear of paralysis resulting from the fact that the ordinary Judges were not bound to reside at the seat of the Court may have a point then at the PCIJ and even now at the ITLOS where only the President is required to permanently reside at the seat of the ITLOS. However, given the convenience of modern communication, this fear no longer has force, and in any event is subordinate to the need to maintain fairness and the appearance of fairness.[45]

51. In my view, the trigger point for the application of the principle of separation of functions and disqualification of the national President should be the very moment when a particular case is presented to the Tribunal and before

---

this article shall be exercised by the President, subject to any subsequent decision of the Court".

43 PCIJ, Series E, ibid., 248. Hudson, n.15 above, 343 and Guyomar, n.6 above, 176-177, noted this decision.

44 PCIJ, Series D, No. 1 (4th edn, 1940), 24; Minutes of the Committee of Jurists (1929, League of Nations Doc.: C.166.M.66.1929.V.), 65.

45 See also Guyomar, n.6 above, 176-177.

the President has a chance to take any action in that case. As highlighted earlier, the President has considerable power in the finalization of the Bench to deal with a particular case, particularly when a Special Chamber is utilized, his or her decisions will have a significant impact on the outcome of a case. In addition, the case management functions usually also have such an impact, if to a lesser extent. Thus, it is important for the national President to be disqualified before these functions are carried out. Finally, this view finds support in the fact that Annex VII, article 3(e) applies the principle of disqualification at the stage of "Bench" formulation—the appointment of arbitrators and/or president to constitute an arbitral tribunal. Of course, choosing such a trigger point will help to promote the appearance of fairness, not just factual fairness.

III.B. Application of the principle when the national State of the President is not a party but is substantially in the same interest as a party in a case

52. Just like late application, the narrow application of a principle may also frustrate its purpose. In our inquiry here, the principle of separation of functions and disqualification of the national President was formulated in the PCIJ and the ICJ for application to the President whose national State is a party in a case. Its application is not demanded expressly under either the Statute or Rules when the national State is not a party in a case, but is very much an "absent party" in the same interest or substantially in the same interest as a party in that case. This issue has come up in the practice of the ICJ. For example, in the *Lockerbie* cases, Libya brought one case against the United States, and another against the United Kingdom. In the case against the United Kingdom, President Jennings, who was a national of the United Kingdom, was disqualified from acting as President. But in the case against the United States, must he be similarly disqualified or not?

53. In the end, according to the *ICJ Yearbook*, President Jennings voluntarily refrained from acting as President in the case against the United States, thus removing the occasion for the Court to decide this question. He "considered that it would be inappropriate, as well as inconvenient for all concerned, if he were to try to preside, as in theory he supposed he might"[46] in that case. This approach was followed by President Schwebel (of US nationality) in a subsequent phase in the *Lockerbie* cases. He "thought it appropriate not to

[46] See ICJYB 1991-1992, 198.

exercise the functions of the Presidency"[47] in the case against the United Kingdom. Under article 32(1) of the ICJ Rules, he was already disqualified from acting as President in the case against the United States. Subsequently in the *Legality of Use of Force* cases, Yugoslavia brought 10 cases against NATO members separately. President Jennings's approach was again followed first by President Schwebel[48] and, subsequently, by President Guillaume[49] (of French nationality); each "considered that it would not be appropriate for him to exercise" the presidential functions in those cases in which his national State was not a party. Of course each was already disqualified under the Rules from acting as President in the case in which his national State was a party. Thus, each time this issue has come up, it has been resolved by the relevant President's own voluntary relinquishment of presidential functions, without a decision by the Court as a whole. The Jennings-Schwebel-Guillaume practice seems to have the effect of preventing awkward questions, if any, from being raised. Perhaps one may venture—I emphasize, venture—that a practice has developed in the ICJ or by the ICJ Presidents,[50] to be more precise, that in similar situations the President is disqualified from, or *should* refrain from, acting as President in a particular case.

54. Although the trend is strong, it is really difficult to assess whether it has been considered a rule. To the extent that the Presidents considered it inappropriate not to refrain from acting as President in the above-discussed cases, the practice is not a matter of desirability, but comes close or can be considered to embody a rule. We perhaps should note that in the 1992 judgment on preliminary objections in the *Nauru* case, although one of the preliminary objections was that the United Kingdom too was responsible (having shared membership with Australia and New Zealand in the authority administering Nauru during the relevant time) and thus an indispensable party, President Jennings remained as President in the case.[51] Perhaps the reason was that no action had been brought against the United Kingdom in a separate case relating to the subject matter. But should this be the decisive factor? The absence of such a case may have resulted from a reason that has nothing to do

---

47 See ICJYB 1997-1998, 250.

48 See ICJYB 1998-1999, 288-289.

49 See ICJYB 2000-2001, 299 (same as above).

50 For general discussions on precedent, see Mohamed Shahabuddeen, Precedent in the World Court (1996).

51 Case concerning Certain Phosphate Lands in Nauru, Preliminary Objections, ICJ Reports 1992, 241.

with what has motivated the practice. In any event, there was no indication that any objection was raised to President Jennings acting as President. Ultimately the *Nauru* judgment on preliminary objections was reached by a comfortable margin and thus presented no occasion for the use of the casting vote, although President Jennings did dissent on the very question relating to the treatment of the preliminary objection based on the legal interests of the United Kingdom.[52] To the extent that the *Legality of Use of Force* cases came after the *Nauru* judgment, what President Jennings did in *Nauru* may be considered to have been weakened or overridden.

55. Neither the ITLOS Statute nor its Rules nor its case law appears to have addressed our particular inquiry here. However, Article 16(1) of the ITLOS Rules is an advancement; it extends the "national State" of the President to cover situations where he or she is a national of a State member of an international organization which is a party to the case or a national of a sponsoring State of an entity other than a State, when that entity is a party in a case.

56. In the light of the fact that the ITLOS Statute and its Rules borrow the framework as well as much of the language from the ICJ Statute and Rules generally and also specifically on this point, one is inclined to argue that the ITLOS should also follow the ICJ practice or that of its Presidents—which should come in the same portmanteau as the ICJ Statute and Rules—so that the President is either disqualified, or should refrain voluntarily, from acting as President in a case when his or her national State, though not a party in a case, is very much in the same interest or substantially in the same interest as a party in that case. Of course, the ICJ practice or that of its Presidents is independently a good practice for the promotion of equality of parties in substance if not in form and this is a sufficient reason for it to be followed at the ITLOS.

57. Article 16(1) of the ITLOS Rules providing for the disqualification of the President from acting as such when he or she is a national of a State member of an international organization which is a party to the case can be considered to have covered, or can be extended logically to cover, the situation when actions are brought against the members of the organization for the acts of that organization, such as in the *Legality of Use of Force* cases or the *Nauru* case, whether or not an action is being brought against the national State of the President separately. After all, the substantive subject matter of the dispute may

52 Ibid., 268, para.72(1)(f); ibid., 301, Diss. Op. of President Jennings.

well be the same in both situations and the responsibility of the organization and the members are intertwined.[53] This reasoning would seem to extend to not just formal international organizations but also alliances, especially in military affairs. In any event, article 16(1) at least shows a tendency in favour of extending generally the application of the principle to the situation where the national State of the President is not a party but is in the same interest or substantially in the same interest as a party in a case.

58. The abovementioned situations all involved real factual connections between the national State of the President and other States that are parties in a case. A more difficult situation would be one that may not involve such factual connections but only a legal position shared by the national State of the President and one of the parties to the case. For example, assuming, *arguendo*, that the ITLOS somehow receives a case between two Asian States about continental shelf delimitation, in which the vitality of a certain principle is the decisive factor[54] and further that the President is of a European nationality and that his national State is widely known for having championed the position that the particular principle in issue has no effect in contemporary international law, will it still be appropriate for the President to act as President and, in all eventualities, even decide the matter by casting vote?

59. This is a difficult question. The practice that has developed among the ICJ Presidents may logically extend to such a situation so that it may be advisable for the President to refrain from acting as such in the case. But this position, if considered as required by law, may extend quite far the concept of party in the same interest or substantially in the same interest. But "quite far" may not be the same as "too far". Indeed, the Jennings-Schwebel-Guillaume practice evinces a tendency to take extra efforts, so far as these are not expressly required under the Statute and the Rules, to ensure equality of the parties, given the importance of fairness and the strong role of the President. This "pro-fairness" nature of the practice is made more obvious from a comparison between the Jennings-Schwebel-Guillaume practice in the *Lockerbie* cases and

53 For an analysis, see Sienho Yee, The Responsibility of States Members of an International Organization for its Conduct as a Result of Membership or Their Normal Conduct Associated with Membership, in: Maurizio Ragazzi (ed.), International Responsibility Today: Essays in Memory of Oscar Schachter (2005), 435-454.

54 For an analysis on some significant factors in delimitation, see SHI Jiuyong, Maritime Delimitation in the Jurisprudence of the International Court of Justice, 9 Chinese JIL (2010), 271-291.

the *Legality of Use of Force* cases and the ICJ's decisions in those cases to accept the appointment of Judges *ad hoc*. The relationship between the United States and the United Kingdom in the *Lockerbie* cases was such to persuade President Jennings and President Schwebel to refrain from acting as President in the case against the United States and the case against the United Kingdom, respectively (as discussed in paragraphs 52 and 53 above), but, apparently, not to persuade the Court to consider the two States as "parties in the same interest" for the purpose of appointment of a Judge *ad hoc* by the United Kingdom in a subsequent phase of the case against it on preliminary objections, although the Bench had already included Judge Schwebel, a national of the United States. The same happened in the *Legality of Use of Force* cases: although President Schwebel and President Guillaume refrained from acting as President in all the related cases, some NATO members were allowed to appoint Judges *ad hoc* in the provisional measures phase, although the Bench in the cases at issue had already included Judges of the nationality of various NATO members. The Court then decided that the Judges *ad hoc* appointed by NATO members should not sit in the preliminary objections phase.[55] Thus, the Jennings-Schwebel-Guillaume practice seems to apply a broader understanding of party in the same interest or substantially in the same interest than did the ICJ itself for the purpose of appointment of Judges *ad hoc*, whether the Court was correct or not. It would not be such a big step for this presidential tendency to be carried over to the situation where the national State of the President, though a non-party State in a case, shares a legal position decisive in that case with a party in it. The implications of such an approach will be very important and can of course be very complicated especially in Asia where many law of the sea issues are being worked out.[56] Yet, in situations where justice not only has to be done but also

---

55 See Lockerbie (Libya v. UK), ICJ Reports 1998, 9, 13, para.9 (for criticisms, see Joint Declaration of Judges Bedjaoui, Guillaume and Ranjeva, ICJ Reports 1998, 32); Legality of Use of Force (Yugoslavia v. Belgium), ICJ Report 1999, 124, 130, para.12 (for criticisms, see Diss. Op. of Judge Kreća, ibid., 217-220); and ICJ Reports 2004, 279, 287, para.18. As far as the Legality of Use of Force cases are concerned, if they were before the ITLOS, article 22 of its Rules would seem, although not so clear, to militate against the appointment of Judges *ad hoc* by NATO members. It is not clear how the ICJ's case law on intervention may be relevant to our inquiry here and I will leave this issue for another day.

56 See, e.g., Agora: Military Activities in the EEZ, 9 Chinese JIL (2010), 1-47; Responses, 10 Chinese JIL (2011), 177-223.

seen done, there is much to commend such a position. In any event, this point is raised here to provoke soul-searching on the part of those who conscientiously search for justice in international affairs.

IV. Suggestion for the consideration of a presidential solemn declaration

60. The uncertainties relating to the timing and scope of the application of the principle of separation of functions and disqualification of the national President in a case may leave a big space where the President is not disqualified as such in a case in which his national State is a party and, thus, his or her national allegiance may play a role. Even when his or her national State is not a party in a related case, there is still room for that allegiance to assume a large proportion with significant effect for the future. Although this is not clear, one may imagine that this could also obtain regarding the President's exercise of functions as the organizational leader.

61. Accordingly, the search for antidotes may need to continue. In the light of the existence of the judicial oath or declaration and of the fact that heads of States or heads of many organizations often have to make an oath, one is struck by the lack of a "presidential oath" or "presidential solemn declaration", to follow the language of judicial "solemn declaration", in the Statute or the Rules of the PCIJ, ICJ or the ITLOS, specifically addressing the office of the President. Nor is there one, it is believed, in the practice of these judicial bodies.[57] Of course, such a presidential declaration, like the existing judicial declaration, would not address the possible national State extension vice alone but the entire relevant conduct of the actor. Or, one may say, the declaration targets the entire relevant conduct in order to prevent a particular vice.

62. Our immediate instinct is to say that the judicial solemn declaration to be made by every Judge is sufficient. An examination, however, may give us an unclear picture. The express terms of the judicial declaration appear to cover only judicial activities, not "presidential activities". The Statute of the ITLOS in article 11 provides that "Every member of the Tribunal shall, before taking up his duties, make a solemn declaration in open session that he will exercise his

---

57 I have made an effort to seek information on practice, and the feedbacks received confirm this belief. A check on the records of the PCIJ 1922 elaboration of the Rules of Court did not reveal any evidence of this issue being discussed. See PCIJ, Series D, No. 2 (1922).

powers impartially and conscientiously", which is similar to the corresponding provisions in the PCIJ and ICJ Statutes. The phrases "every member" and "his powers" would seem to encompass the President and presidential powers when he or she is called upon to exercise them. That is to say, presidential powers can be considered part of the powers of a Member. That is reasonable enough, as the President must first be a "Member". However, the concretization of the solemn declaration by the Judges in the Rules, as discussed above in paragraph 31, seems to make a distinction between the Judge and other persons and focus on the Judge as a declarant only, by using the term "judge" since the very first version of the PCIJ Rules of Court adopted in 1922. Similarly, the terms of the declaration spelled out in article 5(1) of the ITLOS Rules read: "I solemnly declare that I will perform my duties and exercise my powers as judge honourably, faithfully, impartially and conscientiously". Thus, unless one would give the term "as judge" a very broad or macro interpretation, this declaration would not deal with presidential functions as such. It is not clear whether such a broad interpretation would be proper in the light of the fact that every Judge including every Judge *ad hoc* is required to make the same declaration.[58]

63. Most importantly, it may be difficult to consider the right to cast the casting vote as part of ordinary judicial function. As recognized at the PCIJ, the casting vote is of a completely discretionary nature and can be different from the first vote. It may indeed be difficult for one to maintain that, as a matter of ordinary judicial decision-making, one Judge can say both "yes" and "no" to the same question in the same voting in the same case. So the casting vote can be better rationalized on grounds of extraordinary presidential power, distinct from the normal judicial power.[59]

---

58 Earlier in this paper I have argued for a broad concept of what is judicial for the application of the principle of separation of functions and disqualification of the national President. That of course is not to say every act of the President is judicial. Furthermore, in the Rules, "Member" means only elected Judges, while "Judge" is defined to include all Judges, whether elected or appointed (ICJ Rules, art.1; ITLOS Rules art.1), but this of course should not give one the misimpression that "President" is also included in this term, although the President is always a Judge. The use of Judge as including all Judges is more or less a function of the distinction between Members and Judges *ad hoc* and the need for a phrase that can encompass both; it does not aim to deal with presidential functions.

59 I recognize that there can be debate on the nature and exercise of judicial power. But generally discretionary judicial power is shunned. See Ronald

64. So, perhaps, as a matter of interpretation of the relevant provisions in the Statute and the Rules, one might have reason to say that there is some space to which the principle of separation of functions and disqualification of the national President may not apply, which the judicial solemn declaration does not cover, or where the judicial declaration is not sufficient. These provisions in the Statute and Rules leave us some doubt, but, as a whole, they support our assessment.

65. If these interpretive exercises appear very theoretical, practical experience does not weaken our conclusion. The judicial declaration, if it applies to presidential conduct, may have at least in one instance in real life not been effective in preventing "presidential" misconduct in the ICJ, as has been publicly alleged, although in an incident not involving the "national State extension" issue. Andronico O. Adede related that in *South West Africa Cases, Second Phase*, Judge Sir Muhammad Zafrulla Khan (Pakistan) was persuaded to recuse himself, although according to earlier practice he need not,[60] by some conduct unbecoming a President of the ICJ, leading to the lack of a clear majority in favour of Ethiopia and Liberia.[61] Adede wrote:

> Sir Zafrulla Khan is reported to have been furious to learn afterwards that the decision to ask him to disqualify himself from the 1966 proceedings was actively engineered by the President of the Court himself, Sir Percy C. Spender of Australia, in applying Article 24 of the Statute of the Court dealing with disqualification of a member of the Court to sit in a particular case. The President of the Court is said to have taken the position that Sir Zafrulla Khan had to disqualify himself from sitting in the case on the grounds that he had been an *ad hoc* judge for the Applicants in the case before he became a full member of the Court. This position was communicated to Sir Zafrulla by President Spender claiming that it was also the unanimous view of the other members of the Court. But as it turned out, this was a personal view of the President and not, as he made Sir Zafrulla to believe, supported by

Dworkin, Judicial Discretion, 60 The Journal of Philosophy (1963), 624-638. Sometimes the question goes to what really counts as discretion.

60 Ph. Couvreur, Article 17, in Zimmermann et al. (eds.), n.2 above, 348 n.68 (on the previous instance in a similar situation of Judge Charles de Visscher in Diversion of Water from the Meuse, PCIJ, Series A/B, No. 70, 4, 6).

61 Andronico O. Adede, Judicial Settlement in Perspective, in: A.S. Muller et al. (eds), The International Court of Justice (1997), 53.

other members of the Court.[62] Thus, the President of the Court arrogated to himself the power to bring about the disqualification of a member of the Court, thereby ensuring the possibility of the results he personally supported. He succeeded. There was a tie in the Court and, as President, Sir Percy voted twice and broke the tie in favour of the conservative view (the 1962 minority view), rejecting finally, the claim of Ethiopia and Liberia against South Africa. That the President of the Court is reported to have acted in such a fashion will remain one of the very disturbing developments in this much discussed case.[63]

66. If it were true,[64] this story might be proof that the judicial solemn

---

62 Ibid., original footnote 9 from Adede: "From a conversation with a legal assistant to Sir Zafrulla Khan and also from communication on file with the author. From these conversations the author was reminded that the African missions to the UN did, in fact, hold a demonstration at the Pakistan Mission to the UN, convinced that the Pakistani Judge had let them down by disqualifying himself from the case."

63 Ibid., 53.

64 One cannot be sure that Adede was completely accurate. I am quoting him here also for explaining the dynamics in the situation. Judge Sir Muhammad Zafrulla Khan himself was quoted as having made in 1966 this statement included in a memorandum circulated by the Pakistan Mission to the United Nations: "I never disqualified myself. There were no grounds for disqualifying me. The President of the Court was of the view that it would be improper for me to sit as I had at one time been nominated judge *ad hoc* by the Applicant States, though I never sat in that capacity. I disagreed entirely with that view and gave the President my reasons which I still consider were good reasons. But he told me that a large majority of the Judges agreed with him that I should not sit. So I had no option." Quoted in William M. Reisman, Revision of the South Africa Cases: An Analysis of the Grounds of Nullity in the Decision of July 18th, 1966 and Methods of Revision, 7 Virginia JIL (1966), 55-56. Judge Zafrulla Khan did not put anything down in writing about any decision by other Judges, presumably because he did not have personal knowledge of whether such a decision existed; he related only what the President had told him, of which he had personal knowledge. It could be interesting to know what President Spender told the other Judges. Sir Robert Jennings, Article 24, in Zimmermann et al. (eds), n.2 above, 417, 425 (MN 26), said, "There was never any official explanation of this decision or statement of any reasons for it, though it does seem that the President had consulted some other judges." Even if "it does seem" that the President did consult "some

declaration is not effective as a check on presidential conduct, although it may be effective as a check on judicial conduct in the core adjudicative functions. This is significant even though there is no evidence in the history of the PCIJ, ICJ or the ITLOS that any presidential misconduct has been motivated by national allegiance, because there is still room and possibility for national allegiance to take effect. Furthermore, it is true that the same unsatisfactory situation that occurred in the *South West Africa* cases probably will not occur anymore, as a result of article 34 in the 1978 Rules of Court, the remedy "probably induced"[65] by this situation and adopted in its wake by the ICJ and followed by the ITLOS.[66] However, a similarly unsatisfactory situation

other judges", which was of course only a guess as there was a lack of official information and Sir Robert did not present any other information on point, the problem was how many other Judges. It would seem that Judge Zafrulla Khan was telling the truth; otherwise it would have been difficult for him to get elected, less than four years later on 19 February 1970, as President of the ICJ. ICJYB 1960-1970, 7. In any event, the way the entire event unfolded was and is still troubling. The allegation made by Adede or the version given by Judge Zafrualla Khan did seem to present at least an appearance of impropriety on the part of the President, which is compounded by the lack of any official decision mentioned or explanation given on point.

65 Rosenne, Law and Practice, n.6 above, 1058. Article 34(1) reads: "In case of any doubt arising as to the application of Article 17, paragraph 2, of the Statute or in case of a disagreement as to the application of Article 24 of the Statute, the President shall inform the Members of the Court, with whom the decision lies." Before this rule was adopted, the Court seemed to have already formalized its decision-making process on this issue, at least in part. See Legal Consequences for States of the Continued Presence of South Africa in Namibia (South West Africa) notwithstanding Security Council Resolution 276 (1970) (Request for Advisory Opinion), there were published but unreasoned orders rejecting challenges, ICJ Reports 1971, 4, 7, 10. The Court (under President Sir Muhammad Zafrulla Khan) then in the advisory opinion itself provided reasons for these orders, ibid., 18, para.9. After the adoption of article 34 in the Rules, in Legal Consequences of the Construction of a Wall in the Occupied Palestinian Territory (Request for Advisory Opinion), where one Judge was challenged, there was a reasoned, published order of the whole Court (under President Shi Jiuyong), rejecting that challenge. ICJ Reports 2004, 3-6. That order was subsequently noted in the final advisory opinion. ICJ Reports 2004, 136, 142, para.8.

66 ITLOS Rules, art.18(1). See P. Chandrasekhara Rao and Ph. Gautier (eds), Commentary on the Rules, n.5 above, 44-45.

involving a different question might occur. Accordingly, this piece of evidence of the ineffectiveness of the judicial solemn declaration as a check on presidential powers would militate in favor of searching for an additional safeguard.

67. In the light of these factors,[67] it may be of some value to consider the necessity or propriety of a presidential solemn declaration separate from and in addition to the judicial solemn declaration. This suggestion is relevant to any judicial body where no presidential solemn declaration is currently required, as the considerations are often the same. Here of course I am addressing the ITLOS situation only.

68. I recognize that it is impossible to predict how effective the suggested presidential declaration may be in policing presidential conduct. Such a presidential declaration, one may hope, should have the same effect on presidential conduct as the judicial solemn declaration would have on judicial conduct. To the extent that many national Judges and Judges *ad hoc* have voted against their national States or, in the case of non-national Judges *ad hoc*, their appointers,[68] the judicial declaration *may* have had a positive impact. At least, the presidential declaration can be an additional measure out of an overabundance of caution or a prophylactic tool.

---

67 In my analysis here I have focused on the international situation. This can be an interesting issue on a "general principles of law" analysis. I am not attempting that exercise in this paper, as I am only making a suggestion, not an argument, for the consideration of the possibility of a presidential solemn declaration. Furthermore, the international situation may be different from the national systems. In any event, those interested in this suggestion may deploy their comparativistic prowess to mount a "general principles" exercise. Interestingly, the Chief Justice of the United States if promoted from Associate Justice has to take new oaths required for the Chief Justice. See Denis Steven Rutkus and Lorraine H. Tong, The Chief Justice of the United States: Responsibilities of the Office and Process for Appointment (2005), 1, n.2 (US Congressional Research Service, http://assets.opencrs.com/rpts/RL32821_20050317.pdf). Of course, a national system is under the regulation of its own laws and may be very different from another system. In the USA, the office of Chief Justice of the USA is different from that of Associate Justice of the US Supreme Court. The Chief Justice is not elected by his or her equals, but appointed directly by the President of the USA. But should this lead to any difference regarding our inquiry?

68 See, e.g., Schwebel, n.35 above, for information on the voting record of the national Judges and Judges *ad hoc*.

69. Such a presidential solemn declaration can take a form similar to the judicial declaration. We only need to substitute "as President" for "as judge" so that the declaration will read: "I solemnly declare that I will perform my duties and exercise my powers as President honourably, faithfully, impartially and conscientiously." Any Judge who is called upon to perform presidential functions—whether by election or by virtue of the operation of the Statute and Rules—in the whole Tribunal, or a Chamber or a Bench thereof, should be required to make this declaration before exercising these functions. Or the Rules may provide that the President-elect or President-designate by operation of the Statute and Rules becomes the President only upon making the declaration. In the case of a President-elect, this presidential declaration can be made immediately upon election in the presence of the out-going President who usually presides over this process or another Judge who performs the same function. In the case of a President-designate by operation of the Statute and Rules, this presidential declaration can be made before the President of the Tribunal, the Vice-President or the senior Judge, as the case may be. Another procedure or ceremony can also be provided for under the Rules. In any event, all these issues are procedural and subsidiary in nature, if a decision is made in favour of requiring a presidential declaration.

70. If a presidential declaration separate from and in addition to the existing judicial declaration is not considered convenient, another way to deal with this situation may be to bring the language of the Rules into line with that of the Statute by amending the declaration to read "I solemnly declare that I will perform my duties and exercise my powers as Member honourably, faithfully, impartially and conscientiously". This perhaps can allow the argument that whatever duties that a Member is called upon to perform are all covered here including when a Member is called upon to act as President.[69] So the same declaration will be sufficient for all purposes.

A Judge *ad hoc* may be asked to make a similar declaration before the

---

[69] There is a rule stating that all Members are of equal status when they exercise their functions. ICJ Rules, art. 3(1); ITLOS Rules, art. 3. This provision seems to have judicial functions in mind, cf. above para.7, and even here it is interesting as it does not include Judges *ad hoc*. In any event, this rule should not prevent a difference between the President and other Member (see P. Chandrasekhara Rao and Ph. Gautier (eds), Commentary on the Rules, n.5 above, 16) or the term "Member" from including both the President and a normal Member so that the suggested revised declaration may cover both the President and a normal Member, where appropriate.

President of the Tribunal perhaps as "Member of the Bench", so as to preserve the distinction between "Member of the Tribunal" and "Member of the Bench" as well as to allow the possibility, as recognized by some commentators,[70] that a Judge *ad hoc* may be elected President of an *ad hoc* Special Chamber at the ITLOS. It is not clear how this possibility may play out. If, as argued above in paragraph 45, article 16(1) of the ITLOS Rules applies to any Judge *ad hoc*, it would seem pointless for a Judge *ad hoc* whose mission is limited to a particular case to get elected as President but then cannot exercise presidential functions in relation to that very case. In this scenario, a separate formulation of a declaration for Judges *ad hoc* that can cover presidential functions may not be necessary. If, however, article 16(1) does not apply to a Judge *ad hoc*, or at least not to a non-national Judge *ad hoc*, the formulation of the declaration for a Judge *ad hoc* as proposed here will be meaningful and also sufficient.

71. One may wonder whether it is appropriate to have such a presidential declaration as the presidential declarations that exist in the world seem to suggest that they are only made by political personalities. A president of a judicial body is still a judge and has no political agenda but to decide cases only. This does not seem to be a good objection. There is nothing that prohibits a non-political person from making a solemn declaration. Indeed, judges including the judges at the ITLOS, who are eminently non-political, have been required to make such a declaration.

V. Conclusion

72. The functions of the President of the ITLOS are three dimensional: the President is a normal international judge, an organizational leader and a judicial leader in a particular case. The Presidency is a powerful one, perhaps more so than that in other international judicial bodies, and can be a platform for the national State extension vice to take effect.

73. Several antidotes and safeguards exist to combat this, including the relatively short term of office, the judicial solemn declaration and the efforts to equalize the parties by ensuring "national representation" on the Bench in a particular case, and the principle of separation of functions and the disqualification of the national President as President but not as Judge. These have accumulated the wisdom of the systems of the PCIJ and the ICJ and are

70 See ITLOS Rules, art. 31(1); P. Chandrasekhara Rao and Ph. Gautier (eds), Commentary on the Rules, n.5 above, 81; Eiriksson, n.5 above, 44-45.

motivated by the desire to restrain the Presidency somewhat and to put the parties on an equal footing.

74. However, uncertainties remain regarding the timing and scope of the application of the principle of separation of functions and disqualification of the national President. The context of the Statute militates in favor of an early trigger point at the time when a particular case is presented to the Tribunal and before the President has taken any action at all. Furthermore, the context of the Statute and the Rules and their borrowing from the ICJ Statute and Rules favor the view that the ITLOS should also follow the practice of the ICJ or ICJ Presidents in applying the principle, although not expressly required by the Statute, to the situation where the national State of the President is not a party but is in the same interest or substantially in the same interest as a party in a case, if there exist factual connections between the national State of the President and a party in the case before the Tribunal. Probably, the ITLOS should also extend that application to the situation where the national State of the President shares a legal position of decisive importance in the case with one of the parties, though they are not factually connected. Arguably, article 16(1) of the ITLOS Rules may have covered or can be extended logically to cover part of the situations where the President's national State is a member of an international organization, against whose member States actions are being brought for acts of that organization, whether or not an action is also being brought against the President's national State separately.

75. Finally, noting that there is some space to which the principle of separation of functions and disqualification of the national President may not apply, which the judicial solemn declaration does not cover, or where the judicial declaration is not sufficient, the paper has suggested that as a further antidote, the possibility be considered of requiring a presidential solemn declaration (separate and in addition to the judicial one) or revising the current judicial declaration to clearly encompass presidential functions. It is hoped that a presidential declaration or a solemn declaration that encompasses presidential functions clearly would have at least the same effect that a judicial solemn declaration has had on judicial behavior. At least, the presidential declaration can be an additional measure out of an overabundance of caution or a prophylactic tool, perhaps, for a more perfect system of international dispute settlement.

Postscript

The original paper contains this long abstract:

> The functions of the President of the International Tribunal for the Law (ITLOS) of the Sea are three-dimensional: the President is a normal international judge, an organizational leader and a judicial leader in a particular case. The Presidency is a powerful one, perhaps more so than that in other international judicial bodies, and can be a platform for the "national State extension" vice—the President's possible partiality towards his or her national State—to take effect. Several antidotes or safeguards exist to combat this, including the relatively short term of office, the judicial solemn declaration and the efforts to equalize the parties by ensuring "national representation" on the Bench in a case, and the principle of separation of functions and the disqualification of the national President as President but not as Judge. However, uncertainties remain regarding the timing and scope of the application of the principle of separation of functions and disqualification of the national President. The context of the ITLOS Statute and Rules and the good administration of justice militate in favour of an early trigger point at the time when a particular case is first presented to the Tribunal and the widest scope possible for the application of the principle to cover a situation where the national State of the President is not a party but is in the same interest or substantially in the same interest as a party in a case, including the situation where, though not factually connected, the non-party national State of the President and a party share a legal position that is decisive in the case. Finally, the paper suggests that, as a further antidote, the possibility be considered of requiring a presidential solemn declaration (separate from and in addition to the judicial one) or revising the current judicial declaration to encompass presidential functions.

Part III

Responsibility

Chapter 16

The Responsibility of States Members of an International Organization for Its Conduct as a Result of Membership or Their Normal Conduct Associated with Membership[1]

1. Introduction

Given the limited space available to me, I can only aspire to touch upon several conceptual and theoretical or policy considerations on this complex topic. I will first sketch out my precise inquiry on the responsibility[2] of States members of

---

1 This paper was first published in Maurizio Ragazzi (ed.), International Responsibility Today: Essays in Memory of Oscar Schachter (Martinus Nijhoff 2005), 435-454. I was fortunate to have Prof. Oscar Schachter as my adviser in the preparation of my first legal essay: 'The Discretionary Function Exception Under the Foreign Sovereign Immunities Act: When in America, Do the Romans Do as the Romans Wish?', 93 Columbia Law Review (1993), 744-82. Prof. Schachter was a member of the Fifth Commission of the Institut de Droit International that studied the issue discussed here. I am grateful to Prof. Shabtai Rosenne for reading an earlier draft of this essay; to Chris Gray for research assistance on the comparative law analysis; and to Irene Berkey, and the staff members of the law library at the University of Colorado Law School, for assistance in obtaining materials. Several other scholars also spoke with me on various issues addressed in this essay. Full responsibility is mine alone: concurrent or joint and several responsibility does not apply to this essay, which was completed on 18 November 2004.

2 I am familiar with the distinction between 'responsibility' and 'liability' that seems to have taken root in the work of the International Law Commission. See Barboza, 'Liability: Can We Put Humpty-Dumpty Together Again?', 2 Chinese JIL (2002), 499-526. Of course, such a distinction is not completely a happy one, particularly for treaty drafters, see Nordquist (ed.), United Nations

an international organization[3] for its conduct as a result of membership or their normal conduct associated with membership. From time to time, I shall use the term 'member responsibility' to refer to this concept. I will then deal with some essential aspects of the sources of law relevant to the inquiry; the consequences of the separate and independent personality of international organizations and the nature of the responsibility of the States members; the general operational framework of the international legal system and the background rule on State responsibility; types of transactions and types of injuries; some relevant policy considerations; and the standard of conduct and the possible regime of proportionate responsibility.

2. The Inquiry

International organizations are nothing mysterious, whatever personality they may have; they are simply the result of the acts of States in the international sphere. The constituent acts of the members[4] bring the organizations to life. The general rule on the responsibility of a State acting in the international

---

Convention on the Law of the Sea, 1982: A Commentary, iv (1991), 642; and v (1989), 163. I will leave the 'liability' category out of my inquiry, and focus on 'responsibility', even though, in my view, the analysis here also applies to the 'liability' scenarios. The International Law Commission's work on the 'liability' regime is still under way [after the publication of this paper, the Commission adopted the "draft principles on the allocation of loss in the case of transboundary harm arising out of hazardous activities", ILC Report 2006, A/61/10, 106]. However, the prevalent use of the term 'liability' in the sense of 'responsibility' in municipal law and in the literature, and the need to adhere to its original use, will make it necessary for me to use the term 'liability' in this essay, most of the time in the sense of 'responsibility'.

3 The term is used here in the sense as defined by G. Fitzmaurice: the 'term "International organization" means a collectivity of States established by treaty, with a constitution and common organs, having a personality distinct from that of its member-States, and being a subject of international law with treaty-making capacity'. ('First Report on the Law of Treaties' (Doc.A/CN.4/ 101), YILC (1956), ii, 104-28, at 108.) NGOs are not covered in my inquiry.

4 One supposes that a non-State inter-governmental entity (such as an international organization) may become a member of an international organization. I will leave this abnormal situation aside; but, in any event, there is no reason to treat such entities differently than member States, broadly speaking.

sphere (not necessarily excluding national jurisdiction) is, as stated by the Permanent Court of International Justice in *Phosphates in Morocco*, that, once a State has acted wrongfully against another on the international plane, 'international responsibility would be established immediately as between the two States'.[5] That rule, which I shall call 'the *Phosphates* rule', in contrast to the famous *Lotus* rule,[6] has been applied in several subsequent cases before the International Court of Justice.[7] This point is so basic that courts, States and practitioners normally do not feel a need to make it explicit; they treat it as implicit. When they deal with State responsibility, they often first attempt to establish a violation of a substantive obligation, and then proceed to the reparation stage, without making an affirmative and distinct finding that the injuring State is responsible for the violation.[8] Such a point is presumed or

---

5 Phosphates in Morocco, Judgment, 1938, PCIJ, Series A/B, No. 74, 10, at 28.

6 "Lotus", Judgment No. 9, 1927, PCIJ, Series A, No. 10, at 18-20. On the 'Lotus rule' and the contrast between that rule and the 'Phosphates rule', see the considerations developed in this essay below (footnotes 21-24 and the accompanying text). I am using the term 'rule' as including 'principle' throughout this essay to describe the various 'rules'. I have difficulty understanding the distinction between the two as they are used, often unexplained, in international law materials, although I am familiar with the debate on the two terms in general jurisprudence. See, e.g., Hart, The Concept of Law (2nd edn. 1994), 259-68. I think it reasonable to use the term 'rule' this way for these reasons: (1) the various 'principles' described herein are strong and 'conclusive' so as to amount to 'rules' even under the disputed criteria used in general jurisprudence; (2) some theorists such as Hart have argued that the distinction is really a matter of degree (ibid., 262); and (3) Article 38(1)(d) of the Statute of the International Court of Justice uses only 'rules of law'.

7 The International Law Commission listed these as examples: Corfu Channel, Merits, Judgment, ICJ Reports 1949, 4, at 23; Military and Paramilitary Activities in and against Nicaragua (Nicaragua v. United States of America), Merits, Judgment, ICJ Reports 1986, 14, at 142, paras. 283, 149, 292; Gabčíkovo-Nagymaros Project (Hungary/Slovakia), Judgment, ICJ Reports 1997, 7, at 38. The principle was referred to in several other cases. See comment (2) on Article 1 in 'Report of the International Law Commission on the Work of its Fifty-third Session', Gen. Ass. Off. Recs., Fifty-sixth Session, Supp. No. 10 (Doc.A/56/10).

8 For a survey of the case law of the International Court of Justice, see Higgins, 'Issues of State Responsibility before the International Court of Justice', Fitzmaurice (M.) and Sarooshi (eds.), Issues of State Responsibility before International Judicial Institutions (2004), 1-9. She saw an 'absence of a need

taken for granted.

This principle has now been restated in Article 1 of the International Law Commission's Draft Articles on Responsibility of States for Internationally Wrongful Acts (the 'Commission's Draft Articles'), which reads: 'Every internationally wrongful act of a State entails the international responsibility of that State'.[9] While Article 57 would, by fiat of the Commission, exclude the responsibility of States for acts of an international organization from the scope of application of the Draft Articles, the general rule codified in Article 1 would seem to have application outside the sphere where the Commission reigns, and would lead to the conclusion that States may be responsible for the acts of international organizations if the normal conditions for the application of this general rule are met. For example, if a State uses an international organization as its agent, it will be held responsible for the acts of the latter. I intend to address a narrower inquiry: the potential responsibility of States members of an international organization for the acts of that organization as a result of their membership or of their normal conduct associated with their membership.[10]

---

for a "stepping stone" between illegality and remedy' (ibid., 8).

9 The Commission's commentary on this article does not seem to address expressly the issue whether there is a need for a specific rule stating that responsibility would ensue from a violation, although the article and the commentary as a whole suggest that the Commission presumed that there is no such a need.

10 This question is currently pending before the International Court of Justice in the Legality of Use of Force (Kosovo) cases by Serbia and Montenegro against several NATO members. The Court could have dealt with this issue in the Nauru case, ICJ Reports 1992, 240, but the case did not proceed to the end.

Commentary (3) on Article 57 of the International Law Commission's Draft Articles shows that the Commission members had this precise question in mind, but left it for the future topic on the responsibility of international organizations. Then, in that subsequent project, the Commission mentioned the issue in 2002 in 'Report of the International Law Commission on the Work of its Fifty-fourth Session', Gen. Ass. Off. Recs., Fifty-seventh Session, Supp. No. 10 (Doc.A/57/10), 333. The Commission provisionally adopted some draft articles in 2003. Article 1(2) of these draft articles states: 'The present articles also apply to the international responsibility of a State for the internationally wrongful act of an international organization' ('Report of the International Law Commission on the Work of its Fifty-fifth Session', Gen. Ass. Off. Recs., Fifty-eighth Session, Supp. No. 10 (Doc.A/58/10), 34). However, the Commission does not clearly spell out the different types of responsibility under consideration. In fact, the Commission gives the impression (particularly in para. (7) of the commentary), however unclear, that it seems to have in mind only the situation where an organization acts as an unwilling instrument or willing agent of a member State (paras. (6) to (9) of the commentary on draft Article 1(2), particularly para. (7)). Thus, the precise inquiry dealt with here has not yet been expressly included by the Commission in its work, although this topic might be considered to be, arguably, within the ambit of para. (6) of the commentary on draft Article 1(2). The Commission's 2004 Report did not appear to have added anything, although the second report by the Special Rapporteur contained some interesting language in this respect. See Gaja, 'Second Report on Responsibility of International Organizations' (Doc.A/CN.4/541), 3-5.

During the debates at the Sixth Committee in the autumn of 2004, a proposal was made to include expressly this topic in the work of the Commission. See United Nations Press Release GA/L/3268, 9 November 2004 (Statement by Ambassador Allieu Kanu (Sierra Leone)). [After the publication of this paper, the Commission adopted the "draft articles on the responsibility of international organizations", A/66/10, 82. Several draft articles do touch upon our inquiry here. For a summary and discussion of these draft articles, see my paper, 'Member Responsibility' and the ILC Articles on the Responsibility of International Organizations: Some Observations', reprinted as Chapter 17 here in this volume.]

There is a certain amount of law and practice on the topic, as the Commission too has noted. However, it is not clear to what extent the International Tin Council litigation ([1990] 2 A.C. 418 (House of Lords, UK)) and the Westland Helicopters arbitration/litigation (80 ILR 596 (ICC Award, 1985); 80 ILR 622 (Swiss Federal Supreme Court, 1988); 108 ILR 564 (England, High Court, 1994)) are meaningful because the former seems to be based on English domestic law while the latter seems to be based on the internal arrangements of the Arab Organization for Industrialization.

The Institut de Droit International established a commission to study this issue under the title 'The legal consequences for member states of the non-fulfilment by international organizations of their obligations toward third parties', with Rosalyn Higgins as the Rapporteur. The Preliminary, Provisional and Final Reports of the Fifth Commission, and the responses of and the general debate among members (published at 66 Annuaire (1995), i, and 66 Annuaire (1996), ii) are most illuminating. In 1995, the Institut adopted a resolution on the question. Part B of that Resolution, entitled 'Current Law', reads in relevant part as follows:

Article 5

a) The question of the liability of the members of an international organization for its obligations is determined by reference to the Rules of the organization.

b) In particular circumstances, members of an international organization may be liable for its obligations in accordance with a relevant general principle of international law, such as acquiescence or the abuse of rights.

c) In addition, a member State may incur liability to a third party

i) through undertakings by the State, or

ii) if the international organization has acted as the agent of the State, in law or in fact.

Article 6

a) Save as specified in Article 5, there is no general rule of international law whereby States members are, due solely to their membership, liable concurrently or subsidiarily, for the obligations of an international organization of which they are members.

b) No inference of a general rule of international law providing for liability of States is to be deduced from the fact that the Rules of some organizations make specific provision:

i) for the limitation or exclusion of such liability, or

ii) for the dissolution of these organizations.

c) No liability of a State arises merely by virtue of

— having participated in the establishment of an international organization to serve the State's own purposes;

— the fact that the act of the organization giving rise to its liability to a third party is claimed to be ultra vires.

Article 7

Unless the Rules of the organization direct otherwise, no distinction is to be made between claims in contract and other claims for purposes of determining whether any liability exists for member States for the obligations of an international organization.

66 Annuaire (1996), ii, 449 (also available online: <http://www.idi-iil.org/idiE/resolutionsE/1995_lis_02_en.pdf>). I do not intend to address every important issue that one may raise regarding this study. Other useful commentaries include: Higgins, 'The responsibility of states members for the defaults of international organizations: continuing the dialogue', Schlemmer-Schulte and Tung (eds.), Liber Amicorum Ibrahim F.I. Shihata: International Finance and Development Law (2001), 441-8; Seidl-Hohenveldern, 'Liability of member states for acts or omissions of an international organization', ibid., 727-39; Klabbers, An Introduction to International Institutional Law (2002),

If one is to follow the normal inquiry on State responsibility, one may reasonably conclude that the critical question is whether an international organization may be considered an agent of a State member, to some extent at least, so as to bring the acts of that organization into the sphere of the responsibility of a State member. If so, the debate would seem to be on how to define agency. If not, then, the critical question becomes whether membership or the normal conduct associated with their membership may still be the basis for State responsibility.

The normal argument is that an international organization is an independent organization, having independent personality and autonomy. As a result, it is no agent of any one State member, without additional agreement or conduct in addition to the constituent instruments. As a result, the States members are not responsible for the conduct of the organization.

The true story, however, is different. Depending on the *decision-making* arrangements among the States members, one can see a spectrum of scenarios as follows (without attempting to paint an accurate or comprehensive picture):[11]

- Type A, a State member may be driving the decisions of an organization;
- Type B, a State member may control the decision-making of an international organization;
- Type C, a State member may have a veto over the decisions of an international organization, whether or not it has been an active participant in the formulation of a decision;
- Type D, a State member may participate in the decision-making in an

---

300 ff.; Hirsch, The Responsibility of International Organizations toward Third Parties: Some Basic Principles (1995); Schermers and Blokker, International Institutional Law: Unity within Diversity (3rd edn., 1995), 992-5; Amerasinghe, 'Liability to Third Parties of Member States of International Organizations: Practice, Principle and Judicial Precedent', 85 AJIL (1991), 259-80; Sadurska and Chinkin, 'The Collapse of the International Tin Council: A Case of State Responsibility?', 30 Virginia JIL (1990), 845-90.

11 This typology is given here only with a view to illustrating, roughly, the different kinds of involvement of a State member in the decision-making process of an international organization, not to describing the entire constitutional establishment of it such as the amendment procedure, etc. Sometimes the veto is not exercised to prevent unlawful decisions from being taken.

influential way; or

- Type E, a State member may participate in the decision-making but without much influence and may vote against a certain decision.

One can see the movement of a State member from a position of principal to that of pure membership in the international organization. It is not a foregone conclusion that one cannot treat the international organization as the agent of a Type A, B or C State. If one can, the responsibility of the State member may be rested on this ground. Such a way of treating the international organizations in these situations is not unreasonable. As the International Court of Justice has taught us in the *Reparation* advisory opinion, the word 'agent' should be read 'in the most liberal sense'.[12]

The Type D scenario is a difficult one, as the State member plays an influential role in the decision-making of the organization and yet its role does not rise to a level of being the 'principal' for the agent. The organization in a Type E scenario probably cannot be considered an agent of the State member in the strict sense of the term. Assuming that the responsibility of a Type D or E State member for the international organization cannot be rested on grounds of agency, *stricto sensu*, the question will then be whether the State member should still be held responsible for the acts of the international organization for membership and participation in decision-making, or for an additional element, namely, influential participation. This is the focus of my inquiry.

Given the state of the world and the state of the development of international law, one may reasonably argue that States members must shoulder (at least in part) the responsibility for the conduct of an international organization, leaving aside the scope and extent of that responsibility for further fine-tuning. Otherwise, the world would be beautiful for some but ugly for others; States may simply set up an international organization to reap the benefits of organizing their international activities this way and to avoid the responsibility they would have to shoulder if they conduct the same activities without forming an international organization for such purposes. Various issues

---

12 Reparation for Injuries Suffered in the Service of the United Nations, Advisory Opinion, ICJ Reports 1949, 174, at 177 ("The Court understands the word 'agent' in the most liberal sense, that is to say, any person who, whether a paid officia1 or not, and whether permanently employed or not, has been charged by an organ of the Organization with carrying out, or helping to carry out, one of its functions—in short, any person through whom it acts.").

are involved in our inquiry and I shall deal with the more important ones here in this essay.

3. Sources of Law

It is somewhat puzzling to see, sometimes, broad statements to the effect that the responsibility of a State member of an international organization is to be determined by reference to the rules of that organization.[13] One may argue that such rules of an international organization can only be agreements between and among the members themselves, and, as such, have no adverse effect on third parties,[14] particularly when these rules seek to affect the responsibility of the organization or its members toward third parties. Otherwise, States members of an international organization would be able to make rules on responsibility not only for application among themselves but also for the world.

Of course, these rules may inform our consideration of the role of a State member in the organization, in order to determine the type of organizations involved, as discussed above, which would in return inform our consideration of the responsibility of a particular State member involved and the extent thereof. Furthermore, such rules of an organization limiting the responsibility of a State member may be a basis to exclude such responsibility of a State member vis-à-vis a third party. But these responsibility-limiting provisions do not operate as a matter of treaty law; they must borrow some force from other principles. As discussed below, they are not dispositive of the issue, but may have a differing impact on responsibility depending on the types of transactions.

It would seem that only general international law, including customary international law and general principles, may regulate the relationship between an international organization and its States members (at least to some extent, as a floor), on the one hand, and a third party, on the other. The relevant general principles may be found in national legal systems, and they inform our consideration of the issues when appropriate.

Often, one can see arguments to the effect that international law is different from national legal principles on the liability of juridical persons and

---

13 See, e.g., the 1995 Resolution of the Institut, quoted in footnote 10, above.

14 The term 'third parties' is used here to refer to States primarily but with the understanding that an individual can be impacted by the conduct of an international organization, and can always be protected by a State on the international plane.

that, therefore, the latter have no effect in international law. Such a conclusion would appear a bit hasty, although it may be correct. At least, one who asserts such a conclusion owes us an explanation as to why the difference between international law and national legal principles would necessarily require us to reject an international borrowing of these national legal principles.

Another approach equally suspect is that there is a certain form of liability prevalent in the national legal systems, and, therefore, this should also be appropriate on the international plane. While such an approach may have the semblance of 'prevalence' support, closer examination may demand a rule on the international plane different from that existing in national legal systems if the operational framework or premises of the international system are fundamentally different from those of the national systems. In addition, the current emphasis on the similarity or dissimilarity between the activities of private corporations and those of international organizations concerns only part of the story, if it does not take account of the 'operational framework' differences. A closer look may find commonality at a deeper level of either system.

4. The Separate Legal Personality of an International Organization and the Nature of the Responsibility of the States Members

The normal analysis of the issue seems, as far as one can discern from the existing literature, to start with an inquiry into whether the international organization has a separate legal personality. If not, then the States members are responsible. If yes, and if the conduct in dispute is attributable to the international organization, then either the States members are not responsible at all, or their responsibility is subsidiary (which arises only when the organization is unwilling or unable to bear responsibility).[15] It would seem that the above analysis of the sources of law shows that such an approach is not satisfactory.

While the first part—holding States members responsible if there is no separate legal personality—is correct, the second part is questionable. The international legal personality of an international organization is normally endowed by the States members themselves, and, once endowed, may have to be respected by third parties if certain conditions (such as near universality of representation) are met, as the *Reparation*[16] advisory opinion teaches. However,

15 See Klabbers, 'An Introduction', 302.

16 ICJ Reports 1949, 174.

respecting the international personality is one thing; allowing such personality to remove the responsibility of States members is quite another. Or, one may say, respecting such international personality does not need to reach an extent where the responsibility of States members of the international organization is eviscerated; rather, a third State need only recognize the normal rights and obligations of the organization. The responsibility of States members and those of the international organization are not mutually exclusive.

Furthermore, while the 'subsidiary responsibility' idea is relevant, it is not the most important aspect: one may legitimately treat the responsibility of a State member as joint and several or concurrent with that of other members and with that of the international organization so that:

(a) the States members and the international organization are concurrently or jointly and severally responsible for the conduct of the organization to an unlimited extent;
(b) when the organization is unwilling or unable to bear responsibility, the States members must step up; and
(c) more importantly, even when the organization is willing and able to bear responsibility, an aggrieved third party should be allowed, at its own election, to press a claim against a State member, if that aggrieved third party is not able to press the claim directly against the organization itself because of a jurisdictional or another reason, or if that party simply does not wish to press the claim directly against the organization for a strategic or other reason.

A concurrent, or joint and several, responsibility regime is not only reasonable because of these practical reasons that I have just given (which may be described in more beautiful terms), but, more importantly, because it is based on the general operational framework of the international legal system, as discussed below, and the general nature of organizational arrangements. The allocation of the responsibility of an organization among its members, and between the organization and its members, is the business of the members; whether such responsibility should be subsidiary or not is a matter for them, not the aggrieved third party which should not be adversely affected by this allocation. Indemnification or set-off may be sought among its members, and between the organization and its members, according to the rules of the organization.

Of course, an international organization may make an agreement with a third party, where possible, to provide for a special arrangement. However, such an agreement may not be possible, as discussed below, regarding certain types of injury. In any event, such special arrangements concern particular third parties only.

One, of course, may refine the concurrent or joint and several responsibility so that a regime of proportional responsibility is applied. As discussed below, there are many advantages to such a regime, but it is premised on the appropriateness of concurrent or joint and several responsibility as the basic regime.

5. The General Operational Framework of the International Legal System and the Background Rule on State Responsibility

In my view, the operational framework of the international legal system and the general background of the rules holding States responsible for their activities on the international plane support the concurrent or joint and several responsibility regime. I will sketch out these arguments here, while critiquing the contrary arguments.

(a) *The operational framework of the international legal system on State responsibility*

In the existing literature, one can discern a certain amount of ignoring or at least de-emphasizing of the operational framework of the international legal system and the background rule on State responsibility and a concurrent emphasis[17] on the alleged lack of a rule establishing the responsibility of States members for the conduct of international organizations. Such a rule, though 'specific' in substance, has often been termed 'general'. The normal 'first thing first' item for some scholars in their discussions is to point out that one may, of course, easily notice the lack of any rule specifically and affirmatively holding a State member responsible for the conduct of an international organization as a result of its membership or its normal conduct associated with its membership. However,

---

17 See Article 6(a) of the 1995 Resolution of the Institut, footnote 10, above. There were some dissenting voices, but without detailed elaboration, see, e.g., 66 Annuaire (1996), ii, 273 (Rosenne); 274 (Torres Bernárdez; Broms); 313 (Rosenne reiterated his objection; Torres Bernárdez, Sohn, Díez de Velasco, supporting Rosenne); 314 (Rosenne's proposed amendment defeated, 13-15); 319 (Rosenne reiterated his objection; the final vote for the article was one against, two abstentions).

as noted most authoritatively in 1994, 'the reality was that there was also no rule saying that there was *not* liability'.[18] From this state of affairs, it would be a mistake for one to draw the conclusion that there was no such member responsibility in general. It also seems problematic to simply turn to the rules of the international organization alone,[19] as they are only agreements *inter se* among its members and between them and the international organization. Rather, this state of affairs should point one to fall back to the operational framework of the international legal system on State responsibility and to consider the question whether there already has been a background rule from which one may derive a rule providing for responsibility so that there is no need for an affirmative rule written in so many words.

This view finds inspiration and support in the jurisprudence of the International Court of Justice. A similar exercise was done by the Court in the *Nuclear Weapons* advisory opinion, whatever result that the Court reached in that case. There, at paragraph 74, the Court stated: 'The Court not having found a conventional rule of general scope, nor a customary rule specifically proscribing the threat or use of nuclear weapons *per se*, it will now deal with the question whether recourse to nuclear weapons must be considered as illegal in the light of the principles and rules of international humanitarian law applicable in armed conflict and of the law of neutrality'.[20] The Court then proceeded to answer that question. The content of that answer is now familiar to us, and needs no further elaboration. What I would like to emphasize is that the approach adopted by the Court is the one we should follow in our inquiry. In other words, we should consider the precise question of member responsibility in the light of the operational framework of the international legal system and the general background rule on State responsibility.

If we are to conduct the same kind of analysis, which I have previously sketched out in Section 2 of this essay, we may reasonably conclude that the general rule that States normally are responsible for their conduct demands a rule that States are responsible for their conduct in bringing to life an international organization and, therefore, for all the resultant responsibility of that organization or the consequences of the acts or omissions of that

---

18 'Final Report' (Rosalyn Higgins, Rapporteur), 66 Annuaire (1995), i, 462 (emphasis in the original).

19 But see Article 5 of the 1995 Resolution of the Institut, footnote 10, above; 66 Annuaire (1996), ii, 274 (Statement by the Rapporteur).

20 Legality of the Threat or Use of Nuclear Weapons, Advisory Opinion, ICJ Reports 1996, 226, at 256.

orgnization. That is to say bringing to life an international organization is the 'original sin' for which the States members must be responsible. Thus, there is no absence of law on point. Support for this view can be found in the *Phosphates in Morocco* case and its progeny, as discussed in Section 2 above. There, I coined the phrase 'the *Phosphates* rule' to describe what one can derive from these cases.

This nature of things may be the reason why there is no specific rule providing for concurrent or joint and several responsibility: there is no need for such a specific rule. The general background for responsibility is here for the decision-makers to apply, and its eventual application depends on whether such issues are presented, perhaps haphazardly.

Given this general operational framework, one cannot but have sympathy with the argument for a presumption in favor of concurrent or joint and several responsibility. In fact, if this general background of State responsibility is accepted, whatever the particular rules (including constituent instruments) of an international organization may provide for would not be dispositive, because they are particular rules binding upon particular parties only, not third parties. As discussed below, these particular rules may exert an effect in a different way.

A default operational framework opposite to the one that I have found and elaborated here in this essay was presented, as a possibility, in the Preliminary Report (1989) and the Provisional Report (1993) of the Fifth Commission of the *Institut de Droit International.*[21] In the latter Report, it was stated:

> Is the position that the absence of a specific norm (which some would term a positive rule) determining state liability means that there is no liability? Or is the correct position that, unless states can be shown to have excluded or limited their liability, the liability must be presumed to exist? The latter view can only be correct if international law will presume obligations to be incumbent upon states unless the contrary is proved. But this seems to run counter to well established principles: «The rules of law binding upon states … emanate from their own free will as expressed in conventions or by usages generally accepted as

21 See 'Preliminary Report' (Rosalyn Higgins, Rapporteur), 66 Annuaire (1995), i, 286; 'Provisional Report' (Rosalyn Higgins, Rapporteur), ibid., 415-16. It is not clear whether Article 6 of the 1995 Resolution, footnote 10, above, may have adopted this view of the default rule, although one can say that Article 6 simply states, as a statement of an objective fact, the absence of a general rule, without endorsing any theory relating thereto.

> expressing principles of law» (*Lotus Case*, PCIJ Judgment N° 9, 1927, Series A, N° 10). Put differently, obligations resulting from norms of law (rather than from treaty or other agreement) must be shown to exist by reference to the normal sources of international law. The absence of a norm stipulating liability is, on this basis, determinative of the matter, in the sense that obligations will not be attributed to states in the absence of a clear requirement of international law.[22]

With the greatest respect, I beg to differ. All of my arguments presented here so far go against that possibility; so will my additional arguments to be given below. Here I would like to take issue *directly* with both strands of the above quoted statement. The first is the apparent presumption that there is an absence of a norm providing for member responsibility. As argued above, this apparent presumption may be only apparent, but not true.

The second is the fact that the possibility of no 'liability' was rested on the *Lotus* default rule. In my view, this is questionable. Even if the *Lotus* rule is still alive and well these days when State sovereignty has been constantly under attack (against my personal inclinations),[23] I believe it is the wrong basis for a proposition on State responsibility; the *Lotus* rule is one about *primary* conduct (what States can or cannot do lawfully—exercising jurisdiction in that case), not a *secondary* rule of responsibility about the consequences of the primary conduct (whether and how they should be responsible for their conduct).[24] If that is the point, then in our particular inquiry the *Lotus* rule goes to whether States may create an international organization that may engage in certain activities. That is a question different from whether States should be responsible for the consequences of those activities, although the two are related. If one were to look for a default rule on responsibility (after an internationally wrongful act was found), that should be the *Phosphates* rule as described in Section 2 of this essay. That rule, for the reasons previously given, is a good rule. It will take

---

22 66 Annuaire (1995), i, 415-16.

23 I have argued that the phenomenon called State has both intrinsic and instrumental values. See my Towards an International Law of Co-progressiveness (2004), 23-5.

24 This distinction pervades Hart, The Concept of Law (1961) and the Commission's project on State responsibility after García Armador served as the Special Rapporteur. See Crawford, The International Law Commission's Articles on State Responsibility: Introduction, Text and Commentaries (2002), 14-16.

weighty reasons to override it.

(b) *The operational framework on responsibility in national legal systems*

The framework existing in the international legal system is the same as that existing in national legal systems in general, as comparative legal scholars have taught us.[25] Because of this, some have asked why this did not prompt the rejection of limited liability in municipal law. Some other scholars seem to argue that, because of the prevalence of limited liability in national legal systems, limited liability should therefore be accepted in the international legal system, as a number of the constituent instruments of international organizations have provided for. Both approaches forget that the most important thing that makes limited liability prevalent or even possible in national legal systems is that a positive municipal rule (normally legislation) exists to authorize it, and the decisions of the incorporators merely take advantage of a facility made available to them by the government.

In international society, there is no such super-government that can grant such an authority for States to limit the responsibility that may result from their activities such as setting up an international organization. Therefore, it would seem to be impossible to create limited liability international organizations against such a background in international law.[26] Until a rule of customary international law comes into existence authorizing that, the States concluding constituent instruments providing for limited responsibility would seem to be doing nothing more than municipal incorporators contracting for limited liability in a State where there is no positive rule providing for it. The existing attempts to provide for limited responsibility in the constituent instruments of international organizations are thus not yet proof that it is possible to create limited responsibility entities in international law, as some have intimated,[27] but remain attempts only. The fate of these attempts must await further testing in the battle field, as far as third parties are concerned. This operational framework of the national legal systems thus supports the concurrent or joint and several

---

25 Hirsch, The Responsibility, 136 (note 200 and the text thereto).

26 Henry Schermers seemed, at one point in time at least, to hold such a view ('Provisional Report' (Rosalyn Higgins, Rapporteur), 66 Annuaire, i, 397, quoting Schermers, International Institutional Law (1st edn., 1980), 780), but he may have had a change of mind. See Schermers and Blokker, International Institutional Law, 992-5; 1009-11.

27 See 'Provisional Report' (Rosalyn Higgins, Rapporteur), 66 Annuaire, i, 397.

responsibility regime, unless a positive rule exists to permit otherwise.[28] We may resort to this as a general principle of law or as an analogy which one finds no substantial reason to reject. Of course, the attempts to provide for limited liability in the rules of an international organization may have an impact on responsibility in voluntary transactions, as discussed below.

(c) *The need for an ultimate redress for injury*

A general rule of international law, as well as municipal law, is that an injurer must make adequate reparations for an injury wrongfully done to another, as one can infer from the *Chorzów Factory* case.[29] This can be called the '*Factory* rule'. The International Law Commission's Draft Articles took the same position.[30] This rule finds support ultimately in fundamental justice. Such a strong rule should only be modified sparingly and only when an alternative form of redress has been provided for. There is *no* need for philosophers to tell us that the provision for limited liability has not done away with risks or burdens, but simply distributes or shifts them to those who suffer them (a sort of 'rob Peter to pay Paul'), particularly when the burdens are in excess of the ability of the injurers to pay. For this reason, in national legal systems, the rise of limited liability has been accompanied by the rise of various insurance requirements, which goes a long way to make up for the liability in excess of the ability of the injurers, and, more importantly, by a vast welfare system, which serves as the ultimate or the last resort place for the injured persons to get assistance. This way of organizing the society was considered to be conducive to the promotion of economic activities and general progress in social development.

In the international legal system, which is still anarchical, there is no such

---

28 Another reason why the limited liability regime cannot be transposed to the international legal system, as has been pointed out by Hirsch, The Responsibility, 129-36, would be that the domestic corporations and international organizations are not similar; they do different things. In my view, this is not a good enough reason. International organizations can be set up to do basically anything. A rule based on a distinction between functions would thus seem to be somewhat patronizing.

29 Factory at Chorzów, Jurisdiction, Judgment No. 8, 1927, PCIJ, Series A, No. 9, 21.

30 See Article 31 of the Commission's Draft Articles, and the commentaries thereon.

ultimate or last resort place for an injured State to go to for assistance. Until such a place of last resort emerges, there is strong reason to hold the injurer responsible for the injury done. Otherwise, injustice would result because the injured State, through no fault of its own, would be saddled with the risks and injury alone. The injustice will be aggravated by the jurisdictional immunity that many international organizations still enjoy, making it impossible for the injured party even to air its grievances. This would lead to attempts at vengeance and a spiral of violence and chaos.

(d) *Existing regimes in selected areas and the concurrent or joint and several responsibility of States members*

Currently, there are existing regimes[31] concerning space activities that lend support for concurrent or joint and several responsibility of States members. The 1967 Outer Space Treaty provides for concurrent responsibility.[32] The 1972 Liability Convention provides for 'joint and several liability', while setting up a secondary or subsidiary liability regime as the implementation mechanism.[33]

---

31 See Hirsch, The Responsibility, 98-102.

32 Treaty on Principles Governing the Activities of States in the Exploration and Use of Outer Space, Including the Moon and Other Celestial Bodies, 1967, 610 UNTS 205, Article VI (also available online: <http://www.oosa.unvienna.org/Reports/AC105_722E.pdf>, at 6) ('When activities are carried on in outer space, including the Moon and other celestial bodies, by an international organization, responsibility for compliance with this Treaty shall be borne both by the international organization and by the States Parties to the Treaty participating in such organization.').

33 Convention on International Liability for Damage Caused by Space Objects, 1972, 961 UNTS 187, Article XXII(3) (also available online: <http://www.oosa.unvienna.org/Reports/AC105_722E.pdf>, at 17) ('If an international intergovernmental organization is liable for damage by virtue of the provisions of this Convention, that organization and those of its members which are States Parties to this Convention shall be jointly and severally liable; provided, however, that ... (a) Any claim for compensation in respect of such damage shall be first presented to the organization ... (b) Only where the organization has not paid, within a period of six months, any sum agreed or determined to be due as compensation for such damage, may the claimant State invoke the liability of the members which are States Parties to this Convention for the payment of that sum.'). See also the interesting formulations in Article 139(2)

In addition, in environmental law, the *Trail Smelter* case[34] long ago stated, and has since been considered to represent, the general rule that a State must pay for material damage its own citizens caused to another State as a result of activities conducted within the territory of the former. If a State may be held responsible for not properly regulating the conduct of private actors within its borders when that conduct resulted in extraterritorial damage, should the same State be relieved of its responsibility simply because it has organized, together with other States, an international organization that has produced the same damage?

While these special regimes may not be sufficient evidence from which one can infer a general rule, when coupled with the general operational framework discussed above, they can be considered as concrete manifestations of that general framework.[35] These manifestations take on greater importance because these special regimes concern the most important and controversial areas of activities that States care about strongly; these activities have great potential for transboundary damage. Other areas of activities may present lesser problems that States may be able to deal with on their own, and they have decided to pick their more important battles to fight.

6. Types of Transactions and Types of Injuries

The general regime of concurrent or joint and several responsibility should, in principle, operate as a general proposition, but it applies with particular force to

---

and Annex IX, Article 6(2), of the United Nations Convention on the Law of the Sea (1833 UNTS 396).

34 RIAA, iii, 1905, at 1965-6 (arbitral awards of 1938 and 1941).

35 But see Karl Zemanek's personal recollection that the negotiators meant to create something new. (66 Annuaire (1995), i, 328.) On one view, such private recollections have little value. Judge H. Lauterpacht eloquently argued against reliance on the secret state of the mind of the International Court of Justice when it was called upon to interpret a 1950 opinion. He stated: 'It is for this Court, confronted as it is with an apparent gap in the opinion of the Court of 1950 with respect to a situation which calls for clarification, to fill the lacuna by all available means of interpretation. These do not include the knowledge of any particular member of the present Court as to the state of his—or his colleagues'—minds at the time when the Advisory Opinion was rendered in 1950'. Voting Procedure on Questions relating to Reports and Petitions concerning the Territory of South-West Africa, Advisory Opinion, ICJ Reports 1955, 67, at 96 (Separate Opinion of Judge Lauterpacht).

involuntary transactions with international organizations which a third party has entered into or been forced to enter into, without any element of choice, or any chance of taking notice of or appreciating the organizational rules limiting responsibility. This will occur in the 'tort' situation, to use a common law term, or the 'delict' situation, to use a term that international law lawyers like to use more often, including accidental injuries, intentional armed attacks, negligence, etc. In such a situation, the injury is caused by the injurer alone, and the responsibility should stay with the injurer.[36] As was argued above, it would be a gross injustice if the burden of curing the injury would be borne by the injured party.

If the injury or loss occurs in a voluntary transaction with an international organization which a third party has willingly entered into, the picture becomes more complicated, assuming that the third party has freely given its consent. Normally, one may argue that the same concurrent or joint and several responsibility regime can apply even to these transactions. However, if the constituent instrument of the international organization plainly provides that a State member does not shoulder any responsibility of the international organization, then that statement should have effect. That effect, however, is not one that follows from the language itself, but must be buttressed by something more: either the argument that the third party has assumed the risk willingly, or that the content of the agreement regarding the particular transaction has incorporated that statement on responsibility. We can then say that there is a particular agreement (which can be implicit or express) on the responsibility of States members. Such an agreement can also be signed, and may have been, one hopes, signed by all prudent international organizations when contracting with third parties. A constituent instrument itself does not create the "no member responsibility" regime; the second agreement between the international organization and a third party does. The former simply serves to give notice. Notice, of course, entails consequences.

In voluntary transactions, the most important aspect is not a particular

---

36 But see Article 7 of the 1995 Resolution of the Institut, footnote 10, above. One may think that notice by an international organization to the world was most important. Such a notice in my view can only take care of the normal slip and fall incidents (as was discussed in the deliberation of the Institut), not, for example, armed attacks. Notice may serve to warn potential victims not to get on the premises of an international organization. Such a regime does not apply to those victims who may suffer greatly during an air campaign by an international organization.

regime of responsibility, but clear notice. Assuming that every third party's voluntary intent is genuine, the parties may order their lives and their activities accordingly. For this reason, the championing of a clear rule to be stated in the constituent instruments or other rules of international organizations is laudable. However, this approach solves only part of the problem; it does not help those third parties who are involuntarily injured by an international organization, or those third parties who are in a very weak bargaining position so as to become 'wards' of the community, not a far-fetched scenario even in today's world.

7. Some policy considerations

Various other arguments in the nature of policy considerations have been brought to bear on our inquiry. I will briefly mention a few here.

One argument is that imposing concurrent or joint and several responsibility may cause the States members to attempt to influence or control the decision-making of the international organization, thereby reducing or eliminating its autonomy. This is a serious concern; yet it is an *inter-se* issue among the members, and between them and the international organization. Innocent third parties should not be part of this calculation. That is to say, the independence of the international organizations should not be purchased at the expense of innocent third parties, particularly those who are affected involuntarily by the conduct of an international organization. One might also argue that complete autonomy on the part of an international organization may not necessarily be a good thing, and some measure of supervision and control by the States members, not necessarily a bad thing.[37] A concurrent or joint and several responsibility regime may induce the States members to participate more actively in the decision-making of, and the supervision over, the international organization so that it will not become a 'Frankenstein', hurting the world and ultimately its own creators.

Another argument is that imposing concurrent or joint and several responsibility would lead to reluctance on the part of the States to join international organizations and to engage in their international activities. I am not sure whether such a prediction is exaggerated or not. Even if it were true, one must answer the question why such international activities would still be a virtue or appropriate if the benefits resulting from them are not sufficient to pay for the damage.

---

37 On the virtues of supervision, see Sadurska and Chinkin, 'The Collapse'.

Yet another argument is that imposing responsibility on States members will 'draw a line between rich and poor states—the latter already found membership in international organizations a difficult financial burden and would be unable to participate if exposed to liability'.[38] While one may have great sympathy for the poor States, one wonders whether a no-responsibility regime is the best approach to dealing with their plight. Furthermore, one may also take note that the victims are usually poor states, and this argument may have the effect of placing the loss usually on the poor states and thus hurting those states it aims to help.

In each of these policy arguments a wealth-redistribution scheme is embedded, although it might not have been seen clearly. Determining the responsibility regime is nothing less than distributing risks, burdens and the consequences of injuries. These various policy arguments in favor of a 'no member responsibility' regime will have the effect of making innocent third parties bear all the risks, burdens, and injuries alone. This is nothing less than adding insult to injury when injury is forced upon the victim State through no fault of its own. The injustice of such an approach is manifest. International law should not lend a hand to such injustice.

I am not opposed to redistributing wealth; I, in fact, believe that eliminating the extreme disparities in the world is necessary for the world to be safe and peaceful. I am only opposed to leaving all the burdens to the victims. Better and more comprehensive schemes for wealth-redistribution can be devised. That is a task for another day.

8. Conduct of the States Members and Proportionate Responsibility

Some arguments have been made that do not seem to go against the possibility of a concurrent or joint and several responsibility regime but deal with some other issues. These include the fear that, as soon as the possibility exists, responsibility will be always unlimited. This is not necessarily true. The existence of such a regime does not do away with the normal or substantive requirements for responsibility, such as the standard of behavior to which the international organization and its States members are held. That is to say, responsibility only arises after an internationally wrongful act has been found; if every player involved acts reasonably, there generally would be no wrongful act.

---

38 Argument by Ibrahim Shihata, as described in the 'Final Report' (Rosalyn Higgins, Rapporteur), 66 Annuaire (1995), i, 462.

This should be the same whether the regime is one of unlimited or limited responsibility.

Another issue is the 'fictitious' decision-making concern. One commentator has put the issue this way: 'resting the outcome of the issue of concurrent or secondary responsibility on the theory that states members are responsible for the decisions of the organization in one way or another may not only involve a fictitious assumption of participation in decision making, but also raise the question why the minority that is against a certain decision should be held liable in the same way as the majority'.[39] Such a question is worthy of serious consideration. Still it does not really speak to the possibility of imposing concurrent or joint and several responsibility; it deals with how to distribute responsibility among the members of an international organization. One cannot, simply because it is difficult to distribute the responsibility among the members, eliminate it completely.

As to how to formulate a regime for distributing responsibility among the members of an international organization, one can resort to many existing or theoretical approaches. While I do not intend to give a detailed treatment to this issue, I believe a regime of proportionate responsibility would be appropriate, provided that the injured State is always able to obtain full recovery. This would seem most satisfactory because it can pin responsibility more precisely to the conduct of a State member. This seems to be supported by both common sense and by the general trend in tort law in national legal systems. Such a refinement in a responsibility regime may even be necessary in some circumstances. This is so because it is a fundamental principle of international law that reparation is required only if the injury is caused by the internationally wrongful act.[40] That is to say, there must be a causal link between the conduct in dispute and the injury.

As described in Section 2 of this essay, there can be several types of participation in the decision-making process of an international organization, and responsibility should vary accordingly, in proportion to involvement and fault. For example, a Type A, B or C State member may be held responsible to the same extent as the international organization, because, if it were not for its role in the decision-making or its failure to prevent the decision from being adopted when it could do so conclusively by exercising its power to veto it, the

39 Amerasinghe, 'Liability to Third Parties', 278.

40 See Article 31 of the Commission's Draft Articles, and the commentaries thereon.

injury would not have occurred. A Type D State member may be held responsible for a certain proportion of the responsibility because, if it were not for its influential participation, we do not know whether the injury would have occurred. A regime may properly assign no responsibility for a Type E State member or the minority that has voted against a decision because its participation did not promote the decision in a traceable way.

However, it would not be wrong to assign *some*, *but not all,* responsibility to even a Type E State member or the dissenting minority. The ultimate issue is whether an international organization is being established as a sort of agency or instrument of its States members to achieve a certain purpose, in the loose, if not the strict, sense of those two terms. If so, then the States members should be responsible, *to some extent*, for what their agency or instrument does. One can say that responsibility ensues, at the minimum, from participating in the establishment of, or subsequently joining, the organization, which is an affirmative act by any member. That is to say, by participating in the establishment of, or subsequently joining an international organization, a State member lends its assistance to other States members and the organization which ultimately brings about the injury.

Furthermore, it was no doubt clear to the States members, at the time of establishing or joining an international organization, that, as a rule, the participation of the minority as well as that of the majority together give birth to the decisions of the international organization, that in the nature of things the international organization sometimes may take decisions against their will, and that those decisions may lead to consequences and responsibility. With such knowledge, the States members still have proceeded to establish or join the international organization anyway. Accordingly their autonomy in exercising their will should be given effect to the fullest extent so that they should reap the benefits of their acts as well as bear the responsibility for them.

I am not asserting that this must be the regime to be followed. I am simply illustrating how a good regime can be. I am sure the detailed formulations can be refined and improved upon.

9. Conclusion

The general operational framework of the international legal system and the background rule on State responsibility support a concurrent or joint and several responsibility regime for the responsibility of States members for the acts of an international organization as a result of membership or the normal conduct associated with membership. This also finds support in the general operational framework in national legal systems, in the need for an ultimate redress for injuries done, in the limited existing regimes on member responsibility, and in fundamental sense of justice. The arguments for a 'no member responsibility' regime from the independent personality of the international organization, the alleged absence of a rule on point regarding member responsibility, the rules of the international organization, a faulty analogy to limited liability regimes in municipal law, or policy considerations are not sufficiently weighty, for one reason or another.

Currently the development of international law is trending towards an international law of co-progressiveness, all-encompassing and preoccupied with advancements in moral and ethical terms. This manifests itself in the strengthening efforts to pursue individual and State responsibility and to dismantle, to a large extent, the citadel of sovereign immunity. Such a trend militates in favor of concurrent or joint and several responsibility. At the time when the international community is striving to build a fairer world, a concurrent or joint and several responsibility regime may prove to be an important component of that world, as well as an important tool to build it.

Chapter 17

'Member Responsibility' and the ILC Articles on the Responsibility of International Organizations: Some Observations*

1. 'Member Responsibility'

Writing for a book of essays in memory of Oscar Schachter in 2005,[1] my former tutor, Sir Ian Brownlie (as he later became), and I chose to tackle the same subject matter. He wrote on the responsibility of States for the acts of international organizations,[2] and I on the responsibility of member States for an international organization's conduct as a result of membership or their normal conduct associated with membership.[3] Obviously, this topic has its attraction. The fact that we both wrote on this subject led me to revisit this same topic in these essays in his memory. As a strong champion of the rule of law in international affairs, Sir Ian would certainly have been interested in this revisit.

In the 2005 essay, I had focused on the acts of a member State of an international organization that result from membership or are associated with membership, not other kinds of acts that any State may perform, or the

---

* First published at M. Ragazzi (ed.), Responsibility of International Organizations: Essays in Memory of Sir Ian Brownlie (Martinus Nijhoff 2013), 325-336.

1 M. Ragazzi (ed.), International Responsibility Today. Essays in Memory of Oscar Schachter (Leiden and Boston, 2005).

2 I. Brownlie, 'The Responsibility of States for the Acts of International Organizations', ibid., 355-62.

3 S. Yee, 'The Responsibility of States Members of an International Organization for its Conduct as a Result of Membership or their Normal Conduct Associated with Membership', ibid., 435-54. 'Member State' is used interchangeably with 'State member'.

additional acts that a member State may have to perform to be held responsible for acts (including omissions) of an international organization. I termed the responsibility so defined 'member responsibility',[4] and argued for a concurrent or joint and several responsibility regime, while allowing adjustment based on proportionality. I criticized the position that this issue should be decided by the rules of the international organization,[5] and argued for applying general international law. In my view, general international law accords under the rationale of *Reparation*[6] some rights to an international organization with independent personality, but does not limit responsibility to that organization only, an issue that the *Reparation* advisory opinion did not address. I wrote: 'Otherwise, the world would be beautiful for some but ugly for others; States may simply set up an international organization to reap the benefits of organizing their international activities this way and to avoid the responsibility they would have to shoulder if they conduct the same activities without forming an international organization for such purposes.'[7] Rejecting the view that, since no specific rule mandates member responsibility, the *Lotus* rule[8] would preclude such responsibility,[9] I argued that, in the absence of a specific rule on point, the general framework of international law should be resorted to and that relying on the *Lotus* rule (originally recognized in the context of primary rules—whether a State may act in a certain way) in the context of secondary rules (whether or not a State is responsible after it has acted) is inappropriate. The general operational framework of the international legal system on point is the *Phosphates* rule under which, once a State has acted wrongfully against another on the international plane, 'international responsibility would be established immediately as between the two States'.[10] A member State is in some way involved in the wrong

---

4 Ibid., 436.

5 See, e.g., arts. 5-7 in Resolution on the Legal Consequences for Member States of the Non-fulfilment by International Organizations of their Obligations toward Third Parties (Institut de Droit International), 66-II Annuaire (1996), 444-53.

6 Reparation for Injuries Suffered in the Service of the United Nations, Advisory Opinion, ICJ Reports 1949, 174.

7 S. Yee, 'The Responsibility of States Members', n.3 above, 440.

8 'Lotus', Judgment No. 9, 1927, PCIJ, Series A, No. 10.

9 See, e.g., R. Higgins, 'Provisional Report on the legal consequences for member States of the non-fulfilment by international organizations of their obligations toward third parties', 66-I Annuaire (1995), 373-420, at 415-16.

10 Phosphates in Morocco, Judgment, 1938, PCIJ, Series A/B, No. 74, 10, at 28.

committed by that organization and is thus covered by the *Phosphates* rule. By participating in creating or subsequently joining an international organization, a member State is responsible at least in principle or to some extent for the future acts of that organization, or assumes the risk of being so responsible for those acts. Furthermore, the analogy, sometimes relied upon, to the limited liability company regime under national law is misguided, as that regime depends on legislation specifically authorizing such companies, whereas in the international legal system there is no such enabling legislation, thus leading us to the default regime in the national legal system, namely unlimited liability. Pointing out that the rise of limited liability in the national legal order does not eliminate liability or the cost of social activities but embodies a conscious decision to allocate it to someone other than those responsible for it and is usually accompanied by the rise of the welfare State which serves as the final resort place where injured persons who cannot obtain any remedies from the injuring companies or their shareholders may seek assistance, I argued that, since there is no such final resort place in the international system, limited liability would be unfair, and that, until such a final resort place emerges, international law should not allow limited liability.

Shortly after the publication of that essay, the argument for concurrent or joint and several responsibility as the regime for member responsibility did not get reflected in the first set of draft articles provisionally adopted in 2006 by the International Law Commission.[11]Neither did the weaker variant 'subsidiary responsibility'. This proposed regime of member responsibility, however, did have some followers inside and outside the Commission. Subsequent discussions did not manage to change the Commission's essential position, but appeared to shift gear a little and attempted to ensure the ability of the international organization to discharge its responsibility, especially financially. Of course, if the international organization were able and willing to do so—a situation not to be assumed because of various considerations, political, financial as well as procedural (such as immunity)—there would not be any need for member responsibility.[12] Apparently, these combined efforts had

---

11 Report of the International Law Commission on the Work of its Fifty-eighth Session, Gen. Ass. Off. Recs., Sixty-first Session, Supp. No. 10 (A/61/10), 246-92.

12 See A. Pellet, 'The ILC's Articles on State Responsibility for Internationally Wrongful Acts and Related Texts', J. Crawford et al. (eds.), The Law of International Responsibility (Oxford, 2010), 75-94, at 91. See also the statement of Commission member Shinya Murase, A/CN.4/SR.3009, at 10-13.

resulted in the current framework on this issue in the articles on the responsibility of international organizations, which the Commission adopted on second reading in 2011.[13] I will set out this framework and offer some observations in the following pages.

2. The 2011 Articles Framework

The 2011 articles framework on this issue can be considered to have four aspects, short-handed roughly as 'independent personality', 'additional acts approach', 'no member responsibility', and 'remedy-enabling obligations pursuant to the rules of the international organization'. First of all, independent personality is of foundational importance. The 2011 articles provide, in article 2(a), that 'international organization' means 'an organization established by a treaty or other instrument governed by international law and possessing its own international legal personality. International organizations may include as members, in addition to States, other entities.' The most significant point for our purposes is that the organization has independent legal personality, which is considered the fount of its own independent responsibility. Thus the Commission commented:

> The legal personality of an organization which is a precondition of the international responsibility of that organization needs to be "distinct from that of its member States". [Footnote omitted.] This element is reflected in the requirement in article 2, subparagraph (a), that the international legal personality should be the organization's "own", a term that the Commission considers as synonymous with the phrase "distinct from that of its member States". The existence for the organization of a distinct legal personality does not exclude the

13 'Draft articles on the Responsibility of International Organizations, with commentaries 2011', Report of the International Law Commission on the Work of its Sixty-third Session, Gen. Ass. Off. Recs., Sixty-sixth Session, Supp. No. 10 (A/66/10), 69-172. On the status and authority of these articles, see General Commentary, ibid., 67-69, especially para.(5)('The fact that several of the present draft articles are based on limited practice moves the border between codification and progressive development in the direction of the latter').

> possibility of a certain conduct being attributed both to the organization and to one or more of its members or to all its members.[14]

The bulk of the 2011 articles then sets out, almost in parallel to the 2001 articles on State responsibility,[15] the conditions for and the content of the responsibility of international organizations as well as its implementation.

The second aspect of the 2011 articles framework is that the responsibility of a member State in connection with the conduct of an international organization arises only from some acts in addition to membership, which can be termed 'the additional acts approach'. This is set out in Part Five of the 2011 articles, titled 'Responsibility of a State in connection with the conduct of an international organization'. These additional acts fall into two groups. The first group can be committed by any State including a member State of an international organization. This group comprises: aid or assistance by a State in the commission of an internationally wrongful act by an international organization (article 58), direction and control exercised by a State over the commission of an internationally wrongful act by an international organization (article 59), and coercion of an international organization by a State (article 60). This group of acts need not have anything to do with membership in the international organization at issue and need not detain us long here.

The second group of additional acts is limited to those committed by a member State of an international organization: circumvention of international obligations of a member State of an international organization (article 61),[16] and acceptance of responsibility or causing reliance on its responsibility (article 62). This group of acts can be committed by a member State only because of its special position within the international organization, but its membership or its normal conduct as a result of membership does not necessarily rise to the level of these mentioned acts. This is clear from the text of these two articles:

---

14 Ibid., 76, para. (10) (art. 2(a)).

15 'Draft articles on Responsibility of States for Internationally Wrongful Acts, with commentaries 2001', Report of the International Law Commission on the Work of its Fifty-third Session (A/56/10), YILC (2001), vol. II, Part Two, 31-143.

16 How article 17 (Circumvention of international obligations through decisions and authorizations addressed to members) on the responsibility of an international organization in connection with the act of a State or another international organization figures in this framework (see article 40, commentary, para. (1)) is not dealt with here in this short essay.

> Article 61
> Circumvention of international obligations of a State member of an international organization
> 1. A State member of an international organization incurs international responsibility if, by taking advantage of the fact that the organization has competence in relation to the subject-matter of one of the State's international obligations, it circumvents that obligation by causing the organization to commit an act that, if committed by the State, would have constituted a breach of the obligation.
> 2. Paragraph 1 applies whether or not the act in question is internationally wrongful for the international organization.
>
> Article 62
> Responsibility of a State member of an international organization for an internationally wrongful act of that organization
> 1. A State member of an international organization is responsible for an internationally wrongful act of that organization if:
> (a) it has accepted responsibility for that act towards the injured party; or
> (b) it has led the injured party to rely on its responsibility.
> 2. Any international responsibility of a State under paragraph 1 is presumed to be subsidiary.

Naturally one may ask whether membership alone or the normal conduct associated with membership, not rising to the level of the additional acts described above, may give rise to responsibility on the part of a member State for the acts of the organization. There is no article among the Commission's 2011 articles specifically addressing this point. Nevertheless, the commentary to article 62 provides the answer.

That answer constitutes the third aspect of the 2011 articles framework on member responsibility, which essentially is this: there is no member responsibility. The commentary to article 62, in paragraph (2), states:

> Consistently with the approach generally taken by the present draft articles as well as by the articles on the responsibility of States for internationally wrongful acts, article 62 positively identifies those cases in which a State incurs responsibility and does not say when

> responsibility is not deemed to arise. While it would be thus inappropriate to include in the draft a provision stating a residual, and negative, rule for those cases in which responsibility is not considered to arise for a State in connection with the act of an international organization, such a rule is clearly implied. Therefore, membership does not as such entail for member States international responsibility when the organization commits an internationally wrongful act.[17]

The commentary proceeds to find support for this position in the following:

1. 'The view that member States cannot generally be regarded as internationally responsible for the internationally wrongful acts of the organization has been defended by several States in contentious cases';[18]
2. 'A similar view was taken by the majority opinions in the British courts in the litigation concerning the International Tin Council (ITC), albeit incidentally in disputes concerning private contracts';[19] and
3. The *Institut de Droit International* in 1995 adopted the position that, other than some special exceptions, 'there is no general rule of international law whereby States members are, due solely to their membership, liable, concurrently or subsidiarily, for the obligations of an international organization of which they are members'.[20]

The above three aspects of the 2011 articles framework so far point to the conclusion that '[i]nternational organizations having a separate legal personality are in principle the only subjects that bear international responsibility for their international wrongful acts'.[21] And, if the international organization is unable or unwilling to discharge its international obligations, the aggrieved parties will be left with no remedies.

---

17 'Draft articles on the Responsibility of International Organizations', 164, para. (2).

18 Ibid., para. (3).

19 Ibid., para. (4).

20 Ibid., 165, para. (5).

21 Ibid., 132, para. (1) (art. 40).

This unappetizing prospect led to some debate in the Commission.[22] Article 40 was ultimately added to tackle this issue *in some way*, resulting in the fourth aspect of the framework: remedy enabling obligations pursuant to the rules of the international organization. This article reads:

> Article 40
> Ensuring the fulfilment of the obligation to make reparation
> 1. The responsible international organization shall take all appropriate measures in accordance with its rules to ensure that its members provide it with the means for effectively fulfilling its obligations under this Chapter.
> 2. The members of a responsible international organization shall take all the appropriate measures that may be required by the rules of the organization in order to enable the organization to fulfil its obligations under this Chapter.

In short, the responsible international organization 'shall take all appropriate measures' to cause its members to enable it to fulfill its obligations and the members too 'shall take all appropriate measures' to enable it to do so, all pursuant to the rules of the organization. The commentary to this article makes it clear that,

> [w]hen an international organization is responsible for an internationally wrongful act, States and other organizations incur responsibility because of their membership of a responsible organization only according to the conditions stated in articles 17, 61 and 62. The present article does not envisage any further instance in which States and international organizations would be held internationally responsible for the act of the organization of which they are members.[23]

Furthermore, 'no subsidiary obligation of members towards the injured party is considered to arise when the responsible organization is not in a position to

---

22 See A. Pellet, 'The ILC's Articles', n.12 above, 91.

23 'Draft articles on the Responsibility of International Organizations', 132, para. (1) (art. 40).

make reparation'.[24] So the basis for the obligations under article 40, if at all, is the rules of the organization. These rules thus assume an importance that the founders or rule-makers of the organization may or may not have fully appreciated. If these rules provide for no obligations on the part of the members, article 40 may amount to much ado about nothing. If these rules are unclear or simply silent on this question, member States have an implied obligation as provided for under article 40. The commentary to this article explains:

> While the rules of the organization do not necessarily deal with the matter expressly, an obligation for members to finance the organization as part of the general duty to cooperate with the organization may be implied under the relevant rules. As was noted by Judge Sir Gerald Fitzmaurice in his separate opinion in the *Certain Expenses of the United Nations advisory opinion*:
>
> > "Without finance, the Organization could not perform its duties. Therefore, even in the absence of Article 17, paragraph 2, a general obligation for Member States collectively to finance the Organization would have to be read into the Charter, on the basis of the same principle as the Court applied in the *Injuries to United Nations Servants* case, namely 'by necessary implication as being essential to the performance of its [i.e. the Organization's] duties' (*I.C.J. Reports 1949*, at p. 182)."[25]

This part of the commentary thus may function as a rule of interpretation, favoring reading into the silent or unclear rules of the organization an implied obligation to enable remedies.

In summary, under the 2011 articles framework an international organization with independent personality will independently shoulder its own responsibility. A member State will be responsible for acts of that organization only on the basis of some additional acts besides membership rising to the level required under the articles. Membership as such does not entail for member

---

24 Ibid., para. (2).

25 Ibid., 133, para. (5). On the drafting history of this provision, see Giorgio Gaja, Special Rapporteur, Eighth report on responsibility of international organizations, A/CN.4/640, 27-28, paras.82-84; A. Pellet, 'The ILC's Articles', n.12 above, 91.

States international responsibility when the organization commits an internationally wrongful act. That is, there is no member responsibility. The organization shall take appropriate measures to cause its members to enable remedies, and the members shall take appropriate measures to do so, for any internationally wrongful acts committed by the organization, all according to the rules of the organization. If the rules are unclear or silent, an obligation on the part of the members to do so will (or may?) be read into them.

3. Observations

The net effect of the 2011 articles framework is, when worse comes to worst, that there is no member responsibility for the internationally wrongful acts of an international organization, nor are members necessarily required to provide remedies for those acts if the organization cannot or will not do that. Such a prospect I feared and criticized strongly in my 2005 essay, and I will not repeat *all* those arguments here but will highlight some as appropriate.

First of all, I cannot resist stressing that this framework at best is an immature one as it opens up a gap in the international legal system. A mature and fair international legal system would maintain a 'circular whole', under which international legal relations are defined by rights and obligations and any rupture of those relations must be cured by restoring the *status quo ante*, or in a better way. At worst, this framework is really an assertion of might makes right, allowing the coming together of some States to form an organization with independent personality to remove responsibility that would otherwise result for those States if they act separately. It would seem that article 61 on the circumvention of international obligations of a member State of an international organization sets up too high a threshold for circumvention and most likely does not catch the original establishment of an international organization simply for the purposes of risk management. That is to say, below conscious circumvention of obligations there is a vast and important space in which responsibility can and should arise for a member State, but is not envisioned under the 2011 articles framework. All this seems to have been due to the independent personality that the international organization enjoys. Giving such personality so much weight really exalts the form of independent personality over the systemic values of the international community as well as the realities of international life.

Providing no article on the issue of member responsibility, but stating in the commentary that a 'no member responsibility' rule was 'clearly implied' and that 'membership does not as such entail for member States international responsibility when the organization commits an internationally wrongful act', the International Law Commission seemed to be more fortified in its 'no member responsibility' position than was the *Institut de Droit International* commission on this topic in 1994. The *Institut* commission's report expressed the view that there was no specific rule providing for member responsibility, but also noted that 'the reality was that there was also no rule saying that there was *not* liability'.[26] Apparently, because of its stronger position or for another reason, the International Law Commission did not resort to the *Lotus* rule, the reliance on which I criticized in 2005.

Is the International Law Commission's stronger position on this issue now better than the *Institut* commission's position when it was expressed in 1994-1995? Probably not. The three main reasons given by the Commission include the fact that some States have argued against member responsibility in contentious cases, the old *International Tin Council* case which was really decided on the basis of national law,[27] and the *Institut*'s resolution adopted in 1995. The only 'new news' is that regarding a few States' arguments in contentious cases, but there was no indication in the Commission's commentary that those arguments succeeded in any of those cases. This really is too slender a reed to support this stronger position.

The Commission's positions that there is no member responsibility, that 'no subsidiary obligation of members towards the injured party is considered to arise when the responsible organization is not in a position to make reparation', and that '[the "no subsidiary obligation"] approach appears to conform to practice, which does not show any support for the existence of such an obligation under international law', seem to have been reached at the cost of ignoring at least two widely-accepted treaties in force dealing with matters of great importance and gravest magnitude: the Treaty on Principles Governing the Activities of States in the Exploration and Use of Outer Space, Including the Moon and Other Celestial Bodies (1967) and the Convention on International Liability for Damage Caused by Space Objects (1972). The 1967 Treaty provides for concurrent responsibility[28] and now commands the

26 'Final Report (October 1994)' ('The Legal Consequences for Member States of the Non-fulfilment by International Organizations of their Obligations toward Third Parties'), 66-I Annuaire (1995), 461-3, at 462 (emphasis in the original).

27 See S. Yee, 'The Responsibility of States Members', n.3 above, 437, note 10.

28 610 UNTS 205, article VI ('When activities are carried on in outer space, including the Moon and other celestial bodies, by an international organization,

adherence of more than one hundred parties. The 1972 Convention provides for joint and several liability while setting up a secondary or subsidiary liability regime as the implementation mechanism,[29] and is now accepted by almost ninety States parties and three inter-governmental organizations. The Commission's 'no subsidiary obligation' position contradicts in express terms the regime provided in the 1972 Convention. Although not on the issue of making reparation only, the regimes provided in these treaties are stronger, because they deal with responsibility in the case of the 1967 Treaty, or 'liability' in the case of the 1972 Convention, before the distinction between responsibility and liability became popular;[30] the obligation to make reparation naturally follows from the determination of responsibility or liability in the general sense.[31]

Some have tried to rationalize away these important instances of State practice with wide following by labeling these treaties as *lex specialis*. It is not clear why the International Law Commission simply put them out of sight by ignoring them—a computer search in the pages on this topic in its 2011 report does not yield any reference to them. If the reason for ignoring them is the view

---

responsibility for compliance with this Treaty shall be borne both by the international organization and by the States Parties to the Treaty participating in such organization.').

29 961 UNTS 187, article XXII(3) ('If an international intergovernmental organization is liable for damage by virtue of the provisions of this Convention, that organization and those of its members which are States Parties to this Convention shall be jointly and severally liable; provided, however, that… (a) Any claim for compensation in respect of such damage shall be first presented to the organization… (b) Only where the organization has not paid, within a period of six months, any sum agreed or determined to be due as compensation for such damage, may the claimant State invoke the liability of the members which are States Parties to this Convention for the payment of that sum.'). See also the interesting formulations in article 139(2) and Annex IX, article 6(2), of the United Nations Convention on the Law of the Sea (1833 UNTS 396).

30 Apparently, the first proposal to make this distinction at the ILC was made by Kearney at a 1973 session. See J. Barboza, The Environment, Risk and Liability in International Law (Leiden and Boston, 2011), 22.

31 For example, responsibility and 'liability and compensation' are dealt with in the same document in Principles Relevant to the Use of Nuclear Power Sources in Outer Space (A/RES/47/68) of Dec. 14, 1992, Principles 8 ('Responsibility') and 9 ('Liability and Compensation').

that the 1972 Convention deals with 'liability'—in express terms—and not responsibility, this would be a weak reason for doing so. First of all, the 1972 Convention had been adopted before the distinction between responsibility and liability became popular, and the term 'liability' may cover both responsibility and liability in current parlance. Indeed, article III of the 1972 Convention uses the term 'liable' to describe a situation resulting from 'fault', a sign (sufficient, though not necessary) of responsibility.[32] Furthermore, as late as 1995, the *Institut de Droit International* used the terms 'liability' and 'liable' in its resolution on this topic,[33] and the International Law Commission quoted, in this very project on the responsibility of international organizations, the language in which these terms were used when it suited its purposes.[34] Secondly, if States were willing to accept such a regime even in liability situations in current terms, covering acts not in violation of international law, they would be more willing to accept such a regime in responsibility situations, which are narrower in scope and less onerous. Finally, even if this were the reason, it would not justify ignoring the 1967 Treaty, because that treaty in express terms provides in article VI for a concurrent responsibility regime.

Regarding the *lex specialis* contention, I previously argued to the contrary:

> While these special regimes may not be sufficient evidence from which one can infer a general rule, when coupled with the general operational framework discussed above, they can be considered as concrete manifestations of that general framework. These manifestations take on greater importance because these special regimes concern the most important and controversial areas of activities that States care about strongly; these activities have great potential for transboundary damage. Other areas of activities may present lesser problems that States may be

---

32 See the 1972 Convention, cited above, art. III, in full: 'In the event of damage being caused elsewhere than on the surface of the Earth to a space object of one launching State or to persons or property on board such a space object by a space object of another launching State, the latter shall be liable only if the damage is due to its fault or the fault of persons for whom it is responsible.' See also arts. IV and V.

33 Resolution on the Legal Consequences for Member States of the Non-fulfilment by International Organizations of their Obligations toward Third Parties (Institut de Droit International), 66-II Annuaire (1996), 444-53.

34 'Draft articles on the Responsibility of International Organizations', 165, para. (5) and note 353 (art. 62).

> able to deal with on their own, and they have decided to pick their more important battles to fight.[35]

The International Law Commission's positions also ignore the same regimes provided for in several United Nations General Assembly declarations relating to space activities,[36] and in one instance also dealing with nuclear activities in outer space.[37]

Perhaps the consolation prizes that the Commission has given to the world are article 61 on prevention of circumvention of member States' obligations and article 40 on ensuring the fulfillment of the obligation to make reparation. As discussed above, neither represents a substantial victory for member responsibility, but each can be considered a half-step forward in that direction. As to article 61, the intention to circumvent obligations may be too high a threshold and may not cover the original establishment of an international organization and thus may not completely solve my 'beautiful for some but ugly for others' problem,[38] but at least it would catch the overtly villainous States, if any. As to article 40, the 'take all appropriate measures' obligation to enable remedies on the part of the international organization as well as its member States may not rise to the level of 'hard obligations' because under article 40 these obligations are supposed to be pursuant to the rules of the organization which may reject such obligations. The saving grace is probably the suggestion made in the commentary that an implied obligation to enable remedies should be read into silent or unclear rules of the organization. This can be a powerful idea because silent or unclear rules of the organizations are

---

35 S. Yee, 'The Responsibility of States Members', n.3 above, 449.

36 E.g., Declaration of Legal Principles Governing the Activities of States in the Exploration and Use of Outer Space (A/RES/1962 (XVIII)), of Dec. 13, 1963, Principle 5; Principles Governing the Use by States of Artificial Earth Satellites for International Direct Television Broadcasting (A/RES/37/92), of Dec. 10, 1982, Principle 9; Principles Relating to Remote Sensing of the Earth from Outer Space (A/RES/41/65), of Dec. 3, 1986, Principle XIV.

37 Principles Relevant to the Use of Nuclear Power Sources in Outer Space (A/RES/47/68), of Dec. 14, 1992, Principle 8 ('When activities in outer space involving the use of nuclear power sources are carried on by an international organization, responsibility for compliance with the aforesaid Treaty and the recommendations contained in these Principles shall be borne both by the international organization and by the States participating in it.').

38 See text to n.7, above.

the norm, other formulations the exception. This 'rule of interpretation' may nudge the law into the direction of providing for remedies where they are due. Hopefully this suggestion will not engender a rash of attempts at revising the rules of the international organizations so as to clearly reject any obligations on the part of their members. Of course, it would seem that reasonable persons would have a difficult time changing unclear rules or silence to clear rules that would manifestly reject such obligations because it would involve taking a conscious and express decision against responsibility. It may be too much in this day and age when everyone wants to take the moral high ground and few would want to be stamped as shirking all responsibility. Herein lies the power of the commentary or the rule of interpretation implicit in article 40 and its accompanying commentary.

When I was a prospective student scouting around the main building of my future *alma mater* Columbia Law School, I saw an ugly and thus puzzling statue in front of it. I was told by a student guide that that was Pegasus, twisted by the force of reason and physical prowess, and that was the image of law. Is this Pegasus statue a good image of the 2011 articles framework on member responsibility? [39]

---

39 There is a peculiar case in which even members of the coalition of the willing in the Iraqi war, thus not of an international organization with independent personality, seemed to have been held by the European Court of Human Rights as not responsible for acts of that coalition. This is the case of Saddam Hussein. He argued that he was under the jurisdiction within the meaning of the European Convention on Human Rights of twenty-one countries, part of the coalition force holding de facto power in Iraq, and asked the Court for remedies under the Convention. Among other things, the Court held that 'there is no basis in the Convention's jurisprudence and the applicant has not invoked any established principle of international law which would mean that he fell within the respondent States' jurisdiction on the sole basis that those States allegedly formed part (at varying unspecified levels) of a coalition with the US, when the impugned actions were carried out by the US, when security in the zone in which those actions took place was assigned to the US and when the overall command of the coalition was vested in the US.' ECHR, Decision as to the Admissibility of Application No. 23276/04 by Saddam Hussein (4th section, Mar. 14, 2006). The Court proceeded to rule that it did not consider it to be established that there had been or was any jurisdictional link between the applicant and the respondent States or therefore that the applicant was capable of falling within the jurisdiction of those States, within the meaning of article 1 of the Convention and declared the application inadmissible. Ibid.

When the 2011 articles were being considered by the United Nations General Assembly, differing opinions were voiced. Several States[40] expressed support for a concurrent or joint and several responsibility regime. Hopefully in the fullness of time, this member responsibility regime will get a better airing, a better hearing and, ultimately, a better reception, although I am not too optimistic.[41]

Postscript

Shortly after the publication of this short essay, my views expressed in this essay as well as those expressed in an earlier one, reprinted in this volume as Chapter 16, received in-depth analysis and critique from José Manuel Cortés Martín.[42] I will not respond to his interesting arguments now but would note that he concluded his article this way:

> [...] one may even [...] question if the final result makes the world "beautiful for some but ugly for others", in the sense that "States can simply set up an international organization to reap the benefits of organizing their international activities this way and to avoid the responsibilities they would have to shoulder if they conducted the same activities without forming an international organization."[43]

The quoted language, I am delighted to say, comes from me. This would seem to show that at least my views are alive and well.

The volume in which this essay appears—the second festschrift for Brownlie—contains an article by Alan Pellet touching upon similar issues,

40 See, e.g., the comments by India (A/C.6/66/SR.19, paras. 40-41); Iran (A/C.6/66/SR.24, paras. 40 and 43); cf. Vietnam (A/C.6/66/SR.20, paras. 72 and 77).

41 The recent rejection by the United Nations of claims relating to the cholera outbreak in Haiti possibly due to the fault of UN personnel involved in the assistance programs there (Letter of the UN Legal Counsel to Brian Concannon, Esq., dated Feb. 21, 2013, online at <http://opiniojuris.org/wp-content/uploads/LettertoMr.BrianConcannon.pdf>) seems to be additional, weighty evidence showing the need for such a member responsibility regime.

42 José Manuel Cortés Martín, 'The Responsibility of Members Due to Wrongful Acts of International Organizations', 12 Chinese JIL (2013), 679.

43 Ibid., 721, quoting Sienho Yee, n.3 above, 440, and text to n.7 above.

which was made available to me after the publication of the whole volume. Pellet was influential in the debut of the language of the predecessor provision that ultimately became article 40,[44] although its intellectual fatherhood can be traced back to earlier times. In his new essay, Pellet discussed the basis for article 40 of the 2011 articles, and seems to show some ambivalence as to the nature of that basis, i.e., legal or moral. Thus, he said at once this:

> it was indispensable to dissociate the problems of compensation from those of incurring responsibility, although, due to the legal personality of international organizations, the responsibility they incur can only be exclusively theirs, and there can be no question of asserting that States are responsible for an act of an international organization [...][45]

and the following:

> In spite of the use of 'shall' in both paragraphs of Article 40, the terminology used is rather soft, and the duty incumbent on both the organization and its members seems to be subordinated to the 'rules of the organization'. The commentary does not dispel the impression of softness: 'an obligation for members to finance the organization *may be implied under the relevant rules.*' In reality, that obligation is not implied by the rules of the organization, but is the logical and unavoidable consequence from the fact that members States, by conferring legal personality on an international organization, necessarily accept that it could incur responsibility and that it must bear its consequences.[46]

His last sentence is most interesting, as it seems to be stating a position not far from mine, if one can take the 'logical and unavoidable consequence' that Pellet talks about as indicating some legal obligation. But he may be referring to some kind of general moral obligation, taking account of what he said earlier in the same paper, as quoted above. There is also some ambiguity in his last sentence,

---

44 Alain Pellet, n.12 above, 91 (commenting on the drafting of Article 39, which became article 40).

45 Alain Pellet, International Organizations Are Definitely Not States: Cursory Remarks on the ILC Articles on the Responsibility of International Organizations, in: M. Ragazzi (ed), Responsibility of International Organizations: Essays in Memory of Sir Ian Brownlie (2013), 51.

46 Ibid., 53.

especially as to the meanings of the "it" (appearing twice) and "its" and how they relate back to the first half of the sentence.

As one can tell from my two papers (Chapters 16 and 17 in this volume), I am ready to say that member responsibility is already required as a matter of law. Then, at its best, article 40 (plus the interpretive implication or even directive as stated in paragraph 5 of the commentary) would lead to effective remedy for violations, a *practical effect* that simply would, or a result that would coincide with what would, follow from my position. This ideal result would thus be presuming my position as a condition precedent and go a step *beyond* member responsibility; it may be called 'member remedy'. Indeed, the ultimate game is to secure remedy; getting effective remedy—compensation here—is infinitely better than simply a recognition of responsibility.

Of course, another view may be that the effect of article 40 may unfold in another shape, i.e., no remedy at all, which flows from the language of that article, read in its entirety. Furthermore, even its best result does not endorse member responsibility, even if the practical effect is the same, because that ideal result, according to paragraph 5 of the commentary to article 40, comes from 'an obligation for members to finance the organization as part of the general duty to cooperate with the organization',[47] not member responsibility. This view is more accurate in terms of describing what the ILC said, but at the same time shows that member responsibility as an idea may have sufficient force so as to induce such a round-about way to deal with it.

In any event, the resort to the general duty of cooperation may be an empty one, or at least an imperfect one, as such a duty is triggered only after the organization has made a decision to compensate the victims and call for further funding when its coffers are empty. If the organization does not make such a decision or is prevented from so doing because of voting issues such as the effect of a veto or another circumstance, there would be nothing on which members are under a duty to cooperate with the organization and, as a result, no remedy at all for the victims. So banking everything on the duty of co-operation may be a pipe dream on the part of those who are already affected by the force of the member responsibility idea to an extent of wanting to give it some effect and yet not ready to go all the way to ensure that. However, as argued in this paper, if the interpretive implication or directive is applied with some force, it may suffice to secure remedy in most situations, as silence on this issue is the norm in the rules of the international organizations, whatever deeper

47 Text to n.25 above.

motivation—member responsibility or the duty to cooperate with the organization—one may resort to in order to ground the interpretive implication or directive.

Chapter 18

Universal Jurisdiction: Concept, Logic, and Reality*

I. The Concept and Logic of Universal Jurisdiction

1. The perceived abuse in recent years in the resort to universal jurisdiction, particularly over African officials, caused the Group of African States to request in February 2009 the inclusion of an additional item on the "Abuse of the principle of universal jurisdiction" in the agenda of the 63d session of the United Nations General Assembly (UNGA). The request was accepted and universal jurisdiction has been a subject of heated discussion in the UNGA since that time. Debates were conducted on this topic in autumn of 2009. The UNGA then asked governments to submit observations and information on state practice. Again debates were held on the topic in the autumn of 2010. Further information has been sought and further work has been scheduled for 2011.[1]

2. The comments and statements made by governments show that there is great confusion on the concept, the scope and application of universal

---

* First published in: 10 Chinese JIL (2011), 503. The preparation of this article forms part of the work of Research Project No. 08&ZD055 of the China Social Sciences Foundation. The comments of William Schabas and the reviewers of the Chinese JIL on a draft are much appreciated. All opinions are personal. This article was completed on 12 September 2011. The websites cited were current as of this date unless otherwise noted.

1 For the Request and the Explanatory memorandum, see A/63/237 (3 February 2009) and annex ("African Union memo"). For summaries of development and documentation, see UN 6th Committee websites, http://www.un.org/en/ga/sixth/64/UnivJur.shtml; http://www.un.org/en/ga/sixth/65/ScopeAppUniJuri.shtml.

jurisdiction. In order for us to properly understand universal jurisdiction, it will be helpful for us to recap the understanding of jurisdiction in general. Usually jurisdiction has three dimensions: prescriptive, adjudicative, and enforcement. It is said that national criminal jurisdiction[2] is normally justified on several grounds: territoriality, nationality, passive personality or protection of national vital interests. Sometimes the effects of an act upon a State are also assimilated to some of these principles. Sometimes a treaty may be considered an independent justification for the assertion of jurisdiction; whether a treaty without incorporating the normal links such as territoriality is a sufficient justification is a controversial question. Each justification for jurisdiction may inform its exercise and thus leads to a different type of jurisdiction. The different justifications enumerated above thus give rise to different types of jurisdiction generally characterized as territorial, nationality, passive personality and protective jurisdiction.

3. Given these considerations and given the fact that there is no internationally codified definition of universal jurisdiction at present, many proposed definitions and commentaries seem to have defined universal jurisdiction by an "absence" of the normal jurisdictional links to the national legal system attempting to exercise jurisdiction. For example, the Institut de droit international (IDI) in its 2005 resolution on universal jurisdiction, paragraph 1, states:

> Universal jurisdiction in criminal matters, as an additional ground of jurisdiction, means the competence of a State to prosecute alleged offenders and to punish them if convicted, irrespective of the place of commission of the crime and regardless of any link of active or passive nationality, or other grounds of jurisdiction recognized by international law.[3]

In the view of the IDI Rapporteur of the project, "It was [the] absence of link between the crime and the prosecuting State that captured the essence of universal jurisdiction."[4] Similarly, the AU-EU Expert Report on this topic

---

2 This articles deals only with universal criminal jurisdiction.

3 Institut de droit international (IDI), Resolution on universal criminal jurisdiction with regard to the crime of genocide, crimes against humanity and war crimes, adopted in Krakow, 2005 (http://www.idi-iil.org/idiF/resolutionsF/2005_kra_03_fr.pdf), para.1 (hereinafter, "IDI Resolution").

4 Christian Tomuschat, Rapporteur of the IDI Commission on Universal

states:

> Universal criminal jurisdiction is the assertion by one state of its jurisdiction over crimes allegedly committed in the territory of another state by nationals of another state against nationals of another state where the crime alleged poses no direct threat to the vital interests of the state asserting jurisdiction. In other words, universal jurisdiction amounts to the claim by a state to prosecute crimes in circumstances where none of the traditional links of territoriality, nationality, passive personality or the protective principle exists at the time of the commission of the alleged offence.[5]

4. Behind the "absence" façade, however, rests the basis for such an assertion of jurisdiction, normally formulated this way: The alleged crime is an attack on the fundamental values of the international community as a whole (i.e., a violation of *jus cogens* or a species of law that is very close to that genus however described, such as *erga omnes* obligations), so that the crime is a matter of universal concern, considered as such by the international community as a whole, and that every State in the world has an interest in prosecuting the perpetrator.[6] Another instrumental reasoning, which may apply with greater force to some situations than in others, is that the exercise of universal jurisdiction is *necessary* in order to ensure that certain crimes be punished. For example, piracy, normally committed on the high seas, may go unpunished if universal jurisdiction does not exist. As such, these crimes are also of universal concern, perhaps of a slightly different kind. So understood, it would seem better to characterize universal jurisdiction as "universal concern jurisdiction",[7]

Criminal Jurisdiction, as quoted in IDI, 71(II) Annuaire de l'Institut de droit international (2006), 257; see also ibid., 261.

5 AU-EU Expert Report (http://ec.europa.eu/development/icenter/repository/troika_ua_ue_rapport_competence_universelle_EN.pdf), para.8.

6 See generally ALI, Restatement of the Law, Third, Foreign Relations Law of the United States (ALI, Restatement Third), §404 and the associated comments and notes; IDI Resolution, n.3 above; and the IDI deliberations, IDI, 71(II) Annuaire, n.4 above, 199-284; International Association of Penal Law (AIDP), XVIIII Congress in 2009, Resolution on Universal Jurisdiction (http://www.penal.org/?page=mainaidp&id_rubrique=24&id_article=95).

7 See ALI, Restatement Third, §404 ("A state has jurisdiction to define and prescribe punishment for certain offenses recognized by the community of

in some contrast to other forms of jurisdiction such as "territoriality jurisdiction", "nationality jurisdiction" and "national interests protection jurisdiction". These terms would make immediately apparent the justification behind each assertion of jurisdiction. A definition of universal jurisdiction or universal concern jurisdiction should be the exercise of national jurisdiction, based on universal concern, over crimes that attack the fundamental values of international society.[8]

5. The logic of universal concern jurisdiction is easy to understand. Universal concern as a motivating force for national action was propounded by the International Court of Justice in the celebrated *Barcelona Traction* case in 1970.[9] That case was about diplomatic protection, and the Court's celebrated dictum therefore cannot be claimed as direct precedent or immediate support for universal jurisdiction.[10] But that dictum on this point is unmistakably of general applicability and can be considered the elaboration of the *ultimate* rationale for universal jurisdiction. There the Court said:

> 33. When a State admits into its territory foreign investments or foreign nationals, whether natural or juristic persons, it is bound to extend to them the protection of the law and assumes obligations concerning the treatment to be afforded them. These obligations, however, are neither absolute nor unqualified. In particular, an essential distinction should be drawn between the obligations of a State towards the international community as a whole, and those arising vis-à-vis another State in the field of diplomatic protection. By their very nature the former are the concern of all States. In view of the importance of the rights involved, all States can be held to have a legal interest in their protection; they are obligations *erga omnes*.
>
> 34. Such obligations derive, for example, in contemporary international law, from the outlawing of acts of aggression, and of

---

nations as of universal concern, such as piracy, slave trade, attacks on or hijacking of aircraft, genocide, war crimes, and perhaps certain acts of terrorism, even where none of the bases of jurisdiction indicated §402 is present").

8 See ALI, ibid.

9 Case concerning the Barcelona Traction, Light and Power Company, Limited, Second Phase, Judgment, ICJ Reports 1970, 3.

10 See Rosalyn Higgins, Problems and Process: International Law and How We Use it (1994), 57-58.

> genocide, as also from the principles and rules concerning the basic rights of the human person, including protection from slavery and racial discrimination. Some of the corresponding rights of protection have entered into the body of general international law (*Reservations to the Convention on the Prevention and Punishment of the Crime of Genocide, Advisory Opinion, I.C.J. Reports 1951*, p. 23); others are conferred by international instruments of a universal or quasi-universal character.

6. Intended to implement this idea,[11] Article 48 ("Invocation of responsibility by a State other than an injured State") of the International Law Commission's Articles on State Responsibility, adopted in 2001, states: "1. Any State other than an injured State is entitled to invoke the responsibility of another State in accordance with paragraph 2 if: [...] (a) The obligation breached is owed to a group of States including that State, and is established for the protection of a collective interest of the group; or [..] (b) The obligation breached is owed to the international community as a whole."[12]

7. Thus, as a general proposition, there are certain matters in the world that are of universal concern, and this universal concern is sufficient to justify certain action on the part of States. Applied to our inquiry in this article, this rationale alone, or this rationale plus another factor, potentially would justify a State's exercise of universal jurisdiction. However, universal jurisdiction is not a necessary corollary of universal concern, even when that concern assumes *jus cogens* proportions.[13] The sole fact of the violation of a rule that attains the *jus cogens* status does not give rise to the jurisdiction of the International Court of Justice or another international tribunal, as the Court ruled in *Democratic Republic of the Congo v. Rwanda*;[14] nor do violations of *erga omnes* rights or obligations alone, as the Court has also ruled in *East Timor*.[15] Consent alone founds international jurisdiction or the jurisdiction of international courts and tribunals.

---

11 ILC Draft Articles on State Responsibility, art. 48, commentary, para.(8), in ILC Report 2001, A/56/10, 321.

12 ILC Report 2001, ibid., 56.

13 See Paolo Picone, The Distinction between *Jus Cogens* and Obligations *Erga Omnes*, in Enzo Cannizzaro (ed), The Law of Treaties beyond the Vienna Convention (2011), 411, 421-422; but see generally Alexander Orakhelashvili, Peremptory Norms in International Law (2006).

14 Armed Activities on the Territory of the Congo (New Application: 2002) (Democratic Republic of the Congo v. Rwanda), ICJ Reports 2006, para.64.

15 East Timor (Portugal v. Australia), ICJ Reports 1995, 102, para.29.

Although the justification of the exercise of jurisdiction by a national legal order, our inquiry here, was not in issue in either case, the same conclusion may be drawn that the violation of a norm having *jus cogens* or *erga omnes* character does not in itself give rise to universal jurisdiction for the national legal systems. Whether the potential of universal concern in justifying the exercise of national jurisdiction has been realized, or the extent to which it has been, would depend on what crimes would be considered by States generally as crimes of universal concern and whether this universal concern has in fact be also considered by States as sufficient to justify an exercise of such jurisdiction. The answers to these questions will depend on the reality of the international law formation process. This is an issue that needs to be assessed according to the normal sources of law exercise under article 38 of the Statute of the International Court of Justice (ICJ). That exercise will be attempted in Part II of this article. For now, let us briefly consider some general issues that may frame such an evaluation and help us to understand what may have factored into that reality.

8. As the term "universal jurisdiction" has been used by various people to indicate various things in varying degrees of density or looseness, it will be helpful to offer some clarifications on the typology of situations that may constitute universal jurisdiction, properly so-called, or resemble it. To make things clear, the following characterizations, in the order of strength of "universalness", can be used:

1. "Pure universal concern jurisdiction". This form of jurisdiction would be an assertion of jurisdiction based solely on the universal concern character of the crime, without more. This would be the "pure universal jurisdiction" or "true universal jurisdiction". If considered legitimate, this form of jurisdiction would entitle, as far as the jurisdictional requirement is concerned, the prosecuting State to the extradition of the suspect from a foreign State, if other conditions are met.[16] Sometimes "universal jurisdiction *in absentia*" is used to describe this type of jurisdiction but this term can be confused with "trial *in absentia*" and is not preferred here. Included in this form of jurisdiction are: (1) A State unilaterally asserts pure universal jurisdiction; and (2) Hypothetically a treaty allowing States parties to assert pure universal jurisdiction over nationals of non-

---

16 Cf. AIDP, n.6 above, para.II(2); but see 2005 IDI Resolution, n.3 above, para.3(b).

parties for crimes occurring on territories of a third party. In the latter situation, the treaty regime as a whole does not have greater authority in relation to a third State than a particular State party to it, and the treaty granting jurisdiction to the parties to the regime does not add anything to our assessment.

2. "Universal concern plus presence jurisdiction". This is illustrated by a State unilaterally asserts jurisdiction over a non-national who is present in that State for crimes of universal concern that have occurred in a foreign State. This is not universal jurisdiction properly so called, as the presence of suspect may justify this form of jurisdiction as "territorial", to some extent, or "nationality" when the presence of the suspect is prolonged so as to assimilate it to nationality. When the presence of the suspect is fleeting (such as a weekend visit) or brief (such as a medical visit), such an exercise of jurisdiction gives rises to different characterizations: some call it universal jurisdiction, while others claim that this is jurisdiction with some connection. If the absence of a link between the crime and the prosecuting State is the essence of universal jurisdiction, then a fleeting presence of the suspect in the prosecuting State may not disqualify the assertion of jurisdiction as that of universal jurisdiction. However, to the extent that the law about a State asserting jurisdiction based on brief presence is made clear, notice would have been given to any potential suspect. If he or she still comes to that State, voluntarily making that connection, such an exercise of jurisdiction can be considered "non-universal", definitely not "pure universal concern jurisdiction".
3. "Universal concern plus treaty and presence jurisdiction". This situation is similar to Situation 2, with the added obligation or right from a treaty to assert jurisdiction on that basis. An illustration would be a treaty allowing parties to exercise jurisdiction over a national of a third State, if present in the prosecuting State, for crimes of universal concern that have occurred in a third State.
4. "Universal concern plus treaty, presence and intra-regime territoriality or nationality jurisdiction". This is similar to and narrower than Situation 3, with the added requirement that the suspect or the crime must be related to a party to the treaty setting up the regime in terms of territoriality, nationality or victim nationality. An illustration of an intra-regime nationality link would

> be a treaty allowing party A to the treaty to prosecute suspect B, a national of party C to the treaty, who is present in A, for crimes of universal concern that have occurred in State D, a non-party to the treaty. An illustration of an intra-regime territoriality link would be a treaty allowing party A to the treaty to prosecute suspect B, a national of a third State (non-party to the treaty), who is present on the territory of party A, for crimes allegedly took place on the territory of party C to the treaty.

Among these situations, only the first situation is pure or true universal jurisdiction. The second situation moves away from pure and true universal jurisdiction but is closer to it than the other situations. Situations 3 and 4 are not universal jurisdiction in the true sense. The role of universal concern in justifying the exercise of jurisdiction in Situations 2 to 4 is, strictly speaking, redundant. Indeed, if presence triggers a treaty based obligation to exercise jurisdiction, that jurisdiction can be, as described by the Joint Separate Opinion of Judges Higgins, Kooijmans and Buergenthal in *Arrest Warrant*,[17] "really an obligatory territorial jurisdiction over persons". If we were to call these situations "universal jurisdiction", "universal jurisdiction" would be purchased at the price of diluting and cheapening the concept; we would be playing a game of words.

9. Secondly, various factors may inform the international law making process relating to universal jurisdiction, and these result in the reality of the extent of acceptance of it. First of all, universal jurisdiction can be rationalized as a system jurisdiction, for the protection of the interests of the international system including the protection of human rights and the fight against impunity, while employing the national legal systems, *faute de mieux*, to perform that task because of the lack of a central government in what we often call the "international community". In a way, the national legal systems can be considered to be in a situation of "dédoublement fonctionnel".[18] As a result, States hoping to protect the interests of the international system and to contribute to its maintenance and promotion should have incentives to promote

---

17 Joint Separate Opinion of Judges Higgins, Kooijmans and Buergenthal, ICJ Reports 2002, 74-75, para.41.

18 A term from Georges Scelle. See Antonio Cassese, Remarks on Scelle's Theory of "Role Splitting" (dédoublement fonctionnel) in International Law, 1 EJIL (1990), 210.

the establishment and the application of the principle of universal jurisdiction. Furthermore, relating to this systemic consideration, universal criminal jurisdiction would seem to be necessary to implement or enforce *jus cogens*, another important systemic factor. Otherwise, that concept would be toothless. Those States that have recognized the idea of *jus cogens* probably may also have incentives to be friendly to the idea of universal jurisdiction.

10. On the other hand, the exercise of universal jurisdiction may infringe, or at least detract from, the principle of sovereignty and sovereign equality and is easily subjected to political abuse including discrimination as manifested in selective prosecution, thus destabilizing international relations. Because of this, this form of jurisdiction has been described as "dangerous" by none other than Henry Kissinger.[19] Of course, any exercise of universal jurisdiction will most likely favor the big and powerful States.[20] If as claimed by some States and Judge *ad hoc* van den Wyngaert in *Arrest Warrant*, the question is "about what international law requires or allows States to do as 'agents' of the international community when they are confronted with complaints of victims of" heinous crimes,[21] one may immediately question whether such agents should be self-appointed by a particular State itself. This concern assumes a greater proportion if the *Lotus* dictum is allowed to prevail.[22] Furthermore, the political nature of universal jurisdiction is on full display when the attempt to exercise universal jurisdiction by States may indeed be tradable, as in the case of Belgium which decided in 2003 to scuttle its strong universal jurisdiction authorization when threatened by the prospect of the NATO Headquarters moving away.[23] Also,

---

19 Henry Kissinger, The Pitfalls of Universal Jurisdiction, Foreign Affairs (July-August 2001).

20 As pointed out by Shahabuddeen, in IDI Annuaire, n.4 above, 228.

21 Arrest Warrant, diss. op., ICJ Reports 2002, 141, para.5.

22 See Part III below, paras.44-49.

23 5 August 2003 Act on Grave Breaches of International Humanitarian Law. As reported by none other than the person who did the threatening, Donald Rumsfeld, Known and Unknown: A Memoir (2011), 596-598. Rumsfeld reported a "frank and full exchange" with Mr. Andre Flabaut, Belgium's minister of defense, in which Rumsfeld made clear that NATO could move its headquarters again as it did from France when the host was hostile and that the American support for the building of a new NATO headquarters "would evaporate instantly absent a prompt shift in the Belgium government's position". Ibid., 598. Rumsfeld seemed to relish this: "The difference in style between a Chicago-born American and member of the European diplomatic corps was on full display in that conversation. From his demeanor I could tell

the attempt can be shamed away at least to some extent, as, on my view, in the case of Spain which in 2009 dismantled its own strong universal jurisdiction authorization when Judge Garzon began to dig into Spain's old dirty laundry resulting from the Spanish Civil War.[24]

11. Obviously a regime of universal jurisdiction would present severe challenges to national reconciliation efforts such as those made in post-apartheid South Africa or in some Latin American States. As stated by Kissinger[25]:

> It is an important principle that those who commit war crimes or systematically violate human rights should be held accountable. But the consolidation of law, domestic peace, and representative government in a nation struggling to come to terms with a brutal past has a claim as well. The instinct to punish must be related, as in every constitutional democratic political structure, to a system of checks and balances that includes other elements critical to the survival and expansion of democracy.

12. These factors and others[26] not discussed here no doubt have left their imprint in the international law formation process, resulting in the current state of affairs that we will examine in the following pages.

---

he fully understood my point. Within two months of that conversation, the Belgian government repealed their law." Ibid., 598.

24 See Jaclyn Belczyk, Spain parliament passes law limiting reach of universal jurisdiction statute, 16 Oct 2009, http://jurist.law.pitt.edu/paperchase/2009/10/spain-parliament-passes-law-limiting.php; Daniel Woolls, Baltasar Garzon, Spanish Super Judge, Suspended Over Alleged Abuse, AP News (05/14/10), http://www.huffingtonpost.com/2010/05/14/baltasar-garzon-spanish-s_n_576872.html; Scott Horton, The Poet, the Judge, and the Falangists, http://harpers.org/archive/2010/04/hbc-90006895.

25 Kissinger, n.19 above.

26 See generally Luc Reydams, The Rise and Fall of Universal Jurisdiction, Leuven Centre for Global Governance Studies, Working Paper No. 37 (http://ghum.kuleuven.be/ggs/publications/working_papers/new_series/wp 31-40/wp37.pdf, January 2010) ("Leuven Working Paper"); papers by George Fletcher, Louise Arbour, Antonio Cassese and Georges Abi-Saab, in 1 J Intl Criminal Justice (2003), 580-602.

II. The reality of universal jurisdiction in international law

13. Reasonable as the idea of universal jurisdiction sounds, persuasive as its logic appears, one must not forget the teaching that "The life of the law has not been logic: it has been experience".[27] The experience and reality of international relations are such that universal jurisdiction over crimes other than piracy has not been established as a matter of international law.

14. An examination of the status of universal jurisdiction in international law is hampered by a lack of clear statement in the relevant primary official materials and a lack of dispassionate and rigorous analyses of them. Over-exaggerated statements expressing support for universal jurisdiction are often found in the writings of various writers. Closer examination, however, may lead to differing conclusions.[28] Despite various difficulties, such an examination will be attempted in the following pages under the framework of Article 38 of the ICJ Statute, primarily under paragraph 1(a) and 1(b), in terms of treaty practice and customary international law. Since there is no dispute about the lawfulness of universal jurisdiction over piracy under international law, I will not deal with piracy in this article.

II.A. Treaty practice

15. There are numerous treaties dealing with jurisdiction over crimes of universal concern, presenting a formidable task to any conscientious scholars. Literature also abounds regarding how these treaties should be classified and evaluated.[29] The task is made more difficulty by the controversy surrounding what constitutes universal jurisdiction, properly so called. I will first recap the current discussion of the treaty practice with some commentary of my own and

---

27 O.W. Holmes, The Common Law (1886), 1.

28 See generally Luc Reydams, Leuven Working Paper, n.26 above; id., Universal Jurisdiction: International and Municipal Legal Perspectives (2003); William Schabas, Foreword, ibid.; Zdzislaw Galicki, ILC Special Rapporteur, Fourth report on the obligation to extradite or prosecute (aut dedere aut judicare), A/CN.4/648 (31 May 2011), http://daccess-dds-ny.un.org/doc/UNDOC/GEN/N11/358/84/PDF/N1135884.pdf. For an optimistic assessment of the status of universal jurisdiction in international law, see V.D. Degan and Vesna Baric Punda, Universal Jurisdiction: An Option or a Legal Obligation for States, 13 International Law Review of Wuhan University (2010), 66-92.

29 See ILC Special Rapporteur, ibid.; Reydams, ibid.

then attempt to sort through these treaties by giving my typological summary of them.

II.A.i. The current evaluation of treaty practice

16. The first and most eligible modern crime for pure universal jurisdiction is probably genocide. I believe I need not spill any more ink to prove the universal concern character of the crime of genocide. Yet, universal jurisdiction over this crime was expressly debated and rejected twice: first when the UNGA drafted and adopted Resolution 96(I) of 1946 and again when it drafted and adopted the Convention for the Prevention and Punishment of the Crime of Genocide ("Genocide Convention") of 1948.[30] The resultant Article VI of the Convention relies on the traditional territorial jurisdiction and on a yet to be established international court.

17. Those who claim to have found the existence of universal jurisdiction usually seize upon, as their evidence, the various "extradite or prosecute" provisions in a large number of treaties and assert that these embody the existence of universal jurisdiction. This claim is not supported by a close examination of the treaty practice: although the universal concern character of the crimes dealt with may have motivated the conclusion of these treaties (a point few would disagree with), the exercise of jurisdiction may be justified on other grounds. "Extradite or prosecute" is a means of exercising jurisdiction; it is not jurisdiction itself.[31] The ways and means of exercising jurisdiction should not be conflated with jurisdiction itself. The "extradite or prosecute" obligation may apply jurisdiction that has been justified on any basis, whether territoriality, nationality, national vital interests or even universal concern. Thus the adoption of this means of exercise of jurisdiction does not necessarily lead to the finding of a particular kind or basis of jurisdiction itself, but of all the possible kinds utilized.

18. The pivotal point is to identify which kind of jurisdiction that the means ("extradite or prosecute") is utilized to implement. Such an effort reveals no treaty expressly using the "extradite or prosecute" to implement pure universal jurisdiction, and thus no *express* treaty practice support for the idea of

---

30 See William Schabas, Genocide in International Law: The Crime of Crimes (2d edn 2009), 49-116, 411-416.

31 For another formulation of this difference see AU-EU Expert Report, n.5 above, para.11.

pure universal jurisdiction. Having chided the majority for not addressing the issue of jurisdiction and upon an examination of several important treaties, Judges Higgins, Kooijmans and Buergenthal concluded in their Joint Separate Opinion in *Arrest Warrant*[32]:

> 41. The parties to these treaties agreed both to grounds of jurisdiction and as to the obligation to take the measures necessary to establish such jurisdiction. The specified grounds relied on links of nationality of the offender, or the ship or aircraft concerned, or of the victim. See, for example, Article 4 (l), Hague Convention; Article 3 (l), Tokyo Convention; Article 5, Hostages Convention; Article 5, Torture Convention. These may properly be described as treaty-based broad extraterritorial jurisdiction. But in addition to these were the parallel provisions whereby a State party in whose jurisdiction the alleged perpetrator of such offences is found shall prosecute him or extradite him. By the loose use of language the latter has come to be referred to as "universal jurisdiction", though this is really an obligatory territorial jurisdiction over persons, albeit in relation to acts committed elsewhere.

19. Whether the situation where a suspect's presence alone in the prosecuting State that refuses to extradite him or her, whose disputed acts had no link to that State, justifies the exercise of jurisdiction is merely what was described by Judge Higgins, et al., or in fact universal jurisdiction or a conditional form of universal jurisdiction appears to be unsettled. This "mere presence" subsequent to the alleged crime situation is apparently what was contemplated in the provisions of on the repression of "grave breaches" of the Geneva Conventions of 1949 (Articles 49(I)[33]; 50 (II); 129 (III); 146 (IV); 85 (AP(I)). The ICRC in

---

32 Joint Separate Opinion, n.17 above, 74-75, para.41.

33 That articles states in relevant part:

> The High Contracting Parties undertake to enact any legislation necessary to provide effective penal sanctions for persons committing, or ordering to be committed, any of the grave breaches of the present Convention defined in the following Article.
>
> Each High Contracting Party shall be under the obligation to search for persons alleged to have committed, or to have ordered to be committed, such grave breaches, and shall bring such persons, regardless of their nationality, before its own courts. It may also, if it prefers, and in

various statements apparently considered this regime to be one of universal jurisdiction.[34] The ICRC Study on the status of the customary international humanitarian law also seems to believe so.[35] Expressed in another context[36] or in other ways,[37] some governments also seem to treat this situation as "universal jurisdiction".

20. This view apparently also receives the endorsement of the IDI. During the debate on the universal jurisdiction project, the IDI Rapporteur put emphasis on the lack of a link between the crime and the prosecuting State as the criterion for finding universal jurisdiction.[38] Such "mere presence" was apparently not considered to furnish such a link. The final text of the 2005 IDI resolution in paragraph 2 states:

> accordance with the provisions of its own legislation, hand such persons over for trial to another High Contracting Party concerned, provided such High Contracting Party has made out a *prima facie* case.

The term "search for" can be properly interpreted as "search for persons said to be present on its territory". See Jean S. Pictet's commentary, Convention (I) for the Amelioration of the Condition of the Wounded and Sick in Armed Forces in the Field, Geneva, 12 August 1949 (1952), 365-366 (http://www.icrc.org/ihl.nsf/COM/365-570060?OpenDocument).

34 Statement by the ICRC representative in the 6th Committee, A/C.6/65/SR.12 (15 Oct. 2010)), 6, para.42; ICRC Official Statement, 27-08-2003, on the "First Meeting of Experts of States Parties to the Biological and Toxin Weapons Convention, Geneva, 18-29 August 2003", http://www.icrc.org/web/eng/siteeng0.nsf/htmlall/5qkdpf ("It should be recalled that States are already required to exercise universal jurisdiction in respect of 'grave breaches' [of] the 1949 Geneva Conventions and their Additional Protocol I of 1977, which refer to acts committed in situations of armed conflict against protected persons such as wilful killing, torture or inhuman treatment including biological experiments, and making the civilian population or individual civilians the object of attack. Use of biological weapons amounting to such 'grave breaches' would thus require the assertion of universal jurisdiction.").

35 See Jean-Marie Henckaerts & Louise Doswald-Beck (eds), 1 Customary International Humanitarian Law ("ICRC Study"), Rule 157 and the associated support in vol. 2.

36 See views of governments as characterized in E/CN.4/1983/63, paras.22 & 23, on the proposed Convention against Torture.

37 See generally the views of the UK government, as quoted in Ian Brownlie, Principles of Public International Law (7th ed., 2008), 305-306.

38 IDI Annuaire, n.4 above, 257; 261 (Rapporteur).

> Universal jurisdiction is primarily based on customary international law. It can also be established under a multilateral treaty in the relations between the contracting parties, in particular by virtue of clauses which provide that a State party in the territory of which an alleged offender is found shall either extradite or try that person.[39]

The second sentence was adopted despite the objections of some members including Higgins and Abi-Saab.[40]

21. Furthermore, some treaties require that the alleged crimes have significant links to *some* parties to a particular treaty such as territoriality or nationality; these links to the regime as a whole definitely disqualify the "mere presence" situation as an exercise of truly universal jurisdiction. This would be "universal concern plus treaty, presence and intra-regime territoriality or nationality jurisdiction" as highlighted above. Such a situation is a quintessential intra-regime cooperative affair, in the sense that at least one party to the regime can legitimately exercise jurisdiction based on a traditional criterion, and the prosecuting State party is simply performing the function of that other party in its stead, for whatever reason (such as its inability or unwillingness to do so). The regime in essence allows the parties to share their traditional jurisdictional powers, or permits one party to exercise the jurisdictional authority of another party. The Geneva Conventions use broadly worded language ("regardless of their nationality") to describe the "extradite or prosecute" obligation, but the application of those Conventions may—though this is not clear—require that the alleged crime was committed on the territory of one of the parties to the Conventions, thus requiring a first level connection (such as nationality, territoriality, victim nationality, or vital interests) with at least one party to the applicable Convention. In any event, subsequently treaties such as the Convention against Torture and Other Cruel, Inhuman or Degrading Treatment or Punishment of 1984 make it clearer that the "mere presence" of a suspect in the territory of one of the parties is of a secondary nature; the crime or the suspect must have a first level link such as territoriality or nationality with one of the parties to the Convention for the suspect to be subject to some kind of process. This is at least one plausible reading of article 5 of the Convention against Torture. That article reads:

---

39 IDI Resolution, n.3 above.

40 IDI, 71(II) Annuaire, n.4 above, 209-210 (Abi-Saab); 257 (Higgins).

Article 5

1. Each State Party shall take such measures as may be necessary to establish its jurisdiction over the offences referred to in article 4 in the following cases:
   (a) When the offences are committed in any territory under its jurisdiction or on board a ship or aircraft registered in that State;
   (b) When the alleged offender is a national of that State;
   (c) When the victim is a national of that State if that State considers it appropriate.
2. Each State Party shall likewise take such measures as may be necessary to establish its jurisdiction over such offences in cases where the alleged offender is present in any territory under its jurisdiction and it does not extradite him pursuant to article 8 to any of the States mentioned in paragraph 1 of this article.
3. This Convention does not exclude any criminal jurisdiction exercised in accordance with internal law.

Paragraph 1 of this article provides for the obligation to establish jurisdiction based on territoriality, nationality or victim nationality. Paragraph 2 provides for the obligation to prosecute if the suspect is not extradited to "any of the States mentioned in paragraph 1 of this article". One reading of this provision would be that for paragraph 2 to apply, paragraph 1 must have been potentially applicable but the requested State is not willing to extradite the suspect; that is to say, the suspect (or the suspected crime) must have first level links to a State party ("any State mentioned in paragraph 1", which deals with States parties only)—territoriality, nationality or victim nationality—to establish that potential applicability. So read, article 5(2) does not deal with matters outside the province of the regime.

22. A further and clearer illustration of this regime is the Rome Statute of the International Criminal Court, which in article 12 provides for the ICC—which can be considered a cooperative of the States Parties—to take jurisdiction based on territoriality links between the crime and a State party or nationality link between the suspect and a State party.

23. One may argue that there can be an alternative and broader reading of article 49 of Geneva Convention (I) and the corresponding articles in the other Geneva Conventions as well as article 5(2) of the Convention against Torture. This alternative reading would not require first level links between the suspect (and the suspected crime) and a State party for the "extradite or

prosecute" obligation to be triggered. Indeed, article 49 of Geneva Convention (I) is so broadly written that it may be susceptible of the alternative reading. Further, one can imagine a reading of article 5(2) of the Convention against Torture this way: that paragraph 2 is triggered whenever a suspect is not extradited to any State party, irrespective of the reasons for that. Under this reading, whether or not paragraph 1 is potentially applicable is immaterial, although if it is not applicable, it will be because the suspect is a national of a third State accused of a crime occurring on the territory of a third State against a national of a third State and is not extradited to any State party. However, this reading would seem to render part of the language of article 5(2) redundant or unnaturally formulated. If such an alternative reading is accepted, this situation would be the "universal concern plus treaty and presence jurisdiction" as highlighted above.

24. Other examples of this situation include article 4(2) of the 1970 Hague Convention for the Suppression of Unlawful Seizure of Aircraft[41] and article V of the Apartheid Convention.[42] Both can be read as authorizing the

---

41 See Joint Separate Opinion, ICJ Reports 2002, 73, para.35; President Guillaume, Separate Opinion, in his separate opinion, ibid., 38, para.7. There President Guillaume emphasized the obligation to establish jurisdiction so that "the obligation to prosecute was no longer conditional on the existence of jurisdiction on, but rather jurisdiction itself had to be established in order to make prosecution possible", and he seemed to call this "compulsory, albeit subsidiary, universal jurisdiction". He took as the forerunner Article 4(2) of the Hague Convention for the Suppression of Unlawful Seizure of Aircraft of 1970. One may agree with this emphasis if the obligation to establish jurisdiction cannot be considered a logical extension of, or as included in, the term "extradite or prosecute". To prosecute implies the existence of the wherewithal to do so, i.e., the establishment of jurisdiction. In any event, a general promise to take effective measures to repress crimes would have included such an obligation. This is the understanding of the broadly worded Article 49, especially paragraph 1, of the Geneva Convention (I) of 1949 and the corresponding articles in the other Geneva Conventions. Furthermore, Article 4(2) of the Hague Convention for the Suppression of Unlawful Seizure of Aircraft of 1970 expressly requires the presence of the suspect on the territory of the Contracting State, while Article 49 of the Geneva Convention has been construed as requiring the same. That is to say, potentially the 1970 Hague Convention may not be the first on the requirement to establish jurisdiction.

42 Apartheid Convention, art. V, which states: "Persons charged with the acts

exercise of jurisdiction over a suspect, a national of a third State, who is present in the prosecuting State party to the applicable convention for crimes that have occurred in a third State. We cannot be certain that this reading is correct, there does not appear to be any record of these provisions being applied this way either administrative or judicially.

25. However, even this "universal concern plus treaty and presence jurisdiction" is not true or pure universal jurisdiction, as a treaty permission or obligation to exercise jurisdiction and the presence of the suspect are required. Only when a treaty claims to give the parties thereto jurisdiction over crimes and suspects having no link with any of the parties to the treaty, one would see pure universal jurisdiction. For example, if the 1970 Hague Convention would authorize jurisdiction over a national of a third party to the Convention who is not yet present in the prosecuting State party to the Convention for crimes occurring in a third State, that would present a "pure universal concern jurisdiction" scenario. However, no such a treaty is readily found, although I have not done exhaustive research on this. The Judges in the *Arrest Warrant* case (especially those who issued opinions on the issue of universal jurisdiction) and the various scholars who have done thorough research on universal jurisdiction have not reported one either.

26. The phrasing of some treaty provisions may give rise to the impression or the argument that the treaty somehow impliedly recognizes universal jurisdiction. For example, the Second Protocol to the Hague Convention for the Protection of Cultural Property in the Event of Armed

---

enumerated in article II of the present Convention may be tried by a competent tribunal of any State Party to the Convention which may acquire jurisdiction over the person of the accused or by an international penal tribunal having jurisdiction with respect to those States Parties which shall have accepted its jurisdiction." "Acquire jurisdiction over the person of the accused" apparently means his presence. This Convention is quite special both in terms of the circumstances of adoption and the political climate prevailing then. See comment by John Dugard, http://untreaty.un.org/cod/avl/pdf/ha/cspca/cspca_e.pdf, 2 ("The Apartheid Convention allows State parties to prosecute non-nationals for a crime committed in the territory of a non-State party where the accused is physically within the jurisdiction of a State party (arts. 4 and 5). […] No one was prosecuted for the crime of apartheid while apartheid lasted in South Africa. And no one has since been prosecuted for the crime."). But cf. Reydams, Leuven Working Paper, n.26 above, 18, who seemed to characterize the Apartheid Convention, art. V, as granting universal jurisdiction.

Conflict (1999),[43] in article 16(2)(a), states that the Protocol "does not preclude [...] the exercise of jurisdiction under national and international law that may be applicable, or affect the exercise of jurisdiction under customary international law". The ICRC experts on customary international humanitarian law were of the view that

> The Second Protocol to the Hague Convention for the Protection of Cultural Property states that it does not affect "the exercise of jurisdiction under customary international law", which was intended by delegates at the negotiation of the Protocol to refer to the right of States to vest universal jurisdiction in their national courts for war crimes.[44]

The experts did not present evidence from drafting history.

27. It is better not to read this provision this way; it is better to read it as a provision preventing an *a contrario* interpretation of article 16 that it prohibits other forms of exercises of jurisdiction not spelled out in the article. It would be a jump to read it as supporting a particular form of exercise such as universal jurisdiction. Such a meaning would have required affirmative support in the text of the treaty itself. This better interpretation is supported by the similar interpretation generally given to article 5(3) of the Convention against Torture.[45]

II.A.ii. Summary of treaty practice

28. The messy treaty practice and scholarly treatment do not afford much confidence in us when we attempt to distill any rules of customary international law from it. The universal concern character of the crimes under consideration may have motivated the conclusion of a substantial number of treaties, but whatever we would like to say about these treaties, it will be advisable for us to remember that a treaty right or obligation is only applicable to the parties thereto and is subject to a variety of conditions specific to that treaty.[46]

---

43 http://portal.unesco.org/en/ev.php-URL_ID=15207&URL_DO=DO_TOPIC &URL_SECTION=201.html.

44 ICRC Study, n.35 above, vol.1, 605, & n.198.

45 See Joint Separate Opinion, Arrest Warrant, above n.17, paras.34, 38.

46 See Statement of China (Chinese original at: http://www.un.org/en/ga/sixth/65/ScopeAppUniJuri_StatesComments/China.pdf; English translation by the UN at: http://www.un.org/en/ga/sixth/65/ScopeApp UniJuri_StatesComments/China_E.pdf), Observations, para.6.

Nevertheless, data do show that there is no instance of "pure universal concern jurisdiction" being authorized in any treaty. Some treaties authorize or can be interpreted as authorizing "universal concern plus treaty and presence jurisdiction". Even more treaties authorize "universal concern plus treaty, presence and intra-regime territoriality or nationality jurisdiction". But neither of the latter two types can be properly called "universal jurisdiction".

II.B. Customary international law

29. Turning to the customary international law status of universal jurisdiction, one is of course reminded of the requirements as stated in article 38(1)(b) of the ICJ Statute for the finding of such a rule: customary international law is evidenced by a general State practice accepted as law (i.e., *opinio juris*).

30. In this regard, one is struck by the lack of evidence of clear exercise of "pure universal concern" jurisdiction and the seemingly broad support for "universal jurisdiction", loosely described, as evidenced in the various declarations and statements. If the latter were to be taken at face value, there appears to be *opinio juris* for the concept of "universal jurisdiction", loosely used, over genocide, crimes against humanity and serious war crimes. For example, as early as in 1971, a General Assembly resolution was broadly worded so as to be consistent with the idea of universal jurisdiction. There, the GA "*affirms* that refusal by States to cooperation in the arrest, extradition, trial and punishment of persons guilty of war crimes and crimes against humanity is contrary to the purposes and principles of the Charter of the United Nations and to generally recognized norms of international law".[47] Many Western States have made statements supporting the concept of universal jurisdiction.[48] The African Union stated, in a memorandum annexed to the request for the inclusion of universal jurisdiction in the agenda of the 63rd session of the UNGA, that "The principle of universal jurisdiction is well established in international law" and that "The African Union respects this principle, which is enshrined in article 4(h) of the Constitutive Act" but that it was concerned about the uncertain scope and application of the principle and the abuse of it.[49] The American Law

---

47 UNGA Res 2840 (1971).

48 For further info, see AU-EU Expert Report, n.5 above; ICRC Study, n.35 above.

49 A/63/237, annex (Explanatory memorandum), para.1. The States of the Non-aligned Movement seemed to hold a more ambiguous attitude. See A/C.6/64/SR.12 (25 November 2009), paras.20-21; A/C.6/65/SR.10 (13

Institute, a national institute of legal experts, found that universal jurisdiction existed under customary international law over several crimes as early as 1986.[50] The IDI, a world academy of international law experts, also gave its support to the concept or principle of universal jurisdiction in 2005.[51]

31. In any event, data on State conduct asserting universal jurisdiction do not reveal sufficient evidence establishing true universal jurisdiction, other than in cases of piracy. This is more or less the conclusion of the Western judges including Judge Higgins, Kooijmans, Buergenthal, and President Guillaume in *Arrest Warrant* (2002). The Joint Separate Opinion by Higgins, Kooijmans and Buergenthal in *Arrest Warrant* endorsed[52] the opinion of the authors of *Oppenheim's International Law* (9th ed., 1996, 998), that:

> While no general rule of positive international law can as yet be asserted which gives rise to states the right to punish foreign nationals for crimes against humanity in the same way as they are, for instance, entitled to punish acts of piracy, there are clear indications pointing to the gradual evolution of a significant principle of international law to that effect.

Subsequent development has not strengthened the status of universal jurisdiction; rather, it has weakened it, as discussed below, especially in paragraph 34. In a sense, the fortune of universal jurisdiction peaked in 2002 when *Arrest Warrant* was decided.

32. Although some States such as the United Kingdom[53] have asserted universal jurisdiction over war crimes in their military law or regulations in the form of manuals, this assertion does not appear to have attracted general following among States, or have extended to other crimes or to other prosecuting contexts. Indeed, the United Kingdom's military manual even has

---

October 2010), paras.55-56.

50 ALI, Restatement of the Law, Third, the Foreign Relations of the United States, §404 and the comments and notes thereto. The text is reproduced in n.7 above.

51 IDI Resolution, n.3 above.

52 Joint Separate Opinion, n.17 above, para.52.

53 British Manual of Military Law, III (1956), para.637, as quoted in Rosalyn Higgins, Problems and Process (1994), 59-60; see discussion of id., 56-61; Ian Brownlie, Principles of Public International Law (7th ed., 2008), 305-306; UK Ministry of Defence, The Manual of the Law of Armed Conflict (2004), para.16.30.

difficulty persuading its own legislature to implement that idea by statute,[54] and a "clever" solution was found to implement the Rome Statute. The ICRC Study seems to have a broader view of the exercise of "universal jurisdiction" over war crimes.[55] A critical analysis of the data presented may not bear out its assessment.

33. The German legislations including the Code of Crimes against Humanity Law in a complicated way have been considered by one commentator to allow for the possibility of pure universal jurisdiction,[56] with various conditions. This possibility remains a possibility even now, as no such prosecution has been made.

34. The limited support from national legislation for true universal jurisdiction has recently been further diminished. In 2003 and 2009 respectively, Belgium[57] and Spain,[58] the only two States, as commonly believed, that once had clear statutes asserting pure universal jurisdiction and have in fact attempted to exercise that jurisdiction (Germany is not because of the ambiguities in its legislations and its record of non-exercise), have now modified their statutes to condition the exercise of jurisdiction on various links with the forum State.

35. The limited cases from the Western States regarding the attempt to exercise or actual exercise of universal jurisdiction have been described as

---

54 See Ian Brownlie, Principles of Public International Law (7th edn, 2008), 305-306; Rosalyn Higgins, Problems and Process (1994), 59-61.

55 See ICRC Study, n.35 above, Rule 157 and the associated materials.

56 See the description and analysis of this law in Luc Reydams, Universal Jurisdiction (2003), 141-147.

57 5 August 2003 Act on Grave Breaches of International Humanitarian Law (Belgium). See Luc Reydams, Belgium Reneges on Universality: 5 August 2003 Act on Grave Breaches of International Humanitarian Law, 1 J Intl Criminal Justice (2003), 679-689.

58 Ley Orgánica 1/2009, de 3 de noviembre complementaria de la Ley de reforma de la legislación procesal para la implantación de la nueva Oficina judicial, por la que se modifica la Ley Orgánica 6/1985, de 1 de julio, del Poder Judicial (http://noticias.juridicas.com/base_datos/Admin/lo1-2009. html) (Spain). The essence of this new law, as stated by representative of Spain in the UNGA, A/C.6/65/SR.11 (13 Oct. 2010), 4, para.21, is: "judges could only prosecute perpetrators of serious crimes committed anywhere in the world when no other international or third-country court had initiated proceedings against them and when they were present in Spanish territory or when the victim was a Spanish national".

showing the courts had "largely been cautious so far as reliance on universal jurisdiction is concerned".[59] Alternatively, this situation has been described in 2010 by Reydams[60] as follows:

> All in all some two dozen individuals have been tried by courts in Austria, Canada, Germany, Denmark, Belgium, the United Kingdom, the Netherlands, Finland, France, Spain, and Switzerland for "war crimes" committed abroad. Without exception the defendants had taken up permanent residence in the forum state—as refugee, exile, fugitive, or immigrant—and resisted being 'sent back to the countries in which their abominable deeds were done'. In most cases the other states concerned acquiesced in or even supported prosecution. Not to overlook also is the fact that the majority of these cases concerned atrocities committed in the former Yugoslavia and in Rwanda; the prosecutor of the ad hoc international criminal tribunals for these countries and the UN Security Council had encouraged all states to search for and try suspects on their territory (cf. the obligations under the Geneva Conventions). Finally, extradition often was impossible, if not legally then practically.

In addition, the rare examples of express assertion of universal jurisdiction from Israel (*Eichmann*[61]) and United States (*Demjanjuk*[62], recognizing Israel's universal jurisdiction as a basis for extradition) have their value reduced by the special circumstances surrounding these prosecutions of perpetrators from the Nazi era and further by Israel's threats against the use of universal jurisdiction against its own officials and the claim of the United States that other States "*should not even think about*"[63] prosecuting its nationals.

---

59 See the analysis in the Joint Separate Opinion, n.17 above, para.21.

60 Luc Reydams, Leuven Working Paper, n.26 above, 22 (internal footnotes omitted). See also the description of State judicial practice in: The Scope and application of the principle of universal jurisdiction: Report of the Secretary-General prepared on the basis comments and observations of Governments, A/65/181 (29 July 2010), http://daccess-dds-ny.un.org/doc/UNDOC/GEN/N10/467/52/PDF/N1046752.pdf?OpenElement), paras.55-65; 94-107.

61 AG of Israel v. Eichmann, 36 ILR (Supreme Court of Israel, 1962).

62 In re Demjanjuk, 603 F.Supp. 1468 (ND Ohio), affirmed, 776 F.2d 571 (6th Cir. 1985), cert. denied, 457 US 1016 (1986).

63 Reydams, Leuven Working Paper, n.26 above, 22.

36. Finally, it should be noted that no African State has ever exercised universal jurisdiction.[64]

37. But the IDI seems to believe that universal jurisdiction exists under customary international law but it finds it to be conditional on the "presence" of the suspect, as described below.[65] One may find the IDI Resolution extraordinary, as it was passed in 2005 against the background of the *Arrest Warrant* Judgment arresting the over-enthusiasm for universal jurisdiction[66] and Belgium, the captain of universal jurisdiction, abandoning ship by modifying pure universal jurisdiction out of its statute in 2003.[67] That is to say, the trend in favor of pure universal jurisdiction, if at all, was reversing. In any event, the IDI Resolution did not arrest the reversing trend so far, and in 2009 Spain did what Belgium did in 2003.[68]

38. It will be better for us to analyze these cases one by one, but the conscientious judges and scholars have done so and given conflicting assessments of the record. This alone reflects the uncertain state of universal jurisdiction in international law.

39. This state of affairs appears to be susceptible of several interpretations. First of all, the lack of actual exercise of pure universal jurisdiction may be considered to be evidence showing that the nice-sounding support for the concept is really political, rather than evidencing *opinio juris*.

---

64 AU-EU Expert Report, n.5 above, paras.19, 26, 40.

65 IDI Resolution, n.3 above.

66 After the Congo reformulated its claims, the ICJ did not rule in *Arrest Warrant* on the lawfulness of universal jurisdiction; rather, it held that it was unable to find any customary international law exception to the immunity from foreign national jurisdiction and the inviolability that an incumbent foreign minister enjoys, even where that foreign minister is accused of having committed war crimes or crimes against humanity. On the effect of Arrest Warrant, see Alain Pellet, Shaping the Future of International Law: The Role of the World Court in Law-making, in: Mahnoush H. Arsanjani et al. (eds), Looking to the Future: Essays on International Law in Honor of W. Michael Reisman (2011), 1065, 1080 ("the ICJ's Judgment in *Arrest Warrant Case* shows that the Court can also slow down and maybe go as far as durably jeopardizing highly desirable evolutions in the law in force"); Antonio Cassese, n.26 above, 1 J Int'l Criminal Justice, 589–595. On immunities (not discussed in this paper), see, e.g., the reports of the ILC Special Rapporteur Roman Anatolevich Kolodkin and other materials, available at: http://untreaty.un.org/ilc/guide/4_2.htm.

67 See n.57 above.

68 See n.58 above.

40. The support of the African Union as stated in its 2009 memorandum for this concept is further weakened by its expressed reliance on article 4(h) of its Constitutive Act, [69] which, the African Union statement claims, "enshrine[s]"[70] the principle of universal jurisdiction. That article recognizes "the right of the Union to intervene in a Member State pursuant to a decision of the Assembly in respect of grave circumstances, namely: war crimes, genocide and crimes against humanity". This article in fact enshrines an intra-regime collective political action mechanism: it grants the right to the Union to take action in relevant situations, not to any individual State to take action; the action authorized is political collective enforcement action, not judicial enforcement action. It does not say anything about the Union's right to exercise universal jurisdiction, much less that of an individual State to exercise universal jurisdiction. These factors may not have received attention when the statement of the African Union States was formulated.

41. The exchange of views by States so far after the inclusion of universal jurisdiction on the agenda of the UNGA does not strengthen the status of universal jurisdiction. The number of States that have submitted statements to the UNGA is not substantial, only 44 in total, about 25% of the membership of the UN.[71] Nor has this exchange clarified much, as broad and loose language seems to continue to prevail. If anything, this exercise seems to lessen the meager support for the concept. Several States have noted that "the scope and application of universal jurisdiction remained very much a matter of political and legal debate".[72] Some States such as Thailand[73] have made clear statements

69 Text accompany n.49 above.

70 African Union memo, n.1 above, para.1.

71 The statements are available on line here: http://www.un.org/en/ga/sixth/65/ScopeAppUniJuri.shtml. For a summary by these statements, see The Scope and application of the principle of universal jurisdiction: Report of the Secretary-General prepared on the basis comments and observations of Governments, A/65/181 (29 July 2010), http://daccess-dds-ny.un.org/doc/UNDOC/GEN/N10/467/52/PDF/N1046752.pdf?OpenElement. In 2010 China submitted a statement (Statement of China, n.46 above). See also ZHU Lijiang, Chinese Practice in Public International Law: 2009, 9 Chinese JIL (2010), 607, 647, para.75.

72 See, e.g., statement of Malaysia, A/C.6/65/SR.12 (15 Oct. 2010), 5, para.26.

73 See, e.g., statement of Thailand, A/C.6/65/SR.11 (13 Oct. 2010), 3, para.12 ("With the exception of piracy, there was no general consensus among States as to which crimes were subject to universal jurisdiction under customary international law."); Sudan, A/C.6/65/SR.12 (15 Oct. 2010), 4, para.20;

arguing against universal jurisdiction over crimes other than piracy and/or slavery. Even the African Union which clearly expressed support for the "principle" of universal jurisdiction in 2009 seemed to have retreated in 2010 from its earlier position. The statement made on behalf the African Group of States before the 6th Committee in October 2010 said:

> There was as yet no generally accepted definition of universal jurisdiction and no agreement on which crimes, other than piracy and slavery, it should cover or on the conditions under which it would apply. If few States had responded with information about their practice on universal jurisdiction, it was because the principle hardly existed in most domestic jurisdictions.[74]

Furthermore, rather than reiterating that the Constitutive Act of the African Union "enshrined" the principle of universal jurisdiction, the statement now said that "the Constitutive Act of the African Union accorded the Union the power to intervene in the affairs of its member States in situations of genocide, war crimes and crimes against humanity".[75]

42. Secondly, the thin record of actual exercise is evidence that there is no positive rule of customary international law yet in favor of pure universal jurisdiction other than that over piracy.[76] Indeed, there is not even sufficient evidence to prove a customary international law rule permitting the exercise of "universal concern plus presence" jurisdiction.

43. Finally, another interpretation, as put forward in the Joint Separate Opinion of Judge Higgins et al. in *Arrest Warrant*, is that this only shows that States have not "[legislated] to the full scope of the jurisdiction allowed by international law" and that:

> [W]hile none of the national case law to which [the Judges] have referred happens to be based on the exercise of a universal jurisdiction properly so called, there is equally nothing in this case law which evidences an *opinio juris* on the illegality of such a jurisdiction. In short, national

statement of China, n.46 above.

74 A/C.6/65/SR.10 (13 October 2010) (http://daccess-ods.un.org/access.nsf/Get?Open&DS=A/C.6/65/SR.10&Lang=E), para.60.

75 Ibid., para. 61.

76 See Statement of China, n.46 above, Observations, paras.4-5.

legislation and case law—that is, State practice—is neutral as to exercise of universal jurisdiction.[77]

III. Possible application of the *Lotus* dictum

44. Concluding thus, the Joint Separate Opinion by Judge Higgins et al. in *Arrest Warrant* argued in essence that the matter then turns on not whether the exercise of true or pure universal jurisdiction is supported by positive international law, but whether such an exercise is precluded by any prohibitive rule, in application of the *Lotus* dictum which militates in favor of state freedom. Finding no such prohibitive rule, these Judges concluded that a State may exercise pure universal jurisdiction (or "universal jurisdiction *in absentia*").[78]

45. President Guillaume, on the other hand, directly challenged the very dictum itself, at least in its application to the area of criminal jurisdiction. He said in his Separate Opinion in *Arrest Warrant*:[79]

> 14. This argument is hardly persuasive. Indeed the Permanent Court itself, having laid down the general principle cited by Belgium, then asked itself "whether the foregoing considerations really apply as regards criminal jurisdiction". It held that either this might be the case, or alternatively, that: "the exclusively territorial character of law relating to this domain constitutes a principle which, except as otherwise expressly provided, would, *ipso facto,* prevent States from extending the criminal jurisdiction of their courts beyond their frontiers". In the particular case before it, the Permanent Court took the view that it was unnecessary to decide the point. Given that the case involved the collision of a French vessel with a Turkish vessel, the Court confined itself to noting that the effects of the offence in question had made themselves felt on Turkish

---

77 Joint Separate Opinion, n.17 above, para.45. The UK explanation is found in Higgins, Problems and Process (1994), 59-61.

78 See Joint Separate Opinion, n.17 above, paras.49-54, etc.

79 President Guillaume, Separate Opinion in Arrest Warrant, ICJ Reports 2002, 35, 43. For further criticisms of the *Lotus* dictum, see Judge Simma, Declaration, in Accordance with International Law of the Unilateral Declaration of Independence in Respect of Kosovo (Request for Advisory Opinion), ICJ Reports 2010, http://www.icj-cij.org/docket/files/141/15993.pdf; Sienho Yee, Notes on the International Court of Justice (Part 4): The Kosovo Advisory Opinion, 9 Chinese JIL (2010), 763, paras. 22-26.

> territory, and that consequently a criminal prosecution might "be justified from the point of view of this so-called territorial principle".
>
> 15. The absence of a decision by the Permanent Court on the point was understandable in 1927, given the sparse treaty law at that time. The situation is different today, it seems to me—totally different. The adoption of the United Nations Charter proclaiming the sovereign equality of States, and the appearance on the international scene of new States, born of decolonization, have strengthened the territorial principle. International criminal law has itself undergone considerable development and constitutes today an impressive legal *corpus*. It recognizes in many situations the possibility, or indeed the obligation, for a State other than that on whose territory the offence was committed to confer jurisdiction on its courts to prosecute the authors of certain crimes where they are present on its territory. International criminal courts have been created. But at no time has it been envisaged that jurisdiction should be conferred upon the courts of every State in the world to prosecute such crimes, whoever their authors and victims and irrespective of the place where the offender is to be found. To do this would, moreover, risk creating total judicial chaos. It would also be to encourage the arbitrary for the benefit of the powerful, purportedly acting as agent for an ill-defined "international community". Contrary to what is advocated by certain publicists, such a development would represent not an advance in the law but a step backward.

46. There is much force in President Guillaume's view. The *Lotus* dictum was indeed unnecessary in that case and its vitality results from the uncritical recitation to and following of it.

47. To some extent, the debate seems to be about which default rule is the proper one. When the decision was adopted by the Permanent Court of International Justice, States still adhered to the old rule of a right to use of force to settle international disputes. It was probably natural that State freedom was considered paramount and therefore given priority. That apparently was the default rule behind the application of the *Lotus* dictum. In any event, developments since the date of the decision in 1927 militate against following it anymore. Since the first renunciation of the use of force as an instrument of national policy in the Kellogg-Briand Pact of Paris of 1928 and the restatement of this position in Article 2(4) of the UN Charter, State freedom is now subordinated to the territorial integrity and political independence of States.

This is now the grand default rule for the entire international legal system. In the words of President Guillaume, these new developments have strengthened the territorial principle. The *Lotus* dictum therefore can be considered outdated at least as far as criminal jurisdiction is concerned. This is also the view of some IDI members[80] expressed during its deliberations leading to the adoption of the 2005 Resolution on the topic. Indeed, in some areas States have positively by treaty reversed the holding of the PCIJ in *Lotus* regarding criminal jurisdiction.[81]

48. Rejecting the *Lotus* dictum in this context, China expressly states in its statement submitted to the UNGA in 2010 on universal jurisdiction:

> Jurisdiction is an important element of State sovereignty. Under the principle of sovereign equality of States, the establishment and exercise of [jurisdiction] by one State may not impair the sovereignty of other States. Therefore the establishment of a State's [jurisdiction] should have as a prerequisite the existence of valid and adequate connections between that country and the cases involved, and should be limited to a reasonable scope.[82]

49. One cannot but await further development on this point with great interest. Before the *Lotus* dictum is defeated in this area, conceivably the States may prevent its application by making objections to universal jurisdiction, because the basis for its application, according to the Joint Separate Opinion in *Arrest Warrant*, is the fact that there is nothing that evinces an *opinio juris* on the illegality of universal jurisdiction. A State's silent non-support alone for universal jurisdiction will not necessarily prevent it from being applied to the nationals of that State, as the effect of the application of the *Lotus* dictum is such that it may permit a State's exercise of jurisdiction not authorized, but not prohibited either, by international law. This means that making clear objections has its benefits, while "diplomatic" ambiguity or silence may have its perils as far as the application of the *Lotus* dictum is concerned.

---

80 See IDI, 71(II) Annuaire, n.4 above, 245 (The Rapporteur); 258 (Frowein).

81 E.g., 1952 Brussels Convention for the Unification of Certain Rules Relating to Penal Jurisdiction in Matters of Collision or other Incidents of Navigation, art. 1; UNCLOS, art. 97.

82 Statement of China, n.46 above, Observations, para.1, English translation by the UN. This UN translation mistakenly translates "guanxiaquan" into "sovereignty". "Jurisdiction" is used here instead.

IV. Possible limitations on the exercise of universal jurisdiction if permitted

50. From the above analysis, we can see that universal jurisdiction may be a positive tool in the efforts to vindicate the fundamental values of the international community, to promote and protect human rights and to fight impunity. Its negative side is that the exercise of universal jurisdiction is at least in tension with the principle of sovereignty and sovereign equality and is easily subjected to political abuse including discrimination as manifested in selective prosecution, thus destabilizing international relations.[83] If one were to assume, *arguendo*, that this doctrine or principle could be used for whatever reason and to attempt to reap the benefits of the tool while reducing its side effects, one can imagine that the exercise of universal jurisdiction may be placed under a variety of conditions or whether such conditions should be made part of the "definition" of universal jurisdiction, such as (1) limiting that exercise to the most heinous crimes such as, in addition to piracy, slavery, genocide, crimes against humanity and serious war crimes; (2) giving priority to the territorial State, (3) applying the clean-hands doctrine;[84] (4) requiring a decision of the highest State authority to trigger the exercise; (5) respecting applicable immunities of officials and States; (6) possible approval of an international screening mechanism; and (7) the presence of the suspect. These are not discussed herein, except that I will make some comments on the presence requirement or condition.

51. It seems that there is broad support for the point that there is no customary international law rule allowing the exercise of universal jurisdiction without the presence of the suspect.[85] There is insufficient support for the view that the presence of the suspect would legitimize the exercise of "universal jurisdiction", absent support from a treaty. Furthermore, there is disagreement on the temporal point at which the presence requirement is triggered, if the exercise of universal jurisdiction is permitted for some reason. It seems that for Judges Higgins et al. in the *Arrest Warrant* case who still would rely on the *Lotus* dictum, this finding about the role of presence in itself does not show that the

---

83 See Henry Kissinger, n.19 above.

84 See Sienho Yee, The *Tu Quoque* Argument as a Defence to International Crimes, Prosecution, or Punishment, 3 Chinese JIL (2004), 87-133.

85 See statement of Israel, A/C.6/65/SR.12 (15 Oct. 2010), 3, para.9 ("many States agreed that the accused should be present in the territory of the forum State").

presence of the suspect is thereby required for the exercise of universal jurisdiction; for a State to exercise universal jurisdiction, there need be only no prohibitive rule against it. The existence of such a presence requirement in the various treaty provisions on extradite or prosecute—in their view, "*Definitionally, this envisages presence on the territory*"—is no ground for reaching an *a contrario* conclusion so that the presence is required.[86] For these judges, "If it is said that a person must be within the jurisdiction at the time of the trial itself, that may be a prudent guarantee for the right of fair trial but has little to do with bases of jurisdiction recognized under international law".[87] One cannot but note that this view, reducing the presence requirement to the mere procedural requirement of a prudent guarantee for a fair trial is far reaching and extraordinary against the trend in international criminal law shunning trials *in absentia.* Indeed, this trend may evince a certain attitude about or view of the world we live in, rather than a mere quest for a fairer trial. The far reaching effect of the procedural view of the presence requirement will be greater still—perhaps exponentially so—when it is coupled with the application of the *Lotus* dictum, which the Joint Separate Opinion in *Arrest Warrant* argued for, because both are biased in favor of the freedom of the prosecuting State.[88]

52. According to the IDI and others, the trigger point appears earlier. The IDI Resolution, in paragraph 3(b), states:

> Apart from acts of investigation and requests for extradition, the exercise of universal jurisdiction requires the presence of the alleged offender in the territory of the prosecuting State or on board a vessel flying its flag or an aircraft which is registered under its laws, or other lawful forms of control over the alleged offender.

According to the Rapporteur, this paragraph

> rejected the theory of absolute universal jurisdiction, insisting on the presence of the alleged perpetrator on the territory of the prosecuting State. However, it did allow any State to undertake acts of investigation

86 Joint Separate Opinion, n.17 above, in particular, para.57 (emphasis in the original).

87 Joint Separate Opinion, n.17 above, para.56.

88 This has the danger of leading to the maximum freedom of the prosecuting State, a sort of "*Lotus*-maximum", see Sienho Yee, n.79 above, 9 Chinese JIL (2010), 763, para.26.

> which per se did not harm the individual, unlike the issue of an arrest warrant. Likewise, States should be free to request extradition, although there was no obligation for the requested State to comply with such request.[89]

While this approach is reasonable to some extent, there are still three major problems. The first is this: if the requested State is where the suspect holds an official position, it will probably not comply with an extradition request without a tough decision; if this requested State is one different from the suspect's home State (when the suspect/official travels outside), different considerations may be entertained and the request for extradition may well be complied with.

53. The second is that existing judicial assistance or extradition treaties may indeed mandate extradition because under at least some of these treaties the requested State may be required to surrender a suspect if the requesting State has made out a prima facie case in terms of jurisdiction and evidence and pure universal jurisdiction may be considered sufficient to satisfy that jurisdictional requirement. How to reconcile the IDI Rapporteur's view that the requested State is under no obligation (resulting from the universal jurisdiction law itself) to comply with such a request and the requested State's obligation to comply under other species of law becomes a most important question. In other words, should there be, in the context of universal jurisdiction, an exception from the general obligation arising from other species of law to comply with requests?

54. Thirdly, in some countries the initiation of an investigation may result in compulsory judicial processes other than arrest and extradition. This lesser form of compulsory judicial processes can still present serious problems. However, arguing for conditioning the starting of an investigation on the presence of the suspect may be too much and will likely be rejected by many States. Perhaps a compromise position can be to condition the issuance of any compulsory judicial process on the presence of the suspect on the territory of the prosecuting State.

55. This discussion should raise a red flag to any cautious government that the relationship between the possible exercise of universal jurisdiction and all the judicial and police assistance treaties and the implications of the presence requirement on this relationship are a subject calling out for urgent

---

89 IDI Annuaire, n.4 above, 208 (the Rapporteur introducing the draft resolution).

examination. It may wish to attempt to modify these treaties to ensure a relaxed presence requirement will not present a problem for its conduct of international relations.

V. Concluding remarks

56. True or pure universal jurisdiction is jurisdiction solely based on the universal concern character of the crime in issue. The concept and logic of universal jurisdiction is understandable, as each State has an interest in matters of universal concern. Universal jurisdiction can be a powerful instrument for the international system to protect its interests and to protect human rights and fight against impunity. However, the exercise of universal jurisdiction by one State may infringe the sovereignty and sovereign equality of another State and can be abused, thus destabilizing international relations.

57. These pros and cons and others not discussed here have influenced the international law formation process in such a way that so far only universal jurisdiction over piracy has been accepted in international law. There is insufficient support to show that "pure universal concern jurisdiction" exists in international law over other crimes yet. The evidence of State practice on "universal concern plus presence" jurisdiction is not yet substantial so as to afford the finding of a customary international law rule in its favor. Treaty practice providing for "universal concern plus treaty, presence and intra-regime territoriality or nationality jurisdiction" or "universal concern plus treaty and presence jurisdiction" is limited to the particular treaty regime only. In the light of this state of affairs, the possible application of the *Lotus* dictum and the presence requirement—especially the weak, procedural view of it—can be of significance and deserves attention.

58. The movement for "pure universal jurisdiction" has been "trending down" since the conspicuous silence of the ICJ on the legitimacy of that jurisdiction in the *Arrest Warrant* case in 2002, when the Joint Separate Opinion of Judges Higgins et al. found some evolutionary trend toward universal jurisdiction.[90] The subsequent downtrend may have been in no small measure due to the cautious Judgment in that case. That Judgment can be said to have, in an ingenious way, helped to inject some calming elements back into international relations.[91] With Belgium and Spain now having abandoned pure

---

90 Joint Separate Opinion, n.17 above, paras.45-52.

91 For a stronger assessment of the influence of the Arrest Warrant Judgment,

universal jurisdiction by narrowing down their statutes, the universal jurisdiction movement appears to be a moving train without its locomotive.

Postscript

The paper as originally published contains this long abstract:

> The debates in the UNGA since 2009 on universal jurisdiction reveal great confusion on its concept, scope and application. True or pure universal jurisdiction is jurisdiction solely based on the universal concern character of the crime in issue. The concept and logic of universal jurisdiction is understandable, as each State has an interest in matters of universal concern. Universal jurisdiction can be a powerful instrument for the international system to protect its interests and to protect human rights and fight against impunity. However, the exercise of universal jurisdiction by one State may infringe the sovereignty and sovereign equality of another State and can be abused, thus destabilizing international relations. These pros and cons and other factors have influenced the international law formation process in such a way that so far only universal jurisdiction over piracy has been accepted in international law. There is no "pure universal concern jurisdiction" over other crimes yet. The evidence of State practice on "universal concern plus presence" jurisdiction is not yet substantial so as to afford the finding of a customary international law rule. Treaty practice providing for "universal concern plus treaty, presence and intra-regime territoriality or nationality jurisdiction" or "universal concern plus treaty and presence jurisdiction" is limited to the particular treaty regime only. In the light of this state of affairs, the possible application of the *Lotus* dictum and the presence requirement—especially the weak, procedural view of it—can be of significance and deserves attention. The movement for "pure universal jurisdiction" has been "trending down" since the conspicuous silence on the legitimacy of universal jurisdiction in the *Arrest Warrant* case decided by the ICJ in 2002. The subsequent downtrend may have been in no small measure due to the cautious Judgment in that case. That Judgment can be said to have, in an ingenious way, helped to inject some calming elements back into international relations. With Belgium and

---

see Alain Pellet, n.66 above.

Spain now having abandoned pure universal jurisdiction by narrowing down their statutes, the universal jurisdiction movement appears to be a moving train without its locomotive.

Index